D0169387

Sarah Orne Jewett,
an American Persephone

Recipient of the University of New Hampshire
Book Prize for 1988

Sarah Orne Jewett,
an American Persephone

Sarah Way Sherman

Published for University of New Hampshire by
University Press of New England
Hanover and London

University Press of New England

Brandeis University
Brown University
Clark University
University of Connecticut
Dartmouth College
University of New Hampshire
University of Rhode Island
Tufts University
University of Vermont

PS 2133
S 54
1 9 8 9

© 1989 by the Trustees of the University of New Hampshire

All rights reserved. Except for brief quotation in critical articles or reviews, this book, or parts thereof, must not be reproduced in any form without permission in writing from the publisher. For further information contact University Press of New England, Hanover, NH 03755.

Quotations from "Aunt Jennifer's Tigers" are reprinted from THE FACT OF A DOORFRAME, Poems Selected and New, 1950–1984, by Adrienne Rich, by permission of W. W. Norton & Company, Inc. Copyright © 1984 by Adrienne Rich. Copyright © 1975, 1978 by W. W. Norton & Company, Inc. Copyright © 1981 by Adrienne Rich.

Printed in the United States of America
∞

Library of Congress Cataloging-in-Publication Data
Sherman, Sarah Way.
  Sarah Orne Jewett, an American Persephone.
  Bibliography: p.
  Includes index.
  1. Jewett, Sarah Orne, 1849–1909—Criticism and interpretation. 2. Women in literature. I. Title.
PS2133.S54 1989   813'.4   88-40353
ISBN 0–87451–477–0
ISBN 0–87451–484–3 (pbk.)

5   4   3   2

To my grandmother, Peggy Sherman
and to my parents, Joan and Skip Sherman

OCT 15 1993

Contents

Illustrations follow page 46

Preface

Willa Cather once called *The Country of the Pointed Firs* (1896) an American classic able to stand alongside *Huckleberry Finn* and *The Scarlet Letter.*[1] Cather notwithstanding, Sarah Orne Jewett's *Pointed Firs* hasn't gotten that kind of recognition. It may be partly because it doesn't fit the pattern of most American classics, those novels that Nina Baym labeled "melodramas of beset manhood."[2] There's no search for the father, no exploration of untracked wilderness, no hunt to kill the magical beast, let alone an easily discernible plot. Instead, an unmarried writer visits a tiny Maine fishing village, where she hopes to write a book in peace and quiet. Over the course of the summer she becomes intimately acquainted with her landlady, Mrs. Todd, a motherly widow who raises herbs and nurses her neighbors according to ancient remedies. This pastoral interlude closes with the summer itself. As the narrator leaves on her steamer for the city, she looks back over the water for a last glimpse of her friend.

The world described here is a simple one, virtually without conflict. The writer's solitary routine is punctuated by feminine rituals: tea parties, neighborly visits, confidential talks, and reminiscing. The grand event is a family reunion in which the anonymous narrator's adoption by Mrs. Todd is signified by their sharing of a sacramental gingerbread house. The narrator does not fall in love with the local doctor—as the cover of one paperback edition seemed to suggest. In fact, there are no young men around at all, and the only romance is the gently sketched courtship of two people over sixty. Indeed, the primary bonds here are between women—mothers, daughters, cousins, and friends. The chapter describing William Blackett's wedding actually closes not with the married couple but with Mrs. Todd and the narrator watching them sail away, then walking home themselves, holding hands.

I was first introduced to this book as an undergraduate in 1970, the year of the Cambodian invasion; and though I was moved, I wanted a vision a bit more robust. I remember saying in class that it reminded me of my great-grandmother's teacups, lovely but too fragile for use. Now this great-grandmother, Gwendolyn Lawrence, was a tall, white-haired woman who lived in Springfield, Illinois. The family always said that she looked like Queen Mary should have looked. When she went apartment-hunting, landlords took one glance and raised the rent. She was a lady, and so was Jewett. It's a notion I'm still ambivalent about. But while writing this opening I stumbled upon the memory that linked these two women for me. It's a family photograph of my mother and my great-grandmother sitting at the breakfast table in the big Victorian house in Springfield. They are quietly intent on their conversation, obviously pleased with each other, companionable in a rectangle of morning light. And now, after several years of studying Jewett's fiction and Jewett's world, I see the aptness of my original association, for through the matrilineal links of my own mother, grandmothers, and great-grandmothers I am connected to that world, perhaps lost, which Jewett celebrated and which the historian Carroll Smith-Rosenberg has named "the female world of love and ritual."³

Jewett was born and raised within this world. If her art grew beyond its boundaries, its nurture remains visible. Part of my story is how Jewett came to terms with the culture that defined her womanhood, its values and its symbols. Of these symbols, the Greek goddesses Demeter and Persephone were central. Emerson once wrote that the seer is always a sayer; but women have not always had a name for their vision, and sometimes the ability to say shapes the ability to see. In the ancient story of a divine mother and daughter Victorian women found figures for their own experience.

The Country of the Pointed Firs gave this myth new life. At the book's heart is the narrator's recognition of Mrs. Todd, her growing reverence for the other woman's power and numinous presence. Over and over the narrator names that power, that presence. She describes Mrs. Todd as a "sibyl," as a "priestess of experience," as a "personification of some force of Nature." She compares her to Antigone, to Medea, and finally to "the ancient deities" themselves. Through her eyes we see rural Maine become twin to pastoral Greece, the ground from which Demeter and Persephone once rose. Many critics have pointed out the mythic quality of Jewett's work. This book traces its source: a highly self-conscious literary, even religious, tradition—a tradition that gave Jewett the words to say it.⁴

Acknowledgments

Many people helped me write this book, both directly and indirectly. Robert Fisher at Kennett High School first got me writing about myth and American literature. Richard Judd at Marlboro College brought me into American studies and, with Alan Kantrow, introduced me to Sarah Orne Jewett. Geraldine Pittman de Batlle and Audrey Gorton taught me about form and nineteenth-century fiction. At Brown University, Barton St. Armand started me on this particular study with a seminar on local-color writers. David Hirsch, St. Armand, and Mari Jo Buhle then guided my research and patiently read my long dissertation. Later Sharon O'Brien recommended a key work, Nancy Chodorow's *Reproduction of Mothering*. Marjorie Pryse and Mark Savin generously donated both their time and encouragement, while Steve List saw me through some difficult years. Some of this material appeared in *Colby Library Quarterly* and *Lady-Unique-Inclination-of-the-Night*, for which I thank the respective editors, Karin Woodruff Jackson and Kay Turner.

At the University of New Hampshire, Melody Graulich, David Watters, and Jean Kennard were sharp and sympathetic readers, while the Feminist Criticism Reading Group gave me the model of a lively, engaged audience. As administrators, Jean Kennard, Carl Dawson, Michael DePorte, and Cathryn Adamsky offered unflagging support. I am also grateful to the College of Liberal Arts, and Dean Stuart Palmer, for a summer stipend that meant time to revise. Tory Poulin and the English Department staff—Carol Demeritt, Sabina Foote, and Kim Bousquin—provided consistently professional help under sometimes trying circumstances. Roland Goodbody and others at Dimond Library helped me track down illustrations, as did Lorna Condon of the Society for the Preservation of New England Antiquities and Jennifer Rathbun at the Houghton Library. At the last minute Catherine Turnbull and Jeffrey Wescott pitched in as research assistants.

I would like to thank the Society for the Preservation of New England Antiquities for permission to reproduce photographs 6, 8, and 10. The last is the work of Elise Tyson Vaughan, daughter of Emily Davis Tyson and owner of Hamilton House. Sarah Orne Jewett's 1891 letter to Louisa Dresel and portraits from the Jewett family album—photographs 1, 2, and 5—are reproduced courtesy of Special Collections, the University of New Hampshire Library, Durham, New Hampshire. The Barrett Library at the University of Virginia Library gave permission to quote from their Sarah Orne Jewett Collection. Letters by Edward Eastman and Anna L. Dawes are found in the Sarah Orne Jewett Papers in the Rare Book and Manuscript Library at Columbia University. They are quoted with permission. Most important, I would like to thank the Houghton Library at Harvard University for permission to consult their extensive Jewett collection and to quote from manuscripts and letters by Caroline Perry Jewett, Sarah Orne Jewett, Annie Fields, Theophilus Parsons, and Elizabeth Stuart Phelps. Photographs 3, 4, 7, 10, and 11 are also included courtesy of the Houghton Library.

I am especially grateful to University Press of New England. Their copy-editor Marilyn Houston was tactful as well as thorough. Their outside academic readers gave me both encouragement and searching, valuable criticism. If the book is not better for their help, the responsibility is mine, not theirs. At various times Carrie Sherman, Caroline Preston, Christopher Tighlman, Kate Bernhardt, and Lincoln Perry also gave me good advice, not from the specialist's perspective but from the interested, general reader's. I hope I have done well by them. Finally, Jewett's narrator writes that *Pointed Firs* is meant for those who have "a Dunnet Landing of their own." In my friends and family, my husband, Jamie Calderwood, and our son Peter, I do have a Dunnet Landing of my own. This book could not have been written without them.

November 1988   s.w.s.
Kittery, Maine

Sarah Orne Jewett,
an American Persephone

Chapter One

Root-Bound: The Victorian Context

> ... You bring something to the reading of a story that the story
> would go very lame without; but it is those unwritable things that
> the story holds in its heart, if it has any, that makes the true soul
> of it, and these must be understood, and yet how many a story goes
> lame for the lack of such understanding. In France there is such a
> code, such recognitions, such richness of allusions; but here we
> confuse our scaffoldings with our buildings, and—and so!
> —Sarah Orne Jewett, Letter to Sarah Whitman,
> South Berwick, Thursday morning (1894 or 1895).[1]

In his essay "Thick Description," Clifford Geertz argues that culture
is not an entity, "something to which social events, behaviors, institutions can be causally attributed; it is a context, something within
which they can be intelligibly . . . described." This context makes social
behavior intelligible for the ethnologist or historian, but more important, it makes these acts significant for the performers themselves. In
this sense culture consists of "interworked systems of construable
signs," the "socially established structures of meaning in terms of
which people do such things as signal conspiracies and join them or
perceive insults and answer them."[2] Or, I would add, write stories and
read them.

A woman writing these stories confronts two kinds of silence. The
first is a silence imposed by tradition. The second is a silence in language itself. By its very nature language limits expression while it makes
expression possible. Moreover, the language a woman must use bears
the lasting imprint of her culture's history, of gender as well as race
and class divisions. Through the articulation of her experience, a
woman writer helps heal those divisions; she shares the common artistic task of renovating language. Roland Barthes writes: "Like modern
art in its entirety literary writing carries at the same time the alienation
of History and the dream of History; as Necessity, it testifies to the

division of classes; as Freedom, it is the consciousness of this division and the very effect which seeks to surmount it."[3]

In a 1978 talk Elaine Marks argued that Jewett achieved this transcendence by creating characters in *The Country of the Pointed Firs* who were not defined by their gender.[4] I agree with Marks about the achievement but not about the way it was achieved. In the reader's imagination these characters may be freed from their culture's limitations; however, they are freed because its codes are manipulated, neutralized, rendered ambiguous within the text itself. In Jewett's language we may still trace the alienation of history as well as the dream of history. Finally, it is because we, her readers, also possess this history that we may interpret her works. With this key we recognize her swerves and realignments. Without some lines of continuity the words would be unintelligible. No text without its shadow.

And Jewett's texts often are, as Nina Auerbach has suggested, shadowy, devious, and shifty, a "buried language," whispered and subversive, dealing in paradoxes, inversions, and ambiguities.[5] In her work women find voice, the marginal becomes central, and immanence is a means to transcendence. But there is still silence. Her stories of friendship and communion are punctuated by silent moments. However, this is not the silence of repression or frustration but a silence beyond language. It is rich with emotion and full of meaning. Finally, Jewett's art did aim at the unwritable. Juxtaposing image and anecdote, glimpses of landscape and classical myth, she constructed a scaffolding calculated to evoke her story's "true soul," the building in the reader's imagination. Thus, this study focuses not on the text alone but in relation. It deals with the bonds between text and context, between the story and the codes needed to gain its heart.

I

What then is woman's place within these codes? What does she signify and why? In her influential 1972 essay, "Is Female to Male as Nature Is to Culture?," Sherry Ortner suggested some answers.[6] While they may not fit every culture, as Ortner claimed, they do fit Sarah Orne Jewett's. Obsessed with dichotomies and delighted by hierarchy, genteel Victorians sharply differentiated civilized from primitive, white from black, masculine from feminine.

Ortner begins with woman's status as the second sex. Like her precursor, Simone de Beauvoir, she believes that at the basic level of cultural ordering women are "a symbol of something that every culture devalues, something every culture defines as being at a lower order of existence than itself."[7] That "something" is nature, the ground against which culture must define itself. On this differentiation depend all notions of humanness: the distinctive ability to "transcend" the viscous, the random, and the contingent through the creation of symbolic forms. Geertz defined culture in a similar way—as webs of signification, fictions of order. However, Ortner is also dealing with the signification of culture within its own system of meanings. Within that system "culture" is identified with human consciousness and opposed to the (equally cultural) notion of a purely natural world: the cooked versus the raw.

One could argue that not all peoples differentiate between the cultural and the natural worlds as rigidly as modern Westerners do; moreover, that such groups might not devalue women in the ways that Ortner describes. While she acknowledges cultures that do not separate themselves as radically from nature as our own does, Ortner maintains that "the universality of ritual betokens an assertion in all human cultures of the specifically human ability to act upon and regulate, rather than passively move with and be moved by, the givens of natural existence."[8] In his discussion of Sartre's *Nausea,* Frank Kermode singles out this crucial rescue of human meaning from the viscous, "feminine" matrix of inhuman reality. Ortner sees the same process in a ritual's ability to "purify" human activity of its "natural" pollution. But what motivates the association between nature and the female when males are apparently equally "natural"?

A lady supposedly once asked Samuel Johnson why the sexes were so strictly differentiated. His reply: "I cannot conceive, Madame. Can you?" Although she would reject the biological determinism of Johnson's simple, and possibly apocryphal, response, Ortner also thinks a woman's ability to conceive, bear, and care for children to be the prime determinant of her position in the semantic system: "It all begins with the body."[9] "More involved more of the time with 'species life,' " women appear closer to nature than men, "whose physiology frees them more completely for the projects of culture." The biological tie to childbearing, then, keeps women in the domestic sphere and places them in social roles that are perceived as lower on the cultural hierarchy. Perhaps more important, in response to this domestic world and its demands women develop a "different *psychic structure*—and again, this psychic structure . . . is seen as being more 'like nature.' "[10]

As Ortner's colleague, psychologist Nancy Chodorow, argues, the asymmetrical distribution of parenting ensures that men and women develop personalities suited to their traditional roles. For women this means a psychic and cognitive style that is communal rather than individual, concrete rather than abstract. But again, it is a style less valued. For most cultures, "the mother . . . represents . . . regression, passivity, dependence, and lack of orientation to reality, whereas the father represents progression, activity, independence, and reality orientation."[11]

However, feminine symbolism is obviously more diverse and complicated than the simple equation "mother equals regression." Women, whose bodies transform matter into life and whose nurturance transforms infants into human beings, are also associated with the crossing of boundaries: "Women mediate between the social and cultural categories which men have defined; they bridge the gap and make transitions—especially in their role as socializer—between nature and culture."[12] These roles—as transformational vessel, as mediator, as bridge—give to feminine symbols a peculiar ambiguity. Within the semantic system, women occupy that strange, sometimes ambiguous, sometimes anomalous position of the intermediary, the mediating sign, neither raw nor fully cooked.

Psychoanalysts such as Melanie Klein have long known that the experience of the mother, with all of its intensity and lack of reality principle, tends to be projected onto all women (and the world) in two forms. The mother is split in two: the good and the bad. The "bad" regressive mother, infantalizing and death-bearing, becomes the threat from below. From above, the "good" mother offers primary love without restraint or judgment, dissolving the punitive superego, sublimating and transforming the inarticulate infant dependence into wisdom beyond expression.

Thus, women's psychic and cognitive styles, while devalued on the one hand for being "more like nature," may also be valued for being "more like spirit." The communal mode, so important in child rearing and family life, may seem to threaten the universalistic ties and abstract categories on which the public, masculine sphere depends. However, this same intensely "personal, relatively unmediated commitment . . . may also be seen as embodying the cement or synthesizing agent for culture and society from 'above.' " If the public sphere demands categories "that transcend personal loyalties . . . every society must also generate a sense of ultimate moral unity for all members above and beyond those social categories."[13]

These "higher" uses for women's particular psychic mode can be seen in the traditional feminine symbolism for Justice, the Muses, Charity, the Virgin Mary, and so on. However, we are not dealing with actual women ruling over society from above. Instead, we are dealing with symbols that depend on the image of the feminine, Woman, to articulate the crucial distinction between these loyalties and those of every day. But what of the Virgin's disconcerting tendency to become the Whore? Or of a culture's even more disconcerting tendency to condemn in one moment what it idealizes in the next?

Edmund Leach argues that, given a binary opposition, the third or middle term tends to be "the focus of all ritual observance." Mediating between nature and culture, woman appears polluted and threatening; mediating between culture and heaven, she is divine and uplifting. Also working within a structuralist framework, Ortner offers an analogy that helps explain the "polarized ambiguity" of this female imagery. Rather than a simple linear scale from nature to culture, we should think of culture as circular. If we imagine it having a margin that functions as a "continuous periphery, rather than as upper and lower boundaries . . . we can understand the notion that extremes, as we say, meet—that they are easily transformed into one another in symbolic thought and hence seem unstable and ambiguous." We should think of woman's position "not so much as location between culture and nature, as the fact of marginality per se in relation to the 'centers' of culture, and the ambiguity of meaning which is inherent in a marginal position."[14]

Thus, the semantic system's structure is expressed in authoritative cultural patterns that reinforce each other. These patterns, or para-digms, consistently place woman on the margins of culture, whether she is seen as middle term, intermediary, or transformational vessel. What happens, then, when a woman writes from her own "quiet center," as Jewett advised Willa Cather to do? What happens when the "center" is feminine and, by definition, "marginal"? The paradox of the marginal center is crucial to every woman's consciousness, as it is crucial to the consciousness of any person not identified with cultural authority. This "minority" speaks—to quote the title of Lee Edwards and Arlyn Diamond's fine anthology of feminist criticism—with the "authority of experience" but not of culture.[15] Indeed, this is why women seem anomalous within the system as a whole: they are both "other" and "existent," both "sign" and "signmaker." These are the riddles a woman writer poses. And she poses them to herself as much as to others.

Recent historical analysis of Jewett's century seems to confirm Ort-ner's theory. Although Victorian women found their biological roles little changed from time immemorial, their social roles had shifted dramatically. The transformation began with the rise of specialization and professionalism in the eighteenth century, then accelerated with industrialization in the early nineteenth. As men left for their offices and factories, middle-class women stayed at home. The home had been a workplace where women wove cloth, baked bread, made soap. Now these necessities became commodities, and women became consumers rather than producers. As the split between men's and women's work deepened, the distribution of child rearing became even more lopsided and gender codes even more rigid. Victorian convention asserted that men and women were nearly separate species, perhaps complementary but definitely created on different principles for different purposes. More than ever, these principles and purposes kept women on the cultural periphery.

According to historian Barbara Welter, middle-class women became "hostages in the home." Relatively unencumbered by economic responsibilities, they preserved the traditions of an agrarian past while their menfolk forged ahead into the future.[16] Margaret Coxe in her popular advice book, *The Young Lady's Companion* (1839), put it this way: "Man is sent forth to subdue the earth, to obtain command over the elements, to form political communities; and to him, therefore, belong the more hardy and austere virtues . . . but humility, meekness, gentleness, love are also important characteristics of our nature." These kindly traits would be neglected if left to men to cultivate. Luckily, "these principles . . . have been placed more particularly in the keeping of woman; her social condition being evidently more favorable to their full development." This social condition, of course, was woman's place within the home, her "proper sphere." Here she would reign, "vestal virgin in the Christian temple."[17]

And so was born "the angel in the house." The Victorian lady worshiped in the cult of true womanhood displayed "piety, purity, submissiveness and domesticity."[18] Purged of gross sexuality or earthiness—that was relegated to women who engaged in manual labor outside the home—she was defined primarily by her motherhood. Virtually the only productive role left to the middle-class, genteel woman in America was the reproductive: both the physical act and its elaboration through the reproduction of socialized children. Trusted with this moral guardianship, Victorian women found their maternal role one of their few routes to self-esteem and power. However, even that power was subject to severe restrictions. At the same time that their social roles narrowed to child rearing, convention de-emphasized, even tabooed these women's heterosexuality. With their lives increasingly differentiated from their husbands', they turned to their children for emotional gratification—to their children and to their female friends. The result, according to historian Carroll Smith-Rosenberg, was a "female world of love and ritual" in which men played but a "shadowy" part. Maternal love was split from heterosexuality: the latter became nasty, brutish, polluted; the other, a pure love supporting the culture's "highest" values.[19]

Historians still disagree on the effect of these shifts on American women. Some, like Ann Douglas, find Victorian domestic life and ideology ultimately crippling. According to her 1978 study, *The Feminization of American Culture,* these women found themselves disenfranchised and responded with a variety of neurotic and manipulative responses. Disguising their drive for power even from themselves, they used their angelic status for their own ends. However, historians such as Nancy Cott and Smith-Rosenberg see another picture. In their interpretation the Victorian "homosocial" world allowed American women to gain dignity and strength. As Smith-Rosenberg puts it, "Women who had little status or power in the large world of male concerns, possessed status and power in the lives and worlds of other women."[20] Rather than a restrictive ghetto, the domestic sphere could become, for some women at least, a walled garden, one they could cultivate with impunity. For others, it could become a power base in whose name they organized for temperance, women's education, and urban reform.

While its final meaning for historians will probably remain elusive— since individual situations varied from community to community, family to family—nevertheless, we can safely say that the domestic world did become a female subculture.[21] At its heart was the bond between mother and daughter, a bond reproduced in a young girl's and a woman's friendships. Domestic rituals, subtle and obscured from public view, celebrated a woman's passage from girlhood to adolescence to maturity while still affirming the continuity of her experience. These women were bound not only by a common gender but by a shared way of life. Their perspective and values found expression in popular literature. Recently the subject of intense critical scrutiny, these bestsellers often reveal both unacknowledged conflicts and surprisingly subversive themes. Ann Douglas and Mary Kelley, for example, have demonstrated how domestic ideology gave private women a chance for public power. Overtly proclaiming women's obedience and selflessness, sentimentalist writers covertly undermined the masculine hierarchy and substituted their own values for those of male tradition.[22]

Indeed, recent historians seem agreed that sentimentalist writers articulated a feminine ethos, sharply differentiated from the masculine model of Protestant orthodoxy. Elizabeth Ammons, for example, traces a distinctive literary tradition beginning with Stowe's *Uncle Tom's Cabin* in 1852. These works offer a vision of "human community that places the group before the individual, cooperation before competition, love before progress." Moreover, "it is an ideal that, whether Christian or secularized, asserts in the face of capitalist, masculine progress women's belief in the superiority of alternative matrifocal values."[23] The career of Rose Terry Cooke (1827–1892) follows a pattern typical of many such writers. Among the first to make literature out of purely local materials, Cooke earned a place in American literary history as a regionalist pioneer. In her work and in the work of women like her we can see the context in which Sarah Orne Jewett came to literary maturity.

II

In the introduction to her new collection of Cooke's stories, Elizabeth Ammons justly praises "Cooke's biting—sometimes grimly humorous, sometimes simply grim—tales about Calvinism, about domestic violence in American society, and about life as a single woman in rural, white, middle-class New England in the late eighteenth and early nineteenth centuries." Her best work will be remembered for "its aggressive honesty, even its 'ghastly honesty,' which speaks across the century which separates her life from ours."[24] Unfortunately, Cooke was not always free to be honest, nor perhaps was she always of one mind. As Judith Fetterley points out, her work reveals a deep "ambivalence toward the culture she exposes and critiques."[25] The sources of this ambivalence are complex.

Rose Terry Cooke was educated for domesticity at Catharine Beecher's Hartford Seminary. At her graduation in 1843, she became a member of the Congregational Church, a religious commitment she kept all of her life. Like many intelligent middle-class women Cooke initially supported herself by teaching: first in Hartford, then in a Presbyterian school in New Jersey, and finally as a governess for a clergyman's family. She returned home in 1847 and began writing poetry. According to her biographer, Jean Downey, her first major published piece of fiction was "The Mormon's Wife," offered in *Putnam's* in 1855. In the following years her work appeared in *Harper's* and *The Atlantic*. Like Harriet Beecher Stowe, Rose Terry Cooke became an inspiration to young female readers, and writers.[26]

Cooke was always proud of her ability to support herself, but her marriage in 1873 to Rollin H. Cooke, a widower sixteen years her junior, meant constant financial struggle. Her husband was never able to maintain a steady income, and in 1885 his father lost much of Rose Terry Cooke's savings in a disastrous business failure. Pot-boilers and writing for the market were often the only way she could survive. And yet, while Cooke was the financial mainstay of her household, she remained an advocate of True Womanhood and an opponent of woman suffrage. Here, as in the church, her criticism came from inside the institution. She often reminded readers that a woman's place was in the home under the "headship" of a good husband. Many women writers found themselves in just such an ironic situation.

But if many of Cooke's stories are, as Fetterley says, "didactic homilies that extol and idealize the virtues of female self-sacrifice," others, arguably her best, ruthlessly expose the harshness of both Calvinism and patriarchal authority.[27] There is for example, Cooke's portrayal of Deacon Flint, who virtually murders his wife through overwork and starvation. Her sympathetic spinsters, such as "Polly Mariner, Tailoress," paved the way for later characters such as Jewett's Mrs. Todd. Marriage for these women is often destructive.

The story I have chosen to explicate is neither gritty nor particularly realistic; "didactic homily" is more like it. Even so sympathetic a critic as Ammons describes "Root-Bound" as "formulaic and pat." But that formula is what I am after. Published by the Congregational Sunday School and Publishing Society, "Root-Bound" offers a neat paradigm of the domestic world-view and sentimentalist ethos.[28] Moreover, it shows how Cooke's innate honesty brings out surprising twists in a conventional tale. Throughout this parable-like story we can see her grappling with the ideology that defined woman's place in Victorian culture. These are the codes by which women like Jewett were raised.

As the story opens, Mrs. Rush, a wealthy widow, complains to her seamstress, Mary Meyers, that the plants in her conservatory refuse to bloom, although she provides a gardener, brilliant sunlight even in winter, and plenty of space. However, the windows of a small house nearby are filled with blooming flowers. They belong to Mrs. Rockwell, poverty-stricken and crippled. The problem, as Mrs. Rush will learn from this saintly woman, is that her plants have too much freedom. Mrs. Rush had always "had a vague idea that plants should have all the earth that could be afforded them, when they could not riot in the garden." However, as Mrs. Rockwell gently explains, her plants blossom extravagantly because they are firmly bound in place, "so they do their lawful and appointed work, instead of going all over, and playing-like." Even plants that grow in gardens need restriction, she reflects: "Even then I believe folks sometimes cut in the roots of fruit trees to make 'em bear." And, of course, she draws an analogy with people, for this is a parable about domesticity: "It's good for folks and flowers too to be root-bound . . . especially if we want to bring forth good fruit."[29]

Mrs. Rush, as her name indicates, is too busy to concern herself with other people. Her wealth, widowhood, and childlessness give her freedom to travel outside the domestic sphere. She is unburdened by traditional feminine duties. But as the story argues, freedom deprives her of true womanly satisfaction; her life is without bloom. Her "house was superb in its appointments and well ordered, but it was not a home." Although she gives money generously to the church, she and her sister, equally free and unattached, "were of little use in the vineyard." Superficiality and deathly cold permeate her family relationships. Mrs. Rush not only married her husband "without that one thing in her heart that alone sanctifies and justifies marriage—a real devotion," but her only baby died in a railway accident: "She never saw the little waxen image laid on her husband's arm. . . . She had not even a memory of it left."[30] Systematically deprived by the author of every "feminine" attachment—home, husband, child, family—Mrs. Rush suffers for her freedom. She is spiritually dead: "her conscience was asleep, her faith in abeyance."

Then one day, after a "journey of pleasure," Mrs. Rush returns to her house to find her forty-year-old brother about to marry a "sly creature, only half his age." When she argues against it, he retorts, "I haven't had any home since mother died. . . . You and Sue were always wandering around the world. The house had no mistress." He is setting up his own household and will no longer pay his share of the expenses: "At my age, a man wants a settled home." Next comes a letter from her sister "who was in England, to say she was about to enter an order of deaconesses, and devote herself to good works." Again, the sister needs to be root-bound. Of course, poor Mrs. Rush draws the correct conclusion: "If she had stayed where God had appointed her lot, and done her duty in her own place, she would not at once have lost her home and her brother, for she could not keep up this expensive house alone."[31] Part of her punishment is emotional—she loses her family to other attachments; and part is economic—she loses her house and her wealth.

Before describing Mrs. Rush's inevitable conversion and transformation, let us look at her role model, Mrs. Rockwell, and her hierophant to the domestic mysteries, Mary Meyers. Mary cares for a lame, frail mother and finds relief from a drab existence in the homes of her wealthy customers, but she was "so true a Christian that envy and jealousy did not poison her enjoyment of the good belonging to another." Like Mrs. Rockwell, she works within the church and belongs to a stable network of women. When Mrs. Rush expresses a wish to meet Mrs. Rockwell and discover the secret of her blooming plants, the seamstress is eager to bring them together: " 'And I'd love to have you see her, ma'am,' said Mary, her pale, dark face brightening. For, strange to say, Mary Meyers loved Mrs. Rush, though that lady had not an idea that her seamstress ventured so far, and Mary had no thought of expressing herself to that effect."[32] Through this deep sympathy Mary Meyers divines the wealthy woman's emotional deprivation and provides the cure.

In Mrs. Rockwell we have the apotheosis of the domestic woman. Significantly, this saintly figure is not the young angel in the house described by Ruskin or Dickens but a woman past childbearing. She is also confined, literally, to her tiny space. Even the street to her house is "narrow." She lives in a "sunny, bare little room, with a stove in it, two rush-bottomed chairs, a small table, a large rocking-chair, and only a strip of carpet for all furniture." However, if the room itself provides the tightest possible constriction of the domestic boundary, a lowest common denominator of the concept "house," blooming plants fill it to bursting: "across both the south windows rough shelves had been put; and on these, set in old tin cans, broken sugar-bowls, cracked pitchers, starch-boxes, were geraniums, carnations, oxalis, both pink and yellow, and one dark red flowered rose-bush,—all of them in a blaze of bloom."[33]

Centered in this shrine is the saint herself: "In the large chair, with two crutches beside, sat such a sweet-faced woman! Pale and thin, and shabby, her gray hair drawn straight back from her forehead, and her face lined with pain and privation, some loveliness from within shone so brightly from her clear eyes, and played so softly about her patient lips, that Mrs. Rush looked at her with her heart in her eyes."[34] Mrs. Rockwell—her name signifies her rocklike identity as a locus of feminine values—not only binds her plants but picks their flowers as fast as they open, giving them away to sickrooms, funerals, and so on. Her selflessness, however, is repaid; the plants bloom more vigorously than ever: "the more I pick, the more they blossom."

Saddled with an ineffectual husband (a carpenter without "faculty"), her children dead, confined to her rocking chair with hip disease, Mrs. Rockwell suffers some of the same deprivations of family life that Mrs. Rush does, but her crippling and her poverty save her. Her energy is sublimated into selfless works and spiritual blossoming. For example, she is better able to comfort the dying than the local minister. As Mrs. Rockwell describes the death of a friend, her superior faculties become apparent: "She had sort of dreaded it. . . . But I used to tell her the Lord never gives folks dying grace to live by; and, sure enough, it came to her in time of need. She fell asleep in Jesus, as calm as ever you see a baby on its mother's bosom droppin' off without anything but a little soft sigh."[35]

Following Mrs. Rockwell's example—necessarily, I should add, since economy prompts her new domestic confinement—Mrs. Rush blooms: "No longer able to please herself in her own way, she began to follow the way of the Master and try to please him. She took up the duties that lay nearest to her, and so was led out and on till her days were filled with joyful service, and her heart at peace."[36] Having renounced her egotistical life, Mrs. Rush's rebirth is complete. Her sister returns to live with her. She becomes almost a "deacon" to the parish minister.

In this parable of domestic piety several messages can be traced. First, there is the obvious point that freedom and a will of her own cannot make a woman happy. Rather, her life will become sterile and meaningless. No one else—in this case a dead husband and an absent brother—will take responsibility for maintaining those emotional ties that can satisfy her need for intimacy. Further, the wealthy woman who has freedom to travel outside the home, in the public sphere, does not possess meaningful work: her travel is voyeuristic and superficial. And, especially important here, she does not possess true independence, since Mrs. Rush cannot support herself financially when her brother, the male relative, withdraws his funds. Her freedom is both trivial and insecure. Significantly, there is a "realistic" note to this story. Mrs. Rush must be *forced* into her narrow sphere by economic necessity, just as Mrs. Rockwell was originally compelled by the "will of God," who gave her a shiftless husband, hip disease, and poverty. Mrs. Cooke does not go so far as to suggest that women voluntarily take vows of poverty and immobility (although she does come close when she has Mrs. Rush's sister sacrifice the world to become a deaconess).

Read from our own twentieth-century perspective, "Root-Bound" might seem to offer a reactionary message in light of some idea of progress. However, we might also find a covert message for Victorian readers. In Mrs. Rush's failure to thrive before her conversion, Victorian readers may have read a condemnation of the masculine life-style, presented here as isolation and self-absorption—a failure to nurture, hence a failure to grow. The price for Mrs. Rush's spiritual flowering is her selfhood. However, at the close of this story Mrs. Rush is significantly *not* bound within the home; she is rather an active charity worker, virtually a second minister to her church. Once her activities are coded as service to others, Mrs. Rush can range outward into the world again, a confident missionary in the cause of righteousness, bringing domestic sweetness and light into the heart of the masculine

city. Working through a female network and using the domestic ideology, Mrs. Rush has created a public role for herself. Part of that
spiritual flowering comes, I suspect, from increased self-esteem and an
exhilarating sense of moral authority, all safely coded in terms of self-
sacrifice.

There are, of course, some problems with the sentimentalist, domestic strategy. First of all, there is the problem of false consciousness.
If these women were really seeking public power without admitting it
to themselves, then the possibilities for personal confusion as well as
political failure are great. Then there is the problem of proclaiming
moral superiority. William O'Neill and Gail Parker have both remarked
that genteel reformers were too apt to believe their own claims of
purity; as a result they could not deal effectively with the realities of
the political process they were trying to enter. They were unable to
make the compromises with corruption that successful reform entails.[37]

But perhaps most important, the ideology of domesticity often prevented these reformers from making common cause with women whose
background was not middle-class. Women who worked alongside men
in the fields or the factories could not easily claim the mantle of domestic purity. Hence, Sojourner Truth, the ex-slave who argued so
passionately for abolition and women's rights, had to ask her audience,
"Ain't I a woman?" Sojourner Truth demanded her right to speak not
on the basis of her purity but of her humanity. Her criticism was simple
but sweeping; in claiming to be angels women sold themselves short
as people.

Finally, the story's obvious moral—that women's libidinous energy
will destroy their spirituality unless forcibly sublimated—neatly defines
Victorian domestic religion. Suppress the ego, cut the roots—the tale's
imagery is drastic and not a little frightening. Crippling a woman looks
almost like a benign act of the Lord, who in his infinite wisdom has
"influenced" her greater selflessness. The more women are prevented
from the "natural" expression of energy and will—the more they are
forced to attend to the needs of their Lord, the other—the more they
will enter into the feminine world of ethereal, sublimated energy. The
"roots" show us woman's association with the "dirty," "polluted" side
of nature, the earth itself. The more that inescapable connection is
minimized and circumscribed by social convention, the more a woman
will blossom out into that spiritual entity, the flower-like angel hovering
on the boundary of culture. From her position on the periphery she
mediates between the public world and heaven itself. Mrs. Rockwell's
age may be significant here. Past childbearing, she can carry no asso-

ciation with the pollution of actual biological intercourse and reproduction. She has become a mother in a spiritual sense, transferring her
kin-based sympathies to the larger world beyond the home.

Here we can see the ambiguity that Sherry Ortner describes. Situated
on the boundary between culture and "the world beyond," the Victorian angel still retains a subtle association with the natural world.
However, while Victorians celebrated sublimated motherhood, the only
physiological process still open for public examination and elaboration
was death. The genteel woman's absorption with the biological world
was strictly controlled. The lower side of nature—sexual, "red in tooth
and claw"—was not their nature. This depraved world they abjured,
along with the terror of the Calvinist God. The nature they celebrated,
like the maternal deity they turned to, was a cleaned-up, gentler nature.
Death should have no terrors, they reasoned; nature in its fearsome
aspect was an illusion. Grasped by its proper aspect, death becomes a
simple translation into the higher spiritual sphere, a sphere actually
much like this world but better. Continuity, not crisis, governs this
central human experience.

Thus, writers such as Elizabeth Stuart Phelps (Ward) stressed the
similarity between this world and the next. Their preoccupation with
spiritualism and ghostly presences testifies to their blurring of the
boundary between life and death, a boundary sharply marked in Calvinist orthodoxy.[38] In novels such as *Pearl of Orr's Island* and even in
Jewett's later stories such as "The Foreigner" and "Miss Tempy's
Watchers," a female figure moves between the human and spiritual
worlds. Just as women, according to Ortner, mediated between the
natural world and the culture, here they mediate between heaven and
earth. Their flexible ego boundaries correlate with this ability to transcend boundaries. To use Chodorow's language, a richer "inner object
world" and a greater ability to regress to the preoedipal stage (with its
characteristic loss of reality-sense) give the female "medium" her ability
to see the ineffable mysteries of the spirit and the dead.

This then is "Root-Bound"'s paradox: the way down is the way up
(or the way in is the way out) as the periphery of culture circles around
to transform opposites into each other. For if immanence is the way to
transcendence and restriction is the way to freedom, then death is the
way to life and loss is the way to victory; and ultimately, the unknown
woman, hidden in her private world, will be the saint of the world to
come.

And this role brings us to that image of Jesus with the dying woman
sleeping like a baby at his breast. Barbara Welter and Ann Douglas
argue that sentimentalism, which "Root-Bound" certainly represents,

offers a feminized Christianity; its stories substitute new, potentially subversive female images for the conventional male deity.[39] This story implies a gospel of domesticity, and crucial to its dissemination is that network of "sympathetic" women. Mrs. Rush's conversion begins when she looks at Mrs. Rockwell "with her heart in her eyes." It is confirmed when she takes up her role as a kind of missionary within the parish. And, the story suggests, her spiritual development will be complete only when she finally returns to Christ's breast at death. The true "Lord" of this story is the Great Mother, and Mrs. Rockwell is her prophet.

Chapter Two

Mother Texts

While Rose Terry Cooke inscribed her subversive vision within a deceptively realistic fiction, other writers sought more explicit symbols. In the Catholic Madonna, in the Greek Demeter, they found figures equal to their own experience. Henry Adams, however, vehemently denied that America had or even wanted such a feminine iconography. In *The Education* he complained that an "American Virgin" would never dare rule. All of our goddesses were dead or dying. According to Adams, Venus was forgotten even as a name in the Boston of his boyhood, except perhaps as the derivation of venereal disease.[1] Although literary critics have tended to accept Adams's judgment, my own quest revealed that literate Bostonians had been trying to resuscitate dead goddesses for decades. Caroline Healy Dall records that two of Margaret Fuller's 1841 "Conversations on Mythology" were devoted to "Ceres, Proserpina, and Isis, as well as Rhea, Diana, and so on."[2] *The Atlantic Monthly,* which I searched from its first issue to 1900, regularly informed its readers on pre-Christian goddesses and their rituals. By 1869 Thomas Wentworth Higginson felt obliged to apologize to his *Atlantic* audience for presenting them with yet another essay on the subject: "The Greek Goddesses have been very fully discussed. . . . Their genealogies have been ransacked, as if they lived in Boston or Philadelphia."[3]

From Margaret Fuller to T. W. Higginson to Charlotte Perkins Gilman, Americans searched for the Goddess. Whether she was to be revived from deathlike sleep, reborn in modern form, or rediscovered in our own green places wasn't clear. Only one thing was: she was needed. In 1869 Higginson wrote, "we toil among the dust and rubbish, waiting for the goddess and the shrine."[4] And the waiting was sometimes surprisingly literal. Justin Kaplan describes a New Year's Eve party in Hartford where Isabella Beecher Hooker and a crowd of spiritualists huddled upstairs and watched for the dawn of Universal Matriarchy. (A bemused Mark Twain saw some mediums straggling away after the apocalyptic deadline.) Twenty years later Hamilton

Wright Mabie, editor of *Century* magazine, went to the woods hoping
for just a "fleeting glimpse of her face and form." "If I had been a
Greek," he explained, "she would have been at my door. There is a
good deal of paganism . . . we must recover before we realize Goethe's
ideal of living in the whole of things."[5] Moreover, the demand was not
limited to New England or to literary circles. According to historian
Mari Jo Buhle, some midwestern granges even got up their own Eleusinian Mysteries. (Apparently it was a small step from Episcopal fri-
volities like Christmas to the real pagan article.) As for the theory
behind the revivals, T. W. Higginson's "The Greek Goddesses," published in *The Atlantic Monthly* (July 1869), is a good place to start.[6]

I

Higginson opens with this epigram from Carew: "That heroic virtue / For which antiquity hath left no names / But patterns only, such
as Hercules, / Achilles, Theseus."[7] Women need their own patterns:
their own myths for their own virtues. In Greece they had them. The
pantheon comprised a perfect "prism of feminine existence." From
Artemis the young virgin to Aphrodite the lover, from Hera the wife
to Demeter the mother, "an imaginative Greek girl had not an epoch
nor an instant that was not ennobled." Her "life was like a revolving
urn, upon which she could always see one great symbolic image sculp-
tured, though each in its turn gave way to another."[8]

The argument is strikingly similar to one made by twentieth-century
feminists, particularly Mary Daly. For Higginson the culprit wasn't
patriarchy but monotheism. However, the result was the same, for as
soon as monotheism took hold, "it instantly became necessary to say
He or She in speaking of the Highest; and the immediate result was a
masculine Deity, and the dethronement of woman."[9] Religious life lost
the expression of feminine spirituality and its connection to women's
experience. Since Protestant Christianity was the most monotheistic
religion, it was also the most impoverished. While he acknowledges the
social oppression of Greek women, Higginson contrasts their spiritual
wealth to American women's poverty: "In [Greek] temples the sexes
stood equal, goddess was as sublime as god, priestess the peer of priest.
. . . In Protestant Christian Churches, on the other hand, nothing feminine is left but the worshippers, and they indeed are feminine, three
to one."[10]

Given this poverty it is not surprising that Higginson finds modern
women better served by Roman Catholicism: at least Catholics had the
Madonna. Since nineteenth-century American fiction is strewn with
shrines to Mary, Higginson's fellow writers apparently agreed with

him. There's Hawthorne's *The Marble Faun,* where the motherless Hilda tends the Virgin's shrine in a crumbling Roman tower; her task is to keep the sacred flame alive. In *Little Women,* Amy, missing her Marmee, sets up a copy of Raphael's Virgin in a closet, where she sits and meditates on her faults. In Henry James's *The Bostonians,* Olive Chancellor and Verena Tarrant retire to the pastoral village of Marmion, where their cottage displays two conspicuous photographs of the Sistine Madonna and a number of suspicious German books.[11]

With such an embarrassment of Virgins, Henry Adams's complaint about her absence might seem shortsighted, if not perverse. However, the Madonna Adams mourned was the force of "reproductive energy," and when he "asked himself whether he knew of any American artist who had insisted on the power of sex, as every classic had always done . . . he could think only of Walt Whitman; Bret Harte, as far as the magazines would let him venture; and one or two painters, for the flesh-tones." To Adams's contemporaries, "Eve was a tender flower, and Herodias an unfeminine horror." They saw the goddesses of the past "only as reflected emotion, human expression, beauty, purity, taste, scarcely even as sympathy."[12]

Higginson renders this genteel feminine iconography with complete fidelity. According to his anxious assurances, five of his six goddesses are literally virgins. Venus herself is a virgin; Demeter conceives Persephone through an "ineffable idea"; only Hera is initiated—and she has to be because she's married to Jove. Moreover, Higginson averts his gaze from a host of darker deities. There is no Medusa on this revolving urn, no Medea. Where are the Parkae, those scary images of the Fates, sharing their one eye? And where are the ecstatic rioting Bacchantes? The women Higginson eulogizes apparently never retreated with Hecate to the cave of the moon, never heard their sexual fears expressed through Persephone's cries on the Nysian Plain.

Higginson's attitude toward Mary Magdalene, the "sole modern figure" introduced by Christianity into the feminine pantheon (the Virgin is just Demeter revived) is especially revealing: "she has not an ideal interest, but one that is philanthropic alone. . . . if we are looking for the very highest, it cannot be found in the fallen." What American women need is "elevation through contact with the great ideal women of the sky."[13] Clearly, "elevation" can be achieved only by purging women and their symbols of any sexual association. But, to paraphrase Martha Saxton's quip about Bronson Alcott, it is not fair to accuse Higginson of bias. His goddesses were all ladies, but then his gods were always gentlemen.

Thus, Higginson's mythic "prism" reflects the life cycle of aspiring angels in the house. In this genteel pantheon, divinity stems from maternity, not sexuality. For Henry Adams, the Virgin was a descendent of Venus, her power veiled but still radiant. For Higginson, the Virgin was literally a survival of Demeter, whose rising-and-dying daughter has been disguised as a rising-and-dying son. My own research suggests that many, if not most, Victorian women writers agreed with Higginson. While Kate Chopin heralded a return of Aphrodite at the close of the century, writers such as Harriet Beecher Stowe and Louisa May Alcott found the story of Demeter and Persephone a more compelling plot.[14]

Take, for example, *Little Women* (1869). At her wedding, the oldest daughter, Meg, pulls away from her new husband immediately after their vows. She wants to save "the first kiss for Marmee." After the birth of her twins, Meg declares that they have made her "more one" with her mother. The book itself closes with a chapter called "Harvest Time." We see Marmee enthroned in an apple orchard, receiving tributes from her three daughters, all of whom are now mothers. Beth, the daughter who has died, is resurrected in the child who bears her name.[15]

This plot appealed to nineteenth-century writers, as it does to twentieth-century ones, as a paradigm of female development. Indeed, Jungian theorist Erich Neumann's archetypal portrait of the reluctant maiden ravished by the Underworld Prince makes a striking fit with Carroll Smith-Rosenberg's description of the sheltered Victorian daughter separated from her mother's middle-class home through a series of elaborate nuptial rituals, then given over to a husband "in every sense a member of an alien culture." The Victorian bridegroom in his dark suit played, in Smith-Rosenberg's own words, only a "shadowy" part in the Victorian world of women.[16]

However, many writers, like Higginson, averted their eyes from disturbing aspects of the Homeric story. In their genteel version the Prince's sexuality finds no sympathetic counterpart; his bride "suffers" his advances for the sake of her ultimate transfiguration as consecrated mother and domestic priestess. If she is to be a true angel in the house, Persephone must be purged of sexual complicity. Her rape is a tragic event, necessary to her eventual apotheosis, but the shadow is cast off the woman and onto the male; while those darker goddesses, Hecate and Rhea, pledge submission to the risen mother.

The problem with this Victorian version is that Hades is never transformed, the sexual relationship remains a rape, and Persephone's return comes dangerously close to regression. Interpreted as an expression of the actual social situation, rather than as events within the individual psyche, the myth expresses the distance between men and women. The

male world never becomes Persephone's world; she is not co-ruler but
the child of the distant uncle or the subordinate of the rapist/husband.
Only with her mother is she fulfilled. Persephone's original attraction
to the penis-like narcissus is denied, as is her willful straying far from
her mother's call. Nor is her return a transformation of both mother
and daughter; the daughter may have become a mother, but the achievement of consciousness through separation is not stressed. Individuation
is not a goal, whereas communion offers escape from the rigors of
masculine alienation.

Curiously, in *Tanglewood Tales,* Hawthorne's expurgations for children reveal the regressive qualities of the "angel's" gentility. His Persephone is a very young girl carried off by her uncle for no discernible
reason. She remains a child throughout the proceedings, pining away
on Uncle's knees. Here the development of the feminine self has been
arrested at the earliest level; she will remain a child and return to her
mother none the wiser for her experience. The mirror bond is never
broken; the oedipal "third" never penetrates. Like Hilda in *The Marble
Faun,* Hawthorne's Persephone is implacably, even stupidly innocent.[17]

Looking at this genteel version of the myth as a dramatization of
interior psychological events, we could say that the male-identified
world appears more alien to the girl, who is either less able or not
allowed to separate from her mother. Her own ego thus appears more
threatening, and she is more likely to "run away" from it back into
fusion, into the "selfless" nurturing of others. Thus, in one graphic
image Hawthorne's Hilda flees to the Virgin's Tower, safely above the
dangerous revelations of Rome. In Nancy Chodorow's vision of integration, Persephone "marries" both ego and unconscious; in a curious
way she identifies with both, is happy with both. But the angel in the
house regards the "masculine" aspect of her own personality as alien.

In large part this version reflects the extreme patriarchal structure of
middle-class Victorian society. Even if the Victorian lady had wished
to explore the "masculine" world of heterosexuality and self-assertion,
she would have been firmly restrained. The father who "seduced" the
daughter definitely did not allow her freedom but insisted on her obedience and subordination. Thus, we see how the myth—if we stop at
the "rape" without further transformation of the male element—brings
Persephone closer to regression than to integration. Psychologically, the
"arrested" myth denies woman's need for differentiation and ego development. Socially, it denies her roles that require agency or authority,
as well as devaluing or even rejecting her part in heterosexual intercourse. If we look at the imagery of "Root-Bound," we see Persephone's roots in the Underworld of sexuality and freedom drastically

restricted. The rhythmic circulation of life—root, stem, and blossom—
is pinched at the base for the sake of the flower. Although she still
watches over the world of the dead, who return to Jesus "like a child
to its mother," Persephone is no longer free to "riot in the garden,"
the source of her downfall. Her connection with the shadowy Hades is
the shameful secret of the Victorian household; the ladies of "Root-
Bound" are all past that now.

II

So would an American Virgin dare rule? Adams thought not, but
perhaps he underestimated the power not of sex but of sentiment. Higginson, for one, had no doubts on the matter: "Nothing shall drive me
from the belief that there is arising in America, amid all our frivolities,
a type of virgin womanhood, new in history, undescribed in fiction,
from which there may proceed, in generations yet to come, a priesthood
more tender, a majesty more pure and grand, than anything which poet
ever sang or temple enthroned."[18] Higginson then invokes what seems
to have been a common theme: the fusing of the patriarchal and matriarchal symbolism to produce "yet nobler forms, that shall eclipse
those 'fair humanities of old religion'; just as when classic architecture
had reached perfection, there arose the Gothic and made the Greek
seem cold."

The conclusion: women weren't the only ones needing the goddess—
America needed her. If Victorians denied female sexuality, they hailed
maternal "instinct" as a recovered aspect of the Godhead. Writers such
as Harriet Beecher Stowe argued that America needed a more nurturant, more maternal deity. H. M. Alden believed that we needed a religion closer to the earth and more respectful of its processes. And
there often seems to be a covert association between the green world
obliterated by patriarchal civilization and the female domestic sphere—
a pastoral haven in an increasingly industrialized world. For example,
Margaret Coxe's *Young Lady's Companion* told the new housewife
that she was the priestess of a shrine "more sacred than Delphos."[19]

Thus, the Dual Goddess and her Mysteries represented more than a
paradigm of female development. Philosophical discussions of the goddesses almost always defined these deities as products of a primordial
cultural epoch or as symbols of an archaic spiritual ethos. The authority behind this theory of progress was often the German historian
J. J. Bachofen, whose 1861 *Das Mutterrecht* achieved a broad popularity, which it still retains (although it has long been out of favor
among professional anthropologists).[20] In surprisingly lyrical prose
Bachofen evoked a lost matriarchal world founded on the worship of

benevolent earth goddesses. These matriarchs invented the basic structures of civilization—agriculture, marriage, the home—before their rule was overthrown by jealous males. As the Father assumed power, the forms of a new spirituality took hold. The judgment of an otherworldly Jove or Yahweh replaced the nurturance of a chthonic Ishtar, Isis, or Demeter. But beneath the dominant culture the matriarchal ruins remained, surfacing occasionally in a witchcraft scare or mysterious nursery rhyme. Although Bachofen believed the matriarchy's defeat was inevitable and universal, his portrait of this archaic green world was both tender and nostalgic.

However, even before Bachofen's work appeared, the matriarchal theory had caught the Victorian imagination. In her 1840 "Conversations" on classical mythology Margaret Fuller described the Mother Goddess as the guiding force of earliest civilization. Her myths expressed "the progress of a people from an unconscious to a conscious state." Innocence lost could never be fully restored; thus, "Ceres regained her daughter, but only for half the year. Isis found her husband, but dismembered."[21]

H. M. Alden's interpretation of the Eleusinian Mysteries also underscores this link between the feminine deities and the "sorrowful" aspects of human existence. His essay, mentioned above, came out in the *Atlantic* in two installments, September 1859 and August 1860. Like Fuller, Alden came to his conclusions without the aid of J. J. Bachofen. However, unlike either one of these, Alden did not feel that the great feminine goddesses were rendered obsolete by the rise of patriarchal consciousness. Instead, he believed that "all mythology naturally and inevitably flows" about a male and a female center. The religious sentiments always acknowledge a feminine aspect of the Godhead, although her presence might be obscured from view from time to time (just as the masculine aspect might).[22]

The 1870s saw a resurgence of interest in myth and folklore. And again the goddess drew particular attention. Among the pieces published by the *Atlantic,* Lydia Maria Child's "The Intermingling of Religions" (October 1871) is representative. She describes a "universal" need for a sympathetic mediator between mere mortals and "Infinite Being." The One God is too abstract, too distant for human comprehension. She concludes that "almost every ancient nation had some Mother Goddess, whose favor they sought to propitiate by prayers and offerings."[23] As Higginson had, Child discovers that the Madonna is only a disguised Demeter: "When Christianity superseded the old religions, the ancient ideas and forms took new names. . . . Nations that had been accustomed to worship the Goddess of nature as a Mother

Goddess easily transferred their offerings and prayers to the Virgin Mary, their Spiritual Mother."[24]

Other discussions in the *Atlantic* during this period included B. W. Ball's "Woman's Rights in Ancient Athens" (March 1871). Ball, predictably, lamented the low status of women in Greek society but noted that the "chief Aryan divinities, whose worship was most significant, were feminine." Like Child, Ball feels that these goddesses were so beloved because "their jurisdiction . . . came nighest to the concerns and needs of mortal life."[25] Her conclusion that these "divine women of Olympus were worshipped with a devotion . . . equal to the subsequent Christian adoration of the Mater Dolorosa" could have come as no surprise to the magazine's regular readers.

Two decades later writers took the goddess's archaic origins for granted but were uncertain what to make of them. An *Atlantic* review of Tennyson's *Demeter and Other Poems* (1889) adopted a rather orthodox Christian approach (as Tennyson himself had done). Retelling the Eleusinian story, the poet "has touched the lines with an infinite Christian suggestion."[26] In this interpretation the feminine drama is a primitive version of the masculine one. Persephone's ascent from Hades prefigures Christ's own resurrection, and Demeter's prophecy of her daughter's annual return makes "her figure like that of the oracular priestess" who dimly anticipates "the coming of the kinder gods."[27] However, in this same year, 1891, Elizabeth Cady Stanton's "The Matriarchate, or Mother-Age" described the gods of patriarchal Christianity as anything but kindly. And just one year earlier, Sir James George Frazer's *The Golden Bough* had inaugurated a new era in the interpretation of myth and folklore.[28] Frazer, with little regard for the angel in the house, found that Demeter's original prototype was the primordial pig sacrificed at Eleusis to ensure the return of vegetation after winter's devastation. Far from spiritual, maternity, for Frazer, was a dark process indissolubly linked to the fears and urges of a primitive people.

Higginson was right about one thing at least. Writers everywhere were "ransacking" the genealogies of the goddess. In each person's hands the multicolored fragments of the cultural kaleidoscope produced new variants of the ancient patterns. The variants themselves could best be categorized according to their ideas of progress. For Bachofen, the patriarchal forms were the highest; there was nowhere else to go but back, or down. For Elizabeth Cady Stanton and Mathilda Joslyn Gage, the patriarchy was a blasphemous overthrow of the noble matriarchal culture. But it is probably safe to say that most fell in with the ever moderate Higginson, who simply wanted to *balance* the extreme patriarchalism of Protestant Christianity and so arrive at a new fulfillment of the cultural potential.

Thus, many of the authors claiming America's need for the goddess—Margaret Fuller, H. M. Alden, even Elizabeth Cady Stanton and Mathilda Joslyn Gage—close their argument, as Higginson does, by invoking a vision of the matriarchal mother reenthroned beside the patriarchal father. Together the couple ushers in a new age of peace and justice. The conclusion of Elizabeth Cady Stanton's 1891 speech, "The Matriarchate, or Mother-Age," is a good example of this ultimate moment when "the united thought of man and woman will inaugurate a just government, a pure religion, and a happy home; a civilization at last in which ignorance, poverty, and crime will exist no more."[29]

Here again a popular choice for reinstatement as national—or at least New England—goddess was Demeter. The reasons for this choice are complex, but one may be an important shift in the way some New Englanders saw themselves. The Boston of Henry Adams's ancestors saw itself against an Old Testament background—the Puritans were the new Israel—but by the mid-nineteenth century many Boston writers saw their city as the Athens of America. (Such comparisons abound in the pages of the *Atlantic*; one writer even turns the analogy around and describes fourth- and fifth-century Athens as "in some marked respects a community of New England Yankees, prematurely appearing in the recesses of the Eastern Mediterranean."[30]) Now the preeminent rituals of ancient Athens were the Eleusinian Mysteries, which survived for two thousand years. But as Walter Pater's 1876 article on "The Myth of Demeter and Persephone" points out, Demeter and her rites were actually alien "to the genuine traditions of Greek mythology," relics of "that older religion, nearer to the earth, which some have thought they could discern behind the more definitely national religion of Homer."[31] Slowly, the goddess gained the interest and love of the Greeks, "becoming finally the central and most popular subject of their national worship." Judging by my sources, it's clear that several writers hoped that she might enjoy a similar success in Yankee New England.

III

Of course, we now know that the goddess never won a legitimate place in the prim white churches of Maine or Massachusetts. But if Protestants stubbornly refused to make room for Mother, her worship found its way into their faith nevertheless. Describing the newly liberalized Christ of Horace Bushnell and Harriet Beecher Stowe, Ann Douglas remarks, "it is not just that God wants to become a man; He wants to become a woman."[32] And what kind of woman would God want to become? The Madonna would be a good bet, and so would the noble Demeter, *Mater Dolorosa* of the ancient world. Indeed, contemporary descriptions of the feminized Savior make a striking fit not only with the angel in the house, as exemplified by Stowe's Mara Lincoln, but also with Erich Neumann's "Sophia," dual goddess of the Eleusinian Mysteries, archetype of the risen Persephone. According to Douglas, the Christ painted by Horace Bushnell "has found it lonely to be God up there with that power and no love. He prefers earth to heaven, feeling to logic." We recognize this Savior's suffering "because we witness it daily in the responses of a mother to her child."[33]

Compare Bushnell's passage with Neumann's description of the Sophia, who is "living and present nearby, a godhead that can always be summoned and is always ready to intervene."[34] This deity, who also grows out of the "responses of a mother to her child," "does not vanish in the nirvana-like abstraction of a masculine spirit; like the scent of a blossom, her spirit always remains attached to the earthly foundation of reality."[35] Sophia's rituals—the Eleusinian Mysteries—express a cyclical view of life. Transcendence is achieved not by dominating nature through abstract form but by returning to nature with conscious awareness, a transcendence paradoxically achieved through immanence. This pattern matches Ann Douglas's description of the sentimentalist ethos, as expressed in the biographies of Protestant ministers: "'Masculine' attempts at domination and demarcation give way to 'feminine' abilities for assimilation and absorption. The active force of public example is lost in the persuasive rites of protection and dependency established by the nurturing power of memory. Biography is merged with something close to vegetation myth."[36] According to Douglas, liberal ministers and their feminine literary counterparts "were engaged in subordinating historical progress to biological process." And, I would argue, they found paradigms for this process in the myths and mysteries of the "Demetrian" age.

My key text is one Douglas selects as exemplum of the sentimental genre: Harriet Beecher Stowe's *Pearl of Orr's Island* (1862).[37] The novel could best be called a *Bildungsroman,* the story of a soul's education. It also fits the pattern of the quest myth that Neumann and Joseph Campbell analyze.[38] Usually, the quest's heroes leave home to seek a special "boon" or "wisdom," with which they return, enlightening their family and society. Often the protagonists are orphaned, symbolizing their existential loneliness in the world they seek to understand. In this case, Mara Lincoln loses her father in the opening pages; then her mother dies giving birth. Mara comes into the world alone and, in the course of the novel, discovers that her vocation is to die and by dying to become the savior of those she loves. Her ordeals stem primarily from the temptation to become a human, conventional wife, a role that would destroy her deepest identity. Through death and transfiguration Mara comes into her own.

In dramatizing this plot, Stowe, not surprisingly, ran into the problem described later by Higginson. She had to turn to classical and Roman Catholic imagery to find adequate symbols for Mara's situation and ultimate significance. Although I have not found direct evidence for Stowe's sources, internal evidence from the novel suggests she may have been influenced by H. M. Alden's article "The Eleusinia," which appeared in the September 1859 *Atlantic* along with Chapter 22 of *The Minister's Wooing*. (Significantly, Part 1 of Alden's piece was flanked by this installment of Stowe's novel and an article entitled "A Visit to Martha's Vineyard.") A brief outline of Alden's theory will help us see how Stowe incorporated it. Recent critics, such as Elizabeth Ammons and Dorothy Berkson, have demonstrated how seriously Stowe took her commitment to matrifocal values and her belief in the feminizing power of New Testament teachings. What this material suggests is Stowe's conscious adaptation of mythic patterns, a deliberate reworking of the matriarchal mythology.[39]

Alden believes that all of human experience and all of human knowledge revolve about two centers—one masculine, one feminine. These two forces are symbolized in every mythology as "Lord and Lady," *Mater Dolorosa* and *Dominus Salvator*: "in the Hindu *Isi* and *Isana*, the Egyptian *Isis* and *Osiris*, the Assyrian *Venus* and *Adonis*, the *Demeter* and *Dionysus* of Greece, the Roman *Ceres* and *Bacchus*, and *Disa* and *Frey* of Scandinavia."[40]

Although their meaning is spiritual as well as natural, these images display a universal symbolism taken from nature. The *Mater Dolorosa* is inextricably tied to the earth and earthly immanence: "She was the Mother, and hers was the travail of all birth; in sorrow she forever gathered to herself her Fate-conquered children." However, the sun, "Eternal Father, the Revealer of all things," clears the mists that rise from the grief-stricken Earth: "out of darkness and death, he called into birth the flowers and the numberless forest,—even as he himself was every morning born anew out of darkness,—so he called the children of earth to a glorious rising in his light."[41]

Not surprisingly, these figures, "detached from natural symbols," appear in Christendom as the Virgin and her son. However, the ancient faith reached its fullest expression in the Eleusinia, which Alden sees as the source of the Christian sacraments themselves. Greek worshipers gave the mysteries "a profound spiritual meaning" that extended to the "mystic connection of Demeter and Dionysus": "She gave them bread: but they never forgot that she gave them the bread of life. . . . So Dionysus gave them wine, not only to lighten the care of life, but as a token . . . of higher joy which would be given them in some happier world."[42] Demeter's presence at the Eleusinia is the grave, sorrowing weight that tempers the joy of Dionysus, restoring measure to excess and giving due respect to the centrality of death in the universal scheme. She is, Alden writes, the skeleton at every feast, the narrow gate that must be traversed on the way to Paradise. The Lord and Lady are inseparable, just as "the snows of winter are necessary to the blossoms of spring,—the waste of death to the resurrections of life."[43]

Significantly, Alden finds that many religious traditions combine male and female aspects of the Godhead in one implicitly androgynous deity, who suffers but is miraculously transfigured. These gods wander and grieve as Demeter did but are resurrected as Dionysus was. Here Alden's "natural" gender-based symbolism begins to break down. For if Demeter suffers, Persephone rises from the dead. And, of course, Christ also descends into the Underworld following his agony on the cross. His transfiguration is thus balanced by the "feminine" aspect of his divinity. But the most important point to bring away from Alden's interpretation is his strong assertion of a feminine presence in all religious worship: "We do all . . .—Hindu, Egyptian, Greek, or Saxon,—claim kinship with both the earth and the heavens, with the sense of sorrow we kneel upon the earth, with the sense of hope we look into the heavens."[44]

Stowe's adaptation of these Eleusinian patterns gave the feminine faith a human form, gave women a myth to measure their daily lives. Her archetypal portrait of New England life also marked the way for other women writers. Sarah Orne Jewett said that *Pearl of Orr's Island,* which she read when she was only ten, inspired her first book, *Deephaven* (1877). Its themes and imagery recur throughout Jewett's career, up to her greatest work, *The Country of the Pointed Firs* (1896).[45]

IV

Stowe's novel begins with sorrow, not hope. The story is set on Orr's Island in Maine, an old-fashioned community dependent on the sea and sustained by Calvinism. In the opening scene Zephaniah Pennel and his only daughter, Naomi, survey the shining bay and islands from the headlands. Suddenly, before their very eyes, the ship carrying home Naomi's husband is wrecked on the rocks below. Shock brings on the premature birth of Naomi's child. She names it Mara, from the passage in which her biblical namesake says, "Call me not Naomi; call me

Mara; for the Almighty hath dealt very bitterly with me."[46] With this final reproach the mother dies.

Despite these fearful beginnings Mara lies safe in the bosom of a pastoral Israel. Zephaniah Pennel might be called a Hebrew of the Hebrews, for "New England, in her earlier days, founded her institutions on the Hebrew Scriptures." And yet, Stowe adds, New England "bred better Jews than Moses could, because she read Moses with the amendments of Christ."[47] Thus, Grandfather Pennel leads his family in prayer at night, a kindly "priest" in his own home. His wife, however, gives the lie to Calvinist doctrine and suggests the direction Mara will later take: "All she wanted of a child, or in fact of any human creature, was something to love and serve. We leave it entirely up to theologians to reconcile such facts with the theory of total depravity."[48]

Mara, delicate and ethereal, is the joy of her grandparents' lives. She is more refined than other children of the island and preternaturally sensitive. Her closest friend is the "dark" heroine of the tale, the saucy, earthy Sally Kittridge, a sturdy brunette child who gives ample promise of womanly "faculty." One night the tiny Mara has a prophetic dream: she and Sally are playing on the beach when suddenly a woman appears before them. She is wearing a "long white garment" and her face is "very pale, with sweet, serious dark eyes." Clasped in her hand is that of a small bewildered boy, black-eyed and olive-skinned. As Mara wonders, the lady approaches, "looking at her with sweet, sad eyes, till the child seemed to feel them in every fibre of her frame." Then, "as if in blessing," she places the little boy's hand in Mara's and says, "Take him, Mara, he is a playmate for you."[49]

The next morning Sally and Mara do play on the beach, which, after a storm the night before, is littered with seaweed, "what might have been the fringes and fragments of sea-gods' vestures." And there are the mother and child Mara had dreamed of: "Both had been carefully lashed to a spar, but the child was held to the bosom of the woman, with a pressure closer than any knot that mortal hands could tie."[50] The mother—whom we will later discover to be Dolores, Roman Catholic daughter of a tyrannical Spanish-American father—is literally "embedded" in the natural world. Both she and her child "were sunk deep in the sand, into which had streamed the woman's long dark hair, which sparkled with glittering morsels of sand and pebbles, and with ... tiny, brilliant, yellow shells." The association is strengthened by the next paragraph: "A wedding-ring gleamed on the marble hand; but the sea had divorced all human ties, and taken her as bride to itself." In this deathly marriage, the sea has made his bride "a worthy bed, for she was all folded and inwreathed in sand and shells and sea-weeds, and a great, weird-looking heap of kelp . . . lay twined around her like a shroud."[51]

The image evokes the *Mater Dolorosa* described by Alden and numerous other commentators. Dolores is the "sorrowing lady" forever "married" to the natural forces that twine about her and her "fate-conquered children." Curiously, her sorrow is similar to Naomi's despair on her deathbed; both mothers lose all to the sea, symbol of "viscous" contingency. Dolores's association with Catholicism also recalls the Protestant's lost Madonna and her pagan antecedents. However, as the novel will reveal, this *Mater Dolorosa* will be transfigured through a new revelation, for the sorrowing mother's grief will be assuaged by the new dispensation of Mara herself. Mara will become Persephone to Dolores's Demeter; she is the Maiden who mystically becomes the Mother, the Daughter who confronts death and conquers it through love. In Mara are combined the pathos of the Lady and the resurrection of the Lord.

And Mara, the Sophia of Orr's Island, does merge with Dolores. For in her dream the Lady with sweet, sad eyes had entrusted her son to her care. Now that son miraculously lives. He is named Moses, for he was drawn out of the water. As the two are raised side by side, brother and sister in the Pennel household, Mara loves, even idolizes the self-centered Moses from the first. However, her love has always a large admixture of the maternal. During one crisis Mara remembers "that poor mother was lying now silent and peaceful under the turf in the little graveyard not far off, and *she* must care for her boy."[52] As a "strong motherly feeling swells out" Mara's heart, she vows to "somehow save that treasure which had been so mysteriously committed to her." Thus, Moses' name also fits his role in the drama to come, for he is the unenlightened masculine element, the patriarchal soul, a Moses without the amendments of Christ. These amendments will come through Mara herself.

At this point more should be said about the characters of Moses and Mara. Moses' type is of "the first unreflecting stage of development." He is a "true healthy boy" with the "breezy, hearty virtues of a young Newfoundland dog." His moral conscience is unawakened; his sensibilities remain on the physical plane; his "aspirations tend toward manly accomplishments" alone. For him, as for other young men, "sentimental sensibility, delicate perceptions, spiritual aspirations are plants of a later growth."[53] Moses is eager to discover the world around him and to exercise his masculine prerogatives over it. While he also has loved Mara since childhood, his love is "egotistic, exacting, tyrannical, and capricious." Her adoration and service he accepts as his right and

due. However, Stowe shrewdly notes, Moses' swagger hides an inse-
curity quite foreign to the more passive Mara. Thus, "he thought himself quite a man, but the manhood of a boy is only a tiny masquerade,—
a fantastic dreamy prevision of real manhood." Moses is trying on an
abstract role, one that is not yet truly his. On the other hand, Mara
has no such concern about her gender role: she "never thought of
asserting herself as a woman; in fact, she seldom thought of herself at
all, but dreamed and pondered of almost everything else."[54]

Mara is indeed as close to sainthood "as human dust can ever be."
Like her grandmother, she thinks only of others, never of herself. Although she loves Moses dearly, her love has only the faintest tinge of
sexuality, to which human dust is prone. And her dying purges her of
that blush entirely. Central to her character is a precocious maternal
feeling, the sympathetic identification with others. Like other angels in
the house, Mara does retain an association with the natural world; but
as with those other figures, it is a spiritualized nature: "there was not
a moss, not a fern, not an up-springing thing that waved a leaf or threw
forth a flower-bell that was not a well-known friend to her."[55] "A child
of the woods," Mara's genius is not for managing a bustling household
but for painting the "cool shaded flowers" grown up like her own
"delicate life." From years of studying their "veiled and shy habits,"
she has "interwoven their lives with her own."

The risk of pollution such a deep "interweaving" with nature might
bring is averted by the exquisite spiritual perception that guides all of
Mara's relationships. In a passage savoring strongly of Swedenborgian
mysticism, Stowe reflects on the possibility that we may possess alongside our ordinary faculties a "rudimentary one, like the germs of wings
in chrysalis, by which the spiritual world becomes sometimes an object
of perception."[56] In certain highly refined natures such as Mara's, "the
walls of the material are so fine and translucent that the spiritual is
seen through them as through a glass darkly." Since these souls are so
little attached to the physical world that they see *through* to the spiritual one, messages may be sent from the "other side" as well: "It may
be too, that the love which is stronger than death has a power sometimes to make itself heard and felt through the walls of our mortality,
when it would plead for the defenceless ones it has left behind." Stowe
hints at a true spiritual communion linking Dolores to Mara through
the medium of the dream.

A somewhat longer passage elaborates on Mara's marvelous powers.
She is but one of a special group of human beings, most of them
women, "in whom from childhood the spiritual and the reflective pre-
dominate over the physical." Oftentimes, the very fragility of their

connection to the physical plane makes them appear "imperfect specimens of life." And indeed, "many of them pass away in earlier years." However, "in relation to other human beings, they seem to be organized much as birds are in relation to other animals. They are the artists, the poets, the unconscious seers, to whom the purer truths of spiritual instruction are open." Those who survive despite their relatively undeveloped material nature "are the priests and priestesses of the spiritual life, ordained of God to keep the balance between the rude but absolute necessities of physical life and the higher sphere to which that at length must give place."[57] In comparison with Moses, and even with Sally Kittridge, her robust and "earthly" friend, Mara "looks not exactly in ill health, but has that sort of transparent appearance which one fancies might be an attribute of fairies and sylphs."[58]

While descriptions of Mara emphasize this strange transparency, descriptions of the sea surrounding her pastoral island stress over and over its reflective qualities:

Sunday morning rose clear and bright on Harpswell Bay. The whole sea was a waveless, blue looking-glass, streaked with bands of white, and flecked with sailing cloud-shadows from the skies above.

Orr's Island, with its blue-black spruces, its silver firs, its golden larches, its scarlet sumacks, lay on the bosom of the deep like a great many-colored gem on an enchanted mirror.[59]

The sea—symbol of immanence and death—when seen rightly, becomes an "enchanted mirror," revealing not the depths of nature but the flying, sailing clouds of heaven. Interestingly, the sea here has a "bosom," again associating it with the drowned Dolores, who was also bejeweled with the seaweed, sand, and shells of Orr's Island. For one such as Mara, natural immanence, death and decay, will ultimately hold no terrors. She will move *through* physical death to everlasting life. However, that dark passage is one she will have to make.

As an adolescent, Mara has yet another vision of the dead mother, this time sent up by reflections on the sea's surface. Since the context of the experience is important, I will give the quotation in full:

... there are souls sent into this world ... who see the face of everything beautiful through a thick veil of mystery and sadness. The Germans call this yearning of spirit homesickness—the dim remembrances of a spirit once affiliated to some higher sphere. ... as Mara looked pensively into the water, it seemed to her that every incident of her life came up out of its depths to meet her. Her own face reflected in the wavering image, sometimes shaped itself to her gaze in the likeness of the pale lady of her childhood, who seemed to look up at her from the water with dark, mysterious eyes of tender longing.[60]

This strange, evocative passage establishes once again Mara's identification with the "pale lady," Dolores. It also confirms that Mara's
"home" is not the earth but the spiritual world beyond death. Should
Mara herself drown—as her "pensive" absorption suggests she might
even wish to do—she would only be reunited with this tender mother
who is in some mystical way her spiritual self.

That Mara's God might be a maternal one is confirmed in a conversation she has with Moses when they are older and about to be
married. At last awakened to her virtues, Moses tells Mara he worships
her more than God himself. Shocked, she tries to silence him. But he
replies, "Why should you love an unseen and distant Being more than
you do one whom you feel and see, who holds you in his arms, whose
heart beats like your own?"[61] Then, bathed in "clear moonlight," Mara
answers majestically: "God has always been to me not so much like a
father as like a dear and tender mother. . . . I never woke in the night
that I did not feel that He was loving and watching me, and that I
loved him in return. . . . His love is so much a part of my life that I
cannot conceive of life without it. It is the very air I breathe."[62]

As the daughter, priestess, and possibly even the earthly embodiment
of this maternal aspect of the Godhead, Mara is appointed to reveal
her truth and so "balance" human wisdom: "there is a masculine and
a feminine element in all knowledge, and a man and a woman put to
the same study extract only what their nature fits them to see, so that
knowledge can be fully orbed only when the two unite in the search
and share the spoils."[63] Thus, as the two children study their lessons,
"Moses was full of Romulus and Numa" while "Mara pondered the
story of the nymph Egeria—sweet parable, in which lies all we have
been saying."[64] This "sweet parable" is especially revealing for its matriarchal symbolism. According to Frazer's *Golden Bough*, Egeria was
a lesser divinity who lived with Diana in her sacred grove at Nemi.
She was associated with the clear water that cascaded into the lake at
Le Mole and was offered sacrifices by women about to give birth "because she was believed like Diana, to grant them an easy delivery."
More directly relevant to Stowe's purposes, ancient tradition held that
the wise king Numa had secretly consorted with Egeria in the sacred
grove "and that the laws which he gave the Romans had been inspired
by communion with her divinity."[65] In this marriage of patriarchal ruler
with pastoral nymph lies the hope for "fully orbed" wisdom.

Even as tiny children Mara's intuition unerringly corrects Moses'
moral lapses. In a central incident a seven-year-old Moses spoils an
eagle's nest to steal the eggs. Mara worries that the birds will grieve
to find their home and family destroyed, but Moses sees the incident

as warfare: "they're only mad to think they couldn't beat me. I beat them just as the Romans used to beat folks,—I played their nest was a city, and I spoiled it."⁶⁶ When Mara vigorously rejects the pastime of spoiling cities, Moses matter-of-factly replies, "That's because you are a girl,—and I'm a man and men always like war; I've taken one city this afternoon, and mean to take a great many more." Mara's further questioning of his dubious morality leaves his heroic ambitions undisturbed. But Stowe notes that, "little and unformed" as she was, Mara even then was one of those earthly angels "to whom was given the golden rod which measured the New Jerusalem. . . . She had ever in her hands that invisible measuring-rod, which she was laying to the foundations of all actions and thoughts." And as the novel unfolds, there will "come a time when the saucy boy who now steps so superbly, and predominates in virtue of his physical strength and daring, will learn to tremble at the golden measuring-rod, held in the hand of a woman."⁶⁷

Two other crises must intervene before Moses comes to this saving dependency. As a young adolescent he grows restless and anxious for adventure in the wider world beyond Orr's Island. He falls in with a gang of smugglers, who intend to use him to steal his grandfather's savings. Mara, maternally concerned, secretly follows Moses to the midnight meeting where these plans are hatched and arranges for Moses to be shipped away as a crewmate on Captain Kittridge's boat before he loses his immortal soul.

Years later, Moses returns from the sea to find Mara a lovely young woman with beaux of her own. He is falling in love with her but, true to his egotistical and stubborn nature, refuses to admit it. And Mara— who, Stowe tells us, is still a human woman, even though she may be a saint—is not above letting Moses simmer jealously about one of her Bostonian admirers. As a result, Moses spends his summer on Orr's Island idly romancing the pretty and highly flirtatious Sally Kittridge. Although neither is capable of deeper feelings, "Greek meets Greek" as they enjoy their banter and the physical attraction. Both essentially pagan, Moses finds his match in the "wicked elf" in Sally, who is trying out her womanly powers. And these powers are sexual. The two of them are strongly tempted to yield to their attraction. One evening Moses leads Sally along the moonlit beach to his "hermitage." As "the advancing tide drives them up into the little lonely grotto," Sally slips on the "treacherous footing" of the seaweeds' "yellow tresses." As Moses steadies her, he "instinctively . . . threw a meaning into his manner so much more than ever he had before that by the time they had gained the little cove both were really agitated and excited. . . .

'Sally,' said Moses, in a low, earnest whisper, 'you love me,—do you not?' and he tried to pass his arm around her.''[68]

Although she is not present, it is Mara who saves them. On an evening shortly before, Mara had plumbed Sally's heart: "So Mara pressed Sally with the old-times request to stay and sleep with her; for these two, the only young girls in so lonely a neighborhood, had no means of excitement or dissipation beyond this occasionally sleeping together—by which is meant, of course, lying awake all night talking.''[69] In this domestic "grotto," each reveals her inmost self. Sally discovers Mara's love, and they both discover Sally's "hard heart." Sally not only does not love Moses, she wonders if she can ever love anyone. Her chief delight with men is to tease them, for they are "such thumby, blundering creatures, and we can confuse them so." Mara, of course, cannot comprehend this pagan philosophy but is certain that Sally's soul is only undeveloped.

Sure enough, at the critical moment, Sally recalls her sympathy for her saintly friend and refuses Moses' advance. She tells him seriously that they must stop their dangerous trifling. It is actually Mara he loves, not her, and further, Mara loves him. The chastened Moses admits he is "a vile dog, unworthy of either [woman].''[70] For love of Mara, the pagan couple withdraw from the seaside cave: they have begun the painful ascent toward a purer life.

V

As Mara joyfully accepts Moses, it seems the novel will have its happy ending: the right woman gets her man. But now Stowe frustrates her readers' expectations, as she tells them outright. Mara's path will deviate abruptly from this conventional resolution. The couple are to be married when Moses returns from his last voyage. As she waits, Mara grows weaker and weaker. Instead of blissful anticipation, she feels life dwindling away. Even the woodlands affect her "painfully, like the want of sympathy in a dear friend." She finds herself "looking out into the old mossy woods . . . with a yearning pain, as if she wanted help or sympathy to come from their silent recesses.''[71] The natural world can no longer help her; the spiritual one is calling her home. Mara comes to the forest cottage of the two aged spinsters, Miss Ruey and Miss Roxy Toothacre. Miss Roxy, the ancient "sibyl" of Orr's Island, was the midwife who brought Mara into the world and who presides over all of the island's crises of birth, sickness, and death. And this "priestess" confirms Mara's intuition; she is dying.

At first Mara struggles against her fate, but then "victory" is achieved. In a dream she is walking by the shore of Galilee and sees the fishermen mending their nets, just as they did in the Bible (and still do on Orr's Island). She sees Jesus himself going to each one and asking him to "leave all and follow me." And so great is Christ's power that each one does it. But then Jesus comes to her. Mara "feels his eyes in my very soul, and he said, 'Wilt *thou* leave *all* and follow me?'" And Mara cannot answer. She feels a terrible anguish, a consciousness of a "thousand threads" "tied and woven" about her heart. Then the vision of Jesus seems to fade, and she is desolate and alone, "mourning" her loss. Suddenly, "something shone out warm like the sun." Christ has returned for her. "Looking pitifully," he asks her again to follow him: "Every word was so gentle and full of pity, and I looked into his eyes and could not look away; they drew me, they warmed me, and I felt a strange wonderful sense of his greatness and sweetness. It seemed as if I felt within me cord after cord breaking. I felt so free, so happy; and I said, 'I will, I will, and with all my heart;' and I woke then, so happy, so sure of God's love."[72]

This passage seems deliberately to echo Mara's earlier dream of the Sorrowing Lady, Dolores, whose "sweet, sad eyes" she had "felt . . . in every fibre of her frame." This Christ is maternal, intensely feminine; not a judge but a sympathetic, pitying friend who *needs* Mara himself. Equally important he is the Savior Lord of Alden's Eleusinia, the Father sun who warms the resurrected souls of Dolores's "fate-conquered children." Yet another passage echoes the earlier vision of Dolores's face rising out of the reflecting sea.

As Mara transcends the earthly world, she feels "beyond sorrow" forever. She assures her grieving family, friends, and lover that they also will find their sorrows in this life were but blessings preparing their souls for the life to come. For then "the whole weight of life's anguish is lifted, and the soul, seeing the boundless ocean of Divine love, wherein all human hopes and joys and sorrows lie so tenderly upholden, comes and casts the one little drop of its personal will and personal existence with gladness into that fatherly depth."[73] Stowe's language is patriarchal, but the sense of fusion with an ocean of divine love has strongly maternal overtones, especially when we recall "the pale lady who looked up . . . from the water with dark, mysterious eyes of tender longing." This Sorrowing Lady is the necessary balance to the ecstasy of Divine love. In "The Eleusinia," Alden asked what saved the Mysteries from "the ruin inevitably consequent upon all intemperate joy? It was the presence of our Lady, the sorrowing Actheia . . . who subdued the joy of victory, and preserved the strength and holy purity of the great Festival," for only through earthly discipline does the soul become fully aware and worthy of Divine love. Sorrow is the

"narrow gate" to salvation; as Alden concludes, "Demeter was necessary to Dionysus,—as Dionysus to Demeter."[74]

Mara's prolonged dying, her calm acceptance of fate, and her utter
faith in God's love in the world to come are the means to salvation not
only for Moses and Sally but for all those around her. And significantly,
it is sorrow that engenders their coming into grace. As Sally tends her
friend, "the tricksy elf . . . was melting away in the immortal soul, and
the deep pathetic power of a noble heart was being born. Some influence sprung of sorrow is necessary always to perfect beauty in a womanly nature."[75] Within Moses also, "unconsciously, even to himself,
sorrow was doing her ennobling ministry within him, melting off in
her fierce fires trivial ambitions and low desires, and making him feel
the sole worth and value of love."[76] Even the rugged Captain Kittridge,
whose stern Calvinist wife has nearly given him up as a depraved sinner
incapable of conversion, begins through Mara's Christian nurture a
slow growing toward grace. As he tells Moses, "Mis' Kittridge, she
allers talks to me as ef I was a terrible sinner . . . but this 'ere blessed
child, she's so kind o' good and innocent, she kind o' takes it for
granted I'm one o' the Lord's people. . . . It kind o' makes me want to
be."[77]

Mara's feminized religion ignores alienation, ignores sin, and draws
sinners to grace through personal influence. That she has become a
type of Christ himself, a mediator between fallen humankind and the
Creator, Captain Kittridge surmises: "There'll be joy that side o' the
river when she gets acrost. If she'd jest leave a hem o' her garment to
get in by, I'd be glad." And he won't be the only one clinging to Mara's
skirts, for "there'll be a good many fust and last that'll get into the
kingdom for love of her."[78]

For Moses, however, reconciliation to Mara's death is not so easy.
Although sorrow has begun its "unconscious" work, the degree of his
anguish must be in proportion to his egotism, which is considerable.
As Moses comes to see his selfishness and repent his blindness, Mara
reassures him. At first she refuses responsibility for her morality:
" 'Moses, I always knew I loved most. It was my nature; God gave it
to me, and it was a gift for which I give him thanks—not a merit.' "
But then she underscores the social context of their difference: " 'I knew
you had a larger, wider nature than mine,—a wider sphere to live in,
and that you could not live in yours as I did. Mine was all thought and
feeling, and the narrow little duties of this little home. Yours went all
round the world."[79] Does a woman's life lead to sainthood? It sounds
like it. And now, at last Moses recognizes the value of Mara's "narrow
sphere" and the "centripetal" force of her binding love. He realizes,

suddenly, that he had "had a sort of superstitious feeling,—a sacred presentiment about you,—that my spiritual life . . . would come through you."[80]

But knowing Mara's worth, Moses now doubts God's providence in depriving him of her. Here too Mara understands God's mysterious ways. Despite the hidden love she knows Moses has always had for her, still "in all that was deepest and dearest to her," Mara felt always alone. Then, surprisingly, she argues that marriage, far from saving him, might have driven them even further apart: "If we lived together in the commonplace toils of life, you would see only a poor threadbare wife. I might have lost what little charm I ever had for you; but . . . if I die, this will not be." Her conclusion is strangely chilling: "There is something sacred and beautiful in death; and I may have more power over you, when I seem to be gone, than I should have had living."[81] Upon reflection Moses is forced to accept her words as truth for "in all [those] years he could not remember one selfish action,—one unlovely word,—and he thought to himself, 'I hoped to possess this angel as a mortal wife! God forgive my presumption.'"[82]

Mara's justification of the ways of God to man deserves a closer look. The climax of her quest, of this *Bildungsroman,* is the realization of her vocation, which is to save souls, particularly Moses' soul. Curiously, this realization demands what any profession then demanded of women: Mara must give up conventional marriage and family. By making this sacrifice she will not only transcend the natural world, but she will also escape the inevitable devaluation that the conventional feminine role brings. The "narrow" domestic sphere, the "thousand" ties that bind her heart, like the bound roots of Mrs. Rockwell's plants, are finally broken. Always essentially "alone," Mara will now find independence and freedom *outside* both her body and her culture. Like the angelic figures Sherry Ortner describes, Mara rises above the masculine world to symbolize values transcending those of conventional culture. Thus, Mara escapes both the taint of biological reproduction and the devaluation of domesticity, and she does so by transforming the natural and domestic to spiritual symbols.

Stowe uses several "sweet parables" to express this transformation: the meaning of Mara's death and resurrection. As Mara looks for comforting words to give Moses, she remembers "those mysterious words of Him who liveth and was dead, 'Except a corn of wheat fall into the ground and die, it abideth alone; if it *die,* it bringeth forth much fruit.'"[83] Although these are Christ's words, they are the Eleusinian images. And here they are translated into their spiritual terms. Significantly, the fruits that Mara will bring forth are not the human children of a mortal marriage but the immortal souls of those she leaves behind. Hers will be a spiritual motherhood that finds its fulfillment through death, not sexuality.

Mara's transcendence of the body—with its burden of sexuality, pollution, and decay—is represented by another parable, taken from Roman Catholicism: "It is a beautiful legend which one sees often represented in the churches of Europe, that when the grave of the mother of Jesus was opened, it was found full of blossoming lilies,— fit emblems of the thousand flowers of holy thought and purpose which spring up in our hearts from the memory of the sainted dead."[84] Like the Virgin, Mara's death gives us spiritual flowers rather than material decay. Her "victory" turns the salt and bitterness of human immanence to sweetness and light. Here again the "Root-Bound" imagery illuminates Mara's significance. In proportion as Mara is physically weakened and confined, she becomes more spiritually potent. Finally, like Mrs. Rockwell, she is unable to leave her bed; her small bedroom, adorned with flowers, becomes the shrine of a domestic saint. Thus, the earthly "ground" in which her soul is rooted grows smaller and smaller, the roots wound tighter and tighter, until at last the spiritual blossom breaks free and leaves the earth behind. But only by submitting to this ultimate physical experience—death—can Mara be freed.

Until that moment the entire community resembles Bunyan's description of "the land of pleasant waiting which borders the river of death." As Mara crosses that river, her death seems a peaceful return home, a merging with the "ocean of divine love." Her lifeless face seems so joyful that no one would have dared "to call her back." Moses himself is finally reconciled: "Even he that should have been her bridegroom could not at that moment have unsealed the holy charm, and so they bore Mara away, and laid the calm smiling face beneath the soil, by the side of poor Dolores."[85]

Bunyan's image reappears in another "sweet parable," this time a dream that comes to Captain Kittridge the night of Mara's death. In this dream he was walking up and down the shore, heart-broken, for he has lost his "pearl of great price." Then far away he seems to see this mystical pearl, glowing on the wet sands:

I thought it was Mara, but it seemed a great pearl with soft moonlight on it; and I was running for it when some one said "hush," and I saw *Him* a-coming—Jesus of Nazareth, jist as he walked by the sea of Galilee. It was all dark night around Him, but I could see Him by the light that came down from his face, and the long hair was hanging down on his shoulders. He came and took up my pearl and put it on his forehead, and it shone out like a star, and shone into my heart, and I felt happy;—and he looked at me steadily, and rose and rose in the air, and melted in the clouds, and I awoke so happy, and so calm![86]

In this vision are resolved several strains of symbolism. Now that Mara is reunited in the soil with the *Mater Dolorosa,* she also rises above that "poor Lady" to immortal life. The image of the Savior Lord walking over the water is especially appropriate, for now material life is at last transcended. Mara's spirit has moved off the shore and across the water. And she cannot drown, for she is borne up by divine love. Indeed, she is merged with Christ himself. She brings to the sun of the patriarchal Godhead the moonlight and stars of Captain Kittridge's dream. She is the round, glowing pearl of "fully-orbed" wisdom. In this she is most like the Eleusinian Kore. Like Persephone she resolves the "bisexual" triangle of Dolores and Christ, who, like Demeter and Dionysus, are doubles of each other. Now Mara will be forever united with both. Her body will rest eternally in the earth, united with its Mother; her soul will be "married" to its heavenly bridegroom, Christ, who is also King of the Dead.

The heavenly "bisexual triangle" is paralleled by a human one. Like Dolores and Christ, Moses and Sally are doubles, as Stowe acknowledges when she describes their flirtation as "Greek meets Greek." At the triangle's apex is Mara, who transcends the cultural plane that Moses and Sally have not yet reached. Initially Moses has only the virtues of a "Newfoundland dog" or a young "race-colt," and out of Sally's dark eyes peeps a "tricksy elf," not a woman. These two are not only pagan, they are prehuman, unsocialized, incapable of love— until Mara completes her saving ministry. Thus, as Mara leaves the human world behind, Moses and Sally climb painfully toward it from the natural realms below.

For four years after Mara's death Moses and Sally are separated. Together they "worship" their dead friend's memory. They write long letters, telling each other "the same story": "that they were lonely, and that their hearts yearned for the communion of one who could no longer be manifest to the senses."[87] They insist on calling each other "brother and sister," and "each ... was firm that buried love must have no earthly resurrection." However, when Moses comes home at last, he and Sally meet "as fully developed man and woman." They walk together, thoughtfully, back to the grotto of their earlier crisis, where Moses recalls to Sally his "presumption":

"You and I are neither of us what were then. ... We are as different as if we were each another person. We have been trained in another life,—educated by a great sorrow,—is it not so?"
"I know it," said Sally.[88]

Now they are worthy of married love. Moses has found that Sally is "wholly necessary to him." Further, they alone can share their memories of Mara together: "Why should we two, who have a world of thoughts and memories which no one can understand but the other,— why should we, each of us, go on alone." And so the novel has its happy ending after all: "Nor was the wedding less joyful that all felt the presence of a heavenly guest, silent and loving, seeing and blessing all, whose voice seemed to say in every heart,—'He turneth the shadow of death into morning.'"[89]

In this image of bride and groom united under the silent, loving gaze of another woman, the bisexual triangle of female development is repeated. I think of Michael Balint's comment that the goal of adult erotic striving is the return to primary love and communion first experienced through the mother. Here Sally and Moses marry to preserve the sacred communion they found through Mara. As the dark heroine, Sally has sacrificed her dangerous sexual freedom to accept the loving "ties that bind." She will no longer "riot in the garden," teasing and tempting male admirers with her curving figure and dark eyes. She accepts the domestic sphere and is finally capable of Demetrian conjugal love. For his part, Moses has learned to narrow his masculine horizon and to tremble at the golden measuring-rod held in the hand of a woman. The authority of the angel transcends even that of the patriarch.

The Eleusinian images reappear here as well. For their earthly love has indeed been resurrected but in more spiritual form. Moreover, this transformation has been achieved through the purifying discipline of sorrow. And this process recalls the Homeric hymn's description of a similar transformation: Demeter's nurturance of Demophoon. Earlier, Stowe described "sorrow doing her ennobling ministry within [Moses], melting off in her fierce fires trivial ambitions and low desires, and making him feel the worth and value of love."[90] In just this way Demeter lowered the infant prince into the fire to purge away his mortality. And like Demophoon, Moses and Sally will retain their mixed humanity: their characters will now be part nature and part spirit. To be completely purified would be to vanish into the heavenly ether, as Mara herself has done. And yet, though "in nowise may [they] escape the Fates and death, yet glory imperishable will ever be theirs," since, to quote the Homeric hymn, "they have lain on the knees [of the Goddess] and slept within her arms."[91]

The religious ethos of *Pearl of Orr's Island,* as Elizabeth Ammons and Dorothy Berkson argue, bypasses the masculinist aspects of the Calvinist Godhead. The "Father" of this novel does not judge his children, nor does he punish them. Sorrow educates Moses and Sally, and they learn to repent their selfishness. However, this is a growing toward grace, not a terrifying conviction of sin. Insofar as they *feel* their unworthiness, so far are they saved. Evil is only the absence of communion. Through communion with the endlessly forgiving mediator, Mara, they come into the company of the faithful. The book's deviation from the more Calvinistic line of American literature may be seen most clearly by contrasting it with the different resolution of a similar plot. Milly Theale, in Henry James's *The Wings of the Dove* (1902), spreads her wings and blesses Kate Croy and Merton Densher from her deathbed.[92] However, the motivation of this couple is much darker and more destructive than the animal spirits or childish egotism of Sally and Moses. Their growing awareness of Milly's goodness also has a drastically different outcome. There will be no resurrected marriage between them despite the ambiguous blessings of the dove. Instead, the novel's closing lines imply that they will each have to go on alone, working out their repentance through renunciation and regret.

Neither will there be a resurrected marriage for Donatello and Miriam in Hawthorne's *Marble Faun* (1860).[93] Their sin, murder, also is deeply dyed, and their remaining lives will be spent in expiating their crime. However, Hawthorne asserts that they too will be educated by their sorrow. Their "fortunate fall" will humanize them as awareness of their sin disturbs and instructs the virgin consciousness of the dovelike Hilda. However, Hilda, unlike Stowe's Mara, shrinks from further association with the doomed pair, lest her purity be sullied and her faith shaken. For James and Hawthorne, the problems of sin and salvation were more complex and more frightening than they appear in *Pearl of Orr's Island*. Happy endings were harder to come by and answers more ambiguous. The wonderful thing about *Pearl* is that none of the major characters actively brings himself or herself to commit a sin. They repent of their potential for sin but do not deal with the consequences of actually having done so. Everyone seems to be headed for heaven. Indeed, it seems there is no hell to go to.

VI

While Jewett's response to *Pearl of Orr's Island* may be best discovered through analysis of its influence on her own work, her comments on rereading the book in 1889 can give us a head start. In a letter to Annie Fields, Jewett wrote that she was beginning the novel and finding it "as clear and perfectly original and strong" as it had seemed when she was in her "thirteenth or fourteenth year." She complained that Stowe had not been able to finish it in the "same noble key," and she attributed the failure to Stowe's willingness to sacrifice her work for the sake of domestic and maternal duties: "[A writer] must throw everything and everybody aside at times, but a woman made like Mrs. Stowe cannot bring herself to that cold selfishness of the moment for one's work's sake, and the recompense for her loss is a divine touch here and there in an incomplete piece of work."[94]

Jewett's comment subtly rejects the entire premise of Stowe's book and reveals the irony at its heart. Mara is the apotheosis of feminine virtue; but insofar as Stowe actually emulated Mara's life, she failed to tell Mara's story. Novel writing demands "agency," including the writer's "selfish" isolation from others. As de Beauvoir and Ortner insist, art—like other transcendent "masculine" activities—imposes order on the world and creates lasting objects out of the flux of temporal experience. Self-sacrificing Mara will leave no such lasting objects; her glory will survive only in her personal influence, enshrined in the memory of the equally perishable people who knew her. The deeper irony is that what "divine touches" there are in this "incomplete" work got there through Stowe's own deviations from the virtues she prescribes. Sentimentalism, Jewett hints, makes "good" women but bad art.

While this assessment is interesting as an illustration of Jewett's own priorities, a later letter revised her literary critique: "Yesterday I read the Pearl of Orr's Island or rather finished it as I had begun it when I was last at home. I take back all my childish belief that the last half of the book was not so good. The Spanish episode is of thinner texture—but all the rest full of marvelous truth and beauty. I love to find the same delicious pleasure in certain places that I found at *ten*!"[95]

On this later reading, Jewett discovered a new beauty in the last half of the book, which described Mara's prolonged sickness and death. There is a strong possibility that Jewett was moved by those scenes then, as she had not been before, because her own life mirrored them. At that time her mother was bedridden. The description in her unpublished story, "The Christmas Ghosts," of a "golden moment" of loving communion with her dying mother suggests a biographical source for Jewett's new sympathy with Mara's last moments.[96]

Of the characters themselves, Jewett wrote that "the two heroines [are] most lovely especially Sally Kittridge." Then she added, "I cannot help talking about the story still!" That Jewett should single out the darker, "earthier" heroine is significant, but equally so is the fact that she ignores Miss Roxy Toothacre, who seems to have been an inspiration for Mrs. Todd of *The Country of the Pointed Firs*. A quick look at this thread of Stowe's plot reveals the connection.

Miss Roxy is physically homely: "Tall, thin, angular . . . with sharp black eyes, and hair . . . well streaked with gray." Her manner is "vigorous, spicy, and decided." Without husband or wealth, she nonetheless speaks with unquestioned authority: "Was she not a sort of priestess and sibyl in all the most awful straits and mysteries of life? How many births and weddings, and deaths had come and gone under her jurisdiction! And amid weeping or rejoicing, was not Miss Roxy still the master-spirit,—consulted, referred to by all!—was not her word law and precedent?"[97] This role gives Miss Roxy the almost frightening outlines of a more primitive femininity, an image reinforced by her dwelling deep in the woods with her dependent sister. Miss Roxy's apparent coldness also comes from the New England tendency to "betray the uprising of the softer feeling . . . only by an increase of outward asperity." "Shyness" leaves these Puritan descendants "no power of expression for these unwonted guests of the heart."[98] Thus, this stern "master-spirit" hides a maiden tenderness. Stowe compares Miss Roxy to the chestnut burr, for, "hard as it is to handle, no plush of downiest texture can exceed the satin smoothness of the fibres which line its heart."[99] The revelation of this inner sweetness and the "transfiguration" of the "hard-visaged" Miss Roxy will come through Mara.

As Mara feels herself growing weaker, she goes to Miss Roxy's cottage deep in the forest. As she examines the girl, Miss Roxy—priestess and sibyl—"sees" the inevitable death: "The hard-visaged woman sat down on the wash-bench, and, covering her worn, stony visage with her checked apron, sobbed aloud." To Mara, who had always known Miss Roxy as "beneficently impassive in sickness and sorrow . . . it was awful as if one of the Fates had laid down her fatal distaff to cry."[100] Although Miss Roxy, like Dolores, comes from this "darker" feminine tradition, her relation to the Maiden will draw her "upwards" to a higher spirituality:

Mara sprung up impulsively and threw her arms around her neck . . . and the two wept together,—the old grim gray woman holding the soft golden head against her with a convulsive grasp. "Oh, Aunt Roxy, do you love me, too?" said Mara. "I didn't know you did."

"Love ye, Child?" said Miss Roxy; "yes, I love ye like my life. I a'n't one that makes talk about things, but I do; you come into my arms fust of anybody's in this world,—and except poor Hitty [a sister who died when just a year older than Mara], I never loved anybody as I have you."[101]

Following this embrace, Miss Roxy tucks Mara into her own bed. Stowe renders the intimacy of this scene within the pastoral cottage carefully:

Miss Roxy opened the door of a little room, whose white fringy window-curtains were blown inward by breezes from the blue sea, and laid the child down to rest on a clean sweet-smelling bed with as deft and tender care as if she were not a bony, hard-visaged, angular female, in a black mohair frisette.[102]

Thus, Miss Roxy, like Dolores, functions as yet another version of the mother figure. In Neumann's archetypal scheme, she would appear as the "Lady of the Plants," the mantic woman deeply associated with the natural world and mistress of its secrets. In Walter Pater's interpretation she would be the "humanized" image of the *Mater Dolorosa*: the peasant woman hurrying home in the last sad light of evening. In the Homeric hymn itself, Miss Roxy's analogue is Demeter disguised as a "crone" past childbearing. Like Demeter, she hides her divinity beneath a veil of age and ugliness. But Mara's spiritual perceptions can see through this veil, as Metaneira's could not. More important, Miss Roxy's potential divinity is revealed through her sorrow at the loss of the Persephone figure, Mara. And that divinity is finally fulfilled through her communion/fusion with this maiden "daughter."

As Miss Roxy nurses Mara in her last days, "she finished her arrangement by softly smoothing the hair from [Mara's] forehead with a caressing movement most unlike her usual precise business-like proceedings."[103] In response, Mara looks up with a smile and says, "I love you, Aunt Roxy." "Choked with tenderness," Miss Roxy scowls and says she doesn't see how Mara can: "I a'n't nothin' but an old burdock-bush;—love a'n't for me." But Mara "draws her down and kisses her withered cheek." In Mara's eyes Miss Roxy's spirit shines forth; their communion "transfigures" her:

"God sees that you are beautiful, and in the resurrection everyone will see it."

"I was always homely as an owl," said Miss Roxy, unconsciously speaking out what had lain like a stone at the bottom of even her sensible heart. . . . "I made up my mind pretty early that my part in the vineyard was to have had hard work and no posies."

"Well, you will have all the more in heaven;—I love you dearly, and I like your looks, too. You look kind and true and good, and that's beauty in the country where we are going."

Miss Roxy sprang quickly from the bed, and turning her back began to arrange the bottles on the table with great zeal.[104]

Here we see again the curious merging and doubling of roles and generations. As Miss Roxy caresses Mara, Mara sees the Maiden within the Mother. And so Mara, in her turn, mothers Miss Roxy by assuring her of her innate worth and beauty.

This lovely scene, with its uncharacteristic understatement, surely contributed to Jewett's portrayal of Mrs. Todd, who also turns away in moments of deep emotion yet is "transfigured" when the narrator sees her innate wisdom, tenderness, and power. Stowe's treatment of Miss Roxy may also have contributed to Jewett's original conception of her own artistic vocation. A childhood reading of *Pearl* had, Jewett admitted, deeply influenced her first book, *Deephaven*. Her main impulse in writing it was to reveal the inner dignity of "homely" country people, those a sophisticated traveler, or reader, might overlook or even despise. Thus, Jewett must have taken to heart Stowe's admonition to her reader:

Now if Miss Roxy had been like you, my dear young lady—if her soul had been encased in a round, rosy, and comely body, and looked out of tender blue eyes shaded by golden hair, probably the grief and love she felt would have shown themselves only in bursts of feeling most graceful to see, and engaging the sympathy of all; but this same soul, imprisoned in a dry, angular body, stiff and old, and looking out under beetling eyebrows, over withered high cheek bones, could only utter itself by a passionate tempest—unlovely utterance of a lovely impulse—dear only to Him who sees with a Father's heart the real beauty of spirits.[105]

(Needless to say, the human incarnation of this Father was the maternal Mara.) However, Stowe did not make the homely Miss Roxy the heroine of her novel. That place was reserved for the same golden-haired angel her young lady readers expected. But Jewett *did* put "Miss Roxy" at the center of her design. Indeed, one of Jewett's most radical innovations within Stowe's paradigm was to jettison the genteel, virginal heroine and replace her with a middle-aged widow, both earthy and homelike, broad in the beam and lovely in the heart.

Chapter Three

Hearts and Rounds: Jewett in the Community of Women

In 1979 I spent a rainy afternoon with Elizabeth Goodwin, the elderly Berwick woman who cared for the Jewett homestead. She told me of the formal calls she paid with her mother long ago and, best of all, the breakfasts she shared in the Jewett garden with Sarah herself. Seeing Elizabeth go by on the morning trolley, the great writer would wave her off and invite her in. I couldn't help but recall Jewett's own memories of childhood teas with the grandes dames of South Berwick. Even the cakes were the same, the dainty "hearts and rounds" dear to little girls. Face to face with the "visitable past," I gathered my courage and asked what Jewett was really like, what kind of woman she was. Miss Goodwin replied simply, "She was a lady." And that, she seemed to feel, told me everything.

Though surrounded by traffic signs and confronted by a pizza parlor, the Jewett house in South Berwick, Maine, still testifies to the family's social standing. Large, Georgian, white, it stands foursquare in the town's center. An imposing boxwood hedge descends the brick path to the gate which, with its white fence, marks off the grounds from the street beyond. Born in 1849, Jewett grew up in this green enclosed space, first in the little, newer house next door, then in the Jewett house itself. This is a coastal town, linked to the sea by the Piscataqua River, which empties into the Atlantic ten miles south near Portsmouth, New Hampshire. Jewett's paternal grandfather, Captain Theodore F. Jewett (1787–1860), was a wealthy shipowner, and Sarah grew up with the names of his ships a part of the family, "as if they were children who had grown up and gone wandering in the world."[1] Purchased in 1819 as a testament to the Captain's success in the West Indies trade, the house was built for Major John Haggens in 1774 by ship's carpenters. As the story goes, three of them spent a hundred days on the entrance alone. Its carved wainscoting, dentiled cornices, and broad staircase still command respect.

1. Sarah Orne Jewett

2. Sarah Orne Jewett in the garden, Nealley House, South Berwick

3. Sarah Orne Jewett at her desk, South Berwick

4. Sarah Orne Jewett at her front door, South Berwick

5. Theodore Herman Jewett

6. Caroline Perry Jewett

7. Annie Adams Fields

8. Sarah Orne Jewett and Emily Davis
Tyson at Hamilton House, South
Berwick, 1905

10. The Jewett House, South Berwick, Maine

11. Front hall, the Jewett House, South Berwick, Maine

That success left Captain Jewett's family, including Jewett herself, financially independent. This was particularly fortunate since his son, Dr. Theodore Herman Jewett (1815–1878), once considered the most talented among his fellow students, contracted consumption. Although he contributed to medical journals and periodically visited Boston to deliver lectures, Theodore Jewett stayed at home to become the proverbial and well-loved country doctor. Caroline Perry met her husband when he was studying under her father, William Perry, a famous surgeon in Exeter, New Hampshire. After their marriage, the couple settled in South Berwick, visiting distance from her own family. Mrs. Jewett appears to have been genteel, retiring, and dedicated to her family's well-being. In her later years, after Theodore Jewett's unexpected death by heart attack in 1878, she grew more and more feeble, requiring the constant attendance of her daughters: Sarah, Mary Rice Jewett (1847–1930), and Caroline (Carrie) Augusta Jewett (later Eastman) (1855–1897). Caroline Perry Jewett died on October 21, 1891.

Other close and significant family members included Jewett's paternal grandmother, Mary Jewett, who lived with the family until her death when Jewett was five years old. This grandmother, Captain Jewett's third wife, was a stern, uncompromising figure who scrupulously observed the formalities of domestic life. Sarah's early run-ins with her were apparently frightening. Another important figure was her mother's father, William Perry, an old-fashioned Calvinist who impressed a sense of vocation on his children and grandchildren. He had high expectations for these descendants, whether male or female. Jewett later criticized his severity but always valued his encouragement. This extended family included not only parents and grandparents but also cousins, nieces, nephews, aunts, and uncles. Jewett remained especially close in later life to her sister Carrie's son, Theodore Eastman.

Though financially independent, the Jewetts shared in the region's general decline after the failure of the shipping industry. This failure, whose sources reached back to Jefferson's 1807 Embargo, was exacerbated by the rise of railway transportation and the shift of trade after the Civil War. South Berwick, with the rest of the region, lost its claim to a vital role in the New England economy. As Jewett notes in "River Driftwood," South Berwick had once been a center for exporting lumber to the West Indies or Russia: "Not forty years ago there were still twenty gundalows sailing from the landing wharves, while now there are but two."[2] With this decline came the drain of young men from the old ports to the new manufacturing towns, to the burgeoning cities, or off to the West. Jewett's sketches and stories frequently paint the decrepit and now useless sea captains idling by the dilapidated wharves.

Just inland, in the hill country, the somber mood deepened. Here the land was not much good for farming. If families had no access to the sea and therefore could not fish, life was hard and extreme poverty common.

However, being out of the economic mainstream meant the preservation of old ways that otherwise would have been lost. According to Jewett's remarks in *Deephaven*, "From a Mournful Villager," and "River Driftwood," society in these coastal towns was still stratified according to tradition, and class distinctions were carefully observed. Although tourism and nearby mills brought both urban and foreign folk into the local life, the preindustrial world was relatively intact if worse for the wear. Jewett noted several times, with satisfaction, that Berwick, York, and Wells were more like their English counterparts than the America lustily in progress elsewhere.

Jewett herself belonged by birth to the upper level of this society. If not exactly part of the New England aristocracy celebrated in her novel *The Tory Lover,* she was without doubt a member of a privileged class. Tradition, social structure, continuity, order—these all pleased her. Her sketch "From a Mournful Village" laments the passing of the formal front yard and argues the benefits of fences and the delights of privacy: "People do not know what they lose when they make away with reserve, the separateness, the sanctity of the front yard of their grandmothers. It is like writing down the family secrets for anyone to read; it is like having everybody call you by your first name and sitting in any pew in Church. . . . We Americans had better build more fences than take any away from our lives."[3] While she tempered this advice—"there should be gates for charity to go out and in, and kindness and sympathy, too"—nevertheless, Jewett's sentiments leaned to the Tory side. Upon reaching twenty-one she converted from her family's Congregationalism to Episcopalianism and took the sacraments at St. John's Church in Portsmouth. In a letter to a friend she proudly noted the silver chalice preserved through many generations. A Whitman she was not, at least not politically.

However, if Jewett cherished the ways fast becoming extinct, she was not rapaciously opposed to progress. In later life she spent much of her time in Boston and loved cosmopolitan life if not the industrial pollution and foreign immigration that seemed to come with it (although she attempted to treat the Irish and French Canadians sympathetically in several stories). In "Tom's Husband" and "The Two Mr. Browns" she paints the business world of the new manufacturing classes with virtual enthusiasm. The city was not her enemy, though she might be an easier person to understand if it were. Ann Douglas has described her, with other local colorists, as a woman who symbolically burned herself alive to signal her hatred of the new urban/industrial order.[4] This is, to put it mildly, going too far. As we shall see, she was far from a reclusive figure, hidden like Hepzibah Pyncheon in her family manse.

A few things are worth noting here. First, there is Jewett's association with a peripheral, rural world. Divested of the young male population, closer to the "natural" world of preindustrial labor, coastal New England seemed marked by continuity, not change. Clinging tenaciously to the past and tradition, it was, in relation to the rest of America, "feminine." In *Deephaven,* Jewett's first book, the narrator compares the old port town to its old ladies, still maintaining the manners of a lost time. At the same time she notes the relative scarcity of children and young people, except those from inland farms, and comments "that a few years will see Deephaven possessed by two classes instead of the time-honored three."[5] The church is primarily populated by older women, and in one very funny scene the two young heroines attend a lecture on "The Elements of True Manhood" with not one young man in the audience. In fact, the narrator remarks on the parallel between Deephaven and Mrs. Gaskell's *Cranford,* that description of life in a pastoral English village that opens with the line "Cranford was in possession of the Amazons."[6]

Thus, for tourists escaping the rigors of city life, towns like South Berwick and York functioned as analogues to the domestic sphere, "havens in a heartless world." Here, just as in the home, one could find the values of an agrarian past, the continuity of tradition, and perhaps the strategies of a disenfranchised populace eager to "influence" the monied and powerful out of a dollar. For the the young man or woman embedded in a country town there was also the danger of becoming "root-bound." Unlike the summer visitor—a veritable Mrs. Rush able to come and go at will—the native New Englander without money was confined to a small community on the periphery of the larger culture. Whether this confinement was a paradoxical means to spiritual growth or a crippling restriction of human potential is a question Jewett's stories often debate. And because preindustrial New Englanders and middle-class Victorian women faced problems that were in many respects analogous, Jewett's reflections on the former often reveal her struggles with the latter.

For finally, Jewett did not make child rearing her vocation—the motherhood cherished by the cult of true womanhood—nor did she remain within her domestic place. Her deepest bonds were other women; yet rather than share this homosocial life with a heterosexual one, as most Victorians did, she remained single, childless, and relatively free. Although she always asserted her strong attachment to her home, it was not the limit of Jewett's horizon but a place to which she returned. She did not cut back the roots of her will to blossom in the service of others. As a writer she resisted the claims of biology and blossomed instead in the service of an art that transcended, even while describing, the natural world and human relations.

The story of Jewett's initial separation from this domestic world and her development as an artist begins with Theodore Jewett. Nancy Chodorow argues that the father becomes a model of the developing ego for son and daughter alike. As Juliet Mitchell puts it, he is the "third" that breaks the mirror bond between mother and child; he provides the wedge necessary for differentiation.[7] In "Looking Back on Girlhood," Jewett wrote that she could not help believing that her father "recognized, long before I did myself, in what direction the current of purpose in my life was setting."[8] Seeing that she was "given to instant drooping if ever she were shut up in school," Dr. Jewett took his small daughter with him on his rounds in the countryside. As she followed "him about silently, like an undemanding little dog," Dr. Jewett carefully directed Sarah's attention to the subtleties of village and country life. Through his tutelage she learned to observe character, to appreciate the pastoral landscapes through which they passed, and to extend her sympathy "for the dreams of others." And so "the quiet village life, the dull routine of farming or mill life, early became interesting to me. I was taught to find everything that an imaginative child could ask in the simple scenes close at hand." Later, as she composed her "sketches of country life," Jewett remembered "again and again the wise things he said, and the sights he made me see."[9]

Theodore Jewett's nurturance of his daughter's talent extended to literature itself: "He gave me my first and best knowledge of books by his own delight and dependence upon them, and ruled my early attempts at writing by the severity and simplicity of his own good taste."[10] In an 1890 letter to Annie Fields, Jewett commented on Flaubert's *Madame Bovary,* which also probed the life of a country town: "People talk about dwelling upon trivialities and commonplaces in life, but a master writer gives everything weight, and makes you feel the distinction and importance of it. . . . That is one reason why writing about simple country people takes my time and thought."[11] Her father taught her that greatness lay hidden in these rural scenes if one could only see it. Moreover, despite her own apparent limitations—her country background and her gender—Jewett herself could aim for greatness. The description of her father ends with this advice: "I long to impress upon every boy and girl this truth: that it is not one's surroundings that can help or hinder . . . it is having a growing purpose in one's life to make the most of whatever is in one's reach."[12]

However, it was not the books her father recommended that first captured her imagination but women's novels, such as Stowe's *Pearl of Orr's Island* (1862). These were her mother's books: "while I was too young and thoughtless to share an enthusiasm for Sterne, or Fielding, and Smollett or Don Quixote, my mother and grandmother were leading me into the pleasant ways of 'Pride and Prejudice,' and 'The Scenes of Clerical Life,' and the delightful stories of Mrs. Oliphant."[13] Later Jewett appreciated the "severity and simplicity" of Flaubert, whose quotation, as biographers have often noted, was pinned above her desk: "To picture common life as one portrays history."[14] Her father had once give her similar advice: "Don't try to write *about* people and things, tell them just as they are!"[15] As a mature writer Jewett returned to the "pleasant ways" of her mother's and grandmother's fiction, bringing with her the restraint and simplicity she had learned outside. And so the apparent "trivialities and commonplaces" of women's lives were illuminated by a "master writer" who gave "everything weight" and made her readers feel the distinction and importance of it. Like Nan Prince of *A Country Doctor,* Jewett returned to the simple houses the doctor had first taken her to, but now she entered as a healer in her own right. Ultimately, independence did not lead to alienation but allowed Jewett to recreate her bonds with the female world of love and ritual. In her finest work there is a graceful adaptation of the maternal ethos, but Jewett came to this understanding on her own terms, from a new perspective. To appreciate Jewett's return to the community of women we must begin where she began, with her mother.

I

The strange thing about Jewett's relationship to Caroline Perry Jewett is how little we know about it. For a writer who celebrated bonds between women, she was surprisingly reticent about *this* bond, so very basic to her own life. While she openly describes, even celebrates her father, Jewett rarely mentions her mother in any of her writings. She even goes so far as to delete Caroline Jewett's presence in one sketch, "The White Rose Road," that describes a walking tour the two women took up into the hills beyond Berwick.[16] However, I have been able to locate three key documents. All were written after her mother's death in 1891. They include two letters, one to Georgina Halliburton and the other to Thomas Bailey Aldrich. The third document is an unpublished manuscript entitled "The Christmas Ghosts." Highly autobiographical in some of its details, the story describes an encounter between a sympathetic ghost and a woman writer. The setting seems to be the Jewett house in South Berwick. The first draft identifies the ghost as the writer's mother. The second, more finished draft deletes the identification, although their relationship remains essentially the same. The "Christmas Ghosts" is too long to include in its entirety, but I will quote from it at length below.[17]

The letter to Georgina Halliburton is written from London and dated April 22. It was certainly 1892, immediately following her mother's death, because she left with Annie Fields for Europe that year:

... Oh you don't know how I have thought and thought about everything in these long days on shipboard. One is always a child as long as she has her mother to go to—but it seemed to me that I felt "grown up" and older for the first time, then. I do so long to have you feel clear and free in your new conditions dear! It seems to me that with all the difficulty of adjustment, you are going to have a gift of new possibilities, and a certain kind of joy in standing on your own ground. I don't know whether it will seem the best thing to "take Grandma's house" as you said one day, but I find that my thoughts fly back all the time to your having spoken of it or rather to the thought that lay under it of this very standing on your own ground and living your OWN life. One MUST do that as one grows older, and makes one's own decisions. One can have all the sweetness of being a kind of tributary to the lives one loves and can flow into those lives with all the stronger impulse. You will find yourself taking a new attitude now, and with all the loss and pain you will have something that is new and sweet to you.[18]

The letter to Thomas Bailey Aldrich is quoted in F. O. Matthiessen's biography of Jewett. Matthiessen does not give its date or place, nor a location for the manuscript, which I have been so far unable to find elsewhere:

Dear Friend,
    Your letter gives me the comfort of knowing that weakness and age are at an end forever for your dear mother and that her kind and gentle life is done as far as this world goes. Whatever change has come must be for the better since she herself put no hindrance in the way. All this I felt so little while ago when the same loss touched me that my heart is full of instant comprehension. I know how different this loss is from any other. As long as one's mother lives the sense of being lovingly protected never fails, and one is always a child.
    'Tis a strange sense of being alone in the world for the first time. When a larger life opens for those who are nearest and dearest it seems as if a larger life opened for us too. I sometimes remember what Sir Thomas Browne said— about joining both lives together and living in one but for the other. "For seeing there is something of us that must still live on," he begins. I have not seen the page in a long time, but in such days the words come back. It makes a great change in one's life, but it is a change for the better. I never felt so near my mother or kept such a sense of love for her as I have since she died. There

are no bars of shyness or difference or carelessness; it seems as if I had never known my mother before. But it is no use trying to write these things. If I were with you, I should take hold of your hand and not say anything, and I do that now.[19]

Following her father's death in 1878, Jewett had written Lily Munger that she felt "grown up" and no longer a child. It was this earlier death that her biographer, John Eldridge Frost, stresses as the dividing line between childhood and maturity. Certainly the event was traumatic, as a letter at the time to Theophilus Parsons reveals: "In that grave all my ambitions and hopes seem sometimes to be buried."[20] And as Edward Eastman (who married Carrie Jewett) noted in a letter to his mother about Dr. Jewett's death, "the poor girls, how I pity them. . . . I have never known a family which so worshipped their father."[21] However, this sense of "being lovingly protected," of having always "her mother to go to," sustained Jewett's sense of childhood dependence beyond even this deep loss. It was this continuing bond to her mother and the world of childhood emotions that may have prompted her often-quoted line, "Today is my birthday and I am always nine years old." It is a line that was echoed in her adolescent diary, where, at eighteen, she remarked if anyone should ask her age she "should certainly say 10!"[22]

However, what is crucial here is not only Jewett's childlike quality but her attitude toward it: her awareness of its source and its limits, particularly her relief at her mother's death. Somehow, as long as her mother was alive, she could not find her own feet, could not differentiate herself clearly as an individual. This is an almost classic statement of maternal overidentification. The letter to Georgina Halliburton is earnest and insistent. Jewett seems almost to reach and shake the girl, gently of course, but shake her all the same. This death, which to a Victorian woman might be devastating, could be a liberation. Georgina should find "joy in standing on her own ground." "Joy" is a strong word, almost blasphemous, rather like the ecstasy of freedom that grips the newly widowed wife in Kate Chopin's "The Story of an Hour." The emphases on "OWN life" and "One MUST do that" testify to Jewett's own struggle with these issues and her sense of their urgency. Breaking free to her own identity must have been difficult to prompt this intensity. In a much earlier letter to Lily Munger she had advised the younger friend not to leave home for a teaching position in another state. (Lily did anyway.)[23] Now, however, she seems to feel that the threat to self-development may be too great—a woman has to "stand on her own ground and live her own life."

And significantly she urges Georgina *not* to "take Grandma's house," advice that seemingly contradicts the common image of Jewett as the apotheosis of genteel New England domesticity, as well as her own earlier choices. In an often-quoted passage Jewett once said that she hoped to die in her old South Berwick homestead, "with all the chairs in their places." This house had been, in fact, her grandmother's, and Jewett's earliest memories centered on that stern presence. But elsewhere in Jewett's stories and in her life we can find ample evidence of her desire, if not to escape the house, at least to keep its doors and windows open. The images of houses are central in her writing, and the most important ones—such as Mrs. Todd's in *The Country of the Pointed Firs*, Kate Lancaster's in *Deephaven*, Temperance Dent's in "Miss Tempy's Watchers"—are permeable: murmurs from the sea, the scent of garden herbs, moonlight, all drift inside through doors and open windows. And more important, women drift in and out according to their own will. Those who cannot, like Mrs. Hight, the indomitable crippled mother of Esther in *Pointed Firs,* do not gain by confinement but become emotionally crippled, stunted and narrow, manipulative and power-seeking.

In one fascinating sketch, "The Housebreaker," the narrator breaks *out* of her family's house to see the dawn alone.[24] Moving from enclosed domestic spaces to the open natural world, she wanders through the fields and town alone, reflecting on the sleeping village and its natural setting. When she returns to her own bed, it is with a sense of smuggled achievement and renewed pleasure in her domestic place. This story, with its structure of enclosure, escape, and return, reveals the enduring shape of Jewett's vision, with its tension between the solitary watcher/ writer and the social milieu in which she is embedded.

Again, Jewett sought balance for women's lives and her own. Although she appropriated the grand white house in the center of town, she felt free, particularly after her mother's death, to travel to Boston to be with Annie Fields; she left South Berwick for London, France, and Greece. As Jewett advised many younger writers, men and women both, and as she counseled Willa Cather, one must know the world before one can know the parish. She never disowned the parish—it was hers to keep—but she was open to the world beyond and sought experience with a clear conscience.

Thus, although Jewett's 1892 letter to Georgina Halliburton may sound like a testimonial to Emersonian self-reliance, there is an important twist to its ending. Only those with a strong sense of identity, a firm ego, can give fully to others. This is the paradox of mature dependence described by Nancy Chodorow. Fusion with others may be the highest good in a life but only if balanced by a firm sense of self. A weak ego that prevents self-assertion and development stifles, even cripples; a genuinely strong ego can bend without breaking. Jewett's water imagery gracefully conveys the sense of merging, fusing with others. By being fully oneself, centered, differentiated, "one can have all the sweetness of being a kind of tributary to the lives one loves and can flow into those lives with all the stronger impulse." Selfhood does not prevent intimacy but makes it even stronger—advice counter to the ideology of true womanhood, whose advocates had stressed abdication of the individual life. Jewett recognizes the dangers here and wisely steers her friend away from the conventional feminine solutions. Her own solution was apparently confirmed by her mother's death, but she had actually discovered it earlier. In an 1879 letter to Lily Munger, Jewett had written: "Don't forget that the true way of growing is to be taking and giving both. I think we can almost always put these two things together in our relations with one person even. . . . Taking so that one can give again is the true secret of a happy, useful life, don't you think?"[25] It is a message that she was to reiterate and rediscover throughout her fiction. And we see again the rhythm of intimacy, isolation, and return, the balance of independence and communion.

If the letter to Georgina Halliburton focuses on the moment of recognized individuality she experienced at her mother's death, the letter to Aldrich hints at "bars of shyness . . . difference . . . [and] carelessness" in that relationship. It also looks forward to a curious sense of renewed, strengthened intimacy with her mother's memory, even her mother's spirit. Taking up the hints of difficulty first, we can find corresponding suggestions in the extant letters between Jewett and her mother and in other references to her mother's illness.

By the time of Jewett's first trip to Europe she was intimate enough with Annie Fields to call her "Darling" and "Fuffy." However, Jewett's letters home to her mother all refer to her companion as Mrs. Fields, never Annie or even AF. A letter from this trip, written "at sea" on June 1, 1882, also teases her mother for an implied oversolicitousness: "Dear Mother, I might have written sooner but I thought it would be fun not to write any letter for a week. . . . I am afraid it will cause you a *dreadful* disappointment, but I have not been seasick at all!"[26]

An 1888 letter from Caroline Jewett to Sarah picks up the theme of motherly and daughterly solicitousness: "Dear Sarah. The grapes came last night and it seems almost needless to say we enjoy them very much, and we both thank you very much for your kindness in sending them. You are always so thoughtful that I feel as if I did nothing for your pleasure and happiness when you are away."[27] In this letter Mrs. Jewett sends "our love to Mrs. Fields." There is warmth in her tone but also genteel formality and more than a hint of guilt at receiving something from her daughter. The give-and-take Sarah Jewett advocated did not come so easily to her mother.

The possible maternal overidentification seen in these letters is supplemented by the more obvious problem of Mrs. Jewett's invalidism. As early as 1880 her mother's weakness tied Sarah to the home when she would have preferred being in Boston with her beloved Annie Fields. In the following letter to Annie Fields one can sense the frustration and patience that later went into Jewett's portrait of Esther Hight, also tied to a sickly mother and prevented from being with her lover, William Blackett. Here Jewett describes a secret plan she had concocted to escape to Boston for the day:

I came so near seeing you today darling that I miss you all the more because I gave it up. This morning I said to myself why shouldn't I go to you and spend Sunday . . . and it was the loveliest thing in the world to think about, so pretty soon I tumbled out of bed and felt very eager and happy, and I was to take the two o'clock train and reach Charles St. before you came in yourself, and then I didn't exactly know where I would be. You hurried up the stairs to get ready for dinner—Oh darling I cant bear to give up this lovely long evening I might have had with you![28]

The problem was her mother, for as Jewett explains: "You must see that when I came down stairs I found that Mother looked even more pale and tired than when she came home last night and she told me that she was not feeling quite well. By everything she did much plainer than if she had talked a great deal about it."[29]

Realizing that their servant, John, has planned to take a holiday and not wanting to leave her mother alone, Jewett sacrificed her "loveliest thing": "And there is a little crack in my heart that never will be mended until I see you dear." And then, not surprising, "Mother brightened up amazingly after it was too late to go! And I suppose I really might have been away as well as not but it did not look like it and I did what was right then. I feel as if I were tying myself to the rigging this time!" Like Odysseus, Jewett did her duty and turned aside from Annie Fields's siren call, only to have her mother propose that Sarah take a little trip to Exeter to see her grandparents. Needless to say, Sarah met the offer with despair, although a lightly humorous one: "It was dismal to have Mother propose that I should go over to Exeter to spend Sunday!"

Jewett's responsibility for her mother's care extended until 1891. It was a job she shared with her sister Mary. In an 1891 letter to Annie Fields, Jewett writes that she has to watch that Mary does not take on too much of the burden since she, Sarah, can escape to Annie Fields's houses at Manchester-by-the-Sea or Boston.[30] In another letter of that year she writes of Lowell's recent death: "And yet I say to myself again and again how glad I am that the long illness is ended."[31] Letters from this final year of her mother's illness show the strain. In an August 1891 letter to Annie Fields, she describes the visit of a cousin, Alice Gilman: "I only hope that mother will be equal to taking some little pleasure. She has been brighter this evening than for two or three days and more like herself but she has seemed so ill and dull, and could hardly move herself about at all."[32] On September 10, 1891, Jewett says she pities her "poor Uncle Will," who had paid a visit to her mother the day before: "I think that he didn't feel very well himself and he knows so well about this hopeless kind of illness, and he and mother are so fond of each other that it's peculiarly hard when she looks to him for the help that he can't give."[33]

But the clearest picture of Jewett's devotion to her mother during this long and painful illness comes from a letter to Loulie Dresel that was dated South Berwick, 10 January [1891]:

... I have been in town for only one night and I thought that Mrs. Fields looked piteously ill when I first saw her, but I think she is doing well. It was very hard to leave her so soon when I knew what a difference it [would] make if I could only stay but I am needed *so much* here. My dear mother is fairly comfortable now, but very weak indeed and I cannot bear to think of being away for more than a few hours. I begin to feel the need of getting out more. There is so much snow and I have to be so careful of it, that I walk very little and though all the horses need driving I don't really care much for sleighing and so I make excuse whenever I can. As for writing I keep beginning things, and after all I like best to sit by the garden window in my mother's room and talk to her when she likes it, and look out at the snow and the glistening elm twigs. Now that we are not so hurried and anxious about the illness my sister and I feel a little dulled and tired: it has been a terrible strain and sorrow.[34]

The long ordeal ended in October. Jewett's relief at her new independence seems understandable. And it was followed by the new sense of intimacy that she describes in her letter to Aldrich. Her description of moving into that "larger life" after death, in concert with her mother's spirit, brings into play the child's sense of identification and fusion, although now the fusion does not threaten the daughter's freedom and selfhood: "When a larger life opens for those who are nearest and dearest it seems as if a larger life opened for us too. I sometimes remember what Sir Thomas Browne said—about joining both lives together and living in one but for the other." Here Jewett is ostensibly talking about two phases in an individual's life—this world and the world to come—but the association with her own newly expanded life cannot be missed. Nor can the sense of spiritual merging with the lost mother now that the barriers were removed. In a letter of condolence to her cousin Caroline, Jewett reiterates this hope for a deeper intimacy following death: "I wish that I could say anything that would give you a little comfort in so great a loss but couldn't help remembering that your own love and memory comfort you best. And there does come such a new feeling of nearness, and complete understanding. I sometimes think that *mis*-understanding is the only thing to fear!—and all that is forever swept away."[35]

Jewett's faith in life after death naturally supported these hopes. Many years after her father's death she wondered if he celebrated his birthday in heaven, was watching over, or was bored with her.[36] Throughout her stories, the spirits of the dead return to warm the hearts of the living. Temperance Dent's unseen presence brings her two estranged friends together in a moment of sisterly communion; the ghostly vision of Mis' Tolland's mother comforts her daughter's dying moments in a foreign land. Celia Thaxter's letters to Jewett's friend, John Greenleaf Whittier, describe a séance in which Annie Fields and Jewett both were present. At one point, the medium roused the spirit of Annie's husband, James T. Fields, and Celia Thaxter later encountered the ghost of her own mother in an incident that may have contributed to "The Foreigner."[37] Jewett's interest in spiritualism had roots not only in the popular craze of the 1880s and early 1890s but also in her early Swedenborgianism. Through Professor Theophilus Parsons she had been introduced to the mystic's theory of a spiritual world similar to our own, in which angels carry on their lives in pure and perfect sympathy. These are issues that need further discussion, but this faith helps explain Jewett's response to her mother's death.[38]

Finally, there is the lovely closing to the Aldrich letter: "But it is no use trying to write these things. If I were with you, I should take hold of your hand and not say anything, and I do that now." Sympathy goes beyond language. Sharing this loss, so different from any other, demands a physical touch, a return to the personal and particular kindness that the mother herself first granted. This communion reaches back beyond intellectualization, beyond words to a most basic human bond. Significantly, many crucial moments in Jewett's fiction take place in silence, in wordless recognition of emotional intimacy: the preverbal preoedipal world.

These issues, and their resolution, are poignantly expressed in the unpublished sketch "The Christmas Ghosts." Although undated, the piece may have been written soon after Caroline Jewett's death, for in it the spirit of a writer's mother returns to her old home the second Christmas after her death. In the course of the visit, the writer comes to a new sense of her mother's love and of her own life. Since the sketch seems to have a strong autobiographical cast and since it deals so openly with mother/daughter relationships, I will look at it in some detail; its patterns recur throughout Jewett's work.

II

"The Christmas Ghosts" opens on Christmas Eve, near midnight. A solitary "watcher" is sitting awake and writing. As a high wind creaks the trees and brushes the lilac bushes, this watcher feels "curiously . . . alert . . . and expectant." The ghosts who had once lived in the old house are returning through the "familiar gate" to revisit their past. Among them is the ghost most recently removed to that "other country," who, like the others, is moved "to touch the lives of those who were still beloved, to see them, no longer with sorrow and impatience as at first, stumbling through their tasks like stupid children."[39] This ghost, identified in the first draft as the watcher's mother, also wishes to "know if the new relationship could not be understood, if a sense of presence and of love might not be given and taken." As the various ghosts, "quiet home keeping women and hurried men who had known much business by sea and shore" (conventional figures surely), explore the familiar settings, this new ghost comes to the watcher's side, seeking somehow to communicate her presence and to establish a new, "transfigured" bond between them.

The watcher, at first merely expectant, now wishes for some sign from the other "side." With an uncanny intuition she senses the ghosts' entrance and welcomes them silently without even glimpsing their "shining faces." Although the watcher does not know it, "the ghost most dear to her, the ghost who had been the last to die . . . came close to her and smiled wistfully." Then the ghost goes on to look at her old possessions, which her grieving family has not yet put away. Coming upon the heap of Christmas presents, she reflects on the strains the holiday had brought in the past: "I used to worry about the Christmas gifts in those last years when my strength was going, but I like to think about them now: we made us many idols in the old life, but they were only the signs of love. What should we not do for each other if we gave gifts this night?" As the ghost's thoughts turn toward her daughter, the watcher's "heart was filled with the same thought." In this moment she remembers "her dear ghost with such love and longing that their hearts were joined in one golden moment of content."[40]

This moment of blessed fusion recalls to the watcher a similar communion when the ghost was still living. Her memory clearly recalls the

long afternoons Jewett spent "sitting by the garden window" in her
mother's room during Caroline Perry Jewett's last illness:

"I know that she thinks of me this night," said the watcher with great joy: "I
feel that she is near, it cannot be only in remembrance. It is like one summer
day when she was ill and we sat in silence in her room when she turned to me
and smiled; we never had been so near each others hearts as we were then.
The wind was playing in the garden trees, the golden sunset shone in the room:
that was the way in which she said farewell and bade me not forget her and
gave herself to me, as I to her."[41]

In this moment there is a perfect merging; mother and daughter surrender to each other in complete sympathy, affirmed by the golden light
that spills in through the windows. It is a silent moment, recognized
by both.

As in a fairy tale, the watcher now wishes a boon from the ghost:
"How shall we keep Christmas now? . . . What can our gifts be to each
other now, except our love alone? The old way of gifts was but to find
a shape and body for the soul of love!" At this the ghost returns to
the watcher's side. The answer is simple: "The watcher's hands, that
had reached out, dropped empty; but her heart was full. 'I love you, I
love you!' she said and found again and forever what was lost."[42] But
there is one more step to be taken before the watcher can make this
answer her own. The wind dies down and the night grows still. The
ghosts are leaving and the Christmas night is passing. "The watcher
grew strangely afraid, she did not dare to look about the room. She
began to wake from a strange spell. The darkness of the house was
full of dread, the clocks ticked louder and louder." It is another death.
"The house seemed empty and the ghosts were gone." But then, in the
emptiness, a sudden awareness brings the sketch to its close: "And
presently a great joy of love and blessing, the joy of those who know
that love is immortal filled the waiting heart."[43]

Before analyzing the sketch further I would like to look briefly at the
first draft, where Jewett's themes are much more explicit. What is
especially interesting is how Jewett edited this earlier version—how she
reined in its passion and pruned the didactic sections. Because these
revisions reveal so much about Jewett's literary and emotional style, I
have included her deletions as marked.

In the earlier draft, after asking how she should keep Christmas, the
watcher adds, "If you could help me do the best things I can for every
one tomorrow I should be so glad." Underlying this request, of course,
is the question: how shall I be good? The following passage, subse-
quently deleted, shows that Jewett was placing her ghost within both
a religious and a maternal context:

And the ghost who went last came and stood beside her like ~~the f~~ a tall white flame and the heart of that flame was love. ["]~~Dear child thought said the ghost, dear child!" and the sound of her earthly voice came clear to the waking heart's remembrance.~~ "Listen to the love that speaks in your own heart" said the ghost "we were always told the best thing but how little we listened. it never happened that we did not know["]—and as this thought came clear and seemed to answer the anxious question she knew that it was true.[44]

For those who have "crossed the boundary," such misunderstandings and bewilderments are no longer troubling. The dearest ghost can now see past the failures to enduring bonds. It is this she strives to communicate to her waiting daughter.

Now the watcher's strange dread after the ghosts depart has a definite source. As these lines—marked for deletion—explain, she "grew suddenly frightened, because she was left alone." Next we have the image of the ticking clocks and darkened house, which was kept, then this passage, which was not:

But . . . the love that was brought by the dearest ghost of all was unforgotten in her lonely heart. Yes they all live; she is alive, she was here, she loves me! ~~whisper~~ said the only one who was still awake. ~~Wherever she is it she my mother~~ she may be she knows that I love her and that I feel her dear presence when she comes and tomorrow I shall keep Christmas for her sake, and do the things she would do if she were here again.[45]

Here we see Jewett's struggle clearly. She begins, "Wherever she may be it . . ." She takes out "it" and adds "she." Then she takes out "she" and puts in "my mother." Then she scratches out "my mother" and puts in another "she." Jewett completed the passage, but at some point she returned. This time she was decisive. A single line runs straight down the page.

Probably she wanted to delete not only the reference to the mother but also the moralizing. In the revised draft the conclusion is brief and relatively restrained. However, it is also vague. The significance of the love that fills the watcher's heart is not altogether clear. In this earlier version Jewett openly explores the connections between the watcher's experience and Christian conversion:

And a new presence strangely moved her so that she stopped, afraid in the dark and a joy she had never felt wrapped her as if with light and ["]Rejoice for my sake" the presence said. "Christmas is ~~mine~~ ours. ~~You who know and believe are mine,~~ there should be peace and good will, now will you live tomorrow to show them ~~forth~~ to your little world. I know these wonders now and I show them through those who love me ~~to this troubled world~~ as I could not show them when I was in the world."[46]

From an earthly mother, troubled by the petty worries of Christmas presents and weakened by illness, the ghost has become the internal model of divine love. For Her sake, as for Christ's sake, the watcher is brought to the fold of believers. Her redemption comes through her bond to the mother: "Peace and good will, ... Dear ghost and the Master said the same things." The next day, the fruits of this surprising conversion appear:

The watcher of the night went to a person whom she had wronged in thought and tried to her just and kind [sic] and all day long she took joy in doing things that she knew were [illegible word deleted] right but had not wished to do before. She [illegible word] saw her life in a larger way and [illegible word] she set its bounds still wider and so this dear Ghost helped her to live on.[47]

The literary value of "The Christmas Ghosts" may be slight. The first draft seems both overwrought and overwritten, and the second seems relatively insubstantial, despite its control—perhaps why Jewett did not publish it. However, the story expresses some central patterns in Jewett's emotional and intellectual life. On the psychological level we can see clearly the drive toward fusion with the mother and the difficulties of this fusion. Once the mother dies, perfect understanding can be achieved and sustained. Recognition will then be *fully* possible. The feminine cognitive and relational style described by Chodorow clearly is at work here. The watcher's "intuition" makes her aware of the ghostly presence, opens her psyche to communication with the world of spirits. Her ego is permeable; her access to the realm beyond rational consciousness is great.

Further, her communication with divinity comes through a kin-based bond, through intercession by a figure known and loved by her. It is not a lonely vigil or a prostration before a frightening God but a sympathetic communion growing out of a bond nurtured throughout her life. While no longer physical, this attachment grows evenly and gracefully from the natural/biological plane to the spiritual. The conversion, moreover, takes place in the home, amid the familiar, loved objects of their shared lives. The house itself is rich with tradition, rooted in family history. Moreover, it is permeable: open to the sound of the wind in the lilacs and the "flittings" of the returning ghosts. Like the feminine psyche, the house is open to the natural and the spiritual.

In the sketch's conclusion the watcher finds the answer to her questions through acceptance of her mother's enduring presence. In his description of the Eleusinian Mysteries, C. G. Jung describes them as peculiarly feminine initiation rites that articulated women's unique psychic situation. His analysis could apply equally well to the watcher's mystical transformation. He begins with the point Chodorow also makes: daughters experience themselves first as merged with their mothers. This situation produces the curious paradox that "a woman lives earlier as a mother, later as a daughter," a mystery symbolized in the annual renewal of the seed corn: "The psyche pre-existent to the consciousness (e.g. the child) participates in the maternal psyche on the one hand, while on the other it reaches across to the daughter psyche. We could therefore say that every mother contains her daughter in herself and every daughter her mother, and that every woman extends backwards into her mother and forward into her daughter."[48] In the Eleusinian rituals the initiate is brought to experience these ties consciously. The result is the "feeling that her life is spread out over generations—the first step toward the immediate experience and conviction of being outside time, which brings with it a feeling of *immortality*." The individual finds "a place and a meaning in the life of the generations." She is "rescued from her isolation and restored to wholeness."[49]

After her mother's death Jewett apparently did achieve some new sense of wholeness, some new sense of peace with her mother and what her mother represented. This brief sketch reveals new meanings on other levels as well. Here, as in "Root-Bound" and *Pearl of Orr's Island,* salvation is achieved through a woman: Christ is either represented by a mother or becomes maternal himself. Nurture and sympathy replace crisis and conviction. The mother who appears as a "tall white flame whose heart was love" also has archetypal overtones. Like the Virgin or like Persephone, who carries a flaming torch from the Underworld, the dear ghost acts as a Sophia figure, the mother who "has been purged of all gross materiality." Her counsel, in Erich Neumann's phrase, "is a wisdom of loving participation."[50] And like other avatars of the Great Mother archetype, this figure never strays far from earth, never withdraws, but remains ever near to lend her devotees strength and love. Ortner's analysis of feminine iconography also illuminates this image. It is only after the mother is physically dead that apotheosis is achieved. The pollution of biology is finally purged.

III

If the bond between mother and daughter was the heart of the Victorian woman's domestic world, the boundaries of this world extended to include female relatives and friends. A boy's attachments might reach out beyond the family to a peer group, but they were more horizontal, in keeping with his future social role. A young woman, however, was initiated into the complexities of intergenerational ties. Her life, as Jung's quote suggests, stretched upward to touch those of grandparents, aunts, and uncles, then downward to include younger siblings, cousins, nieces, and nephews. In a letter to Mrs. Whitman, written in 1894 or 1895, Jewett commented on Mrs. Kemble and her contemporaries: "I look upon that generation as the one to which I really belong,—I who was brought up with grandfathers and granduncles and aunts for my best playmates. They were not the wine that one can get at so much the dozen now!"[51] Jewett's very real intimacy with these older people might be anomalous in a male writer, but it was not at all unusual in a Victorian woman of her class and time. Picking up the threads of her mother's friendships after Caroline Jewett died, Jewett wrote that she found a "double sweetness" in this responsibility.[52] As she came to terms with her mother's death by internalizing the maternal presence, so she found a new continuity by appropriating her mother's network of friends.

Jewett's bonds to her sisters, Caroline and Mary, were particularly strong. The voluminous correspondence between them, much of it in the Jewett collection at the Houghton Library, testifies to the sisters' steadfast concern for each other's welfare and their drive to communicate even everyday experience. When Mary inherited their grandfather's South Berwick house, Sarah moved with her. These two unmarried women now had command of the patriarchal mansion. Mary took the grand bedroom fronting the street; Sarah, the smaller, more private room in back, where she crossed her riding crops over the mantel. There they lived out their days—Jewett until her death in 1909 (after prolonged weakness following a carriage accident in 1902), Mary until 1930, when she left the house to her sister's son Theodore. When their mother, still next door, began her final illness, the sisters assumed her care together. And when Caroline Eastman died in 1898, Jewett wrote to Grace Norton: "It is impossible to get over the feeling that something of me died and not the living brightness and affectionateness of my sister. I have been reading Madame Darmesteter's Life of Renan with great pleasure lately and I keep remembering one of the last sentences— The important thing in life is not our misery, our despair, however crushing, but the one good moment which outweighs it all."[53]

Like "The Christmas Ghosts," the letter expresses a sense of merged lives. Love brings a mystical participation in another's essence. The "one good moment which outweighs it all" recalls that golden moment of communion Jewett's "watcher" shares with the "dear ghost." These epiphanies became the source of Jewett's strength, the focal point of her life and fiction. *The Country of the Pointed Firs* may actually be structured around a series of such epiphanies: each chapter moving toward some subtle instance of sympathetic understanding and recognition. At times this bond seems nearly telepathic. As Mrs. Todd steers her boat toward Green Island, Mrs. Blackett is intuitively aware of her daughter's approach:

I looked, and could see a tiny flutter in the doorway, but a quicker signal had made its way from the heart on shore to the heart on the sea.

"How do you suppose she knows it's me?" said Mrs. Todd, with a tender smile on her broad face. "There, you never get over bein' a child long's you have a mother to go to. Look at the chimney, now; she's gone right in an' brightened up the fire."[54]

This passage echoes Jewett's letter to Thomas Bailey Aldrich and shows how her mother's death shaped the characterization of Mrs. Todd and Mrs. Blackett. However, as "The Christmas Ghosts" reveals, not even death could deprive you of a mother. No one need ever "get over bein' a child." Though her own mother is long since gone, Mrs. Blackett beams with youthful expectancy and pleasure; the child within her is always accessible.

There was, however, one female relative Jewett remembered with less affection: her paternal grandmother. Although Mary Jewett died when Sarah was only five, she apparently left a lasting imprint on the little girl's imagination. In "From a Mournful Villager," Jewett describes her as a "proud and solemn woman," who "hated my mischief, and rightly thought my elder sister a much better child than I. I used to be afraid of her when I was in the house."[55] Fortunately, Sarah could escape this woman's frightening authority. When she was outdoors, she "forgot I was under anybody's rule. . . . I was first cousin to a caterpillar if they called me to come in, and I was own sister to a giddy-minded bobolink when I ran away across the fields, as I used to do very often."[56] When she was older, she could roam the fields or ride her horse as fast and as far as she wished, through woods and country villages. In "River Driftwood" she describes her boat trip down the Piscataqua. As a young lady she still joined the town boys sledding down the snowy hills. But as a very little girl she was confined to the yards, barns, and sheds of the Berwick house.

In one unhappy incident Sarah's curiosity got the better of her. About four years old, she found a bud just opening on a "cherished tea-rose bush." Anxious to please, she "snapped it off at once," rushed inside to her invalid grandmother, and "showed her proudly what was crumpled in my warm little fist. I can see it now!—it had no stem at all, and for many days afterward I was bowed down with a sense of my guilt and shame, for I was made to understand it was an awful thing to have blighted and broken a treasured flower like that."[57]

Obviously, the older Jewett still did not repent her "grave sin," but her stories do reveal a curious reverberation from this incident. Her heroines often make their symbolic mark on the house of an older, forbidding woman by filling it with freshly cut flowers. In *Deephaven* Kate Lancaster and a guest put wildflowers in nearly every vase, thereby routing the gloom left by a now dead but once highly proper aunt. In *A Country Doctor* one of Nan Prince's first acts when she arrives at her proud aunt's formal house is to cut flowers from the garden and display them. In "Miss Sydney's Flowers," one of Jewett's earliest stories, the young woman softens a stern older woman's heart, then persuades her to give her splendid hothouse flowers away to the needy and sick. The elder Mrs. Jewett's unbending formality evidently acquainted Sarah with at least one negative aspect of the feminine domestic scene: a proud authority figure willing to arbitrate matters of proper behavior and gentility, the forbidding judge in the "cult of true womanhood." Her traits can be found in Miss Prince and Mrs. Fraley of *A Country Doctor* and possibly in other figures, such as Mrs. Hight in *The Country of the Pointed Firs*.

The death of this powerful woman also left its impression. In keeping with Victorian deathbed rituals, Sarah and the rest of the family were called to the grandmother's side for farewells. However, Sarah would not go: "My grandmother was dying, whatever that might be, and she was taking leave of every one—she was ceremonious even then. I did not dare go with the rest; I had an intense curiosity to see what dying might be like, but I was afraid to be there with her, and I was also afraid to be alone."[58] All by herself while the others paid their respects, Sarah saw the December sky darken. Sitting on the doorstep and crying, she heard the next-door bell ring over and over. "I suppose I was afraid to answer the summons. . . . All the world had been still before, and the bell sounded loud and awful through the empty house. It seemed as if the messenger from an unknown world had come to the wrong house to call my grandmother away."[59]

At last her family came trooping back, "awed and tearful." They found the little five-year-old girl "waiting in the cold, alone, and afraid more of this world than next," and were "very good" to her. The funeral, however, provided Sarah with "vast entertainment": "It was the first grand public occasion in which I had any share."[60] While there are many sources for Jewett's preoccupation with funeral processions, deathbed scenes, and messengers from the "other world," these very early memories anchor it in emotional experience. Dying was frightening and fascinating, the first great ceremony she ever encountered, an initiation based on a biological event in a society where many biological events were obscured or actually hidden.

While these relationships within her own family were obviously intense and often ambivalent, Jewett's greatest book celebrates the love between a writer much like herself and a woman from a much less privileged background. Mrs. Todd's guidance and adoption of the narrator in *Pointed Firs* is certainly influenced by Jewett's own relationships with her mother, with Annie Fields, and with other close friends. However, this friendship brings the narrator out of a genteel, ladylike setting—one in which Jewett's grandmother would have been comfortable—and initiates her into a world with a very different model for woman's character and woman's work.

Jewett had known women like Mrs. Todd since childhood. In the sketch "An Autumn Holiday," she describes a visit with Miss Polly Marsh and her sister, Mrs. Snow, survivors of an older, preindustrial world. As she comes up to the door of their house in the woods, Jewett finds them "stepping back and forward together spinning yarn at a pair of big wheels. The wheels made such a noise with their whir and creak, and my friends were talking so fast as they twisted and turned the yarn, that they did not hear my footsteps, and I stood in the doorway watching them, it was such a quaint and pretty sight."[61]

Once aware of Jewett's presence, the sisters stop and settle down to visit, being sure to take up their knitting, "For neither of them were ever known to be idle." Polly Marsh, whom Jewett calls Aunt Polly, "was a famous nurse and often in demand all through that part of the country." During one of Jewett's own childhood illnesses, Aunt Polly came to the South Berwick house to nurse her, leaving Jewett with one of "her pleasantest memories." In these sisters Jewett knew the real-life models for the Miss Roxy and Miss Ruey of Stowe's *Pearl of Orr's Island*.

This brief description of their "autumn holiday" together is in Jewett's finest style: restrained yet blissfully pastoral. The subtle merging of work with friendly talk, set in a homely interior filled with Indian summer sunlight, recalls similar scenes in *Pointed Firs*:

Aunt Polly brought me some of her gingerbread, which she knew I liked, and a stout little pitcher of milk, and we sat together for a while, gossiping and enjoying ourselves. I told all the village news I could think of, and I was just tired enough to know it, and to be contented to sit still for a while in the comfortable three-cornered chair by the little front window. The October sunshine lay along the clean kitchen floor, and Aunt Polly darted from her chair occasionally to catch stray little wisps of wool which the breeze from the door blew along from the wheels.[62]

Jewett appears almost enchanted by the setting. With her milk and gingerbread, her sleepiness and contentment, her seat on the "three-cornered chair," she seems like some fairy-tale heroine: a Goldilocks or Red-Riding-Hood given refuge in some magical cottage immune to time.

And indeed, we can see in this pastoral setting the older balance and harmony of qualities that were to become polarized in the industrial age. This home is both private and public at once. It is centered on the family and the kinship between sisters, but it is also a place of productive work that will be valued outside the family. In the work itself there is a balancing of "male" and "female" qualities. The women approach their tasks straightforwardly, with a sense of urgency and achievement. However, they structure their work loosely, punctuating it with the friendly communion of gossip. The sisters themselves, as we discover through their tales, are wonderful judges of character, sharp-eyed, and full of spunk. There is no question that they value themselves, their work, and their world. In their lives Jewett saw not only strength and love but a model for their integration.

Although domestic ideology argued that these working women could not keep their spiritual bloom, Mrs. Todd surely does. In *Pointed Firs* the association with manual labor and the natural world is not a source of contamination but, paradoxically, a means to transcendence. The ramifications of this association between transcendence and immanence are complex. In "Root-Bound" the association is there but at the price of restriction. Later chapters of this book will explore how Jewett resolved this central issue. In her pastoral vision, women like Mrs. Todd move freely within nature, outside the domestic circumference, yet escape pollution. They are neither bodiless nor angels, but divinity is still theirs.

Chapter Four

Hearts and Rounds, Part 2

Turning to Jewett's friendships is to focus on her life's very center. In *Not Under Forty,* Willa Cather wrote that Jewett "had never been one of those who 'live to write.' She lived for a great many things, and the stories by which we know her were but one of preoccupations . . . friendship occupied perhaps the first place in her life."[1] That Jewett's life centered on these friendships points up the fact that it did not center on a husband nor on children of her own. These conventional sources of love Jewett passed quietly by.[2] A diary entry dated 1867 describes the wedding of her "Cousin Nelly," Helen Gilman Nichols. The event, highly ritualized, apparently brought out strongly mixed feelings in Jewett, then eighteen years old. Her voice in these passages is surprisingly childish: "You old diary let me tell you I am going to [the wedding] and my mamma is going with me. I am going to carry the Dore Tennyson's Elaine [her bridal gift] and Mary got it in Boston for that purpose. My dress is good and has a regular train to it. Oh dear I cannot believe I am grown up. It doesn't seem as if I was at all. I do believe that if any one should ask me how old I was and I didn't think I should say, ten."[3] (She then goes on to describe how she fails to live up to ladylike expectations: her sins, such as not keeping Sunday solemnly, are all quite venial.) As the wedding looms larger, Jewett's dread of "growing up" seems to accelerate. Soon after the last entry, she writes: "But I have really something to write now which is My dear darling Cousin Nelly came up yesterday. . . . I hate to have her married for which I can give no definite reason. She came at eleven and Mary and I went to the depôt for her. I didn't know what to say or do I was so glad to see her."[4]

Although the actual ceremony impressed Jewett with its flowers, costumes, and pomp, her description poignantly expresses the ambivalence provoked by the change in her "dear darling Cousin Nelly": "After Helen Williams Gilman was no more they up and congratulated her and then we had bride cake and the most splendid collation I ever saw."[5] Carroll Smith-Rosenberg notes that marriage was a "particularly traumatic" event for a young Victorian woman, who was separated from everything dear and familiar only to live with the member of a virtually alien culture. Whether or not Helen Gilman felt that way, certainly Jewett, the observer, did. To her, marriage seemed a kind of death in which the girl she had known was somehow annihilated— and the annihilation celebrated with cake and wine. Jewett's response, revealed in her first diary entry, was bewilderment about her own readiness to undergo any such ritual separation and transformation. No, she had rather stay ten years old, a much safer place.

Josephine Donovan locates the source of Jewett's childlike and childish behavior in just this desire to escape the demands of conventional womanhood. In *Deephaven* the two heroines wish to "copy the Ladies of Llangollen and remove ourselves from society and its distractions." The Ladies of Llangollen, Lady Eleanor Butler and Miss Sarah Ponsby, were two friends of the late eighteenth century who became famous by running away from high society to a pastoral Welsh farm, where they led a lyrical domestic life. Donovan sees the desire to emulate them as an "escapist theme that recurs in Jewett's work . . . [which] probably reflects a desire not to have to conform to the role demands that 'adulthood' required in Victorian America."[6] I agree with Donovan's interpretation and would add to it Jewett's need to recapture that sense of fusion, primary love, first experienced with her mother. Return to childhood is not necessarily always an escape but may also be a return to the source of one's well-being, a perpetual renewal and reaffirmation. For Jewett, love would always retain the structure of that first attachment, whether she took the role of mother or daughter. But this structure does not preclude the achievement of emotional maturity nor its expression.

Two 1876 letters from a friend, Anna L. Dawes, present a more adult critique of marriage. Although Jewett's reply is not available, the letters' tone assumes its reader's agreement; apparently, these were views that Jewett would not find shocking and might even second: "So Leslie and Wallace are about to marry. And then, having their cake, are going to eat it in Europe. To all appearances the raisins are almost too thick therein. Still I am too much pleased for them to be very envious. Are you going down to the wedding? I greatly regret I can't be there to disturb the morning [illegible word] of the guests."[7] Several months after the ceremony, Anna writes:

Our bride is an old married woman by this time, and apparently likes it better than ever. I don't feel particularly attracted do you? I always did admire Saint Paul, and I agree with him that the unmarried state is "better." I am not strong minded either! And Alice is on the other side. Happy mortal! I think it is just the thing for her too don't you . . . A fine family that is and what fine attachés they have too. Did our girls find better husbands than George Little and Wallace Pierce?[8]

Anna's attitude toward the whole affair is flippant. She finds little genuine good in the marriage; even the specific benefits she mentions are crassly conventional: good connections. Alice has gone over to "the other side," and I doubt that Anna Dawes envies the "happy mortal" one bit. Her preference for the "better" state of chastity advocated by Saint Paul carries a scent of superiority, as does the entire letter, whose style is both condescending and amused.

Jewett, as far as the evidence shows, was never this sarcastic about the patriarchal institution of marriage. But she seems to have agreed with her friend, in spirit if not in tone. In "The New Wife," an undated poem in the Houghton manuscript collection, she puts the matter another way:

> On the little island see the cows a feeding
> There all the [illegible word] grow that a man may need.
> There you and I shall live, man and wife together
> King and queen of farmer folk! but she did not heed.
>
> Looking backward over the waste of water
> Still she saw the homeward hills on a fading shore
> Life was all before her, yet there lay behind her
> All she knew and all she left. Love had shut the door.
>
> Love had set the waters wide. Love had made her lonely
> All at once she turned away from a love so dear
> Row, row the boat and catch the wind a-quarter
> Row, row the boat. I see the shore come near![9]

Nothing could be clearer: love makes the new wife "lonely," "shuts the door," and "sets the waters wide." Marriage separates you from everything familiar, everything known; marriage is a kind of death. Like Nan in *A Country Doctor,* like the unnamed wife here, Jewett must have felt relief at her escape.

The direct, although probably unconscious link, childhood and female friendship, also appears in Jewett's often-quoted letter to Sara Norton. Since the line "This is my birthday and I am always nine years old" is usually quoted separately, I will give most of the letter below to show the full context. The date is September 3, 1897, Jewett's forty-eighth birthday:

> . . . This is my birthday and I am always nine years old—not like George Sand, who begins a letter—no, no! I mean Madame de Sévigné!!—'5 fevrier 16—; il y a aujourd'hui mille ans que je suis née!' . . . I feel deep in my heart all that you say in your letter. One feels how easy it is for friends to slip away

out of this world and leave us lonely. And such good days as you have are too good to be looked for often. There is something transfiguring in the best of friendship. One remembers the story of the transfiguration in the New Testament, and sees over and over in life what the great shining hours can do, and how one goes down from the mountain where they are, into the fret of everyday life again, but strong in remembrance. I once heard Mr. Brooks [Phillips Brooks of Trinity Church, Boston] preach a great sermon about this: That nobody could stay on the mount, but every one knew it, and went his way with courage by reason of such moments. You cannot think what a sermon it was![10]

The contrast between Jewett's sense of being nine years old and Madame Sévigné's sense of being a thousand points up the playful quality of this remark. Drawing on her Emersonian and Romantic sympathies, Jewett stresses her closeness to an archetypal child/primitive. Rather than being burdened by history, she wishes to keep some essential freshness and spontaneity: the perpetual renewal of life found through a childlike vision. Of course, the remark also expresses her fears that such freedom would be lost if she were to venture beyond the boundary of puberty. Why not be perpetually sixteen, or eighteen? The dread she felt at Nelly Gilman's wedding is now submerged, but the choice remains the same.

Replacing the dread is this hymn to friendship and those moments of transfiguration that sustained her. The question of whether or not to marry was answered; she would do without husband and family. In fact, she had no need of them, for in friendship she found everything. In the opening page of *The Country of the Pointed Firs* she writes: "The process of falling in love at first sight is as final as it is swift. . . . But the growth of true friendship may be a lifelong affair."[11] Friendship, finally, was greater, more enduring, than love itself; it comprised love and carried it to a higher, spiritual plane—echoes of Plato and Emerson. Those "shining hours," "golden moments," were at once moments of emotional intimacy and spiritual communion. In her doctrines of friendship Jewett fused religious redemption and sensuous/emotional satisfaction. Grace comes only from these "personal" and "particular" bonds. Even when this epiphany comes through communion with nature, nature is personified. "She is first cousin to a caterpillar . . . own sister to a giddy-minded bobolink." Even here the ties are kin-based, sympathetic.

A letter to Sarah Whitman reveals how seriously Jewett took these commitments:

. . . I have been thinking of you with deep love in these last days. It could have been easier not to speak but I must tell you as if it were the first time how much I love you, dear. It breaks my heart to see you so tired. When we are together it seems as if we only played at friendship with the old Greek players' mask held over our faces, but in my heart there is something that can never dull nor time keep from being yours nor ever come to the end of this world.[12]

If the letter to Sarah Whitman expresses pain at the absence of communion, at the loss of fusion with a dear friend, another letter describes the forging of a new bond through a "shining" moment of intuitive sympathy. The friend is Madame Marie Thérèse Blanc-Bentzon, a French writer in America to gather material. Recalling Madame Blanc's first visit to South Berwick, Jewett begins with the budding awareness of intimacy: "We were very near to each other. I remember the wonder of it filling my heart as we were walking along a favorite bit of road of mine between two pastures and beside the scattered pines. 'What is this?' she would ask, and I would say 'juniper' or 'bayberry.' 'I have read of it' and she would smile soberly as if she met an old friend for the first time."[13]

To meet an old friend for the first time: Jewett's paradox encloses an almost uncanny recognition. She senses the other woman's openness, her desire to be *in* this place, Jewett's place. At last awareness blooms into speech: "I stopped short and faced her and there we stood in the narrow road together. *How did we come to be walking here together* I cried! I am made of this spot, but you!—How came this afternoon to be *ours*?" The answer is silence but a silence full of meaning: "She smiled at me most as if she knew, but both understood that only Those who are wiser than we give gifts like that; that we were close enough though Berwick and the *Quartier* . . . might be far enough apart."

I

At first Jewett's circle of friends encompassed schoolmates and girls from neighboring towns. Like many young Victorian women Jewett adopted a younger friend, to whom she wrote solemn didactic letters full of wise counsel and moral uplift. Jewett's "dear little girl" was Lily Munger, daughter of the Reverend C. Munger of Farmington, Maine.[14] But even before this correspondence, which dates from 1876 to 1880, Jewett had several "crushes" on other girls, including Kate Birckhead of Newport, Rhode Island, who was the model for Kate Lancaster in *Deephaven*. In her 1872 diary Jewett writes that "she would do anything to demonstrate the depth of her feeling for Kate."[15] Another intense and perhaps difficult friendship developed with Harriet Waters Preston from Newburyport, Massachusetts. Little seems to be known about this relationship, except that it was important during the time Jewett lost her father and was publishing her first book, *Deephaven*.

Preston was a critic for the *Atlantic Monthly* and an author in her own right. According to John Eldridge Frost, there was some misunderstanding between the two women, and they ceased contact after 1877.[16]

About this time Jewett met Annie Fields, wife of *Atlantic* publisher James T. Fields. Apparently they were brought together through the auspices of the *Atlantic* editors, such as William Dean Howells, who had accepted Jewett's first stories for publication. The earliest letter from Jewett to Annie Fields in the Houghton collection is dated December 4, 1877. Although it is chatty and familiar, the language does not bear the marks of the intimacy that was to develop later, most noticeably after 1881. Following the death of James Fields and Jewett's father, the most important men in both women's lives, their relationship blossomed into a "pure and passionate" friendship that endured until Jewett's death in 1909.[17]

In her study *Surpassing the Love of Men,* Lillian Faderman sees Sarah and Annie's friendship as the model of what was then called the "Boston marriage," "a long-term monogamous relationship between two otherwise unmarried women."[18] Assessing these unions is difficult from a twentieth-century perspective. As Carroll Smith-Rosenberg points out, these are pre-Freudian lives, without our concepts of deviance and normalcy—and with a greater tolerance for same-sex attachments than our own society.[19] Because of this different historical context the term "lesbian" may be misleading. Moreover, the important thing is not whether these relationships were explicitly sexual—something we will never know and that seems unlikely given their unself-conscious quality. Rather, as Faderman puts it, the important thing is that "these women spent their lives primarily with other women, they gave to other women the bulk of their energy and attention, and they formed powerful emotional ties with other women." In fact, Faderman argues that because genteel Boston, a "sex-hating society," believed "love between women was asexual, unsullied by the evils of carnality," it could see this love "as ideal and admire, and even envy, it as the British had admired and envied the Ladies of Llangollen a hundred years earlier."[20]

Although Annie Fields remained the central figure in Jewett's life, theirs was not an exclusive relationship. There was room for several other intensely affectionate, loving friendships. The women with whom Jewett formed bonds in her maturity are impressive. They reveal not only Jewett's charm but also the emergence of a network of professional women whose lives centered not on their families and domestic duties but on their cultural, public contributions, whether paid or voluntary. Some of the most important included Sarah Whitman, an artist who worked in stained glass and was a founder of Radcliffe College; Sally

Norton, a cellist; Louise Imogen Guiney, a poet and essayist; Alice Brown, a short-story writer; Celia Thaxter, a poet and story writer; and Louise Chandler Moulton, a poet. Thaxter, in particular, was a cherished friend.[21]

The connection to Annie Fields, along with Sarah's own efforts to publish and win recognition, brought Jewett out of the provinces and into the heart of American literary life. In an interesting unpublished piece called "Outgrown Friends," the narrator defends this shifting of affections as an unavoidable part of growing: "We are not wrong in looking at friendship as a means toward an end; that end being the formulation and development of the young man's character. . . . Often times our friends seem like the rounds of a ladder which help us raise ourselves, our ascent to the level of each giving us a wider view."[22] Annie Fields lifted her young friend very high indeed on this developmental ladder. Through her and other literary contacts Jewett was introduced to virtually everyone of any consequence in American letters and to many leading figures in Britain and Europe as well. With Annie Fields she met Tennyson, traveled through France and Greece, had tea with Henry James at Lamb House.

Although she never severed her bond to South Berwick, Jewett's rapid formation of new ties and a new identity did not occur without pain. According to John Eldridge Frost, her sisters and local friends wondered if she wasn't becoming uppity and too good for them. While she nowhere describes these feelings carefully, Jewett notes in a diary entry for July 17, 1872, that she is "restless and unhappy." In an undated 1874 entry she writes about an "unaccountable melancholy" and "loneliness."[23] An unpublished fragment entitled "For Country Girls" mentions briefly a time of self-doubt and emotional awkwardness: "When I was very young and went from my quiet country home into busy city houses, I used to suffer very much from a sense of unrelatedness to my surroundings."[24] Without more evidence it is difficult to assess the source of this "unaccountable melancholy" or sense of "unrelatedness." Some feelings, obviously, stemmed from the adjustment to urban life with its pressures on a relatively inexperienced girl to perform according to very high standards. After 1878 some of her pain came from grief over her beloved father's death. But this cannot account for the earlier diary entries. Whatever the source of her sufferings, however, solace came through her connection to Annie Fields. As early as 1880 Jewett wrote to the older woman: "I am the most placid and serene of all your friends and I forget that I ever was a girl who couldn't go to sleep at night."[25]

"Outgrown Friends" and another unpublished piece, "For Country

Girls," while not directly autobiographical, give us a fairly good idea of what Annie Fields meant to Jewett in those early years. In "Outgrown Friends," for example, Jewett counsels her reader on how to manage friendships with younger people: "There are many young persons who being in advance of or not finding exactly the sympathy they need in friends their own age become very devoted to and dependent upon some older person." The older friend should not be surprised, Jewett warns, if a younger one outgrows the dependent role to become self-reliant, able to "give as much as they receive." This, in fact, should be the aim of the older friend, just as a parent protects a child but urges it to grow. Thus, Jewett stresses tolerance and patience: "They may be undeveloped and possibly a little conceited and given to tiresome introspection. They may give undue attention to their fits of blues." Rather than criticizing, Jewett advises the older friend to listen well and "teach them to be their best selves": "They would be contented with little from your hands, a little petting and comforting when they are discouraged and discontented and praise when they come to you conquerors from a fight of which the details may be wearisome."[26]

In "For Country Girls," Sarah Jewett takes on the role of mentor herself. She tells her young audience to read widely to overcome their provincialism. They should listen to the wisdom of older people but not be frightened of them just because they *are* older. "Remember," Jewett writes, "that every-body has an easily wounded personality, and is more or less uncomfortable with a new acquaintance." The important thing is to believe in yourself and to act. She recommends Ulysses S. Grant's *Autobiography* as a guide to positive action (the enemy is just as frightened of you as you are of the enemy). And, she reassures her readers, "our time of painful self-consciousness will be soon outgrown if we do not foster it and creep too far into our shells of sensitiveness and self-accusation and even suspicion." The only way to grow up is to come out of that shell of isolation and self-doubt: "To become more entirely yourself will allow you to forget yourself."[27] Through Annie Fields's careful nurture and encouragement, the shy young writer from South Berwick did indeed become "more entirely herself."

II

Among the many things Annie Adams Fields had in common with Sarah Orne Jewett was a distinguished physician for a father; in her case, Dr. Zabdiel Boylston Adams, descended from Henry Adams of Braintree. Annie Fields's mother was Sarah May Holland, also of an old Massachusetts Bay Colony family. When only twenty, Annie married James T. Fields, a family friend and relative by marriage. Nearly seventeen years older than his wife, Fields could remember the days when he had dandled her on his knee. According to W. S. Tryon, "she was ever his 'dear child,' and she, in turn, looked up to her husband with an almost childlike trust."[28] Their marriage in 1854 propelled Annie Fields onto the center stage of American literary life. Later editor of the *Atlantic,* Fields was a junior partner in the publishing firm of Ticknor and Fields (he would become senior partner in 1864). At home the young wife entertained Hawthorne and Whittier, Dickens and Matthew Arnold, Howells and Samuel Clemens, as well as the various Jameses. She travelled across Europe with her husband, meeting Tennyson, Browning, and Leigh Hunt along the way. Her gifts as a hostess were legendary. F. O. Matthiessen describes the graceful house at Boston's 148 Charles Street (now a parking garage) as "the nearest approach ever made to an American salon."[29] Willa Cather's essay "148 Charles Street" memorializes this house overflowing with books and paintings, its windows overlooking the Charles River and the Promenade. In Annie Fields, Cather found what Henry James once called "the visitable past." Surviving well into the twentieth century, she was a last link to the writers of the American Renaissance.[30]

However, Annie Fields was an author in her own right. And despite the apparent harmony of her marriage, Judith Roman's study of her diaries reveals Annie Fields's early frustration at having her literary ambitions overwhelmed by the wifely duties of a hostess and housekeeper.[31] Her poetry, primarily on themes from classical literature and mythology, appeared frequently in the *Atlantic* and was collected in two volumes, *Under the Olive* (1881) and *The Singing Shepherd* (1895). She also translated from the Greek and the German, supporting her work with careful reading of scholars such as Hegel, Fichte, and Pater. Two of her longer dramatic poems are especially interesting. *The Return of Persephone* (1877), which I will discuss below, was adapted largely from the Homeric hymn to Demeter. *Orpheus: A Masque* (1900) reworked the traditional story of Orpheus's descent to the Underworld. In her relationship to Sarah Jewett, Annie not only gave support but found it as well.

Aside from the arts, women such as Fields and Jewett still had few acceptable public occupations. One area where they could assert their talents was charity work (the route taken by the heroine of "Root-Bound"). A lady could be a manager or an executive *if* she was serving others and she was not paid. Here Annie Fields excelled. As part of the temperance movement she helped open coffee houses in the slums during the early 1870s. In 1875 she and Mrs. James Lodge founded the cooperative Society of Visitors among the Poor. According to W. S. Tryon, they adapted the concepts of Octavia Hill, a British social welfare organizer who stressed "the investigation of applicants, personal visits, and 'charity in the form of work,' rather than mere almsgiving."[32] (Individual purpose and firsthand acquaintance would later be important principles in Sarah Jewett's attitude toward country life and working-class people.) In 1879 Annie Fields helped found the Associated Charities of Boston, which she directed until 1894. Her book on social welfare principles, *How to Help the Poor* (1883), sold twenty-two thousand copies in its first two years of publication. Upon her death in 1915, Annie Fields left forty thousand dollars to the organization she had nurtured. She had no children. Although she was never a very active or radical feminist, she did support Boston's moderate woman suffrage movement, which also included the *Atlantic* editor Thomas Wentworth Higginson.

By all accounts Annie Fields was a lovely woman, even in old age. After her husband's death she always wore a mourning veil, black or lavender. She and "Jamie" had been devoted to each other. According to Harriet Prescott Spofford, "before his death, Mr. Fields suggested Sarah Orne Jewett as a possible friend and companion for his wife in the future. . . . Because she had lost the best of life, Mrs. Fields did not give up life itself."[33] Victorian Americans, as Carroll Smith-Rosenberg noted, did not find their heterosexual and homosocial worlds incompatible. Here a husband himself recommended the woman who would replace him. And so, as Henry James wrote, Jewett "came to Mrs. Fields as an adoptive daughter, both a sharer and a sustainer."[34] Earlier Annie Fields had come to her husband as an "adoptive daughter"; now she would begin by playing the parental role.

Sarah Jewett and Annie Fields were already friends before James Fields's death in April 1881. Jewett's first letter to Annie Fields is dated 1877, the year she revised and published the *Deephaven* sketches (which had originally appeared in the *Atlantic*). In the summer of 1880 she evidently paid a long visit to the Fields's house in Manchester-by-the-Sea. In a letter dated September 8, 1880, Jewett says she misses her hostess, addressed as "Dear Mrs. Fields," and that she likes to think of their time together. It is here that Jewett describes herself as "the most placid and serene of all your friends."[35] However, although the two women had become close, their relationship was still fairly formal. Jewett was just one of Annie Fields's many friends.

On January 12, 1881, Jewett writes:

I am looking forward with the greatest pleasure to being with you for a few days, and I hope you will let me come by and play that it is still January, the time when you asked me to come. We do not like to leave my mother alone in the winter. It is so very lonely for her, and just now my sister Mary is gone for a little while. . . . Your *Under the Olive* is already more and more of a pleasure to me. . . . Will you believe that I do wish very much to see you and I am always

Yours affectionately,
S.O.J.[36]

While warm, the tone here is still distanced. The opening bears the marks of a genteel form letter; the closing is one Jewett used routinely for good friends but not intimates. As her comment about *Under the Olive* shows—and Jewett goes on to discuss the book's reviews, which she has been "eagerly" reading in various newspapers—the two women were fast becoming literary colleagues.

Apparently, Jewett spent much of the 1881 winter with Annie Fields and therefore must have been with her during the ordeal of James Fields's death. In Letter 4 of the Houghton Library's collection of their correspondence there is marked change. "Dear Mrs. Fields" has become "Dearest Fuff," and Jewett has become "Pinny" or simply "Pin."[37] The letter is dated 1881, probably by Annie Fields herself. There is no month or day given. When did the shift take place? Another letter, dated June 1882, offers a clue: "Oh my dear darling I had forgotten that we loved each other so much a year ago, for it all seems so new to me everyday. There is so much for us to remember already— But a year ago last winter seems a great way off for us to have loved so much since."[38] Sometime in the winter of 1881, in the wake of James Fields's death, Annie Fields and Sarah Jewett fell in love.

While their personal correspondence gives us the most intimate sense of their relationship, a manuscript fragment in the Houghton Library describes Annie Fields as Jewett first saw her. Entitled "The Friendship of Women," the sketch portrays a heroic woman, who can only be Annie Fields herself. The nameless figure has a "strength of character, heroic resolve when she saw that [some] service was needed for her beloved Boston." Further, she possessed "an exquisite early beauty and an autumnal beauty and charm distinction [sic] that made her the beloved and chosen companion of the great men and women of her time. From Irving and Thackeray to [blank left here] have been her guest."[39] The sketch itself captures the flavor of the two women's early friendship:

Almost every one of the truly majestic women that I have seen were short and heavily built—but she was of at least five foot seven and looked a head taller than most women. There was something severe and even hard in her face that gave a look of great power, but children always ran to her like an old friend as we walked in the village. We never thought of kissing each other in those first weeks nor did we kiss without thinking as most women do, but she always give [sic] [me? illegible word] her hand when we met and before we parted she would sometime keep it in hers in a half conscious affectionate way and once she put her arm about my shoulders as we stood looking down at the sea.[40]

The sensuous attraction and tension in this passage is clear. The "majestic" woman's strength and beauty are equally valued. Her bearing indicates "great power," but she still holds a maternal attraction for children. The figure that Jewett paints is that of a fully integrated woman—warm and strong. Annie Fields pointed the way to maturity, a new way of being feminine that encouraged selfhood without sacrificing intimacy.

From my readings of Jewett's correspondence and from Smith-Rosenberg's historical evidence, it appears that such passionate friendships preserved the tenderness, sensuousness, and security of mother-daughter bonds. However, as Judith Roman describes it, the secret of Annie and Sarah's friendship "lay in its complete reciprocity and in their ability to create for themselves a form of marriage in which all roles were interchangeable and neither partner was limited by the relationship." Finally, neither the conventional term "marriage" nor the traditional hierarchy of parent and child can contain this complex union, which was both "intimate and unconfining."[41]

Henry James's perspective on Jewett's relationship to Annie Fields is especially pertinent here. James's sister Alice lived for many years in a Boston marriage with Katharine Loring, and his portrait of a similar bond in *The Bostonians* is scathing.[42] However, his view of the Jewett/Fields relationship was much more sympathetic. They had visited him in Sussex, and later, in his reminiscences of Mrs. Fields, he recalled their impression on him: "nothing could have more warmed the ancient faith of their confessingly a bit disoriented countryman than the association of the elder and the younger lady in such an emphasized susceptibility. Their reach together was of the firmest and easiest."[43] Given James's probing vision—he was indeed a man "on whom nothing was lost"—his disorientation seems reasonable. But one also gathers from this glimpse that their "emphasized susceptibility" was accompanied by a serene unconsciousness of social unacceptability or pathological implication.[44]

The difference in sensibility appeared acutely when Annie Fields edited Sarah's letters after Jewett's death in 1909. Mark Howe advised careful deletion of Jewett's endearments and childlike affection, in effect censoring her expressions of love for Annie. As Faderman notes, such a need to cover up would have "astonished" Jewett: "in the context of her time, her love for Annie was very fine." However, Faderman goes on to say that "Willa Cather, who was almost twenty-five years her junior and came of age in a different environment, knew that what Jewett's generation would have seen as admirable, hers would consider abnormal."[45] Annie herself ventures an apology for Jewett's childlike voice in her introduction to the *Letters,* which she compares to Swift's letters to Stella. She finds the same use of the "little language," the "same joy and repose in friendship." Fields's description is revealing: "This 'little language,' the private 'cuddling' of lovers, of mothers, and children, since the world began, was native also to her."[46] A letter from Jewett reveals these dialects, and their dynamics, in all of their complexity. To show the interwoven voices, I will quote the letter in full:

This is a lazy loitering Pinny Lawson who came over to the house directly after dinner to write as fast as she could but she got hold of the top of her dear T. L.'s letters and has been reading one more and one more until a great piece of the afternoon is gone. Oh my dear darling I had forgotten that we loved each other so much a year ago, for it all seems so new to me every-day. There is so much for us to remember already—But a year ago last winter seems a great way off for us to have lived so much since. . . . I have had a hard time of worry and hard work since you went away on Monday. I wish I could be idle all the rest of June, that is not feel forced to do things. But I suppose it cannot be and the only thing possible in a busy life is to rest *in* one's work since one cannot rest *from* it. I think a good deal about the long story but it has not really taken hold of me yet. I do get so impatient with myself dear Fuffy. I am always straying off on wrong roads and I am so wicked about things. This is one of the times when I think despairingly about my faults and see little chance of their ever being mended. But Fuffy to have patience with Pin and please to love her! (I have been reading Under the Olive a good deal in this last day or two and I can't begin to tell you how beautiful it is to me— and how helpful. I long to hear you read from it again. And when I think it was my dear little Fuffy who wrote it—It is like remembering that I have dared to talk nonsense and hug and play generally with a something that turned itself into a whole world of beautiful things—Fuffy and the poet are a funny pair to live in the same skin you know, ladies! Oh Pinny to go to work! An idle and thriftless Pinny to whom the rest of the Lawsons are industrious.[47]

Demonstrating a fluid movement from adult to infantile personae, Jewett's voice and syntax shift dramatically according to the role she is playing vis-à-vis Fields. As a lover, and equal, she addresses her in the conventional language of lovers, "my dear darling." As Pinny, play-mate of Fuffy, she speaks in infantile dialect: "Oh Pinny to go to work!" As Pinny, "daughter" of the all-wise Annie Fields, she speaks in a near-adult voice about her despair, "I do get so impatient with myself dear Fuffy. . . . I am so wicked about things." Then she dips down into her child voice: "But Fuffy to have patience with Pin and please to love her!" Then she sprints upward to her adult-voice and discusses Annie Fields's book, *Under the Olive*.

Apparently these rapid shifts alerted Jewett herself to the strange dynamic at work, for she now marvels at how the adult and child can coexist in the same person. "Fuffy" and the "poet" are a "funny pair" who "live in the same skin"—just as Sarah Jewett and "Pinny" share the same body. Curiously, Jewett wonders at her "daring" in hugging and playing with "something" capable of "turning itself into a whole world." The mystery lies in the transformation from mother-playmate, with whom sensuous intimacy and maternal regression is possible, into poet, a solitary self, majestic and transcendent. However, even the poet's role retains traces of the maternal bond. As Erich Neumann points out, the maternal image often becomes unconsciously associated with the world itself. The "other" is feminine. When her poetic power is revealed, Annie Fields becomes an image of totality. Again, Jewett describes Annie Fields as somehow larger than life, overwhelming— feminine images often rooted in infantile memories.[48]

Jewett's deep dependency on Annie Fields brought with it a fear of abandonment, as expressed in a letter from 1882 or 1883:

I had such a wretched dream last night that I have felt very happy by contrast since I waked up and found it wasn't true. I thought you had gone back to Europe to stay all winter, and I didn't know what I should do without you. I was wandering about in the house on Charles St. and the sun was shining into your room and it was so full of sunshine and so *empty,* and poor Pin did almost break her heart and was so rejoiced when she waked up. It was a great surprise to find it wasn't true for there never was a dream that seemed more real and sorrowful. . . . (I am all alone just now . . . and I wish I had you here for an hour all to myself.)[49]

Although the Fields/Jewett relationship may not have been exclusive, there can be no doubt about its primacy in each's life. And there can be no doubt about its passion. There were no "bars of shyness or indifference" here, as in Jewett's relationship to her mother. She ex-presses her desire without inhibition. In 1883 she writes: "I shall be with you tomorrow—your dear birthday. How I am looking forward to Thursday evening. I don't care whether there is starlight or a fog— yes dear, I will bring the last sketch and give it its last touches if you think I had better spend any more time on it. I am tired of writing things—I want now to paint things and drive things—and *kiss* things!"[50] Although the shifts are more subtle than in the earlier one, this letter also reveals the different roles Annie Fields played for Sarah: she is at once lover and literary adviser.

Another letter, undated, shows that Jewett could take on the maternal role herself when needed: "I waked up to a great worry about you on your hill in this gray windy morning and felt as I couldn't have you there another minute. Oh do come away if [it's] so cold and windy darling Fuff—I do hope *you* don't get cold or tired or *hungry*! without your Pinny to make a fuss!"[51] Even here, however, the tone is decidedly childish: a little girl playing "Mama."

While Annie Fields obviously participated in this play—"Fuffy" and "T.L." were roles she relished—her letters are less exuberant. She often refers to her "Pinny" as "darling" or "my dearest child," but she is less apt to speak in baby talk herself, more apt to use the adult voice of a lover or loving friend. Her comments on Jewett's story "The Queen's Twin" are written in her usual tone: "And the woman of imagination shining with a lovely little flame in that lonely place—Yes, dear, it is *charming* & charming, & charming!"[52] Moreover, according to Judith Roman, "unlike Jewett's, Annie's expressions of love do not seem to have included requests for Sarah's prompt return, and she does not dwell on their separation for long in her letters."[53]

Finally, the strength of these two women's bond lay in its graceful balance. Annie Fields's friendship brought both nurturance and detached criticism. While it obviously was not a direct outcome of her loss, Jewett's attachment to the older woman seems to have replaced her attachment to her father. As mentor, Annie Fields assumed the authoritative role that Dr. Jewett had played earlier. She read her young friend's manuscripts and commented on both their style and substance. Further, she widened Jewett's horizons. Now they were not the rounds of a country doctor but the social circles of an aristocratic literary woman. In Annie Fields, Jewett found encouragement for her ambition and ultimately a peer who respected her vocation.

As Sharon O'Brien's fine biography of Willa Cather reveals, this was a gift that did not end with Jewett but was passed to a new generation. Jewett met Willa Cather in 1908, and in that last year of her life she provided for the younger artist much of the same loving advice that had steadied her own course of development. Although Annie Fields was a much more inhibiting figure to Cather, we can see clearly that what Fields had done for Jewett—taken a provincial, uncertain young woman and given her the care and confidence necessary to bloom— Jewett did for Cather. As O'Brien writes, Jewett became a "maternal figure who offered Cather love and support without the coerciveness of the mother-daughter bond." Here also roles were fluid, for "in Sarah Orne Jewett, Cather found many people: a female literary precursor, a woman writer whom she could respect, a mentor, and an encouraging friend. Offering Cather an American and a female literary tradition as well as friendship, Jewett helped the younger woman to unleash her creative powers."⁵⁴ Caroll Smith-Rosenberg discovered that nineteenth-century women's friendships extended outward in concentric circles from the mother-daughter bond: older girls adopting younger ones, who in their turn reproduced this mothering by extending themselves to their own "daughters." In Annie Fields, Sarah Jewett, and Willa Cather we find yet another version of these circles: an Eleusinian chain of caring.

III

Not surprisingly, friends of Annie Fields and Sarah Jewett found the figures of Demeter and Persephone particularly appropriate to their characters. In "Godspeed," a poem written on the occasion of the couple's departure for Europe, John Greenleaf Whittier represents Fields as "her in whom / All graces and sweet charities unite, / The old Greek beauty set in holier light." Jewett he cast as the Maiden, "her for whom New England's by-ways bloom, / Who walks among us welcome as the Spring, / Calling up blossoms where her light feet stray."⁵⁵

Fields especially seems to have evoked Demetrian images. In *A Little Book of Friends* (1916), Harriet Prescott Spofford writes that "the words Demeter spoke to her Persephone were the keynote" of Annie Fields's life: "But as thou goest pluck blossoms from thy path / And strew them in the places without bloom." Spofford places Annie Fields at the center of an intimate circle of female friends. Social position, beauty, and talent allowed her to "bask in the receipt of love and worship," yet she "was always sending comfort to those sitting in darkness." Even Annie Fields's poetry recalled the Eleusinian imagery: she "infused humanity and to-day into the thoughts and fancies of a dead world, and made old legends live with new life in an atmosphere as high as joy, and as deep as sorrow." Spofford recalls the "seldom moment she read to you, in a voice like the voice of the dove her Demeter sang about, or like the double flute, you think, that one of her own Greek girls might be breathing through."⁵⁶

Fields first published her version of the Demeter–Persephone myth in 1877.⁵⁷ Unlike Higginson, she stressed the transformation of innocent virgin to mature woman, a transformation achieved through sexuality and death. Her resurrected Kore is no longer the blithe, unformed girl Demeter had known but a woman wiser than her mother, a goddess surpassing the feminine deities who gave her birth. The poem affirms the daughter's need for separation as well as love—an interpretation significantly different from the developmental pattern of Harriet Beecher Stowe's *Pearl*. If these were Annie Fields's values, they came to be Sarah Jewett's as well. In "The Return of Persephone" we can see the qualities that drew the younger artist to the older one and that made Annie Fields the wise mentor she was.

The transformation from child to woman is first heralded in the image of a seductive narcissus, which Persephone tells her mother she has seen growing "down by the cool /Dark stream where you have bid me not to stray." In this forbidden place "grow tall, strange purple blooms, though some / Are white, / White as warm lilies, and the purple dark / As streams that flow to Bacchus!" Persephone begs permission to gather them, but her mother emphatically forbids it. Instead, Demeter sets her daughter to weaving a magical fabric made of "the warp and woof of dusky circumstance." She reflects that Persephone "lackest yet one thing" and tells her to "revolve" in her heart: "How joy and grief spring from one common root."[58] This 'one thing" Persephone will learn through her sojourn with Hades in the Underworld.

As in the Homeric hymn, Annie Fields's Maiden strays from her duty to join the ocean nymphs at play before dawn. She sees again the "wondrous flowers" growing by the ocean and is caught by the first light of Helios, the dawn. As Persephone falls unconscious from the sun's rays, Annie Fields brings Hades, or Aidoneus, on the scene to rescue, not rape, her. Like the gentlemanly suitor who comes courting in Emily Dickinson's poem "Because I Could Not Stop for Death," Death addresses his charge with consummate tact: "Come with me, lady, where the shadows cool / Will lay their quiet hands upon thy brow. / The chariot and the horses are mine own; / I will convey thee whither thou shalt sleep."[59]

Persephone does not awaken until safely beneath the earth. At once she cries out for her mother: "Bring thou me back to her! / Wilt not? Then will I call to her, and she,— / And she, though hidden in her inmost cave, / Or swept by clashing sheaths of the grown corn, / Would hear, and come, and answer."[60] Persephone's cry evokes the double aspect of Demeter: As Hecate, moon goddess in her cave, and as Demeter, earth goddess of the harvest. (Walter Pater's analysis of the evolution of Demeter from the "monstrous" goddesses of the caves and chthonian mysteries also echoes in this passage.)

From this point the poem follows the plot of the Homeric hymn: Demeter's search, her questioning of Helios and the various gods, her interludes at the well of Eleusis and the palace of Keleus (Celeus), with her ritual purification of Demophoon. The nurture of Demophoon is particularly interesting because the infant prince is presented as a substitute for the lost daughter. Demeter hopes to save this child from Aidoneus: "For I will nourish and hold thee safe, / That others may

not weep as I have done. . . . Drink the warm milk of my late tenderness, / Grown greater for the sorrows I have known." Demeter prepares
the fire "afresh" for him, but this fire is actually the embers of her
motherly love and sorrow. She "will blow the ashes of my love, and
lay thee there / To purify and strengthen for thy day. / Work, charm!
Work, fire! / 'T is thus a man / Is made."⁶¹

Taking the baby prince into her arms and placing him beneath her
robe, Demeter croons a lullaby suffused with maternal tenderness.

> I cover my head
> With the veil of my grief;
> But beneath, beneath,
> Sleep beauty and youth,
> And my pain is fled.
> Close, baby, close!
> I feel thy soft hands
> Nestle and steal
> Round the waves of my breast⁶²

As the baby nurses at her breast, Demeter returns to "eternal" youth
and beauty. The scene recalls Nancy Chodorow's theory: the mother
recovers her own experience of mothering by identifying with her child.
In this fusion both find the fulfillment of primary love. The image of
the beautiful Maiden hidden within the aged nurse also recalls Miss
Roxy Toothacre, whose lovely heart Mara recognizes in another moment of maternal communion.

But Demeter still has not forgotten her daughter, and in act 4 her
grief awakens sympathy in "Father Helios," who calls on "the god of
darkness" to yield Persephone. Here Annie Fields clearly builds on the
nature/vegetation symbolism that H. M. Alden, and later Walter Pater,
analyzed. As the "Father Sun" "bends his rays slowly and caressingly
upon [Demeter]; a blush suffuses the whole heaven and the deeps of
the sea." From this caress of the sun upon the earth comes the return
of spring: "And Aidoneus bids his love return / For a brief space to
soothe her mother's heart." Significantly, it is Hades who urges Persephone to return. And Persephone's answer reveals she is now Death's
loving wife: "I would away, since thou, my love, dost bid."⁶³ Her
allegiance is now to both mother and husband, a dual loyalty that
Persephone openly admits:

> To [Demeter] belongs a portion of the fruit,
> Pomegranate, which thy love hast given to me,
> And eating I have learned to know the seed
> Shall fall, the many many seeds shall fall
> Into the dark earth, then grow again to light.⁶⁴

She will return both to comfort Demeter and to reassure her. As Persephone tells her husband, Demeter "shall know what calm abides with thee." When the leaves fall and the green world freezes,

> We do but smile and brood on the new birth
> Within the fallen seed; here do we watch
> The life that ever lives, yet living rests,
> Thus to renew itself and bring again,
> Not the old past,—ah no! but tenderer yet
> The same old beauty with a heart renewed.[65]

Reunited with her daughter, Demeter throws aside the veil of age. She now appears "in the perfect beauty of womanhood, wearing full-blown roses." Her joy is beyond all bounds for, as she tells Persephone, "There is no life, no light, when thou art gone." But Persephone, with her darker wisdom, gently chides her mother: "Fond mother, say not so! Thou found'st the child / Demophoon, and fed'st thy hungry heart; / Or when that joy was snatched thou still didst feel / A new keen grace in making others glad." These pleasures will forever remain, but none of her mother's glories "feeding every sense" can keep Persephone from Hades and his shadows, "for there is also love, and there is calm."[66]

This is not what the jealous Demeter wants to hear. She wonders impatiently why her daughter "dwells on sorrows that have been!" Persephone tries to explain: "in that shade the seeds put forth again / Which thou, neglectful, hid'st in thy rich heart. / Hence is it sorrow may no longer be / A sorrow there." But Demeter will have none of this philosophy: "Look not at me with thy compassionate eyes! / Thou, love, art here, and gladness is on all." Persephone patiently reminds her mother that she remains only until "the steeds of Aidoneus come." However, "he is kind . . . and stays his solemn call / And leaves us to our gladness."[67] This evocation of Hades as a *loving* husband is too much for Demeter, who cries out, "Art thou not mine! / Then wherefore dost thou bring these darksome thoughts / Into our sunshine." And Persephone, resigning herself to her mother's love and blindness, replies: "Am I not also his! / Let me not grieve thee, mother, this sweet day! / Hold me once more upon thy blessed breast, / As when I was a child and knew but thee. / Perchance thou dost not know the world of shades!"[68]

At last it is autumn. The mother and daughter, in a "forsaken garden," hear the stamping of Aidoneus's horses. Persephone, readying herself, comforts her mother with the promise to return. And Demeter, in the closing lines, accepts this faith:

She will return, my darling will return!
Forever changing, evermore the same!
O ye who dwell in the dust, awake and sing!
She will return, my darling will return! [69]

The patterns of Annie Fields's adaptation suggest that Persephone's mature wisdom surpasses the narrow range of her mother's affection. In Neumann's archetypal scheme, Demeter is not the "highest" form of the feminine but an intermediate link between the "elementary feminine" and the Sophia. "A Lady of the Plants," Demeter is still associated with natural maternity. Embedded in biology her attachments are kin-based and subvert the "higher" forms of culture. As Higginson commented, Demeter would sacrifice the whole world for her daughter. Like other "dark" heroines, Demeter is subject to the sorrows of death and decay. However, Persephone, by descending into death and seeing its transformation of the seed into ever-new forms, transcends this narrow sphere. Having entered into these experiences fully, and re-emerging, she urges the *Mater Dolorosa* to see beyond the limited perspective of earthly attachment. She reminds Demeter of her *adoptive* child, Demophoon, and admonishes her to extend her sympathies beyond her family, to find her joy beyond immediate, sensuous life. Thus, Demeter has all the strengths and faults of the original matriarchs that Bachofen described. But Persephone will extend her maternal sympathies not just to her own offspring but to the entire world.

Equally important, Persephone transcends the "devalued" sphere of natural maternity through separation from her mother. Although Hades appears as her husband, his role seems less sexual than shadowy. Hades teaches Persephone to accept death, not sex; to understand isolation, not sensuality. The sensuous roses are associated with the mother, not the husband. And the Persephone who returns to her mother has always the double consciousness of the individuated self: she will return to her mother's breast knowing always that she must leave it. As she tells Hades, Persephone will laugh in the old "girlish" way to make her mother smile, but Persephone is no longer the girl she was. And so Our Lady of Sorrows yields to the Resurrected Maiden, who gazes with a calm smile upon the continuity of life beyond death.

IV

Dedicated to "the memory of my mother," "The Return of Persephone" was collected in *Under the Olive* (1881), along with poems on Theocritus, Herakles, Helena, Artemis, and a host of other classical figures both historical and mythological. Many of these were adapted from ancient sources and copiously footnoted with extracts from scholarly texts such as Hegel's *Philosophy of History* and Max Muller's *Upanishad*. For "Aphrodite of Melos," Annie Fields chose this passage from Margaret Fuller's *Woman in the Nineteenth Century* (1845): "We would have every path thrown open as freely to woman as to man. Were this done and the slight temporary fermentation allowed to subside, we believe that the divine would ascend into nature to a height unknown in the history of the past ages; and nature, thus instructed, would regulate the spheres, not only so as to avoid collision, but to bring forth ravishing harmony."[70]

Like so many in American literary circles, Annie Fields put her faith in a new spiritual harmony to be born through the elevation of the feminine and its "marriage" with masculine authority. Like Higginson and H. M. Alden, whose essays her husband published, Annie Fields also found a feminine religious tradition in Greece. The implication that its dying and rising goddess prefigured the Christian rising and dying god was not lost on her. And yet she presents the myth not as a pagan precursor but as a female complement. Her support comes from Walter Pater. The notes for "The Return of Persephone" include a long quotation from his essay, "The Myth of Demeter and Persephone": "This myth illustrates the power of the Greek religion as a religion of pure ideas . . . which . . . because they arose naturally out of man and embodied in adequate symbols his deepest thoughts concerning his physical and spiritual life, maintained their hold through many changes, and are still not without a solemnizing power even for the modern mind."[71] Thus, there is a "place in our culture, at once legitimate and possible" for these Greek goddesses and the ethos they symbolized. Their mysteries and their wisdom can be recovered, even welcomed as "recognized and habitual inhabitants" of our modern minds. Once accepted, they will exercise their powers over us, as they did over the "earlier and simpler races of their worshippers" and so "elevate and purify our sentiments."

In a later poem, "The Mysteries of Eleusis," Annie Fields describes this recovery of the female mythos. She begins by speculating on what the initiates saw as they "chased forms of mortal breath / From awful room to awful room." What revelation came "in that moment of despair"? No one has ever "voiced the dreadful word . . . or made the secret heard." The "Old books say Demeter came / And smiled upon them, and her smile / Burned all their sorrow in its flame, / Yet left them here awhile."[72] Longing to recapture this moment, the lost vision of an ancient culture, the poet invokes the goddess directly: "Mother of the shadowed sphere, / Where we dwell and suffer now." Her faith is rewarded: "Lo! the initiate days are here, / Bright is thy dawn-lit brow."[73] As the circle of friends enclosing Sarah Jewett and Annie Fields came to know, the goddess is neither dead nor dying. Initiation into her mysteries is here and now. But first we must know her name.

Chapter Five

Honey from Ashes: Pastoral As Woman's Place

In 1900 Jewett traveled with Annie Fields from Brindisi down the Apennines to Corfu, on to Greece, along the southern shore to the Gulf of Corinth. Of the Orpheus and Eurydice at Pompeii she wrote, "There is nothing so beautiful." Then from Athens: "When I remember what my feelings have been toward the Orpheus and Eurydice and the Bacchic Dance, and then see these wonderful marbles here, row upon row, it is quite too much for a plain heart to bear."[1] In these classic figures Jewett saw the ideal of her own art: "It isn't the least bit of use to try to write about these marbles, but they are simply the most human and affecting and beautiful things in the world. The partings, the promises, are immortal and sacred, they are Life and not only Lives; and yet the character in them is almost more than the art to me, being a plain story-writer, but full of hopes and dreams."[2]

Earlier in her career Jewett had found these qualities in the pastoral poets. Her notes for a story, tentatively called "A Modern Idyll," make the link explicit. An aging married couple return to the country for a small holiday. As they leave the road and cross the fields on foot, they recall their courtship and married life together, their progress from simpler, poorer days to their present prosperity. At the house of an acquaintance they "are given bread & honey and fruit—and come home at night happy and tired and full of country pleasure but liking their home best."[3]

As in Jewett's finest sketches, the point is subtle, a matter of perspective rather than conflict and resolution. When the couple return home, "they have for once a consciousness of their life in general and seem to watch and *review* their course all the way, instead of being occupied and intent upon details." The notes conclude: "Do all this in the manner of Theocritus—."[4] While Annie Fields aimed to make "the old legends live with new life," Jewett aimed to infuse her own moment with classical dignity. To the painting of everyday life she brought the "manner" of the pastoral poets and the patterns of Greek mythology. Here "the partings, the promises are immortal and sacred, they are Life and not only Lives."

Jewett's first book and her best are both pastorals. The protagonists of *Deephaven* and *The Country of the Pointed Firs* simply spend a summer in the country. Nothing much happens to them here, as nothing much happens to the married couple in "A Modern Idyll." And yet their awareness is subtly transformed. Separated from their accustomed lives, they come to see themselves freshly. Equally important, they enter into country life, participate in its festivals and domestic ceremonies. By the summer's close these women have a deepened sympathy for the place and its people. They return to the city changed. With Josephine Donovan and others I believe much of this change stems from their quiet, almost subliminal initiation into a feminine world and its mysteries.[5]

This chapter explores these mysteries and their source. It begins with Walter Pater, for it was Pater who showed Jewett how to make the connection between rural Maine and the Eleusinian goddesses of ancient Greece. His essay on Demeter and Persephone described them as "the peculiar creation of countrypeople of high impressionability, dreaming over their work in spring or autumn, half consciously touched by a sense of its sacredness."[6] Pater believed this pastoral, matriarchal consciousness would always be with us wherever and whenever men and women lived close to the earth and in harmony with its forces: "The temper of a people engaged in the occupations of the country, so permanent, so "near to nature," is at all times alike; and the habitual solemnity which Wordsworth found in the peasant of Cumberland, and Francois Millet in the peasant of Brittany may well have had its prototype in early Greece."[7] And so Maine could be to Boston what early Greece had been to Athens. As the narrator of *Pointed Firs* sees, Mrs. Todd "might have walked the primeval fields of Sicily; her strong gingham skirts might at that very moment bend the slender stalks of asphodel . . . instead of the wind-brushed grass of New England."[8]

I

Pater's essay "The Myth of Demeter and Persephone" appeared in the *Fortnightly Review* for January and February 1876 and was later collected in *Greek Studies* (1894). It provides a translation of the Homeric hymn, an analysis of the myth's origins, and a thorough iconographical history. Although he uses a developmental scheme similar to Bachofen's, Pater leaves the political theory behind to focus on the myth's psychological sources. In this he is more "modern" than Bachofen and seems in many ways closer to Jung and Erich Neumann.

Like Neumann, Pater locates the source of the goddesses in participation mystique. These figures are generated out of the religious instincts, at first vague and dreamlike, that still move people living in the pastoral recesses of society. Their inspiration lies in those feelings such as "most of us have on the first warmer days in spring when we seem to feel the genial processes of nature at work; as if just below the mould, and in the hard wood of the trees were circulating some spirit of life, akin to that which makes its energies felt within ourselves."[9] Thus, "Demeter—Demeter and Persephone at first, in a sort of confused union—is the earth, in the fixed order of its annual changes, but also in all their incidents and detail, of the growth and decay of its children."[10]

Following Bachofen's lead, Pater then divides Demeter's development into two stages. The earliest is "that older religion, nearer the earth, which some have thought they could discern, behind the more definitely national mythology of Homer."[11] Before the cultivation of land and the invention of marriage, when survival depended on the gathering of food, Demeter is "the goddess of the fertility of the earth in its wildness." Still merged with the most ancient mother figures—Gaia, Rhea, and Cybele—Demeter is "the goddess of dark caves . . . and not wholly free from monstrous form."[12] Pater's description anticipates Neumann's portrait of the "elementary feminine" with its archetypal images of bellies, caves, and primordial hills. Pre-Homeric (or preoedipal in Freudian terms), this goddess is "uroboric," almost featureless, and often frightening.

The second stage comes with the invention of marriage, motherright, agriculture, and the settled community. Demeter emerges from the earlier mother goddesses and assumes the traditional form later fixed and celebrated by the classical poets. Inspired by the realities of "country-life," she reigns over the tilled fields and initiates humanity into the mysteries of the seed, which flowers, dies, returns to the earth, and is reborn. She presides over marriage and childbirth and, in her aspect as Persephone, over death and the dead as well. Under her gaze the simple acts of domestic and agricultural life become celebrations in her worship. These images fall into the "transformative" stage of Neumann's scheme: the Ladies of the Plants and Animals with their domestic mysteries and mantic powers.

These "half-conscious" stages of mythical thinking provide the material for the next phase of the goddess's development; now the poets take this "vague instinctive product of the popular imagination, and handle it with purely literary interest."[13] The various aspects of the goddess become clearly differentiated; Demeter and Persephone assume distinct roles in relation to each other. The elements of the traditional plots are simplified or expanded, "incidents and emotions . . . weave themselves into a pathetic story," and the outline of the whole becomes fixed and definite.[14]

The artistic process creates the goddess of the Homeric hymn to Demeter, of Hesiod's *Works and Days,* and Theocritus's *Idylls.* Pater identifies her "three ideal forms" in the statues discovered at Cnidus in 1857. The first statue is Persephone, as goddess of the dead; the second, "Demeter enthroned"; and the third, "a portrait-statue of a priestess of Demeter . . . [which] may represent Demeter herself, Demeter Archoea, Ceres Deserta, the *mater dolorosa* of the Greeks."[15] This aspect of Demeter, the *Mater Dolorosa,* impressed Pater as the most powerful as it was also the most "humanized." Here the divine is revealed *through* the human, which is transfigured by its power. The three faces of the goddess, but particularly the third, became for Pater the equivalent of the Sophia described by Neumann. And, like the Sophia, they prepare the way for the next step.

In this final "ethical" phase the myth with its divine figures and traditional plot "is realized as an abstract symbol . . . of moral and spiritual conditions."[16] Now the peculiar merging of life and death, the mysteries of the seed—ritually revealed in the ear of wheat silently upheld at Eleusis—assume a "higher" meaning. So Hesiod identifies the two goddesses, "the goddess of summer and the goddess of death—Kore and Persephone, that strange dual being . . . full of purpose for the duly chasted intelligence. *Awake and sing, ye that dwell in the dust.*"[17]

II

Jewett appears to have read Pater's essay in 1876. In the midst of revising the *Atlantic* sketches that became *Deephaven,* she began her friendship with Annie Fields. Annie was also writing. Her project: "The Return of Persephone," a poem deeply influenced by Pater's interpretation and later footnoted with extracts from his essay. One of Jewett's additions to *Deephaven* reveals the influence of both sources. In this new passage, *Deephaven*'s heroines, two young literary ladies from Boston, stay up late one night retelling the myth of Demeter and Persephone. Their translation appears to be Pater's, but even more important, so does their interpretation.[18]

During their summer in Deephaven, Kate Brandon and Helen Denis quickly discover the "high impressionability" of its citizens, the impressionability so central to Pater's thesis. The young women are regaled with tales of ghosts and clairvoyance. From Mrs. Bonny they learn of herbal potions and their mysterious healing powers. The old sailors consult the moon on all questions, and Captain Sands "could tell some stories which were considered incredible even by a Deephaven audience, to whom the marvelous was of everyday occurrence."[19] Deephaven's familiarity with the marvelous prompts Helen to reflect on the influence of its pastoral setting. At first, for example, she thought men who spent their entire lives on the sea would find it very commonplace. Now she sees her mistake: "They are in awe of the sea and of its mysteries, and of what it hides away from us. . . . If they have not seen the sea serpent, they believe . . . that other people have."[20] Their investigations culminate in a conversation with Captain Sands.

After confiding his deep belief in extrasensory perception, the Captain explains: "An' we've got some faculty or other that we don't know much about. We've got some way of sending our thought like a bullet that goes out of a gun and it hits. . . . And some folks is scared, and some more thinks it is all nonsense and laughs."[21] This undeveloped faculty is the same intuition that "saw" the primitive goddesses rising out of the Greek landscape. It is the same vision that linked Mara Lincoln to the drowned Dolores through the medium of a dream. In fact, Captain Sands describes a theory of spiritual evolution similar to Harriet Beecher Stowe's: "It makes me think 'o them little black polliwogs that turns into frogs in the fresh-water puddles in the ma'sh. There's a time before their tails drop off and their legs have sprouted out, when they don't get any use o' their legs, and I dare say they're in their way consider'ble."[22] He imagines that someday we will find out what these strange and troublesome faculties are for, but until then "we might depend on 'em more than we do."

Captain Sands's speech comes midway through the book and marks a critical point in the heroines' initiation into the ethos of Deephaven. At first Helen and Kate would have seen the captain's theories as fancy run wild, but now their growing respect makes them receptive to his vision. That night the two young women reflect on what they have learned. This passage, which centers on the Demeter–Persephone myth itself, provides a key to the structure and meaning of *Deephaven*. Since my analysis depends on the dynamics of the passage as a whole, I will first quote it in full:

Later that evening Kate and I drifted into a long talk about the captain's stories and these mysterious powers of which we know so little. It was somewhat chilly in the house, and we had kindled a fire in the fireplace, which at first made a blaze which lighted the old room royally, and then quieted down into red coals and lazy puffs of smoke. We had carried the lights away, and sat with our feet on the fender, and Kate's great dog was lying between us on the rug. I remember the evening so well; we could see the stars through the window plainer and plainer as the fire went down, and we could hear the noise of the sea.

"Do you remember in the old myth of Demeter and Persephone," Kate asked me, "where Demeter takes care of the child and gives it ambrosia and hides it in the fire, because she loves it and wishes to make it immortal, and to give it eternal youth; and then the mother finds it out and cries in terror to hinder her, and the goddess angrily throws the child down and rushes away? And he had to share the common destiny of mankind, though he always had some wonderful inscrutable grace and wisdom, because a goddess had loved him and held him in her arms. I always thought that part of the story beautiful where Demeter throws off her disguise and is no longer an old woman and the great house is filled with brightness like lightning, and she rushes out through the halls with her yellow hair waving over her shoulders, and the people would give anything to bring her back again and to undo their mistake."

"I knew it almost all by heart once," said Kate, "and I am always finding a new meaning in it. I was just thinking that it may be that we all have given to us more or less of another nature, as the child had whom Demeter wished to make like the gods. I believe old Captain Sands is right, and we have these instincts which defy all our wisdom and for which we never can frame any laws. We may laugh at them, but we are always meeting them, and one cannot help knowing that it has been through all history. They are powers which are imperfectly developed in this life, but one cannot help the thought that the mystery of this world may be the commonplace of the next."

"I wonder," said I, "why it is that one hears so much more of such things from simple country people. They believe in dreams, and they have a kind of fetichism and believe so heartily in supernatural causes. I suppose nothing could shake Mrs. Patton's faith in warnings. There is no end of absurdity in it, and yet there is one side of such lives for which one cannot help having reverence; they live so much nearer to nature than people who are in cities, and there is a soberness about country people oftentimes that one cannot help noticing.

"I wonder if they are unconsciously awed by the strength and purpose in the world about them, and the mysterious creative power which is at work with them on their familiar farms. In their simple life they take their instincts for truths, and perhaps they are not always so far wrong as we imagine. Because they are so instinctive and unreasoning, they may have a more complete sympathy with Nature, and may hear her voices when wiser ears are deaf. They have much in common, after all, with the plants which grow up out of the ground and the wild creatures which depend upon their instincts wholly."

"I think," said Kate, "that the more one lives out of doors the more personality there seems to be in what we call inanimate things. The strength of the hills and the voice of the waves are no longer only grand poetical sentences, but an expression of something real, and more and more one finds God himself in the world, and believes that we may read the thoughts that He writes for us in the book of Nature." And after this we were silent for a while, and in the meantime it grew very late, and we watched the fire until there were only a few sparks left in the ashes. The stars faded away and the moon came up out of the sea, and we barred the great hall door and went up stairs to bed. The lighthouse lamp burned steadily, and it was the only light that had not been blown out in all Deephaven.[23]

Jewett, like Kate Lancaster, was always finding a new meaning to this myth. Its scene of ritual transformation and recognition appears again and again in her fiction. As her artistic needs change, so does the internal alignment of its elements. Perhaps the best place to begin our analysis is with the dialogue's interpretation of the pastoral ethos.

This ethos is identical with the "matriarchal consciousness" described successively by Bachofen, Pater, and Neumann. Country people, because they are "so instinctive and unreasoning. . . . have a more complete sympathy with Nature and may hear her voices when wiser ears are deaf." The voice of Nature may be heard only through instinct and intuition. And these are faculties "which defy all our wisdom and for which we can never frame any laws." They are not rational but grounded in the unconscious, which is our link to the natural world itself. Only by diving beneath the rational intellect and civilized ego, down to this earthy stratum of the personality can we rediscover this sympathy with Nature herself. Country people—chthonic, still rooted in the earth—depend on these instincts, these "roots" that still "grip down" into the soil like the plants that awaken in spring by the contagious hospital of William Carlos Williams's poem. For them truth is not abstract but organic, instinctual; a matter of sympathy, not intellect.

Country people are "unconsciously awed by the strength and purpose in the world about them, and the mysterious creative power which is at work on their familiar farms." This is close to H. M. Alden's description of the Eleusinian Lord and Lady. These people learn their "lessons" through participation in the cycles of life. They are educated by their sorrow over nature's inevitable death and enlightened by their joy in its annual resurrection. For these people, and for the two young women who reflect on them, the way down—into the natural world— is the way up. In the pastoral/matriarchal ethos, transcendence is found through immanence.

Thus, the voice of Nature is the voice of God—when Nature is perceived from the right perspective. And this perspective is a respectful communion, a sense of dependence on a divine indwelling spirit. The voice of Nature does not speak in words, in articulate language, but in feeling, as a mother "speaks" to her infant child. These are not "grand poetical sentences, but an expression of something real." The resolutely emotional basis of this notion is undercut somewhat by Kate's reflection that the more one participates in nature, the "more one finds God himself in the world, and believes that we may read the thoughts that He writes for us in the book of Nature." Kate seems to shift from a "matriarchal" stress on sympathy and intuition, devaluing the "grand poetical sentence," to an apparently contradictory desire to "read" the "book" of a male God. Suddenly we have Logos, the word and law, whereas just a moment before we had a warm, living Presence infusing the living world with loving sympathy.

This shift shows that *Deephaven*'s innovative perspective was partially unconscious and unfocused. Earlier we saw a similar problem in the language and conceptual structure of *Pearl of Orr's Island*. Mara says she worships a God who is like a mother to her, but her allegiance, and Stowe's allegiance, to her culture's semantic system is such that she cannot change the gender of the divine pronoun from *he* to *she*. As Thomas Wentworth Higginson pointed out, monotheism drastically limits our perception of the Godhead's potentialities. Since God must be a single being, in a patriarchal society that being must be male; hence, all thought and speech about the divine must struggle with the associations and structures that this male gender imposes. In this dialogue we see two women moving toward a radically feminine concept of divinity, only to have their own language subtly rein them in and direct them back to the fold.

However, even in this first book Jewett's practice as writer—and Helen's practice as narrator—stresses communion over speech. Speech is a means to communion, just as the differentiated ego is a stage in the progress toward integration. Life begins out of silence, grows into consciousness, and then, illuminated, returns to silence. And so, their dialogue having brought them to a moment of understanding, Kate and Helen "were silent for a while, . . . and watched the fire until there were only a few sparks left in the ashes." If we have read this passage carefully and sympathized with it, we should know that this silence is not empty but rich with feeling. The writer has shaped a vessel to contain meaningful silence, to suggest a communion that is itself ineffable. Even in this early work Jewett's success at this suggestion is considerable. By *The Country of the Pointed Firs* she will know enough not to mention the thoughts God writes in His book.

Their summer in Deephaven is teaching Kate and Helen *how* to see and hear, for "the more one lives out of doors the more personality there seems to be in what we call inanimate things." This blossoming perception is subtly mirrored in the setting of the dialogue itself. As they begin their conversation, Kate and Helen are enclosed by the space. The fire on the hearth illuminates their intimacy but also shuts out their awareness of the landscape beyond the house. As their meditation deepens and brings their latent awareness of the pastoral ethos to consciousness, the fire dies down, and their sense of the natural world outside becomes progressively clearer: "We could see the stars through the window plainer and plainer as the fire went down, and we could hear the noise of the sea." As they sit in numinous silence at the close of their dialogue, the walls of the house seem to have become transparent, even to have dissolved. The fire is "only a few sparks . . . in the ashes." The stars themselves have faded. Only when the archetypal "moon comes up out of the sea" do they finally replace the boundary that has been lowered between themselves and the mysterious world outside: "We barred the great hall door and went up stairs to bed." As they sleep through the night, "the lighthouse lamp burned steadily, and it was the only light that had not been blown out in all Deephaven."

This final light, which is placed so strategically at the close of this passage, as if to signal its centrality, appears again at the close of the final chapter. In *The Country of the Pointed Firs* it will be reborn as Green Island, the home of Mrs. Blackett, which rises "like a beacon out of the sea." It represents human order but does so to nurture human life. As a domestic space it maintains the proper balance between enclosure and openness, between public and private (it is both a home and a business, a place of work and love). And so it symbolizes the harmonious blending of male and female elements, exemplified by the harmonious coexistence of its mistress and master with their blooming family. Thus, the lighthouse is Deephaven's pastoral, just as Green Island is Dunnet Landing's pastoral. On the periphery of Deephaven, the lighthouse establishes a separate center. It is the *axis mundi,* "navel" of its own world. In "A White Heron" its incarnation is the great pine that rises "like a mainmast to the voyaging earth." Self-sufficient, the lighthouse is embedded in the earth but rises through the air to shine in the sky like a human star. Surrounded by the sea, it links underworld, earth, and sky. Like the torch-bearing Persephone, who also illuminates the three realms, the lighthouse symbolizes the pastoral, matriarchal ethos.

The centrality of this image is reinforced by *Deephaven*'s closing lines: "Turning, we should see the lighthouse lamp shine out over the water, and the great sea would move and speak to us lazily in its idle high-tide sleep."[24] This ethos does not forsake its roots in irrational nature but nurtures intuition as a means to wisdom and communion with divinity. Here the light of this "Eleusinian" consciousness—the consciousness of Sophia and the Dual Goddess—shines out over the water as if to embrace it. The sea, as if in reply, "speaks" out of its sleep of unconsciousness. These are not the grand poetical sentences that God wrote, nor are they the "noises" the sea made when the dialogue began, when the walls of the house still kept the two women from awareness of the world outside. But these are words of sleep, spoken "lazily." They are the speech of dream, reverie, intuition, the speech hidden within the "silence" of communion and the "noise" of nature. And this brings me to Kate's retelling of the myth itself.

III

The episode Kate selects, Demeter's nursing of Demophoon, is a feminine creation myth: the story of how human beings came to have spiritual natures. In Erich Neumann's analysis of feminine mysteries he divides them into three groups: (1) biological mysteries of blood transformation: menstruation, pregnancy, birth, lactation; (2) domestic mysteries of material transformation: "preservation, formation, nourishment, and transformation"; and (3) the psychic mysteries of spiritual transformation. The last group Neumann divides into the mysteries of death, vegetation, inspiration, and intoxication.[25] All may be signified through the symbolic logic of cooking: the transformation of raw, unformed nature first into physically human forms, then into cultural forms, then into spiritual forms. In this particular mythic action Demeter adopts Demophoon as her own, holds him to her breast, then feeds him ambrosia (in Annie Fields's adaptation she gives him her own milk). Finally, she lowers the infant into the fire to burn away his mortality and make him a god. Her magic encompasses every level of the feminine mysteries, culminating in the final image of "cooking" the child by literally placing him on the hearth.

The interruption of this process results in Demophoon emerging not as a god, but as a mortal possessed of "some wonderful inscrutable grace and wisdom, because a goddess has loved him and held him in her arms." Kate and Helen agree that this myth describes the mixed nature not only of Demophoon but of all human beings, who have given to them "more or less of another nature, as the child whom Demeter wished to make like the gods." Kate and Helen, as well as the country people they have observed, possess this other, incompletely developed spiritual nature, which illuminates their perceptions and draws them into sympathetic communications with Nature, the goddess herself. Here again, there is a strange undermining of traditional patriarchal structures. According to the biblical account of the Creation, humanity's spiritual nature is a gift not from a goddess but from God himself. And our souls are "half-baked," not because the goddess's aim was thwarted but because of our own transgressions. Now humanity gains its divinity directly from the maternal hand and through a domestic baptism by fire.

The divinity that Demeter wished to confer on Demophoon is "eternal youth." Accordingly, those who have "more or less" of this nature can revive the divine child within themselves. Its psychological source is primary love. Human beings have this potential because once a "divine mother" held them in her arms. However, the full promise of this incomparable love could never be realized. Metaneira plays the role of the "bad mother" who forces the child to separate from her and frustrates its desire for fusion. In a curious way she seems to play the father's role as well. Identified with the Prince, she breaks the bond between Demeter and Demophoon, whose very names mirror each other. Despite her intrusion, however, the experience grants Demophoon the power to return partially or periodically to the goddess. And as we have seen, Jewett felt her own life was redeemed by these moments of communion. The characters she portrays most lovingly are those in whom the child is still a living presence, who are not only nurturing but also playful, capable of receiving love as well as giving it.

The double aspect of the goddess herself is central here, for what Helen finds "most beautiful" in the myth is the moment when Demeter "throws off her disguise and is no longer an old woman, and the great house is filled with brightness like lightning." Critical to this scene is Metaneira's failure to recognize the goddess hidden within the aged peasant. Demeter herself reconciles the same polarities as the divine child. She too unites the natural and the divine: the decaying, biological body of the crone and the immortal fire of divinity. In one transfigured moment, she resolves the polarized ambiguity of feminine imagery: the light heroine is hidden *within* the dark one.

This image of Demeter corresponds to Pater's description of the goddess "humanized." Here she is the *Mater Dolorosa*. Grieving for her lost daughter, she is veiled in the dark lineaments of the peasant, the aged woman past the years of childbearing. Pater discovered her outlines in the third statue at Cnidos, a "portrait statue of a priestess of Demeter." For Pater the *Mater Dolorosa* is so powerful because she marks the culmination of the process that created her. That is, the goddess herself rose out of the impressions of people close to the earth; she was their personification of that "mysterious creative power at work with them on their familiar farms." But since they themselves are chthonic people, growing "like plants" out of the ground, these same powers are at work within themselves. If Demeter's divinity may be glimpsed "circulating like a spirit" beneath the bark of trees, animating the sprouting seeds, and gathering the decaying husks back into herself, why should not this power animate the pastoral woman herself?

She too is rooted in the earth and participates in its rhythms of birth and death. To the sympathetic eye this countrywoman may also reveal the divinity of Nature. And the observer who recognizes her may, like the country people Kate describes, be "unconsciously awed by the strength and purpose" she reveals.

The country people described by Pater and Jewett recognize and worship their goddess because they participate sympathetically in her essence; they are nurtured at the breast of nature and gain their living from her body. Because they are so close to her, they are close to the goddess within themselves. Thus, to recognize the goddess, in a mystical way one must *be* her, in the same way that an infant—male or female—*is* the mother. This is the Eleusinian Mystery. The organ of perception is the thing perceived. What we are dealing with is not an object, differentiated from all others, but a *way* of seeing that unites observer and object in a moment of communion. Through this sympathetic identification the common spirit that animates both is felt, and the original union is restored. I recall Carl Jung's analysis of the "Eleusinian emotions," in which the initiate *becomes* the mother. This mystery, according to Károly Kerényi, was accessible to the male as well, for he too began life identified with a "feminine source of life."

A literary example we have already seen comes from Stowe's *Pearl of Orr's Island*. Mara is able to recognize the spiritual beauty of Miss Roxy, whereas Metaneira cannot see the divinity of the disguised Demeter. But Mara can see the Maiden in Miss Roxy because she herself is a type of the Divine Maiden. The union of the two women is fusion of identities, a return in a sense to the mirror-bond of mother and child. Here again the feminine imagery corresponds to the imagery of the landscape, which in a pastoral reflects "spiritual truths" as a mirror does.

However, Metaneira fails to recognize the goddess. In the countrywoman she sees only the devalued crone. This failure shows us the extent of her alienation from the natural world that Demeter incarnates. Metaneira herself is the male-identified wife of the civilized prince of Eleusis: a "city" woman, adjunct to the patriarchy. To her the natural world seems a source of pollution, but she then cannot heal her child. Her denial of these mysterious feminine powers results in her blindness; to her distorted vision divinity appears grotesque. Demeter rages at Metaneira's "witlessness," her failure to comprehend the boon offered her son. But when the goddess reveals herself to Metaneira, the "enlightenment" produces terror rather than ecstasy.

Kate and Helen, as my next chapter will show, come dangerously close to Metaneira's failure of vision. Even in this passage their attitude is complex. They admit that only now are they learning to "reverence" that "hidden" side of the country people they meet. They have glimpsed divinity in their Deephaven acquaintances, but Kate and Helen still cannot help condescending to them. They still find "no end of absurdity" in their "superstitions" and prophecies. This is the image of peasant as yokel: illiterate, foolish, dirty. Like Metaneira, Kate or Helen might well snatch the infant prince out of the crazy nursemaid's hands. If their story of Demeter's transformation demonstrates Kate's and Helen's potential for sympathetic communion with these country-women, the text does not show them fully capable of it. Their actual encounters with countrywomen present them as humorous grotesques who may reveal a surprising humanity but not a shining divinity. In *The Country of the Pointed Firs*, however, the potential, even the prophecy of this dialogue is fulfilled. The anonymous narrator not only discusses the myth but lives it—she sees the goddess in the homely form of Mrs. Todd.[26]

IV

The link between Mrs. Todd and Pater's Demeter is both rich and complex. Its heart is Pater's description of that third statue at Cnidus: "The Homeric Hymn had its sculptural motifs, the great gestures of Demeter who was ever the stately goddess. . . . With the sentiment of that monumental Homeric presence this statue is penetrated, uniting a certain solemnity of attitude and bearing to a profound piteousness, an unrivalled pathos of expression."[27] This "monumental" presence expresses a strength and a sorrow, both deeply human. Demeter veiled becomes "the very type of the wandering woman, going so grandly indeed . . . yet so human in her anguish that we seem to recognize some far descended shadow of her, in the homely figure of the roughly clad French peasant woman, who, in one of Corot's pictures, is hasting along under a sad light as the day goes out behind some little hill."[28]

Pointed Firs echoes the images, sometimes the very rhythms of Pater's description. Mrs. Todd rises, "grand and architectural," before the narrator, who, in this passage, portrays her as another incarnation of the wandering woman. The setting is a field on Green Island, over-looking the sea:

Mrs. Todd looked away from me and presently rose and went by herself. There was something lonely and solitary about her great determined shape. . . . It is not often given in a noisy world to come to a place of great grief and silence. An absolute, archaic grief possessed this country-woman; she seemed like the renewal of some ancient soul, with her sorrows and the remoteness of a daily life, busied with rustic simplicities and the scents of primeval herbs.[29]

The "far descended shadow" of Pater's description has become "the renewal of some historic soul," while the "profound piteousness, an unrivalled pathos" has become "an absolute, archaic grief." More echoes appear in this passage:

Close at hand, Mrs. Todd seemed able and warm-hearted and quite absorbed in her bustling industries, but her distant figure looked mateless and appealing, with something about it that was strangely self-possessed and mysterious. Now and then she stopped to pick something,—it may have been her favorite pennyroyal,—and at last I lost sight of her as she slowly crossed an open space and disappeared again behind a dark clump of juniper and pointed firs.[30]

This last glimpse of Mrs. Todd, as the narrator's boat leaves Dunnet Landing at the summer's close, recalls Pater's French peasant, "so human in her anguish," who "is hasting along under a sad light as the day goes out behind some little hill."

And finally, in "The Queen's Twin," we find the passage with which I opened this chapter. There Mrs. Todd is described as "the personification" of "some force of Nature." Like Demeter herself, "she might have walked the primeval fields of Sicily; her strong gingham skirts might at that very moment bend the slender stalks of asphodel and be fragrant with the trodden thyme, instead of the brown, wind-brushed grass of New England and the frost-bitten golden-rod."[31]

Mrs. Todd, as well as Demeter, is a Lady of the Plants. Deeply sympathetic with the natural world, she makes her living by both raising herbs and gathering them. Her work marks the transition from the most ancient matriarchal world, before the invention of agriculture. There Demeter was "the goddess of the fertility of the earth in its wildness."[32] And like the earliest forms of Demeter, which Walter Pater describes, Mrs. Todd "knows the magic power of certain plants cut from her bosom, to bane or bless, and . . . herself presides over the springs, also coming from the secret places of the earth."[33] Demeter's own speech to Metaneira would suit her well: "Never, methinks, by folly of his nurse shall charm or sorcery harm him; for I know an antidote stronger than the wild wood herb and a goodly salve for the venomed spells."[34] At this point in the hymn Demeter asks Metaneira to mix her a "potion" of "meal mixed with water and mint," a type of the potion that Mrs. Todd will later mix for the narrator, who tastes a mysterious herb in its depths.

The most curious of the analogies between goddesses and landlady is their size. Mrs. Todd is a large woman, broad as a door. While not heavy enough to sink a boat or hinder her movement, she is undoubtedly big and fleshy. The source of this motif—as central to her characterization as her mantic power or her mysterious mint—may also be found in the Homeric hymn and Pater's analysis. Still linked to the ancient fertility goddesses preceding her, Demeter is "the goddess of the dark caves . . . and not wholly free from monstrous form."[35] In the hierarchy of feminine imagery described by Neumann, the Lady of the Plants mediates between the formless, prehuman figures of the "primary feminine" and the spiritualized figure of her own "daughter," Persephone, the Dual Goddess, also known as Sophia. In the shadows of the Homeric hymn stand Demeter's own mothers: Rhea, Cybele, and Hecate, goddess of the moon.

Significantly, Helen neglects to mention that in the passage she found so beautiful not only does Demeter reveal her identity in a blaze of light but she also rises up to her full height. In the Homeric hymn, when Demeter first enters the house of Celeus, "the goddess stood on the threshold, her head touching the roof-beam, and she filled the doorway with light divine."[36] Although awed by this intimation of the old woman's divinity, Metaneira still remains blind. And she remains blind until the enraged goddess forces her to see: "Therewith the Goddess changed her shape and height, and cast off old age, and beauty breathed about her, and sweet scent was breathed from her fragrant robes, and afar shone the light from the deathless body of the Goddess, the yellow hair flowing about her shoulders, so that the goodly house was filled by the splendor as of . . . fire, and forth from the halls went she."[37]

The terror inspired by this vision is linked to the power of primary feminine: the original mother whose shapeless form rose like a mountain or cave before the tiny undifferentiated infant. It is a primary, uroboric vision, the dark side of the good mother, the side she shows to those who deny her or are still too undeveloped to look on her directly. Like Medusa, the primary mother must be seen through the mirror of differentiated consciousness; to return to her directly is to risk loss of ego, regression to infancy or even to the prehuman, perhaps to the stone figures of the Perseus myth. But to those prepared to recognize the goddess, the sense of the numinous is marked by bliss, not terror. Her height is not the outline of a monster but the aura of transfiguration. The "sweet scent" is that sensuous link to the natural world that feminine divinity never loses. Even the most "spiritualized" images of the feminine keep this link, accompanying them "like the scent of a flower," sometimes in their association with an actual flower: rose, lotus, or lily.

The passage that echoes this mythic pattern most clearly comes at the close of the first chapter of *Pointed Firs*. The narrator, an educated city woman, has returned to Dunnet Landing for the summer. Here she describes the beginning of a "deeper intimacy" between herself and her landlady:

I do not know what herb of the night it was that used sometimes to send out a penetrating odor late in the evening, after the dew had fallen, and the moon was high, and the cool air came up from the sea. Then Mrs. Todd would feel that she must talk to somebody, and I was only too glad to listen. We both fell under the spell, and she either stood outside the window, or made an errand to my sitting-room, and told, it might be very commonplace news of the day, or, as happened one misty summer night, all that lay deepest in her heart.[38]

The setting of this conversation closely resembles the setting of the *Deephaven* dialogue. There is the growing intimacy between two close female friends. They are enclosed by a house whose walls are permeable to the natural world outside. Again it is night, marked by the presence of the moon and sea. However, instead of two young women of the same social class, enclosed by a formal house, we have an urban lady in the pastoral house of a "peasant." And she is not interpreting a myth *about* country people but listening sympathetically as a flesh-and-blood countrywoman reveals "what lies deepest in her heart." She is the guest in this woman's home; the countrywoman is the authority, while the city woman is not a detached observer but a receptive listener emotionally moved by what she hears.

And that story has certain parallels to the rejection of Demeter by Metaneira. Like the disguised Demeter, Mrs. Todd had become attached to a man who was, conventionally, "far above her." As in the myth, the mother of this male of a "high family" rejects the countrywoman:

"No, dear, him I speak of could never think of me," she said. "When we was young together his mother didn't favor the match, an' done everything she could to part us; and folks thought we both married well, but 't wa'n't what either one of us wanted most; an' now we're left alone again, an' might have had each other all the time. He was above bein' a seafarin' man, an' prospered more than most; he come of a high family, an' my lot was plain an' hard-workin'. I ain't seen him for some years; he's forgot our youthful feelin's, I expect, but a woman's heart is different; them feelin's comes back when you think you've done with 'em, as sure as spring comes with the year. An' I've always had ways of hearin' about him."[39]

Mrs. Todd's sorrow has never left her. Those "youthful feelings" of love and sorrow, mixed together like Persephone's blooms of white and purple, remain with her always, returning "as sure as spring comes with the year." She is both youthful maiden and sorrowing *Mater Dolorosa:* "She stood in the centre of a braided rug, and its rings of black and gray seemed to circle about her feet in the dim light. Her height and massiveness in the low room gave her the look of a huge sibyl, while the strange fragrance of the mysterious herb blew in from the little garden."[40]

Like Demeter, Mrs. Todd's image expands, becoming "huge" and filling the "low room." Unlike Metaneira, however, the narrator's sympathy allows her to see Mrs. Todd's divinity, which "lies deepest in her heart." We could even say that the narrator's sympathy is itself the "eye" that sees the goddess. For the power that fills and "expands" the numinous image is a surge of emotion: the narrator's sympathy with the other woman's love and sorrow. Here, as in the recognition scene between Mara and Miss Roxy, the observer "sees" the soul of the speaker because she herself participates in its essence.

As for other motifs, the scent of the mysterious herb blowing in from the little garden recalls the "sweet scent" given off by Demeter's robes. Mrs. Todd's chthonian qualities are most apparent in the "rings of black and gray" that "circle about her feet." The associations here are complex. The image recalls the dark waters of the uroboric goddesses whose viscous tides pull the unwary down: the sad Dolores in *Pearl of Orr's Island* or even "poor Adeline" of *A Country Doctor*. The rings also seem to circle inward, as if emphasizing Mrs. Todd's centrality: a dark halo about the chthonic feet rather than a solar aurora about the spiritual head. This too would be appropriate for a Lady of the Plants, who personifies the darker mysteries of nature. Other associations of the black and gray circles include the writhing snakes that surround Medusa and the shadowy "snood" that veils Hecate, the moon goddess who hides in her cave. This shadow veils Demeter's own face in her sorrowing search for her daughter.

But the "dark" quality of Mrs. Todd is most clear in her name. She is a "far descended shadow" not only of Demeter but also of Persephone, who could herself be described as "Mrs. Todd," a wife of Death. We are dealing with a dual goddess, both Mother and Maiden, and appropriately, Mrs. Todd's mother, Mrs. Blackett, *also* seems to be a wife to Death. She too has a dual nature: mother to her children but with a heart always childlike.

Pater's Demeter personifies the Greek countryside. She gives form to a people's experience of their fields and changing seasons. Personification also shapes the strange image of Mrs. Todd standing "outside the window" to tell her story. In some mysterious sense Mrs. Todd *is* the landscape outside the window, which "speaks" to the narrator as the sea "speaks in its idle high-tide sleep" at the close of *Deephaven*. This landscape now penetrates to the narrator's room with the moon-

light and the "cool air . . . from the sea," and finally, with that "strange
fragrance of the mysterious herb blowing in from the little garden."
And if the landscape should speak of what lay deepest in its heart,
what would it say? Here it tells of desertion by a male lover, the ambitious sons and sea captains whose ships lie rotting on the beach.
These men once loved this place, but now they are gone.

Actually, we have been prepared for this identification of Mrs. Todd
with her setting from the very first paragraph, which closes: "When
one really knows a village like this and its surroundings, it is like
becoming acquainted with a single person. The process of falling in
love at first sight is as final as it is swift in such a case, but the growth
of true friendship may be a lifelong affair."[41] Mrs. Todd rises out of
her surroundings, chthonic as her own pennyroyal. Through love of
her the narrator will become an adopted sister and daughter, finally an
initiate and "humble follower" of this "great soul."

V

That the setting should, in some mysterious way, be personified as
a woman is not so strange when we consider its mythic logic. The
pastoral is, in many ways, *about* its setting, and that setting is defined
by its relationship to the more urban world that frames it. This relationship calls into play patterns of association that link the pastoral
world with woman. While Pater shows us the emotional sources of this
setting's "femininity," a structuralist analysis reveals the semantic ones.

While the relationship between country and city is rarely addressed
directly in *Country of the Pointed Firs,* it is highlighted in *Deephaven.*
Helen Denis carefully correlates Deephaven with preindustrial American society. It is "utterly out of fashion." Since the disastrous embargo
of 1807 the harbor has been filling in with sand, and the shores are
littered with decaying dories, wherries, and whaleboats. But if it has
lost its former glory, Deephaven has not accepted change with the rest
of the country: "It was not in the least American. There was no excitement about anything; there were no manufactories; nobody seemed
in the least hurry. The only foreigners were a few standard sailors. I
do not know when a house or a new building of any kind has been
built; the men were farmers, and went outward in boats, or inward in
fishwagons."[42] Its manners seem to belong to the days before the embargo; the democratic passions of the Jacksonian era did not touch this
"quaint" little fishing village, and Helen finds it curious "how clearly
the gradations of society were defined." In fact, with its clinging to
tradition, class, and memory, Deephaven seems more like a "lazy English seaside town than any other." The two visitors feel they have

somehow stepped back in time, for "it seemed as if all the clocks in Deephaven, and the people with them, had stopped years ago." Further, there seem to be no young people to give a sense of the future. Small children are equally absent; the town seems largely populated by older women, with a few stray fishermen and retired sea captains. The preponderance of elderly ladies often reminds Kate and Helen of *Cranford,* Mrs. Gaskell's novel about a similar English village peacefully subject to Amazon rule.[43]

The grotesque aspect of this Amazonian culture is suggested by the juxtaposition of a sideshow featuring "The Kentucky Giantess" and a lecture discussing "The Elements of True Manhood." In a paradigm of the book's action, our tourist heroines attend a circus sideshow exhibiting the largest woman on earth: a pitiful creature who, it turns out, is actually a local woman abandoned by her family and unable to care for herself. She has been taken up by a huckster and put on display. Kate and Helen are at first ashamed to gawk at her, but their local friend, Mrs. Kew, persuades them to enter the tent, where she is surprised to find that the giantess is actually a Deephaven native, her old school friend, Marilly. And so they discover a human being instead of a monster. The giantess seems a comic/pathetic image of the region itself: an inflated feminine dependent, unable to care for herself and forced to earn a living by exhibiting herself to tourists.

This interpretation is reinforced by the second half of the chapter, which contrasts the sideshow with another comic/pathetic performance. This time an earnest pedant addresses a local audience at ponderous length on "The Elements of True Manhood." His speech is filled with stirring allusions to the inspiration of Benjamin Franklin and other great inventors, leaders, and patriarchs of the past. However, as Kate and Helen are all too aware, there is not one young man in the audience. A straggly regiment of elderly ladies, doddering old men, children, and dogs make up the hall, which is filled with impenetrable gloom. The absurdity of the situation moves the heroines to near-helpless giggles and demonstrates again the decline of "true manhood" in the Deephaven parish.

With the book's close, the town itself has become identified with elderly ladies like Miss Honora Carew; the deference due to one is due the other: " 'Dear old Deephaven,' said Kate, gently. . . . 'It makes me think of one of its own ladies, with its clinging to the old fashions and its respect for what used to be respectable when it was young. I cannot make fun of what was once dear to somebody, and which realized somebody's ideas of beauty or fitness.' "[44]

Looking back on *Deephaven* in 1893, Jewett described the impulse behind it as "an attempt to explain the past and present to each other."[45] As a young woman, Jewett remembers, she was "possessed by a dark fear that townspeople and countrypeople would never understand one another, or learn to profit by their new relationship." While Jewett wished to reveal the true provincial character to her literate readers, she also wished to preserve the country ways she then believed to be declining, even to be on the edge of extinction. However, from the perspective of 1893 an older Jewett felt that this danger was exaggerated: "That all the individuality and quaint personal characteristics of rural New England were so easily swept away, or are even now dying out, we can refuse to believe. It appears, even, that they are better nourished, and shine brighter by contrast than in former years."[46]

This perception that the "quaint personal characteristics of rural New England" would "shine brighter by contrast" gives us the key to a structuralist interpretation of Jewett's pastoral writing, perhaps even of the genre. For, as Leo Marx writes in his *The Machine in the Garden*, the pastoral is defined by its mediation between the wilderness and the city. Within these boundaries its territory is framed. Further, this setting—its landscapes, houses, and people—is all of a piece. Each element signifies the same concept, for, to use structuralist terms, they all belong to the same paradigmatic set. And moreover, as Annette Kolodny has shown, this paradigmatic set is same occupied by the term "woman."[47] "Woman" also mediates between nature and culture, here represented by wilderness and city. Moreover, the correlation extends the various levels of mediation described by Sherry Ortner. She argues that women are associated with nature because of their bodies, their social roles, and finally, their psychic structures. Their analogies appear in the pastoral setting as its landscapes, its households, and finally its women. Within our semantic system, woman's place is pastoral.

However, one person's pastoral is another person's Boston. In structuralist terms, the meaning of "pastoral" is "arbitrary."[48] Jewett is especially sensitive to the ironies of this sliding semantic scale:

> The Deephaven people use to say sometimes complacently that certain things or certain people were "as dull as East Parish." Kate and I grew curious to see that part of the world which was considered duller than Deephaven itself; . . . one day we went there.
> It was like Deephaven, only on a smaller scale.[49]

In *The Country of the Pointed Firs*, Jewett uses this motif again. Upon the narrator's return from Green Island, Dunnet Landing "seemed large and noisy and oppressive as we came ashore. Such is the power of contrast; for the village was so still that I could hear the shy whip-

poorwills singing that night as I lay awake in my downstairs bedroom."
Green Island is to Dunnet Landing as Dunnet Landing is to Boston.[50]

The images of women also lie along a sliding scale. They too shift
according to the larger structure. Thus, context may allow a female
figure to signify a conventionally male concept. Given the terms "lady,"
"countrywoman," and "nature," "lady" will signify culture. She is
more "cooked," less "raw" than the "countrywoman," who therefore
mediates between "nature" and "lady." In *Deephaven* the "savage"
Mrs. Bonny is to the "peasant" Mrs. Kew as Mrs. Kew is to the
"aristocratic" Miss Chauncy. And in a quiet way, Mrs. Todd is to Mrs.
Blackett as the narrator is to Mrs. Todd: Almira had to leave Green
Island to find "scope" for her ambitions, just as the narrator must leave
Dunnet Landing at the summer's end.

These sliding scales allow Jewett to articulate subtle cultural shad-
ings, including gradations of social class. In particular, they help her
distinguish between two types of pastoral: what I will call the classic
and the decadent. Before analyzing the setting's links to the feminine
in more detail, I will try to define these two types. While there are
examples of the decadent pastoral in *Pointed Firs,* it is much more
important to *Deephaven,* where both types appear side by side. For
that reason I will primarily use *Deephaven* to illustrate Jewett's pastoral
iconography.

Both the decadent and the classic pastoral settings are defined by
their position on the periphery of the urban, patriarchal world and by
their mediation between that world and the wilderness. However, the
classic pastoral describes a world recognized by Theocritus, Virgil, and
later, George Sand. This is the rural world of the peasant who follows
immemorial tradition and earns a subsistence through toil directly on
the body of the natural world: through farming, shepherding, fishing,
gathering, spinning, cooking, weaving. This is also the "Demetrian"
world described by Bachofen: ordered life has supplanted savagery, but
dependence on the earth is still deeply felt. In the "matriarchal age"
this world was central, but in pastoral literature it is always seen in
retrospect. "Our old home," it is framed by an urban patriarchal society whose complexities have relegated it to the periphery.

The decadent pastoral setting is also a center that has become peripheral. However, this was an *urban* center, patriarchal in Bachofen's
terms. It is now defined as pastoral not because its people take their
living from the earth and are therefore closer to nature; it is defined
as pastoral simply because it has been supplanted by a new center of
authority. In contrast to this new authority, the decadent center *seems*
pastoral. Like the Protestant ministers described by Ann Douglas, the

patriarchs of the declining society appear disenfranchised, "feminized." Further, the decadent pastoral society appears to be closer to nature only because it is declining, even dying. Thus, it is associated with decay, retrogression, the past—with immanence and contingency rather than with progress and transcendence. Here culture has failed to redeem humanity from the viscous pull of nature, which reasserts its claim over human achievements.

While this distinction seems to be only semiconscious in *Deephaven*, its oppositions structure large sections of the book. For example, following the introductory chapter, which gets the two heroines from Boston to Deephaven, Chapter 2 is titled "The Brandon House and the Lighthouse," and Chapter 3 contrasts "My Lady Brandon and the Widow Jim." In each we have the genteel, aristocratic society—represented by the Brandon house and its late mistress—juxtaposed with the rural, "peasant" society—represented by the Deephaven Lighthouse and the Widow Jim, Katharine Brandon's servant. Later chapters are structured on similar or related juxtapositions, such as the contrast, already discussed, between "The Kentucky Giantess" and the lecturer on "The Elements of True Manhood." Picking up the themes of chapters 2 and 3, Chapter 10 describes Mrs. Bonny, a shrewd, earthy countrywoman living deep in the woods above Deephaven, and the chapter immediately following introduces Miss Chauncy, a gently mad lady of the decaying gentry.

Turning to the levels of imagery mentioned earlier, we can see the link between classic pastoral and the feminine most clearly in the households of *Deephaven*. Countrywomen and their husbands still play roles less polarized between private and public. Through human labor each transforms raw materials into objects for human use: through farming, toolmaking, baking, herding, weaving, fishing, sewing, cooking itself. Hence, the differentiation between male and female is less marked than in industrial societies. Men's work, as well as women's, is relatively dependent on natural forces. In fishing: the tides, moon, storms, waves, the fish themselves. In farming: the cycles of heat, drought, rain, frost, insects, and disease. In the pastoral world men's psyches are less sharply differentiated from women's; they too feel their deep dependence on the cycles of birth, death, and decay. They too share the Eleusinian vision and participate in the life of the Demetrian Mother.

This softer differentiation of male and female spheres shapes the image of the rural household, which is at once a place of family love and productive work. The boundaries between public and private are lowered. The walls of the house itself may seem permeable to the natural world. For example, the lighthouse of Mrs. Kew is both a home and a place of business. She and her husband live and work in the same space, which is firmly grounded on its island and open to the sea air. The eccentric Mrs. Bonny, who makes and sells her butter, lives in a cottage in a forest clearing. The natural world edges right up to her door and even wanders across the threshold in the form of some inquisitive chickens. Not only does the barnyard penetrate her household, but Mrs. Bonny's household extends into the barnyard, where her patient horse stands dressed in his mistress's cast-off bonnet. Mrs. Bonny seems to be on the messy boundary between the tidy pastoral and the chaotic wilderness.

The decadent pastoral presents another picture. Here the association between the decadent pastoral society and the feminine comes from the disenfranchisement of male authority. The old shipping magnates and the retired sea captains no longer have their firms and ships to command. Like Captain Littlepage of Dunnet Landing, Deephaven patriarchs can no longer explore their horizons but are confined to the narrow sphere of the home. Unlike the farmers and fishermen of the classic pastoral, these men *would* rule the abstract, public spaces, but they are no longer theirs to command. The ambitious young men of Deephaven have all left for the cities, the factories, or the West. And as Helen and Kate point out, only the elderly and the feminine remain behind.

The loss of authority affects primarily the male members of the family; genteel wives, aunts, mothers, and sisters still rule their domestic havens, impoverished but entrenched to the last. As the crest turns back, the domestic sphere of the patriarchal social structure comes to the fore. As one aging captain ruefully comments, women are the captains ashore. If Deephaven ships no longer sail for Canton, tea is still savored in Miss Honora Carew's parlor and a "power of china" is carefully stowed in Lady Brandon's cupboard. However, the Brandon house is pastoral only because it savors of tradition and retrogression: "feminine" continuity rather than "masculine" progress. It is not open to the natural world, however. Indeed, as we shall see in the next chapter, its formality stifles instinctual freedom, just as its heavy curtains and moldy wallpaper present forbidding boundaries between its interior space and the natural world outside.

The Chauncy mansion shows us the decadent pastoral in its full, extreme bloom: the bloom of decay. The Chauncy family, once one of the wealthiest in Deephaven, lost its fortune along with the others. All of its members, save Miss Chauncy, are dead; the fortune is gone. Mad, she stays on in the house, which is crumbling beneath her in New

England gothic style, reminiscent of Poe's House of Usher. Here the boundary between the natural and the cultural is permeable because the house and the culture it represents are dying. Too rotted to support human weight, the floorboards in the lower rooms threaten to drop unwary explorers onto the soggy ground below.

The fence that separated this estate from the world outside "had been a grand affair in its day, though now it could scarcely stand alone." Reinforcing the pastoral associations, Kate and Helen must enter the apparently deserted house by "climbing over the boards which were put up like pasture bars against the wide front gateway."[51] As they advance, they see the fate of the Brandon house if its downward course is not checked. The furniture is all missing, and there are only blank spaces on the walls where the portraits once hung. An ignorant maid appears, but she cannot say where all of the glorious trappings have gone, "only it would all fall into the cellar soon. But the old lady was proud as Lucifer, and wouldn't hear of moving out."

In fact, nature has already begun to take possession. As they look into the room at the foot of the stairs: "Three old hens and a rooster marched toward us with great solemnity. . . . The cobwebs hung in the room as they often do in old barns, in long grey festoons; the lilacs outside grew close against the windows where the shutters were not drawn, and the light in the room was greenish and dim."[52] Unlike the hens in Mrs. Bonny's cottage, these hens do not "belong" in these formal spaces; they are symptoms of nature's transformational power. And so, the narrator humorously implies, they march with "great solemnity" as if aware that soon they will be sovereigns of this reclaimed territory.

While the imagery of these households gives us a fairly straightforward analogy to the "feminine," the landscape imagery is more subtle. It evokes not only the feminine psyche but also the feminine body: a body whose boundaries blur, whose outlines are suffused with emotion. There are many variations on the classic pastoral landscape in *Deephaven*, but the following seems typical, particularly in its association of spiritual renewal with biological regeneration. As Helen and Kate travel inland to visit Mrs. Bonny, they pass

through a grove of young beeches; the last year's whitish leaves lay thick on the ground, and the new leaves made so close a roof overhead that the light was strangely purple, as if it had come through a great church window of stained glass. After this we went through some hemlock growth, where, on the lower branches, the pale green of the new shoots and the dark green of the old made an exquisite contrast to each other.[53]

The association of a grove with a cathedral is a convention in romantic writing. Jewett uses it again, more subtly, in her description of the Bowden Reunion. These leaves seem to border on heaven, whose light transforms them into stained glass. Within this sacred grove Kate and Helen are embedded within a womblike round of leaves. The human figure is enclosed by an earth and sky made of one substance. The juxtaposition of dead leaves on the ground and new leaves overhead is echoed in the "exquisite contrast" of the "new shoots" and the dark green needles of former growths. This is a grove sacred to the dying and rising deities—to Persephone as much as to Diana and Dionysus.

In the hills above Deephaven, however, the heroines discover the border where pastoral passes into wilderness. As we shall see later, this border perhaps comes at Mrs. Bonny's house, but it is definitely crossed in Chapter 11, titled "In Shadow": "After we were three or four miles from Deephaven, the country looked very different. The shore was so rocky that there were almost no places where a boat could put in, so there were no fishermen in the region, and the farms were scattered wide apart; the land was so poor that even the trees looked hungry."[54] There is less promise of renewal here; the "exquisite contrast" of light and dark is missing. The landscape is no longer nurturing but virtually hostile to human life. These fields do not offer themselves up to the farmer for plowing; instead the rocky hills threaten to swallow the tiny figures who try to wrest a living from them. Here lives the Terrible Mother, who might just as easily cannibalize her children as feed them.

The decadent pastoral landscape, significantly, includes the artifacts of culture:

By and by the Deephaven warehouses will fall and be used for firewood by the fisher people, and the wharves will be worn away by the tides. The few old gentlefolks who still linger will be dead then; and I wonder if some day Kate Lancaster and I will go down to Deephaven for the sake of old times, and read the epitaphs in the burying ground, look out to sea, and talk quietly about the girls who were so happy there one summer long ago.[55]

There is loss of differentiation here, but it is loss of differentiation between nature and culture. Human constructions are literally dissolving back into their formless natural components. Nature is undoing what culture has wrought, but there are no new forms to contrast with this decay. This is the pastoral of ruin, in the tradition of Thomas Cole's paintings on the course of empire. Now the proud structures of civilization are leveled; their outlines are softened and blurred by wildflowers and tangled vines. The image recalls the warning of Bachofen's *Mother-Right*: once the peak of patriarchy is achieved, the crest of civilization may turn back, reverting to earlier forms, even to the oozy tides themselves.

In the decadent pastoral, nature pollutes. These "feminine" settings maintain the patriarchal association of nature with the viscous, the chaotic, the inhuman—finally, with death. Here decay "cooks" culture, returning its human forms to nature. I am reminded of the character in Sherwood Anderson's *Winesburg, Ohio* who suddenly realizes that all the world is on fire: decay is a slow burning. The decadent pastoral ends in ashes: dust to dust, ashes to ashes. The younger Jewett was right to fear it, as Sartre feared the *matrix, materia* without spirit.

But even in *Deephaven* Jewett saw the sources of renewal. In classic pastoral landscapes the way "down" into nature is paradoxically the way "up" into spirit, for nature and spirit are perfectly blended. Each is a mirror of the other. Immanence and transcendence are not opposed but complementary. One boundary faces the city, another the unredeemed wilderness; but another mysterious boundary is the interface of nature and spirit:

One still evening . . . there was a bank of heavy gray clouds in the west shutting down like a curtain, and the sea was silver-colored. You could look under and beyond the curtain of clouds into the palest, clearest yellow sky. There was a little black boat in the distance drifting slowly, climbing one white wave after another, as if it were bound into that other world beyond, but presently the sun came out from behind the clouds, and the dazzling golden light changed the look of everything, and it was the time to say one thought it a beautiful sunset; while before one could only keep very still, and watch the boat, and wonder if heaven would not be somehow like that far, faint color which was neither sea nor sky.[56]

The tiny black figure on the boat seems embedded in an enveloping veil of gray and silver. As in the earlier description of the grove, there is no differentiation between earth and sky; both seem of the same essence. And it is through this nearly insubstantial, if material, veil that the human figure is moving toward the golden "other world beyond." There is no movement, as of flight, to rise *above* the earth into the sky; indeed this is a fusion of earth and sky. But shining under and *through* this veil is a "far, faint color" neither sea nor sky. That far, faint color is the light of heavenly spirit toward which the figure toils. And these colors—the dim gleam of spiritual gold through a dulling curtain of earthy gray—would become Jewett's most characteristic hues. For this fusion of gray and gold, spiritual honey and material ashes, produces the "dun" that lends its name to Dunport of *A Country Doctor* and to Dunnet Landing of *The Country of the Pointed Firs*. It recalls that moment Kate Brandon found "most beautiful," the moment when

Demeter's divinity breaks through her material disguise, filling the halls with light.

And yet, significantly, it is the moment when sea and sky cannot be differentiated that the narrator celebrates in her description, not the next moment when the sun makes the distinction clear. Jewett prefers the boundaries blurred: boundaries between sky and earth, earth and house, house and woman, woman and woman. These moments of participation mystique, of fusion and dissolve, return to the original communion between mother and child. They are primordial, preoedipal; they are the moment when one can "only keep very still." They are also beyond, because before, speech. This prior moment is ineffable; only when the sun of consciousness appears to make distinctions is it "time to say one thought it a beautiful sunset." Before the possibilities of speech, one could only "wonder." It is this moment of communion— of wonder—that transforms death.

For death is still in Arcadia. Indeed death is Arcadia's seed-filled core. Demeter is not only a loving mother, but a *Mater Dolorosa,* the "skeleton at the Dionysian feast." But now death is unutterably changed by the Eleusinian vision: the continuity of generations, the persistence of love, a wisdom born of incarnation. The Wife of Hades and the Goddess of Spring are one. Mrs. Todd, who *is* Mrs. Death, turns her power to healing, and Mrs. Blackett shines with a light that defies her name. While the decadent pastoral gives us rot, classic pastoral gives us honey. In the logic of Lévi-Strauss, this world is neither raw nor cooked but—like the milk and honey that flow through its mythic fields—both raw and cooked at once, naturally supernatural. Its ground *is* anomalous, taboo—not because it is polluted but because it is sacred.

Chapter Six

Deephaven: *Ambivalence in Arcadia*

According to Northrop Frye's *The Anatomy of Criticism,* members of a paradigmatic set exist within the same metaphorical body, conceptually identical. Mrs. Todd and her cottage, Dunnet Landing and its shores, even her pennyroyal are conceptual equivalents. All signify the pastoral, and all exist "within the same body." And this body is a feminine body, the body of the good mother, the "white hotel" where we have all stayed—to paraphrase both Freud and D. M. Thomas. Indeed, Mrs. Todd's cottage *is* a white hotel to which the vacationing narrator returns. In this "quaint little house" she lives "with as much comfort and unconsciousness as if it were a larger body, or a double shell, in whose simple convolutions Mrs. Todd and I had secreted ourselves."[1]

In Jewett's first book, Kate and Helen begin to sense a "personality" speaking through the landscape around them. But they do not see its soul in another person. Their goddess lives only in detached, intellectual interpretations of ancient myth, not incarnated in present flesh. *Deephaven* shows us pastoral landscapes, even houses (such as the Deephaven lighthouse), suffused with mythic power. But as the following chapters will show, a figure comparable to Mrs. Todd or Mrs. Blackett is missing. Kate and Helen are more apt to see Deephaven's women as pathetic or comic, even grotesque.

An explanation may lie in Erich Neumann's theory that the differentiation of archetypal images reflects the relative differentiation of the consciousness perceiving them. Insofar as the subject's ego is undeveloped and insecure, the feminine appears as the Terrible Mother, looming, both cavernous and carnivorous. Her gravitational pull threatens to swallow the barely differentiated ego. Communion with the mother promises "oceanic bliss," but the ego risks drowning to achieve it. On the other hand, if the ego is fully differentiated and secure, flexible without being rigid, then the maternal figure loses its monstrous quality. The feminine appears not threatening but numinous. Thus, a character's unconscious relationship to the mother shapes her perception of the pastoral landscape and its people.[2]

There is deep connection, then, between the developmental plot of the female *Bildungsroman* and the apparently simpler plot of the pastoral. The correlation appears when they are seen against the background of the Demeter-Persephone myth. The *Bildungsroman* follows the mythic pattern in the most straightforward fashion: the daughter's initial innocence, her separation, and return.[3] However, the pastoral begins with the separation already accomplished; it describes only the return. The outsider must be restored to union with nature, with the "mother" that culture supplanted. Thus, the first chapter of *The Country of the Pointed Firs* is actually named "The Return," a title that echoes Annie Fields's own work, "The Return of Persephone."

However, *Deephaven* was written before Jewett had decisively rejected her mother's role. In many ways it is an experimental novel. Jewett is experimenting with her artistic detachment from South Berwick, and her two heroines are experimenting with their temporary connection to Deephaven. In a curious reversal, an emerging author not quite separated from her parents and home imagines her heroines as not quite connected to them. Like their author, these characters are not young enough to merge unconsciously with their "hostess" nor separate enough to return the love their "hostess" gives them.

I

Looking back on her first book from the perspective of 1893, Jewett "frankly confesses" that certain "sentences . . . make her feel as if she were the grandmother of the author of *Deephaven* and her heroines."[4] That Jewett should see herself as the grandmother of her earlier self *and* of her heroines is significant. First, it reveals quite clearly the autobiographical source of the book. Second, it reveals the deeper sense in which the female author identifies her heroine as her daughter. Judith Kegan Gardiner has used Nancy Chodorow's research and that of others to explore the connection between women's writing and women's mothering:

> . . . the text and its female hero begin as narcissistic extensions of the author. . . . Thus the author may define herself through the text while creating her female hero. This can be a positive, therapeutic relationship, like learning to be a mother, that is, learning to experience oneself as one's own cared-for child and as one's own caring mother while simultaneously learning to experience one's creation as other, as separate from the self.[5]

In another article, "The Heroine as Her Author's Daughter," Gardiner develops this insight with particular reference to the female *Bil-*

dungsroman.[6] She sees the tendency of women writers to kill off their heroines' mothers as a strategy to give their fictional daughters open horizons. Identified with her heroine, the author vicariously gains her own freedom from the mother. But as her heroine's literary creator, the author also has the curious power to mother her fictional self. An example may be the moment in "A White Heron" when the narrator speaks directly to Sylvia. Like an ideal mother, the narrator guides her "daughter"'s vision toward the crucial epiphany. Other instances include the wishful thinking that underlies Nan Prince's liberation from both mother and grandmother, then her possession of the androgynous father. Jewett seems to reconstruct her own life through the creation of a fictional self.

What makes Jewett's 1893 comment particularly interesting, however, is that she seems conscious of her maternal relationship to her characters and to her earlier self. Moreover, she is conscious that the quality of this relationship may shift. Helen Denis and Kate Brandon were, Jewett implies, "narcissistic extensions" of their author. Now she bends an indulgent eye on all three and "begs her readers not to smile with her over those sentences . . . so the callow wings of what thought itself to be wisdom and the childish soul of sentiment will still be happy and untroubled."[7] Significantly, Jewett describes herself not as the author's mother but her grandmother, at two removes from identification. As a woman grows older, she thinks back through the generations: to move forward into the future is paradoxically to go deeper into the psyche, discovering there one's link to the generations farthest back. I would like to turn now to that younger self, and to Kate Lancaster and Helen Denis, "those 'two young ladies of virtue and honour, bearing an inviolable friendship for each other,' as two others, less fortunate, are described in the preface to Clarissa Harlowe."[8]

Perhaps the most important thing about these heroines is that there are two of them. Jewett has split her own persona. Helen Denis, the narrator, is the young writer gathering material in a strange place. Kate Lancaster is the returned native, niece of Miss Brandon and rightful mistress of the grand old house in Deephaven. Looking at Helen Denis first, we see that she presents herself as an outsider, an outsider everywhere. Not only is she not "root-bound," she has no roots at all: "I have the good fortune and the misfortune to belong to the navy,—that is, my father does,—and my life has been consequently an unsettled one, except during the years of my school life, when my friendship with Kate began." Far from disliking her "unsettled" situation, Helen believes that "it is easy for me to be content, and to feel at home anywhere."⁹ In the effort to set her heroine free, Jewett sets her almost in space.

Although Helen's parents are not dead, as Nan Prince's are, they have no presence, either real or felt. Helen seems to exist only in relationship to Kate Lancaster, the true heroine of the story. Given this omission, it is interesting that Jewett dedicated this first book to "my father and mother, my two best friends, and also to all my other friends, whose names I say to myself lovingly, though I do not write them here."¹⁰ After Jewett had scoured the parental presence out of her narrator's life, it is curious that she should dedicate the book to her parents. However, they are described specifically as "best friends": this is the privileged relationship in *Deephaven*. By referring to her own parents in this way, Jewett is, of course, paying them a compliment, but she is also denying their parenthood, their power. Indeed, after her father died only a year later, Jewett wrote that only then did she feel "grown up," only then did she realize the enormous influence her father had had on her. In 1877 the shadow of this recognition had not yet fallen.

But if Helen Denis does not have parents close at hand (and notice that she is identified with her father: *she* "belongs to the navy"), Helen does have Kate Lancaster. She says that she "should be happy in any town if I were living there with Kate." The relationship between these two young women is highly narcissistic. Helen admires her friend extravagantly, tells us about her at great length (to Jewett's later embarrassment), and yet somehow cannot seem to particularize her: "I will not praise my friend as I can praise her, or say half the things I might say honestly. She is fresh and good and true, and enjoys life so heartily. She is so childlike without being childish; and I do not tell you that she is faultless, but when she makes mistakes she is sorrier and more ready to hopefully try again than any girl I know."¹¹ Barely a page later Helen again picks up the theme and praises Kate's "unusual power of winning people's confidence, and of knowing with surest instinct how to meet them on their own ground." Here, and in Kate's "childlike" quality, I sense Jewett's own characteristics emerging. As Helen elaborates: "It is the girl's being so genuinely sympathetic and interested which makes every one ready to talk to her and be friends with her; just as the sun-shine makes it easy for flowers to grow which the chilly winds hinder."¹²

Josephine Donovan and others have suggested that Kate Lancaster had her source in Kate Birckhead, a friend to whom Jewett was deeply attached at the time. However, Kate Lancaster also reflects Jewett:

Jewett as her best, idealized self. It is Kate Lancaster who is the rightful mistress of the large house in *Deephaven,* the house that seems so closely modeled on the Jewett homestead. And it is Kate who is the intimate of the local people, who listens to their stories with the sympathetic, yet curiously reserved air proper to a lady of the manor. Thus, Helen and Kate seem to me almost mirror images, Siamese twins. Helen never describes a moment alone without Kate. Indeed, if Helen Denis seems a somewhat blurry version of Jewett's artist-persona, then Kate Lancaster is an equally blurry version of her "rooted" self.

Nancy Chodorow's work accounts for this quality. She sees this type of intense friendship, which played an important part in Jewett's own girlhood, as a strategic defense against maternal overidentification. The doubling provides intimacy apart from the mother, but the lack of differentiation indicates the weakness of each girl's identity. The delight adolescent girls take in dressing alike, sounding alike, sharing their secrets are all common manifestations of their desire to mirror each other.

Chodorow's analysis draws on the earlier work of Helene Deutsch, who "describes a variety of ploys which pre-pubertal girls use to effect their individuation and independence."[13] One ploy is outright rejection: "A girl may become very critical of her family, especially of her mother, and may idealize the mother or the family of a friend." The daughter resolves her ambivalence by "splitting the good and bad aspects of objects: her mother and home represent bad, the extrafamilial world, good." Another tactic may be to create an identity through opposition. She may choose, "a woman teacher, another adult woman or older girl, or characters in books and films, and contrast them with her mother."[14] Here also the daughter splits the good and bad aspects of the mother and projects the good elsewhere. She also attempts to create "arbitrary boundaries by negative identification (I am what she is not)."

In *A Country Doctor* Nan uses this second tactic to differentiate herself from Adeline and from all other women, for that matter. However, Chodorow believes that in both of these tactics the daughter "has fled to intense identification-idealization-object loves, all the while expressing her feelings of dependence on a primary identification with this mother."[15] And so, despite Nan's rejection of Adeline, she still returns to her mother's grave and is standing firmly on that ground in the novel's final image. In the same way, Mara Lincoln is united with Dolores in the grave at the end of *The Pearl of Orr's Island.* Even transcendence cannot finally separate you from the mother: the "ground" of your being.

The daughter's third tactic, one adopted by "many pre-pubertal girls," is to bond with a best friend who shares her tastes, her values, her life—a friend whom she loves and imitates: "This friend in part counteracts the feelings of self-diffusion which result from the intensely experienced . . . identification-attachments in which the girl has engaged." She can then "continue to experience merging, while at the same time denying feelings of merging with her mother."[16] This is the way chosen by Helen Denis and Kate Lancaster. Accompanied and protected by the best friend and double, Jewett's heroine can return to the Deephaven homestead, can penetrate the houses of the local women, can look at the "mother" directly. However, true communion is always with the friend. Perhaps Kate and Helen together add up to one Sarah Jewett: newly self-conscious, possessed of the "mirror" within the psyche, but not yet ready for full separation.

The deep dependency in Kate and Helen's friendship appears in the book's opening lines:

It happened that the morning when this story begins I had waked up feeling sorry, and as if something dreadful were going to happen. There did not seem to be any good reason for it, so I undertook to discourage myself more thinking that it would soon be time to leave, and how much I should miss being with Kate and my other friends. My mind was still disquieted when I went down to breakfast; but beside my plate I found, with a hoped-for letter from my father, a note from Kate. To this day I have never known any explanation of that depression of my spirits, and I hope that the good luck which followed will help some reader to lose fear, and to smile at such shadows if any chance to come.[17]

Surely, this is a very disingenuous beginning. Helen's inability to recognize that her depression comes from the anticipated separation from Kate seems peculiar, especially since she features this depression and its alleviation so prominently. The final advice to the reader hardly makes any sense at all. Helen seems to say that the depression was meaningless, a freak, because, you see, she was not abandoned after all. Here come the letters from her father (not her mother) and her friend. Therefore, her fears were absurd, only shadows. However, it is important to keep this shadow in mind, for it begins the book. And if Helen refuses to acknowledge its significance, the signal is clear, and only "Kate Lancaster's Plan," as the chapter is entitled, saves Helen from "something dreadful."

Kate's note invites Helen to come around to her Boston town house, which Helen soon opens with her own latchkey. There she interrupts her friend practicing the piano in the parlor (these are genteel, rather wealthy young women) and receives a "solemn" kiss of greeting: "We are not sentimental girls, and are both much adverse to indiscriminate kissing, though I have not the adroit habit of shying in which Kate is proficient. It would sometimes be impolite in any one else, but she shies so affectionately."[18] We are clearly in the homosocial world described by Carroll Smith-Rosenberg. Significantly, these two young women do not seem to play mother-child roles with each other. They have a twin-like quality to them, but they also seem to be more or less equals in the relationship. Kate does not, for example, call Helen her "dear child," as Jewett was apt to do with her younger friends.

The plan that Kate Lancaster now unveils says a great deal about both characters. Kate's great-aunt, for whom she was named, died six months earlier. Ancient, last of her generation, she left her inheritance to Kate's mother. The estate includes both shipping wharves and "a charming old house" furnished by the Brandon sea captains. As Kate describes her ancestress, the outlines of Jewett's paternal grandmother again emerge. Miss Katherine was a severe woman, averse to all fri-volities. According to Kate, her house was equally sedate: "I have been there but little, for when I was a child my aunt found no pleasure in the society of noisy children who upset her treasures, and when I was older she did not care to see strangers, and after I left school she grew more and more feeble."[19]

Unlike Miss Sydney in Jewett's earlier story, this woman dies without blooming. She never comes to know the great-niece who might have thawed her heart. Now her house is empty. However, Kate's plan is that the two friends should take it over a summer:

"It might be dull in Deephaven for two young ladies who were fond of gay society and dependent upon excitement, I suppose; but for two little girls who were fond of each other and could play in the boats, and dig and build houses in the sea sand, and gather shells, and carry their dolls wherever they went, what could be pleasanter?"

"Nothing," said I, promptly.[20]

The attraction is clear: regression to childhood and escape from inhibition, from grown-up gentility. Now the house is theirs alone, no strings attached. In "Miss Sydney's Flowers" and *A Country Doctor,* the young woman must enter the sacred precinct alone and timidly; she may bring freshly cut flowers inside or open the windows to the outer air, but she does not come into possession of the space itself (although Nan does use Dr. Leslie's parlor so casually that the house-keeper disapproves). Now the wicked witch is dead, and the house (at last!) belongs to those who know how to use it. They will be living in the aristocratic homestead, but there is nothing to prevent them from shedding their ladylike roles and rollicking on the beach like contented six-year-olds.

As even Helen notices, freedom from convention makes their identities seem fluid: "Sometimes at Deephaven we were between six and seven years old, but at other times we felt irreparably grown-up, and as if we carried a crushing weight of care and duty." When Helen attempts to get a fix on their "true" age, her voice has an unconvincing ring: "In reality we were both twenty-four, and it is a pleasant age, though I think next year is sure to be pleasanter, for we do not mind growing older, since we have lost nothing that we mourn about and are gaining much."[21] I can imagine that this was one of the passages for which Jewett begged her reader's indulgence. The Jewett who had lost both father and mother was well aware of what time could take away. But significantly, her own sense of never losing her childhood— of being "always nine years old"—is stated clearly here. Jewett's letters to Annie Fields also show this curious fluidity in her personality, a subtle and mercurial shifting from adult to adolescent to child and back again.

As Helen describes it, the friendship between the two girls grows even deeper over the summer. Always together, they are often alone but "such good friends that we often were silent for a long time, when mere acquaintances would have felt compelled to talk and try to entertain each other."[22] As is so often true in Jewett's work, silence is the highest form of communication. The almost mystical identification of these two friends is lyrically evoked in this description of them rowing home from the lighthouse at twilight, "far out from land":

... with our faces turned from the Light, it seemed as if we were alone, and the sea shoreless; and as the darkness closed round us softly, we watched the stars come out, and were always glad to see Kate's star, and my star, which we had chosen when we were children. I used long ago to be sure of one thing—that, however far away heaven might be, it could not be out of sight of the stars. Sometimes in the evening we waited out at sea for the moonrise, and then we would take the oars again and go slowly in, once in a while singing or talking, but oftenest silent.[23]

The intimacy is palpable; the two girls wish to lose themselves in the darkness, which "closed round" them "softly." They lose the sense of boundaries, the sight of shore, and feel alone in the world. Just the two of them, embraced by the motherly night. Again there is the repeated "we," no need to differentiate one friend from the other. Each has her star, but Kate is to Helen as one star to another.

II

While the two friends find it easy to merge with the mother as manifested in nature—the gentle sea and twilight—the mother as house or as person is another matter. They must first deal with the Brandon homestead, a formidable presence. As Mrs. Kew explains, Miss Katharine "set a great deal by the house, and she kept everything just as it used to be in her mother's day."[24] This is a matrilineal system: the legacy of the foremothers is passed down to Miss Katharine, who left it in turn to Kate's mother. Eventually, the book implies, all this will be Kate's. But to come to terms with the house also means to come to terms with Miss Katharine's spirit. This quiet process, nearly subliminal, gives what development there is to Kate's character.

At first, the house appears almost hostile to the two visitors, as Miss Brandon herself had appeared to the noisy child Kate once was: "It was impossible to imagine any children in the old place; everything was for grown people; even the stair railing was too high to slide down on."[25] Helen adds that the chairs themselves looked "as if they had been put, at the furnishing of the house, in their places, and there they meant to remain." Many years later Jewett wrote that she hoped she would die at home, in the South Berwick house, with its chairs all "in their places." Tradition comforted her then, but now her heroines find it inhibiting, even frightening. The "dismal" best chamber arouses their "dread" and thoughts of ghosts. The huge old bed and heavy furniture "were draped in some old fashioned kind of white cloth which always seemed to be waving and moving about of itself. The carpet was most singularly colored with dark reds and indescribable grays and browns, and the pattern, after a whole summer's study, could never be followed with one's eye."[26]

This carpet with its unintelligible pattern recalls "The Yellow Wallpaper." And one senses that if a young woman *were* shut up in this best chamber, the results would not be far different from what Charlotte Perkins Gilman imagined, especially since the carpet is matched by an equally "dreadful" wallpaper, captured a century ago in a French prize: "Part of the figure was shaggy, and therein little spiders found habitation, and went visiting their acquaintances across the shiny places. The color was an unearthly pink and a forbidding maroon, with dim white spots which gave it the appearance of having moulded."[27] Part of this wallpaper's design is its decay: a sign of the decadent pastoral. The boundaries between nature and culture are breaking down, and the little spiders have established their own social etiquette.

The association of the decayed gentility with death is reinforced immediately: "It made you low-spirited to look long in the mirror; and the great lounge one could not have cheerful associations with, after hearing that Miss Brandon herself did not like it, having seen so many of her relatives lie there dead. . . . The only picture was one of the Maid of Orleans tied with an unnecessarily strong rope to a very stout stake."[28] The wonderful image of the martyred Maid of Orleans suggests the fate that might befall some other rebellious young women. This threat follows the two friends around the house, even into the sacred shrine of hospitality itself. Something about that best parlor reminds them of "an invisible funeral." Indeed, "all the portraits which hung there had for some unaccountable reason taken a violent dislike to us, and followed us suspiciously with their eyes."[29] To see oneself reflected in this domestic mirror might well make one "low-spirited." The whole house binds, restricts, with "an unnecessarily strong rope."

However, one room seems warmer and more open. Helen finds a place by the chimney to write. In this corner she always keeps a "bunch of fresh green ferns in a tall champagne glass." Among the furnishings she discovers "the largest sofa I ever saw . . . broad enough for Kate and me to lie on together, and very high and square; but there was a pile of soft cushions at one end." Snuggled into this womblike couch, facing the fireplace, Kate and Helen overcome the oppression of the house and its spirits. One of the portraits even seems to like them, "a young girl who seemed solitary and forlorn among the rest in the room, who were all middle-aged. For their part they looked amiable, but rather unhappy, as if she had come in and interrupted their conversation."[30] Quick to appreciate any reflection of themselves, Kate and Helen "both grew fond of her, and it seemed, when we went in the last morning on purpose to take leave of her, as if she looked at us imploringly. She was soon afterward boxed up, and now enjoys society after her own heart in Kate's room in Boston."

The discovery of a kindred spirit among the grown-ups foreshadows their deepening sympathy for the late Miss Brandon. She too may have been a "maiden" bound by circumstance and martyred by convention. In an escritoire they uncover a packet of letters, an ivory miniature, and a lock of brown hair. Hidden away with them is a faded twig of wild rose. It may be the remains of Miss Katharine's one romance, her love for a sailor lost at sea and never openly mourned. At first, Kate and Helen intend to read her letters and uncover the stern aunt's secret, but finally they replace the packet carefully, without untying it. And, Helen adds, she's glad they did.

But the two friends do read one set of Miss Katharine's letters, those from "her girl friends written in the boarding-school vacations, and just after she finished school." One packet reveals a tragedy that Kate and Helen can appreciate. Its few letters are bound with black ribbon, and the girlish handwriting notes, " 'My dearest friend, Dolly Mc-Allister, died September 3, 1809, aged eighteen.' " The letters seem to have been opened many times. The one Kate and Helen read begins: "My dear, delightful Kitten: I am quite overjoyed to find my father has business which will force him to go to Deephaven next week, and he kindly says if there be no more rain I may ride with him to see you, for if there is danger of spattering my gown, and he bids me stay at home, I shall go galloping after him and overtake him when it is too late to send me back. I have so much to tell you."[31]

There are a number of interesting things revealed by this letter. First, of course, is the love for "Kitty" which prompts Dolly to defy her father and go "galloping" off, spattering her gown in the process. In these letters Kate and Helen see themselves projected into the past: two little girls, romping and rebellious. Curiously, the date of Dolly McAllister's death echoes Jewett's own birthdate: September 3, 1849. She has Dolly die exactly forty years before her own birth—perhaps an unconscious way of associating herself with this "ancestress."

Helen's curiosity about Kitty—"such a bright, nice girl"—is immediately piqued, and she wonders what their visit was like. But most important, the friends begin to have some sympathy at last for their dead hostess: "Poor Miss Katharine! It made us sad to look over these treasures of her girlhood." Their dawning awareness of Miss Brandon's loneliness, her missed life, begins to transform Kate's memory. In particular she recalls days when her aunt would be pensive and quiet. Although Kate then thought she was cross, she now realizes, with a sense of shame, that her aunt was sad: "She would open that piano and sit there until late. . . . There was one tune which I am sure had a history: there was a sweet wild cadence in it, and she would come back to it again and again."[32] This "sweet wild cadence" may well have expressed all that Miss Katharine had lost. Newly aware of this hidden possibility, Kate now remembers many things that had been meaningless or mysterious to her as a child: "I was afraid of her when I was a little girl, but I think if I had grown up sooner, I should have enjoyed her heartily. It never used to occur to me that she had a spark of tenderness or of sentiment, until just before she was ill, but I have been growing more fond of her ever since."[33] Kate now wonders if perhaps she might have given the older woman more pleasure.

However, their growing sympathy with Miss Brandon comes in large part from making the dead woman over in their own image. In many ways Kate's summer in the Brandon house is an act of appropriation. She discovers the maiden hidden among the middle-aged portraits, then takes her home to Boston. In the final chapter Helen reflects on her affection for Deephaven and its past. Since this passage sums up so much, I will quote it in full:

I was thinking today how many girls have grown up in this house, and that their places have been ours; we have inherited their pleasures, and perhaps have carried on work which they began. We sit in somebody's favorite chair and look out of the windows at the sea, and have our wishes and our hopes and plans just as they did before us. Something of them still lingers where their lives were spent. We are often reminded of our friends who have died; why are we not reminded as surely of strangers in such a house as this,—finding some trace of the lives which were lived among the sights we see and the things we handle, as the incense of many masses lingers in some old cathedral, and one catches the spirit of longing and prayer where so many heavy hearts have brought their burdens and gone away comforted.[34]

In this rather strange description, the house as domestic shrine becomes a cathedral almost morbidly possessed by spirits of the undead. While Helen's tone is reverential and hushed, I cannot help but remember the original "dread" with which she approached the best chamber and her sense of the parlor's "invisible funeral." As in *The Country of the Pointed Firs,* the narrator imaginatively puts herself in the place of another. However, in the later book the narrator actually sits in the living woman's rocking chair and looks out over a real ocean. Here the chair's owner is unnamed, but if it is anyone, it is Miss Katharine, safely dead. Indeed, part of the summer's effort has been not to celebrate the old woman but to exorcise her. Musing on Helen's comments, Kate says, "When I first came here . . . it used to seem very sad to me to find Aunt Katharine's little trinkets lying about the house." Now, however, the spirit of the house has changed: " 'I think the next dweller in this house ought to find a decided atmosphere of contentment,' said [Helen]. 'Have you ever thought that it took us some time to make it your house instead of Miss Brandon's? It used to seem to me that it was still under her management, that she was its mistress; but now it belongs to you, and if I were ever to come back without you I should find you here.' "[35]

The subtext of *Deephaven* is not return to the mother, at least not to Miss Brandon, but combat with the mother's spirit. The only way to win is to turn her into oneself—find the maiden in the mother—or appropriate her space. To merge with the mother is risking demonic possession. In just this way the undifferentiated daughter fears "drowning" in the mother, fears that by identifying with the mother she will *become* the mother and lose her sense of difference, of selfhood. Of course, the issue is complicated by the type of woman Miss Brandon was: her gentility, her coldness, her loneliness. In this formality and restriction Kate and Helen see only death. There is deep ambivalence here. The two heroines protest how much they respect old ways and old women, but throughout the book there resounds a shudder of dread at these moldy rooms and dusty trinkets—and a convulsive, hardly stifled urge to escape.[36]

III

This ambivalence can be clearly seen in the early descriptions of Miss Honora Carew, who is the living supervisor of Miss Brandon's tradition. Before introducing Miss Carew, with her "honorable" name and ways, Helen carefully announces her allegiance to the ladies of this world: "There is something immensely respectable about the gentlewomen of the old school. . . . Their position in society is much like that of the King's Chapel in its busy street in Boston." She admits that approaching a woman like Miss Brandon would not have been easy, but an invitation to take tea with the great lady would have made her proud. And yet the ritualistic and aristocratic associations of the King's Chapel raise some questions. Helen wonders whether the women of her own, more democratic generation "will seem to have such superior elegance of behavior; if we shall receive so much respect and be so much valued."[37]

Whatever their democratic inclinations, for now the two young women find themselves "Miss Brandon's representatives in Deephaven society, and this was no slight responsibility." Part of their duties as young ladies is to be sociable with their class. And so they accept their invitation to tea at Miss Carew's, a woman Helen defends vociferously: "That was a house where one might find the best society, and the most charming manners and good breeding, and if I were asked to tell you what I mean by the word 'lady,' I should ask you to go . . . to call upon Miss Honora Carew."[38] Well. This same Miss Carew comes off less well in another passage. Despite its few disadvantages, such as an uncomfortable distance from the railway, Miss Carew asserts that " 'the tone of Deephaven society had always been very high, and it was very nice there had never been any manufacturing element introduced. She could not feel too grateful, herself, that there was no disagreeable foreign population.' "[39] In other words, Miss Honora is a snob and a xenophobe. When Kate suggests rather timidly that perhaps these modern trends might bring "some pleasant new people . . . into town," Miss Carew seems doubtful: "I am growing old. I should not care to enlarge my acquaintance to any great extent." It seems highly unlikely that even if she were not growing old these newcomers would enter her social circle.

Class is carefully marked in *Deephaven*, as it is in most of Jewett's work, but in this novel I think we can also see a sharp conflict between gender roles and class identification. Kate and Helen know they belong to Miss Brandon's and Miss Carew's class, but belonging demands that they play a role they find restrictive and stultifying. They praise it, but as soon as possible they subvert it. For example, the tea party at Miss Carew's. Helen describes it lyrically. They sit in the garden and talk with the lady and her bachelor brother. As twilight falls, Mr. Dick reads from the psalms to the assembled household: servants, guests, and family. As Kate and Helen walk home in the moonlight, they reflect on the evening's strange sense of having "nothing to do with the present, or the hurry of modern life. I have never heard that psalm since without it bringing back that summer night in Deephaven, the beautiful quaint old room, and Kate and I feeling so young and worldly, by contrast."[40]

It is the small aside, "by contrast," that gives them away. Much of their pleasure in this scene comes not from their merging into the ceremony but from their sense of difference: their youth, their worldliness, their contrast. It is appropriate that this chapter on "Deephaven Society" ends on a distinctively nongenteel note: "When the moon is very bright and other people grow sentimental, we only remember that it is a fine night to catch hake."[41] The sudden appearance of hake might seem inappropriate, but in fact it is through fishing and their connection to the fisherfolk that Kate and Helen shake themselves free of aristocratic doldrums.

Earlier I noted the distinction between classic pastoral and decadent. The classic pastoral involves the "peasant," working-class people of Deephaven. As often as they can, Kate and Helen shed their aristocratic costumes and head for the beach. After all, it was not to take tea that they came to Deephaven but to dig in the sand. The fluidity of their social identity appears in numerous passages. There are the genteel young ladies who take tea with Miss Carew, all the while aware of their contrast. Then there are the little girls playing with their dolls or giggling on the big couch before the fire. But there are other selves as well. Kate and Helen appear almost protean, willing themselves into a myriad of shapes and guises, deliberately refusing definition and playfully exploring the territory, social as well as geographical. There are two aspects to their freedom: their refusal to grow up and their masquerade as working-class women.

Their clothing is a major signifier of class: "When we first went out we were somewhat interesting on account of our clothes, which were of a later pattern than had been adopted generally in Deephaven. We used to take great pleasure in arraying ourselves on high days and holidays, since when we went wandering on shore, or our sailing or rowing, we did not always dress as befitted our position in the town.

Fish scales and blackberry briars so soon disfigure one's clothes."[42] They take a certain delight in this sliding scale of dress. Costumed ambiguously, they make "long expeditions" to the "suburbs of Deephaven." To introduce themselves to the country people, they ask at houses for water. More interested in satisfying their own curiosity, they find it "amusing to see the curiosity we aroused. . . . I must confess that at first we were often naughty enough to wait until we have been severely cross-examined before we gave a definite account of ourselves. Kate was very clever at making unsatisfactory answers when she cared to do so."[43] A wiser Helen now admits that this was insensitive of them, considering how few were these country people's pleasures. Nevertheless, a sense of masquerade is important here, as is a sense of voyeurism.

The two girls come to know "almost all the fisher people at the shore, even old Dinnet."[44] They befriend Captain Sands, who takes them fishing as he had once taken his daughter Louisa (despite his wife's misgivings). With him they crack their clams like old hands and brag that they are not afraid to get their clothing wet in the rain. They gain the confidence of the old sailor, Danny, who tells them how he was nursed back to life by a Peruvian nun, the nearest he had ever come to having a mother, and of his little Kitty, whom he himself had mothered back to life and lost. Kate and Helen even overhear the conversation of the "ancient mariners" who sunned "themselves like turtles on one of the wharves": "Once we were impertinent enough to hide ourselves for a while just round the corner of the warehouse, but we were afraid or ashamed to try it again, though the conversation was inconceivably edifying."[45] Pucklike, the two twenty-four-year-old women "look forward to a certain Saturday as if we had been little schoolboys, for on that day we were to go to a circus at Denby." The circus itself provides a wealth of picturesque scenes: "All the young men of the region had brought their girls, and some of these countless pairs of country lovers we watched a great deal, as they 'kept company' with each other with more or less depth of satisfaction with each other."[46]

In her discussion of Jewett's work, Ann Douglas sees the narrator of *Pointed Firs* as a writer primarily in search of material. I am not sure I would agree with her about that book, but the comment seems fair here. Kate and Helen want the freedom of the working class but see working-class people themselves as picturesque curios.[47] If it were not anachronistic I could imagine them snapping their Polaroids and comparing their shots: "As for our first Sunday at church, it must be in vain to ask you to imagine our delight when we heard the tuning of a bass viol in the gallery just before the service. We pressed each other's hands most tenderly, looked up at the singers' seats, and then trusted ourselves to look at each other. It was more than we had hoped for."[48] This is Helen as the young artist. Her vocation is not quite defined, but she is busily collecting settings and characters, getting ready to write once winter comes. Kate and Helen look at each other with the consciousness of their "difference" and the "value" of the event—a value only an outsider could appreciate. Their friendship contributes both to their distance from the scene and to their consciousness of that distance. At the same time their friendship insulates them from loneliness and vulnerability.

Kate and Helen seem to hold this attitude toward upper and working class alike. However, they acknowledge their permanent tie—the tie of blood and kin—to the aristocrats. Their attempts to appropriate the freedom of the working class, without a similar loyalty, shows their behavior in a less pleasant light. I have in mind a strange masquerade from "The Brandon House and the Lighthouse." We have seen how morbid the Brandon house is and how dreary Miss Katharine's life had been there. The chapter's second half takes us out of the decadent pastoral into the classic: to the lighthouse and the motherly Mrs. Kew.

Here life is free and easy. On this particular day Kate is dressed "in a costume we both frequently wore, of gray skirts and blue sailor jacket, and her boots [are] much worse for wear." Not only has she discarded the restrictive finery of genteel womanhood, but "the celebrated Lancaster complexion [is] rather darkened by the sun."[49] This is not the lily-white skin of the leisured lady. In fact, Kate and Helen have spent the afternoon fishing and are cozily listening to Mrs. Kew spin tales when a boatload of tourists shows up to see the lighthouse. Since Mrs. Kew has lamed herself temporarily, Kate offers to lead the way up the steep stairs. Mrs. Kew wants to know what questions the visitors ask, and on this pretext Helen follows the party a few minutes later, apparently hiding herself on the stairs. The conversation she overhears indicates that Kate is having some quiet fun at the expense of the young women from Boston:

> "Don't you get tired staying here?"
> "No, indeed!" said Kate.
> "Is that your sister downstairs!"
> "No, I have no sister."
> "I should think you would wish she was. Aren't you ever lonesome?"
> "Everybody is, sometimes," said Kate.
> "But it's such a lonesome place!"[50]

Although Kate does not lie outright to these shopgirls, she certainly lies by omission. She pretends to be the lighthouse keeper's daughter and so gains the attention and sympathy of the naive city girls. She appears strong and brave, a self-sufficient maid of the seas, perhaps a precursor of "poor Joanna." The motive for the deception is not clear, but the fib reveals a recurring theme of Jewett's work: the genteel woman's adoption by a peasant family. Kate cannot resist playing a role that comes so easily to her imagination.

And apparently she plays it very well. The visitors offer to pay her for showing them around, an offer Kate "pleasantly" refuses. Then as Kate closes the doors, one of the girls stays behind with her.

You're real good to show us the things. I guess you'll think I'm silly, but I do like you ever so much! I wish you would come to Boston. I'm in a real nice store . . . and they will want new saleswomen in October. Perhaps you could board with me. I've got a real comfortable room, and I suppose I might have more things, for I get good pay; but I like to send money home to mother. . . . If you will tell me what your name is, I'll find out for certain about the place, and write you. My name's Mary Wendell.[51]

Although from a different class, Mary Wendell lives by values that Kate and Helen recognize readily. She is reaching down to a girl poorer than herself and offering both friendship and city life. But she *is* of a different class:

I knew by Kate's voice that this had touched her. "You are very kind; thank you heartily," said she; "but I cannot go and work with you. I should like to know more about you. I live in Boston too; my friend and I are staying over in Deephaven for the summer only." And she held out her hand to the girl, whose face had changed from its first expression of earnest good humor to a very startled one; and when she noticed Kate's hand, and a ring of hers, which had been turned around, she looked really frightened.[52]

It might seem polite for Kate now to apologize for encouraging the visitor's misconception, but this is not what happens. Instead, the awed shopgirl begs Kate's pardon:

"Oh, will you please excuse me?" said she, blushing. "I ought to have known better; but you showed us around so willing, and I never thought of your not living here. I didn't mean to be rude."

"Of course you did not, and you were not. I am very glad you said it, and glad that you like me" said Kate; and just then the party called the girl and she hurried away, and I joined Kate. "Then you heard it all. That was worth having!" said she. "She was such an honest little soul, and I mean to look for her when I get home."[53]

In what way was the shopgirl's sympathy and embarrassment something "worth having"? Here again the two friends seem to be collecting specimens for study, material for the picturesque sketches to come. I find Mary Wendell's fright at the sight of Kate's ring an almost sinister touch. The shopgirl has transgressed class lines by speaking familiarly to a social superior. And even though the "lady" was not dressed like one, even though her ring was turned around, she is still sacred. Kate, of course, generously overlooks any rudeness on Mary Wendell's part but never acknowledges her own exploitation of the other young woman's sympathy and gullibility. There may also be an echo here of the mythic scene that Kate later describes to Helen: the unveiling of Demeter before Metaneira. Like Demeter, Kate has hidden her "true" stature under the costume of a peasant; when Demeter reveals her power, Metaneira is frightened and awed. But Kate's power is only her money and her class, not her spirituality. Unfortunately, these tend to be confused in this book.

IV

And here I believe we come to the unspoken center around which these two heroines travel. While they resist the genteel roles that the ancestress offers them, they are also reluctant to give up their class prerogatives. They escape from Miss Carew's tea party to Mrs. Kew's lighthouse, but the role as lighthouse keeper's daughter is only a masquerade after all. There is still the ring, and the winter in Boston. The tan will fade. They have no intention of committing themselves to a working woman's life. Nevertheless, the two young women are still on a bewildered quest for the mother they are determined to resist. On their progress through Deephaven's domestic spaces and pastoral landscapes they encounter a confusing series of maternal figures, many of them grotesque, several of them indistinguishable. There is not only Miss Brandon but also Miss Carew and Miss Chauncy, not only Mrs. Kew but also Mrs. Patton and Mrs. Dockum. (Significantly, none of the "ladies" has ever married, whereas all the working-class women have.) Insulated by their friendship, Kate and Helen do not find communion in the world they explore. They remain voyeurs, almost exploitive, rather than becoming fully committed and initiated, truly adopted members of the society to which they have "returned." At times it seems almost as if they were moving through a funhouse where fragments of their own personalities were reflected back at them in distorted ways. Only in each other can they see the "true" reflection.

The central conflict, not very successfully resolved, is the heroines' problematic fear of the aristocratic, genteel, feminine role—as well as the adult women who embody that role. The second, closely related conflict is their problematic attraction to the free "enfranchised" countrywomen like Mrs. Kew. These women have a native dignity and chthonic vitality; however, according to the Victorian cult of true womanhood, they are devalued by their earthiness and manual labor, as well as by their implied sexuality. Thus, although the multiple images of women do have a funhouse effect, they have a symbolic logic. First the "mothers" may be divided by class: working women and ladies. At the extremes of the cultural categories are the light and dark heroines: virgin and whore. These figures are represented more subtly here by Miss Chauncy, the mad angel in the house, and Mrs. Bonny, the dirty witch of the woods. Mediating between them we have figures of the pastoral center. Miss Carew and Mrs. Kew offer more moderate examples of the qualities exaggerated in Miss Chauncy and Mrs. Bonny. Thus, Mrs. Kew represents the pastoral countrywoman of the classic mode, and Miss Carew, whose name echoes Mrs. Kew's, is her aristocratic counterpart, the priestess of the decadent pastoral society.

The interaction of the heroines with these various "mothers" may be deciphered using the code articulated in the myth that Kate herself retells. As we saw earlier, that passage from the Homeric hymn to Demeter defined mortal life as an intermediate state. Humanity is partially raw (material nature) and partially cooked (immortal spirit). The proportion of these qualities—earth and spirit, raw and cooked—defines the gradations of feminine imagery: landscapes, houses, and the women themselves. Finally, this code expresses the relationship between the maternal figures and our heroines. It does so through the human equivalent of Demeter's own ritual: the domestic ceremony of preparing, serving, and sharing food. The quality of food each woman offers—its mode of service and state of transformation (how raw? how cooked?)—is correlated with the quality of the woman herself, particularly with her suitability as a "mother" for Helen and Kate.

The feminine mysteries are mysteries of transformation: from raw blood to infant, from unsocialized infant to cultured human being, from human being to heavenly spirit. And while they resist possession by the Terrible Mother of the primary feminine, Kate and Helen need the transformative feminine: the mother who holds the secret of growth and change. In their search for her, the two heroines, rather like Goldilocks, try the porridge of every woman in Deephaven. The dynamics of their quest can best be seen by looking at the extremes—Mrs. Bonny and Miss Chauncy—just as Goldilocks knew which porridge was right only after finding one too hot and the other too cold.

Now the plot of their quest for the transformative mother parallels, as the Demeter–Persephone myth itself does, the quest for insight into the relationship between death and life. The Eleusinian Mysteries resolve in one revelation both problems: the daughter's difference from/identity with the mother and the living's difference from/identity with the dead. In the Eleusinian vision of the seed of corn there is continuity within change, a mystical merging without loss of individuality.

Kate and Helen retell the Demeter–Persephone myth at the close of Chapter 9, "Cunner-Fishing." In the following chapters Kate and Helen penetrate deeper into the pastoral/chthonic world, confronting the death that is in Arcadia, then the spiritual continuity that transcends the cycles of birth and death. The journey has three parts. The first is their visit to Mrs. Bonny, the woman on the boundary of nature and culture. The second is their observation of a rural funeral and sobering insight into human immanence. The third is their encounter with Miss Chauncy and the revelation of a spirit that escapes physical decay. In Miss Chauncy's ruined mansion Kate confronts her own identity within the great chain of feminine being. After that there is little to do but pack for home.

V

The perfect pastoral mediation is honey, which is both raw and cooked at once, an anomalous and sacred blending of nature and spirit. Its true incarnation is Mrs. Todd, fully woman and fully divine. In Mrs. Bonny, however, the recipe has gone askew, and the result is a delightful grotesque: too much nature, not enough spirit. On the highest hill in the region, she lives on the very boundary of Deephaven. However, she fails to mediate between nature and culture, which are jumbled in strange and humorous juxtapositions wherever she goes. Earlier I described her house, filled with straggling chickens, and her horse, who sports one of his mistress's cast-off bonnets. Mrs. Bonny herself appears in a ludicrous assemblage of costumes:

a man's coat, cut off so that it made an odd short jacket, and a pair of men's boots much the worse for wear; also, some short skirts, beside two or three aprons, the inner one being a dress apron, as she took off the outer ones, and threw them into a corner; and on her head was a tight cap, with strings to tie under her chin. I thought it was a nightcap, and that she had forgotten to take it off, and dreaded her mortification if she should suddenly have become conscious of it; but I need not have troubled myself, for while we were with her she pulled it on and tied it tighter, as if she considered it ornamental.[54]

While Kate and Helen masquerade successfully in their various costumes, Mrs. Bonny subverts the entire sartorial code. She piles on her bits of information indiscriminately, subverting all of their cultural meanings and purposes. Men's coats and boots, domestic aprons, nightcaps,—are all promiscuously thrown together in a chaotic *bricolage* whose only significance is Mrs. Bonny herself: unique and subversive, virtually savage. Helen sees "something so wild and unconventional about Mrs. Bonny that it was like talking with a good-natured Indian. We used to carry her offerings of tobacco, for she was a great smoker and advised us to try it." Like other pastoral figures, she is a part of the Deephaven landscape. (As Mrs. Patton, for one, explains, "I ain't likely to move away from Deephaven, after I've held by the place so long. I've got as many roots as the big ellum.") And like the "savages" themselves, Mrs. Bonny "knew all the herbs and trees and the harmless wild creatures who lived among them, by heart; and she had an amazing store of tradition and superstition, which made her so entertaining to us."[55]

But an unconventional woman close to nature risks getting dirty. Culture purifies nature and cleanses the feminine of pollution. Domesticity not only mediates between nature and culture but transforms one into the other. In Mrs. Bonny's hands this process is subverted, and the result is not order but anarchy and ambiguity. Mrs. Bonny's cooking is particularly suspect. Although she used to ride down into Deephaven on her little black horse to sell berries and eggs, homemade butter and choke pears preserved in molasses, her reputation for negligent housekeeping preceded her: "None of the wise women of the town would touch her butter especially, so it was always a joke when she coaxed a new resident or a strange shipmaster into buying her wares."[56]

Our two Goldilocks know enough not to expect or accept a cooked meal from Mrs. Bonny. Kate does remember once gathering wild berries with her as a child—this type of food is especially appropriate because no transformation is involved before eating. Now, however, they would like a drink of water from her spring: again the food itself is raw and unmediated. However, they would also like a tumbler to drink from, and they turn to their disorganized hostess with the request. At first Mrs. Bonny is not so sure she can find her glass. Watching her clump onto a rickety chair and rummage about in her cupboard over the fireplace, Helen is afraid that Mrs. Bonny will tumble in and "disappear altogether." But at last she returns with her domestic treasures, which she sets on the mantelpiece or casually drops on the floor: "There were bunches of dried herbs, a tin horn, a lump of tallow in a broken plate, a newspaper, and an old boot, with a number of turkey wings tied together, several bottles, and a steel trap, and finally, such a tumbler! which she produced with triumph, before stepping down."[57] Obviously, we are a long way from Miss Brandon's "power of china" and her well-dusted cupboards scented with ancient spice cake. Not only has the tumbler been embedded in chaos, but chaos is embedded in it. When she empties it onto the table, out comes "a mixture of old buttons and squash seeds, beside a lump of beeswax which she said she had lost, and now pocketed with satisfaction. She wiped the tumbler on her apron and handed it to Kate, but we were not so thirsty as we had been."[58] From such a dirty vessel Kate and Helen cannot drink, no matter how pure the water.

Raw, rooted in nature, and virtually defined by it, Mrs. Bonny seems almost oblivious to the transcendent vision of Christianity. She claims to be a practicing Calvinist, but the ground of her faith is amusingly revealed in her reminiscences of the old-time preachers: " 'Parson Reid, he's a worthy creatur', but he never seems to have nothin' to say about foreordination and them p'ints. Old Parson Padelford was the man! I used to set under his preachin' a good deal; I had an aunt living down to East Parish. He'd get you worked up, and he'd shut the Bible and preach the hair off your head. . . . Couldn't understand more nor a quarter part what he said,' said Mrs. Bonny admiringly."[59] As the girls are about to leave with their guide, the Rev. Mr. Lorimer, they stop a moment to look at the view from Mrs. Bonny's doorstep. Pleased by their appreciation, Mrs. Bonny describes the sunrise for them:

"Why the sun is all yaller and red, and them low lands topped with fog! Yes, it's nice weather, good growin' weather, this week. Corn and all the rest of the trade looks first-rate. I call it a forrard season. It's just such weather we read of, ain't it?"

"I don't remember where, just at this moment," said Mr. Lorimer.

"Why, in the almanac, bless ye!" said she, with a tone of pity in her grum [sic] voice; could it be he didn't know,—the Deephaven minister![60]

Practical, down-to-earth Mrs. Bonny knows the true good book is the almanac; nature's hieroglyphics spell first-rate trade. While Helen's treatment of Mrs. Bonny is affectionate and very funny, it would be hard to imagine the kind of love and communion between them that grows up between Mrs. Todd and her summer visitor. Mrs. Bonny is a wonderful sketch for the developing artist but not a spiritual mother for the developing daughter.

VI

If the visit with Mrs. Bonny brings us to the edge of culture, the following chapter, "In Shadow," shows us death on the other side. Mrs. Bonny's comical messes demonstrate that nature's design is to subvert design, but in this chapter we have the hint of a "design of darkness to appall." Mrs. Bonny's food may carry a taint, the seed of decay hidden in all mortal things. Now Helen and Kate see that seed bloom. They are traveling through the landscape of the Terrible Mother. The land resists cultivation and refuses its dependents shelter. The people are poor. Those who are ambitious leave for the city and factories.

Those who stay out of loyalty for their place—a sense of "roots"—are not rewarded: "It is all very well to say that they knew nothing better, that it was the only life of which they knew anything; there was too often a look of disappointment of their faces."[61] Even the pastoral's sliding scale will not make the sum come out right. These people are deprived by any standard. On the older ones Kate and Helen notice a "hard look, as if they had always to be on the alert and must fight for their place in the world. One could forgive and pity their petty sharpness, which showed itself in trifling bargains, when one understood how much a single dollar seemed where dollars came so rarely."[62] Closeness to nature cannot sweeten these lives or fill with spirituality people whose physical lives are so impoverished. Kate and Helen see their own privilege reflected in the young women they meet: "We used to pity the young girls so much. It was plain that those who knew how much easier and pleasanter our lives were could not help envying us."[63]

Traveling deeper into this territory, they find something perhaps more dreadful than death: despair. Earlier in the summer they had met a family struggling like the others but in even more desperate circumstances. The husband's health was failing. Once he was a boat builder; now there was no demand for his skill. The family's only hope was the oldest son, gone to Boston to work in a box shop. After the father had taken care of their horses, Kate and Helen gave him more money for his services than he asked. The gesture touched him deeply:

"I hope ye may never know what it is to earn every dollar as hard as I have. . . . I've done the best I could," said the man, with the tears coming into his eyes. . . . "I'm willin' and my woman is, but everything seems to have been ag'in' us; we never seem to get forehanded. It looks sometimes as if the Lord had forgot us, but my woman never wants me to say that; she says He ain't, and that we might be worse off,—but I don't know."[64]

As the summer progresses, the girls think back on this man and his impoverished family. They intend to call again, but something or other always interferes, and it is not until late October that they return to the farmhouse up in the rocky hills. Both husband and wife are dead. They have returned only in time for the man's funeral.

They encounter a country couple who tell Kate and Helen the story. The wife died of a fever in early August. And the husband, without her support and faith, turned quickly to drink. This couple have come for the funeral and for two of the children; the rest will be boarded with another family nearby. The wife of the couple is the dead man's half-sister, but she begrudges the burden two children will lay on her. While her husband timidly urges that perhaps the children have some redeeming qualities, she reveals a streak of resentment, perhaps even cruelty: "'I can't stand to hear men folks talking on what they don't know nothing about,' said she. 'The ways of Providence is dreadful myster'ous,' she went on with a whine. . . . 'We've had a hard row, and we've just our own children off our hands and able to do for themselves, and now here are these two to be fetched up.'"[65] Mothering without money is "a hard row." Whatever is given to the children must be taken away from the parent, who becomes the cruel stepmother of fairy tales.

Later Kate and Helen reflect on the situation compassionately, aware of how little control any of these people have over their fate. They try to think of what help they could give the orphaned children: "we were afraid they would be told so many times that it was lucky they did not have to go to the poorhouse." However, they are able to pity the hard-pressed Marthy "in spite of her bitterness": "Poor soul! She looked like a person to whom nobody had ever been very kind, and for whom life had no pleasures." Kate and Helen cannot help but see the injustice: "I suppose what would be prosperity to him [the dead man] would be miserably insufficient for some other people." The two friends begin to have an uncomfortable sense of their own guilt: "we wished we had come again soon, for we might have helped them so much more if we had only known."[66] And they realize with a pang how heavily this irrevocable shadow will fall across the innocent children left behind: "'What a pitiful ending it is,' said Kate. 'Do you realize the family is broken up, and the children are to be half strangers to each other? Did you not notice that they seemed very fond of each other when we saw them in the summer? There was not half the roughness and apparent carelessness of one another which one so often sees in the country.'"[67] But the central lesson stands out clearly to them: the despair of the husband who had lost control of his life: "The thoughts of winter, and of the little children, and of the struggles he had already come through against poverty and disappointment were terrible thoughts; and like a boat adrift at sea, the waves of his misery brought him against the rocks, and his simple life was wrecked."[68]

At this moment Kate and Helen look at a very dark riddle indeed, a shadow wiser heads than theirs have been unable to pierce. Perhaps they should not be blamed for turning away, to answers they can understand. Kate averts her gaze from the dead man's tragedy and trains it on the conventional Christian solution. She cannot consider any earthly action that might have made his world more just, but there is another way:

How seldom life in this world seems to be a success! Among rich or poor only here and there one touches satisfaction, though the one who seems to have made an utter failure may really be the greater conqueror. And, Helen, I find that I understand better and better how unsatisfactory, how purposeless and disastrous, any life must be which is not a Christian life? It is like being always in the dark, and wandering one knows not where, if one is not learning more and more what it is to have a friendship with God.[69]

And so we are directed, finally, away from economics and back to faith. This man suffered most, perhaps, because he lost his faith. In the dark, overwhelmed by the "waves" of his misery, he was broken on the rocks and drowned. This is truly the world of the shadowy Fates: nature as the cruel stepmother who withholds her love without reason and devours her children as casually as she bears them. Only otherworldly faith can bring light to this darkness and guide the way out of the labyrinth.

Since the funeral is to be that day, Kate and Helen consider attending it, but then, in a reversal of their usual practice, decide to forgo: "We have no right there, and it would seem as if we were merely curious, and were afraid our presence would make the people ill at ease, the minister especially. It would be an intrusion." Instead, they watch the funeral procession from a nearby hillside: "A strange shadow had fallen over everything." As they see the few mourners walking in line with the pastor, the two girls sense "something piteous about this. . . . 'He's gone, ain't he?' said someone near us. That was it,—*gone*." Now the landscape seems suspended, waiting: "It was like a November day, for the air felt cold and bleak. There were some great sea fowl high in the air, fighting their way toward the sea against the wind, giving now and then a wild, far-off ringing cry."[70] The funeral procession, the landscape, the lost and despairing family, all coalesce in a single moment of recognition:

To Kate and me there came a sudden consciousness of the mystery and inevitableness of death; it was not fear, thank God! but a thought of how certain it was that some day it would be mystery to us no longer. And there was a thought, too, of the limitation of this present life; we were waiting, in company with the people, the great sea, and the rocks and fields themselves, on this side the boundary. We knew just how close to this familiar, everyday world might be the other, which at times before had seemed so far away, out of reach of even our thoughts, beyond the distant stars.[71]

This evocative passage shows again Jewett's skill with landscape description. What is particularly curious is the separation of this world from the other world "beyond the boundary." There is a good deal of Professor Theophilus Parsons's Swedenborgian philosophy here but also a sense that somehow spirit has forsaken these fields and rocks and waves, which all must *wait* to be rewarded after death. Put your faith not in this world but in the world to come. The message is reiterated even more strongly in the next chapter, "Miss Chauncy."

VII

After Kate and Helen step over the boards put up like pasture bars before the apparently abandoned Chauncy mansion, they encounter an apparition of the past: "On the threshold there stood a stately old woman who looked surprised at the sight of us. . . . She was dressed in a rusty black satin gown, with a scant, short skirt and huge sleeves; on her head was a great black bonnet with a high crown and close brim."[72] The girls' first impulse is to run, but after a breathless moment both sides recover their wits. Kate and Helen, anxious to hide their original intention, quickly ask directions back to Deephaven.

Once home, they ask Miss Honora Carew for Miss Chauncy's story. The Chauncys were a highly educated, very wealthy shipping family, "utterly ruined at the time of the embargo." Local rumor had it that Miss Chauncy's father had broken a promise to a sailor, who cursed the entire family. Subsequent events bear out the rumor. Mr. Chauncy became partially insane. Then, according to Miss Carew, one of Sally Chauncy's brothers, a naval officer, young and handsome, "asked her one day if she could get on without him, and she said yes, thinking he meant to go back to sea; but in a few minutes she heard the noise of a pistol in his room, and hurried in to find him lying dead on the floor."[73] Yet another brother went mad and was "chained for years in one of the upper chambers, a dangerous prisoner."

Considering the burden of her history, it is hardly surprising that Miss Sally is partly demented herself. However, her insanity descended in two phases. As a fairly young woman, the only survivor in her family, she lost her reason and was hospitalized. To pay her keep, her guardian sold all of the contents of the house: furniture, china, carpets, portraits, all of the accumulated wealth that still enriches the Brandon house. No one expected Sally Chauncy to recover, but one spring day, like Persephone released from Hades, Miss Chauncy "without a thought of what was awaiting her, ran eagerly into her home. It was a terrible shock, and she never has recovered from it."[74]

As the house gently decays around her, Miss Chauncy lives on, "harmless" but mad. Miss Carew comments that she seems to be contented there, "and does not realize her troubles; though she lives mostly in the past, and has little idea of the present." Sensing Kate and Helen's curiosity, Miss Carew suggests that she give them some delicacies and a message to carry by way of introduction: "I hope she will be talkative, for I am sure you would enjoy her."[75] In just a few days Kate and Helen are on their way to East Parish with their basket.

As they wait with the maid in the entry, their second meeting with Miss Chauncy confirms her otherworldliness: "'Sophia,' said she, 'where are the gentry waiting?' And just then she came in sight round the turn of the staircase. She wore the same great black bonnet and satin gown, and looked more old-fashioned and ghostly than before. She was not tall, but very erect, in spite of her great age, and her eyes seemed to 'look through you' in an uncanny way."[76] Helen comments that she had "seen few more elegant women. . . . Thoroughly at her ease, she had the manner of a lady of the olden times, using the quaint fashion of speech which had been taught in her girlhood." The epitome of early Victorian gentility, Miss Chauncy's "delicately shaped" hands testify to her leisure, however impoverished, "and she folded them in her lap, as no doubt she had learned to do at boarding school so many years before."[77]

As they make polite conversation, Miss Chauncy's bewilderment becomes apparent. She asks after the local gentry—the Carews, Mr. Lorimer, and Kate's own aunt, Miss Brandon. When informed of that lady's death, she will have none of it: "Ah, they say every one is 'dead,' nowadays. I do not comprehend the silly idea!" Rather than accept its finality, she prefers to think death merely a social "excuse": "She could come to me if she chose, but she always was a ceremonious body, and I go abroad but seldom now; so perhaps she waits my visit."[78] Kate and Helen do their best to play along when the ancient lady asks about old Deephaven acquaintances and the Boston families of her youth: "I think every one of whom she spoke was dead, but we assured her that they were all well and prosperous, and we hoped we told the truth."[79]

Before looking at Miss Chauncy's relationship to Kate and Helen, I would like to place her within the pastoral framework. Earlier I described her house as an example of the decadent pastoral. Its decay is physically "cooking" cultural forms back to their natural components. The sagging floors, cobwebbed ceilings, and molding walls testify to the house's slow degeneration. However, Miss Chauncy herself manages to escape the viscous downward tide. To her mad eyes the house remains eternally whole and herself eternally young. She is "incapable of comparing the end of her life with the beginning," and as she paces back and forth on her ruined garden terrace, "the ranks of lilies and the conserve roses were still in bloom for her."[80]

Kate and Helen learn of Miss Chauncy's death early the following winter. Too frail to care for herself, and the house uninhabitable, she had been boarded out in the town. But Miss Chauncy would not allow herself to be separated from her home. Defiant, she ran away from her caretakers, broke into her house through the cellar, "where she had to wade through half-frozen water, and then went upstairs, where she seated herself at a window and called joyfully to the people who went by, asking them to come see her, as she had got home again."[81] During the fatal illness that follows, Miss Chauncy "said over and over again how good God had always been to her." Unlike the impoverished man who drank himself to death up in the hill country, Miss Chauncy does not give in to despair. While he "broke up" on the rocks and drowned, she determinedly, if dementedly, wades through the rising waters and returns to her house joyful. She affirms God's goodness and denies the reality of her suffering. But the price is her sanity and perhaps her physical life. Moreover, denial of the "shadow" in life is also the denial of history. Miss Chauncy has no true memory, which plays such an important role in the chain of "love and dependence" that links the women in *Pointed Firs*. There communion is forged through the sharing of loss and sorrow. This consolation Miss Chauncy does not have. She has the promise of the world to come, but she has lost her bearings in this one:

Mr. Lorimer spoke of her simple goodness, and told us that though she had no other sense of time, and hardly knew if it were summer or winter, she was sure when Sunday came. . . . "She may be a lesson to us," added the old minister reverently, "for, though bewildered in mind, bereft of riches and friends and all that makes this world dear to many of us, she was still steadfast in her simple faith, and was never heard to complain of any of the burdens which God had given her."[82]

The revelation of Miss Chauncy's simple faith comes earlier in the chapter, in a scene like many others in Jewett's fiction:

I remember, just now, as I write, one summer afternoon when Kate and I had lingered later than usual, and we sat in the upper room looking out on the river and the shore beyond, where the light had begun to grow golden as the day drew near sunset. Miss Sally had opened the great book [her well-worn Bible] at random and read slowly, "In my Father's house are many mansions"; then, looking off for a moment at a leaf which had drifted in the window recess, she repeated it: "In my Father's house are many mansions; if it were not so, I would have told you." Then she went on slowly to the end of the chapter, and . . . she fell into a reverie, and the tears came to our eyes as we watched her look of perfect content. Through all her clouded years the promises of God had been her only certainty.[83]

Sally Chauncy's true mansion is neither the rotting hulk that entombs her nor the pristine building of her childhood but the heavenly mansion of her Father. Her body seems physically bound within the earthly house that she cannot leave. Although the image may be morbid, she is a mad angel in the house, a root-bound saint whose roots and the pot that binds them are both rotting away. But as decay draws both house and the lady down toward death, Miss Chauncy's spirit is escaping upward. If the classic pastoral reveals the fusion of matter and spirit, the decadent pastoral shows them separating. Earth returns to earth and spirit to spirit. Thus, as the cultural forms that enclose her dissolve, Miss Chauncy's faith purifies her, even perfects her. Unlike Demophoon, who never was completely purified, immortal, Miss Chauncy will be. Her mortality utterly consumed in the slow fire of decay, her spirit will escape like a puff of smoke from the cinders. Even now she cannot recognize the signs of immanence: death, history, time itself, all are foreign to her. She cannot grasp the seasonal cycles; Sunday is the only day she recognizes. If Mrs. Bonny, nearly savage, is too close to nature, Miss Chauncy, nearly angelic, is too far away. Mrs. Bonny's dishes are too dirty: her food is polluted. Miss Chauncy's dishes, however, are imaginary: her food is ethereal. Thus, Miss Carew warns Kate and Helen not to accept an invitation to luncheon; there is not enough for her to share. The invitation, at any rate, would not be for a meal in this world but in *illo tempore,* that magical past where Miss Chauncy dwells alone.

However, there is an Eleusinian moment of recognition here. Soon after Kate and Helen introduce themselves to Miss Chauncy and offer their message from Miss Carew as credentials, "Something happened which touched us both inexpressibly: she sat for some time watching Kate with a bewildered look, which at last faded away, a smile coming in its place. 'I think you are like my mother,' she said, 'did any one ever say to you that you are like my mother?'"[84] This moment is clearly structured on that Eleusinian recognition of the "mother" in the "daughter." As Carl Jung described the mystery, "every mother contains her daughter in herself and every daughter her mother, and . . . every woman extends backwards into her mother and forwards into her daughter."[85] The conscious recognition of these ties results in the initiate's "feeling that her life is spread out over generations—the first step toward the immediate experience and conviction of being outside time, which brings with it a feeling of *immortality*." As I have pointed out earlier, this sense of immortality is *not* otherworldly but remains grounded, incarnated. The Eleusinian epiphany restores "the lives of her ancestors who, through the bridge of the momentary individual, pass down into the generation of the future." However, the individual is not lost in this process but given meaning and place; she is "rescued from her isolation and restored to wholeness."[86]

The dynamics of the Demeter–Persephone myth illuminate the Eleusinian moment as it appears in *Deephaven*. Persephone's separation from the mother and marriage to the father/lover are central to the mystery. For now she returns to her mother, carrying the torch of consciousness, the knowledge of her difference. Persephone is greater than Demeter alone because she possesses awareness acquired through separation, as well as love affirmed through return. However, patriarchy prevents the angel in the house from developing a fully differentiated ego. Hence, the "male" remains an authoritative father and/or frightening rapist. The return to the mother becomes a kind of regression to childhood. The genteel Persephone remains eternally the Maiden; she never develops into her full stature as goddess greater than Demeter and Hades themselves.[87]

I believe that we see something of this problem in Miss Chauncy. Her Eleusinian recognition is presented as a deeply moving epiphany; however, it seems as much madness as insight. Coming closer to Kate Lancaster, whom she has never seen before, Miss Chauncy scrutinizes her carefully for the resemblance to the lost mother:

"Will you let me see your forehead? Yes; and your hair is only a little darker." Kate had risen when Miss Chauncy did, and they stood side by side. There was a tone in the old lady's voice which brought tears to my eyes. She stood there some minutes looking at Kate. I wonder what her thoughts were. There was a kinship it seemed to me, not of blood, only that they were of the same stamp and rank: Miss Chauncy of the old generation and Kate Lancaster of the new.[88]

In most of Jewett's work, when there is this type of recognition, it is not between actual kin but between women who have adopted each other. The roles of mother and daughter were not purely biological but social and emotional, finally spiritual. Here we see this pattern again. However, the recognition is based on physical resemblance and, more important, on "stamp and rank." Kate is Miss Brandon's representative, the latest avatar of her class. At this moment generations of *ladies* are being celebrated: the reproduction of aristocratic womanhood. But something is awry: "Miss Chauncy turned to me, saying, 'Look up at the portrait and you will see the likeness too, I think.' But when she turned and saw the bare wainscoting of the room, she looked puzzled and the bright flash which had lighted up her face was gone in an instant, and she sat down again in her window seat; but we were glad she had forgotten."[89] The portrait of Miss Chauncy's own mother is gone. In fact, the society that gave Miss Chauncy her identity and place has disappeared.

Throughout their acquaintance with her, Miss Chauncy persists in confusing Kate with Katharine Brandon and talks as if the dead were alive and well. In her perception of the ancestress in the descendant we might have another example of Eleusinian insight. However, the crucial sense of separation is lacking. Persephone's merging with the mother is a paradoxical instance of identity within difference. In the great chain of being, the initiate is to be rescued from isolation and placed within the stream of generations but is also to find her place there, as herself. The boundaries of the individual are to become flexible, permeable, but they are not to disappear. However, Miss Chauncy's insight is bewildered, mad; the boundaries are not flexible but confused. She recognizes Kate *only* insofar as Kate represents her class but not as Kate exists individually, in her difference. Miss Chauncy's gaze is "uncanny"; her eyes seem to "look through you."

In this example the return to the mother is regressive, a loss of individual identity and consciousness. Thus, Miss Chauncy denies her age and her suffering. She is still the Maiden and will be eternally. She cannot grow up. Far from offering herself as a mother to her visitors, she looks for her own mother in them. It is they who bring her food. When Kate and Helen are brought up to her bedroom, the result is not the wonderful scene of sympathy and adoption that unfolds on Green Island. Helen's narration reveals her own mixed motives clearly. After lamenting the sorry collection of old furniture, she focuses on one "tall, handsome chest of drawers, which I should have liked much to ransack. The brass handles and trimming were blackened, and the wood looked like ebony." Symbol of the Chauncys' mysterious history, this chest beckons Helen "to climb up" on it like a child and peer into its secrets: "it seemed to me I could at once put my hand on a package of 'papers relating to the embargo.'"[90]

Reading this passage, I cannot help recalling Henry James's story "The Aspern Papers." Miss Chauncy is indeed the "visitable past," and Helen's motives are not entirely pure, as witnessed by her desire to "ransack." The sense that the connection between hostess and guests is not full communion is reinforced by the description of Miss Chauncy reading from her Bible. In "The Town Poor," "The Christmas Ghosts," or *Pointed Firs,* women gather together in a bedroom, flooded by golden light and overlooking a pastoral landscape. However, Miss Chauncy is not thinking of her guests but musing on the world to come. She is communing with her Father in heaven, who has prepared his mansion for her. Forgotten, the girls watch her reverie. They are moved, but hers is a moment they cannot share.

Miss Chauncy's faith is directly connected to this failure. She is an adjunct to the decayed patriarchy. As an angel in the house, she has embraced the restriction of her freedom necessary to her gentility. Root-bound, she fails when her house fails. And her house must fail when the patriarchal structure supporting it fails. She cannot work; she is too weak to stand alone. As the men in her family are destroyed, she must stand by and watch. Indeed, her one admission of self-sufficiency is brutally punished by her brother's suicide. Miss Chauncy's denial of suffering is intrinsically related to her utter unfitness to survive inde-pendently. If her own father cannot provide the house in which she makes sense, then her heavenly father must provide.

Miss Chauncy's religion is the patriarchal, otherworldly spiritualism described by Bachofen. Unlike Mrs. Bonny she has no root in the earth; she has no chthonic vitality. The pastoral wisdom of Mrs. Todd and of Persephone herself sees identity in difference but also life within death. The cycles of the seasons, like the cycles of the generations, absorb and transform death without denying it. It is a dark passage to a deeper wisdom. However, Miss Chauncy can no longer tell summer from winter, nor death from life. Kate and Helen revere this faith, which they describe as Miss Chauncy's only "sanity." To me, however, it looks like more of the same madness. In a sense Miss Chauncy is the Maid of Orleans prefigured in the Brandon house portrait. Tied to her house, she is condemned to destruction along with it. A martyr to the lost cause of her genteel society, finally purged of physicality, she awaits her reward from the Father above.

VIII

Earlier I remarked that Kate and Helen were on a bewildered quest for the mother. Clearly, Miss Chauncy is no more the right candidate than Miss Bonny. Neither offers her guests the proper food; in neither case is there true communion. When Kate and Helen turn away from the extremes toward the pastoral center, there is more possibility for this communion. They take tea with Honora Carew and are treated to enormous savory meals by Mrs. Kew. Mrs. Patton, the Widow Jim, revives Miss Katharine's spice cake for them, using an ancient recipe that she has preserved. In these instances we are closer to the sacra-mental meals of "The Town Poor," "Miss Tempy's Watchers," or *Pointed Firs*. For example, Miss Carew is a sane representative of the world gone to seed in Miss Chauncy's mansion. Her ceremonious tea party is deeply impressive, even though Helen admits that "nothing very wonderful happened." An old-fashioned maid hands the tea around, and afterward the little group sits in the twilight idly talking, gazing over the garden: "Kate and I took much pleasure in choosing our teapoys; hers had a mandarin parading on top, and mine a flight

of birds and a pagoda; and we used them often afterward.'⁹¹ The
emphasis on the vessels rather than the meal makes sense. In this genteel
world, form is crucial: the vessels are prized, while the food itself is
ethereal. When Kate and Helen explore the Brandon house, they discover so much china that they can only imagine "that the lives of her
grandmothers must have been spent in giving tea parties."⁹² (Altogether
they count ten sets of cups, a variety of odd pieces, and a full collection
of pitchers.) As we have seen earlier, Mrs. Bonny's one tumbler is far
removed from the "mandarin" teapoy of Miss Carew. In "The Best
China Saucer," also from this period, Mrs. Bonny's stand-in, Jane Sim-
mons, breaks the dainty tea set of Nelly's genteel mother. This opposition also appears in the dinner Miss Bonny offers Kate and Helen:
her menu includes "meat-tea" made from a freshly killed chicken.
(They refuse the invitation.)

However, Mrs. Kew is closer to the center than Mrs. Bonny. And at
her lighthouse the two young women enjoy some hearty meals, accompanied by humorous stories and high spirits. However, the china is
never described and the food is not particularized. Helen stresses the
importance of both Mrs. Kew and Miss Carew, but the women themselves remain vague and unrealized. It is the extremes that fascinate
her. Miss Chauncy and Mrs. Bonny are the characters who arouse
Helen's imagination and evoke her narrative skill. Here the strangeness
of the pastoral setting is most clearly revealed. Here too, perhaps, Helen
and Kate are most aware of their own distance and therefore of their
own pleasure.

Their undifferentiated role within this society—and their pleasure
in it—is also signified by their own meals. They can always retreat to
the house of the dead aunt, a house where no rules apply. They liberate
Miss Brandon's lovely old India china from its careful packing and sit
wherever they like at the grand round table: "I must confess that we
were apt to have either a feast or famine, for at first we often forgot
to provide our dinners. If this were the case Maggie was sure to make
us wait for as much ceremony as she thought necessary for one of Mrs.
Lancaster's dinner parties."⁹³ In their retreat to girlhood, Kate and
Helen often forget to take responsibility for themselves. Economically
secure, yet without a mother or father at the head of the table, they
provide unpredictable meals. The food, when it does appear, is apt to
be as capricious as their costumes. At times the local fishing people
bring them some of the day's catch. Other days they may give a formal
dinner party themselves. Then again they may arouse the wonder of
the neighborhood by gathering wild mushrooms and fearlessly consuming them. Again the point is simple. In gustatory code, they are

liberated from established conventions. The two heroines can subvert the dining room if they like, even if their maid tries to keep them in line. And this subversion depends on their lack of commitment to the place and its people. They are floating free.

When Nan Prince comes to Dunport and confronts *her* aunt, Anna Prince, the scene is very different. Compare the tea party in *A Country Doctor* with the one in *Deephaven*. Kate and Helen are spectators, observers. Guests of Miss Carew, they are in no way responsible to her. Nan Prince, however, is called to account for her behavior and severely reprimanded. Kate and Helen break the genteel code innocently, childishly. Drawn to the rustic working women of the neighborhood, they are engaged in a kind of masquerade. Nan Prince breaks this code in earnest and becomes a professional woman herself. For her the stakes are higher. At Mrs. Fraley's tea party Nan defies decorum, and her hostess, by arguing her own cause. There is no feminine communion here because harmony would mean Nan's abdication of her own identity and freedom. There is superficial communion at Miss Carew's tea party because Kate and Helen repress their "contrast," knowing they can easily escape without Miss Carew's authority following them. Blissfully uncommitted, they can avoid choice, and its price. The result again is play, masquerade.

The conflicts that Kate and Helen have avoided appear in the final chapter, "Last Days in Deephaven": "It was very sad work to us— saying good-by to our friends, and we tried to make believe that we should spend the next summer in Deephaven, and we meant at any rate to go down for a visit."[94] There is an interesting duplicity here: a clue to the heroines' true allegiance, which is to the city, not to Deephaven. Much as they enjoyed their summer there, they will not return. Like the couple in "A Modern Idyll" they have discovered that they like their own home best. As they reflect on the Ladies of Llangollen and consider the choice to "remove ourselves from society and its distractions," the answer is clear. As Kate puts it, "I wonder if we should grow very lazy if we stayed here all year round; village life is not stimulating, and there would not be much to do in winter,—though I do not believe that need be true; one may be busy and useful in any place."[95] Kate's thinking starts to get a bit tangled; she does not want to reject country life overtly. Helen picks up the theme: "'I suppose if we really belonged in Deephaven we should think it a hard fate, and not enjoy it half so much as we have this summer,' said I. 'Our idea of happiness would be making long visits in Boston. . . . We should have the blues dreadfully, and think there was no society here, and wonder why we had to live in such a town.'"[96]

This vision, of course, is the pastoral without the "frame" of urban society, without the contrast. It is also the pastoral from the perspective of the insider, for whom it is not periphery but center. Further, this insider has no access to the world beyond, no freedom of movement. In many ways this picture of monotony, narrowed horizons, and dreary prospects recalls the situation of the impoverished family living in the hills above Deephaven, or the young girls who envy Kate and Helen their advantages. Deephaven is their world out of necessity, and they long for wider horizons. In a curious way the description could also apply to the genteel domestic women whose "circumference" is equally restricted. While Kate and Helen are careful not to reject Miss Carew outright, nor to criticize the stiffness of Miss Brandon's way of life (*A Country Doctor* is not at all ambiguous on these points), they do sympathize with the portrait of the young girl from the Brandon house. In fact, they take her back with them to Boston, where she enjoys "society after her own heart in Kate's room." However, neither Kate nor Helen have made a conscious choice between conventional gentility and freedom. They are still able to play at being "little girls."

And so, just as Kate turned her eyes away from tragedy in the chapter "In Shadow," she turns them away now. Rejecting Helen's "gloomy picture" with a laugh, she admits they could have been thoroughly bored by Deephaven's quiet, old-fashioned ways. That they were not has led her to understand something " 'better than I ever did before,— it is that success and happiness are not things of chance with us, but of choice. . . . Sometimes it is a conscious choice, but oftener unconscious. I suppose we educate ourselves for taking the best of life or the worst, do not you?' "⁹⁷ While a similar philosophy guided Jewett all of her life, here it is stated with a certain callousness. The problem concerns not only themselves but anyone forced to live in Deephaven as a type of "hard fate." However, Kate and Helen have the economic power to come and go as they please. This issue is not addressed in Kate's reply. Whenever she comes up against economic reality, she retreats to the power of positive thinking or otherworldly Christianity.

Kate's and Helen's own freedom from these economic realities is graphically illustrated in their leave-taking. Winter is setting in, and the landscape is changing. A northeast wind begins to blow, and to Helen it seems "that the sea would never be quiet and smooth and blue again, with soft white clouds sailing over it in the sky. It was a treacherous sea; it was wicked; it had all the trembling land in its power; if only it dared to send its great waves ashore."⁹⁸ These icy winds bring suffering with them; the old people on shore feel it in their rheumatic joints. Miss Chauncy herself will die in the winter cold. Now it is time to go home; this is no fun at all: "There was one day, it must be confessed, when a biting, icy fog was blown inshore, that Kate and I were willing to admit that we could be as comfortable in town, and it was almost time for sealskin jackets."⁹⁹ Inner choice cannot ward off a stiff ocean wind or icy fog, but a sealskin jacket and cozy town house will do nicely.

What is difficult for Helen and Kate to feel for Deephaven's people, they can express for the landscape itself: "In the front yards we saw the flower beds black with frost, except a few brave pansies which had kept green. . . . we picked some of these little flowers to put between the leaves of a book and take away with us." Helen admits that they "loved Deephaven all the more in those last days, with a bit of compassion in our tenderness for the dear old town which had so little to amuse it. So long a winter was coming, but we thought with a sigh how pleasant it would be in the spring."¹⁰⁰ Here they acknowledge the inevitability of death and sorrow, but when dealing with poor people they tend to judge more harshly. They are a bit like Miss Chauncy herself: unwilling to confront the reality of loss and death. In this denial there is a childlike quality. If they turn their backs on Deephaven as it slips slowly down, they can imagine it renewed in spring. They can also offer a quiet fib to their friends whose "hard fate" keeps them in place through "so long a winter." They pretend to be returning for another summer, but they know it is not true. Kate and Helen want to preserve Deephaven's spirit in art but not to be swallowed up in the vortex of its decay. Thus, they must not identify themselves too closely, must not let themselves be possessed by their hostess. And they do escape intact. Kate has made the Brandon house her own; she has exorcised her great-aunt's spirit. But Kate is not truly going to take Katharine Brandon's place. Our heroines rescue the maiden's portrait from the moldering house and leave Deephaven to its fate.

Chapter Seven

Ascending Spiral

If Jewett's first book reveals her ambivalence toward both the pastoral world and the feminine community, works written after her father's death in 1878 show a new resolution. By the mid-1880s she consolidated her identity as a professional writer and decisively rejected both conventional domesticity and marriage. Rather than the pastoral of *Deephaven*, *A Country Doctor* (1884) is a *Bildungsroman* tracing the steps by which the heroine's self unfolds: her separation, testing, and realization. The narrative result, as Elizabeth Ammons argues for the contemporaneous story "A White Heron" (1886), may be a more linear, hierarchical plot—indeed a more masculine plot, since the model for this development is most apt to be male even if the resolution of the self's journey is a transformation of traditionally masculine values.[1] Thus, while Kate and Helen play at various roles and avoid too close an identification with any one maternal figure, the heroines of this period actively and seriously seek new roles for themselves. More often than not, they turn to a "father" for guidance. The problem is whether this resolution is final or adequate.

Because of their close ties to Jewett's own development, both *A Country Doctor* and "A White Heron" have recently come under close critical scrutiny. Louis Renza even gives "A White Heron" a whole book, treating it from nearly every conceivable angle.[2] As Renza sees it, the story is a kind of "rebus" in which each critic reads his or her own message. I will first present my own, then look briefly at its difference from other current interpretations, before going on to *A Country Doctor,* the book in which Jewett comes closest to describing her development as a writer.

I

Unlike Kate and Helen of *Deephaven,* nine-year-old Sylvia is working class. She comes from an unnamed city, a manufacturing center where, shy and faltering, she has grown "afraid of folks." Adopted by her widowed grandmother, she finds a new home on the very boundary of civilization. Their tiny house is entirely surrounded by woods, but unlike Mrs. Bonny's in *Deephaven,* "this was the best thrift of an old-fashioned homestead."[3] Sylvia's response to this pastoral setting is a burst of growth and bloom: "It seemed as if she had never been alive at all before she came to live at the farm. She thought often with wistful compassion of a wretched dry geranium that belonged to a town neighbor." But Sylvia's great love is not the tidy cottage but the woods themselves.

As the story opens at twilight, she is lazily driving home a loitering cow, Mistress Mooly. Dreamy and sleepy, Sylvia "feels as if she were a part of the gray shadows and moving leaves." Her peaceful reverie is accompanied by the sounds of birds and the soft, sweet air. Idly, she remembers "the noisy town . . . and the great red-faced boy who used to chase and frighten her." This last memory, however, breaks into her mood, and she "hurries along the path to escape from the shadow of the trees."[4] Structurally, we have an initial set of pastoral oppositions and associations. The city is linked with manufacturing and the "red-faced boy" who chases Sylvia. In the woods, however, we have Mistress Mooly, the placid female "companion" whom Sylvia herself now chases home in a friendly spirit. From confinement and masculine domination, she has found a peaceful freedom and bovine communion. The complication enters with a "clear whistle . . . Not a bird's whistle, which would have a sort of friendliness, but a boy's whistle, determined and somewhat aggressive." Sylvia tries to hide, but "the enemy" discovers her.

Carrying a gun and full game bag, the stranger is a young hunter searching for a place to eat and spend the night. Approached, Sylvia is frightened into silence and trembling. When asked her name, "she hangs her head as if the stem of it were broken." Nevertheless, he persuades her to take him home, where her grandmother cheerfully supplies him with supper and a bed. After their meal, as the companionable grandmother gossips with the young man, she tells him of Sylvia's remarkable sympathy for the wild creatures, how at home she is in the woods: "There ain't a foot o'ground she don't know her way over, and the wild creatur's counts her one o' themselves." Birds in particular seem tame in Sylvy's presence, and "she'd 'a' scanted herself of her own meals to have plenty to throw out amongst 'em" if the grandmother had not prevented it. The guest is suddenly interested, for he is "'making a collection of birds myself. I have been at it ever since I was a boy.' (Mrs. Tilley smiled) [a lovely Jewett touch]."[5] In fact, the young ornithologist has collected "dozens and dozens" of birds, which he has killed, stuffed, and classified.

At this point the two paradigmatic sets of oppositions have expanded. We have on the one hand Sylvia's relationship to nature, which is communal and nurturing: she domesticates the natural creatures by feeding them out of her own substance. Then there is the ornithologist's relationship, which gives us conventional masculine terms. Literally bringing the machine into the garden, he masters the natural world through technology, shooting the birds with his gun. Then he forcibly transforms their fragile, decaying bodies into the permanent, if lifeless, figures of his collection. Finally, he brings abstract rational order to bear on the apparently random flux of nature through his ornithological categories. Now he is in quest of a small white heron, rarely seen in their region.

As he describes the heron, Sylvia, who has been more preoccupied with a hop toad than the conversation, feels "her heart give a wild beat . . . she knew that strange white bird, and had once stolen softly near where it stood in some bright green swamp grass, away over at the other side of the woods. There was an open place where the sunshine always seemed strangely yellow and hot, where tall, nodding rushes grew, and her grandmother had warned her that she might sink into the soft black mud underneath and never be heard of more."[6]

The house in the woods, like another grandmother's house in "Little Red Riding Hood," stands on the periphery of civilization and mediates between nature and culture, as pastoral settings always have. The heron's nest lies beyond its imagined gate, "on the other side of the woods," where the viscous black swamp threatens to swallow the unwary. But beyond this danger lies the salt marshes, "and beyond those was the sea, the sea which Sylvia wondered and dreamed about, but had never looked upon. As this landscape flashes through her thoughts, the guest offers the impoverished family ten dollars if Sylvia can lead him to the white heron: "No amount of thought, that night, could decide how many wished-for treasures the ten dollars, so lightly spoken of, would buy."[7] In addition to a formidable arsenal that includes scientific knowledge and technological mastery, the young man has money, the power to transform tangible realities into commodities quantified and suitable for exchange.

Sylvia accompanies the young man the next day. Proving "most kind and sympathetic," he instructs her on the lives and habits of the birds she has known only as companions. Then he makes her a gift of a jackknife, "which she thought as great a treasure as if she were a desert islander." Although she overcomes her initial fear, she still "would have liked him vastly better without his gun; she could not understand why he killed the very birds he seemed to like so much." While this mystery is unanswered and remains so, Sylvia begins to fall in love: "She had never seen anybody so charming and delightful; the woman's heart, asleep in the child, was vaguely thrilled by the dream of love." While Sylvia is only a child, still "some premonition of that great power stirred and swayed these young foresters who traversed the solemn woodlands with soft-footed silent care."[8] All day long Sylvia trails the admired leader; she speaks only when spoken to. When night falls, they have still not found the heron, but the "woman's heart" is awakened.

That night, urged on by her desire to be recognized by the hunter and by the glory of the promised ten dollars, Sylvia breaks out of the house before dawn to search for the heron alone.[9] She remembers a tall pine "at the farther edge of the woods, where the land was highest." This pine, "the last of its generation," may have been left as a boundary marker, for although a new generation of maples, pines, and white oaks surround it, "the stately head of this old pine towered above them all." Although Sylvia is already adept at climbing trees, she has never ventured so far as this one's top, but she believes that whoever did would see the ocean: "Now she thought of the tree with a new excitement, for why, if one climbed it at break of day, could not one see all the world, and easily discover where the white heron flew, and mark the place, and find the hidden nest?"[10]

Whereas before Sylvia had merely "laid her hand on the great rough bark and looked up wistfully at those dark boughs," now she is moved by new forces: "What a spirit of adventure, what wild ambition! What fancied triumph and delight and glory for the later morning when she could make known the secret!" Before the hunter's entrance Sylvia had loitered entranced in sleepy communion with the woods, birds, and the matronly Mistress Mooly. Her satisfactions were sweet but muted. Her identity was dissolved in the life of the forest whose name she bears. Her attachment to the hunter separates her from this fusion. When he first asks her name, her head "hangs from its stem" like a broken blossom, and the syllables are barely audible. But now her attraction to the hunter has brought her out of this undifferentiated, aimless communion to follow his lead. She looks at the natural world with new eyes, naming its creatures and mastering its ways through abstract classification.

In the hunter are merged the figures of both father and lover. Older than Sylvia, he leads and patronizes easily; but still a young man, he also bears the promise of Sylvia's future lover. And in the complex relationship of father to daughter, he offers himself as a model of agency, of differentiated ego, but at the same time promises to become her lover and so keep to himself the role of master and leader. Thus, for love *and* emulation of him she literally wakes up from her sleep filled with new ambitions. However, this new attachment threatens the world where Sylvia found her first contentment: "Alas, if the great wave of human interest which flooded for the first time this dull little life should sweep away the satisfactions of an existence heart to heart with the nature and the dumb life of the forest!"[11]

Before dawn Sylvia acts upon "her great design" and "steals" out of the house. As the "huge tree" "sleeps in the paling moonlight," Sylvia begins her climb "with utmost bravery." Still, she is associated with the creature she seeks: "her bare feet and fingers . . . pinched and held like bird's claws to the monstrous ladder reaching up, up, almost to the sky itself."[12] As she tackles the neighboring oak, disturbing its nests, "a bird fluttered off its nest, and a red squirrel ran to and fro and scolded pettishly at the harmless housebreaker." Then she makes the "dangerous pass from one tree to another" and the "great enterprise really begins."

At first the stately pine resists her: "the sharp dry twigs caught and held her and scratched like angry talons, the pitch made her thin little fingers clumsy and stiff as she went round and round the tree's great stem, higher and higher upward."[13] *Both* Sylvia and the tree are described as birds. The language suggests that Sylvia, pine, and heron share in some common identity. But she is somehow in conflict with the tree, which resists mastery: "The tree seemed to lengthen itself out as she went up, and to reach farther and farther upward. It was like a great mainmast to the voyaging earth." But then the tree seems suddenly to acquiesce in the little girl's ascent, even to encourage her, as if *it* identified with her quest: "it must truly have been amazed that morning as it felt this determined spark of human spirit creeping and climbing from higher branch to branch. Who knows how steadily the least twigs held themselves to advantage this light, weak creature on her way!"[14] In a curious sense the tree feels kinship with this "spark of human spirit," claims her as its own, as if through her vision it too will find fulfillment: "The old pine must have loved his new dependent. More than all the hawks, and bats, and moths, and even the sweet-voiced thrushes, was the brave, beating heart of the solitary gray-eyed child. And the tree stood still and held away the winds that June morning while the dawn grew bright in the east."[15]

Spiraling upward through this leafy matrix, Sylvia carries the frail spark of human spirit to its fulfillment. "When the last thorny bough was past, and she stood trembling and tired but wholly triumphant, high in the treetop," "Sylvia's face was like a pale star, if one had seen it from the ground." In a vaguely Hegelian sense, the story reveals nature seeking to know itself, see itself through human eyes. From "the ground" Sylvia's face is as transcendent as the stars, and her vision encompasses all the world:

Yes, there was the sea with the dawning sun making a golden dazzle over it, and toward that glorious east flew two hawks with slow-moving pinions. How low they looked in the air from that height when before one had only seen them far up, and dark against the blue sky. Their gray feathers were soft as moths . . . and Sylvia felt as if she too could go flying away among the clouds. Westward, the woodlands and farms reached miles and miles into the distance; here and there were church steeples, and white villages; truly it was a vast and awesome world.[16]

Again, in a way as curious as the old pine's nurturance, the narrator has become Sylvia's mentor and guide. Indeed, between the two of them—the pine that supports Sylvia's slight frame and the narrator who guides her eyes and instructs her awareness—Sylvia has gained a set of spiritual parents.[17] The narrator urges Sylvia not to "send an arrow of light and consciousness from her eager eyes." Consciousness and light are described as destructive arrows. The narrator implies that Sylvia should seek not mastery through them but aim for communion instead.

Her epiphany and initiation are completed: "The child gives a long sigh a minute later when a company of shouting catbirds comes also to the tree, and vexed by their fluttering and lawlessness the solemn heron goes away. She knows his secret now, the wild, light, slender bird that floats and wavers, and goes back like an arrow presently to his home in the green world beneath."[18] The repetition so soon of the arrow image is interesting. Sylvia is an anomaly in the natural world. She sympathizes with it, but her participation in its life will be significantly different from that of most biological creatures, which kill to survive and mate to reproduce—as does the heron, which arrow-like flies back to its mate.

Sylvia descends painfully from the heights, "wondering over and over again what the stranger would say to her, and what he would think when she told him how to find his way straight to the heron's nest." With this sentence the verb tense begins a subtle shift downward into the past from the ecstatic present of Sylvia's vision. Suddenly we are back in the house and watching the old grandmother discover the empty bed. We see the young hunter wakened, hoping he can persuade the shy little girl to tell where the nest is. Then, as Sylvia appears, "her old frock torn and tattered, and smeared with pine pitch," the verb tense again shifts upward to the present, stressing its urgency: "The splendid moment has come to speak of the dead hemlock tree by the green marsh." This is Sylvia's second crisis; her decision is the fruit of her vision. She will not speak, "though the old grandmother fretfully rebukes her, and the young man's kind appealing eyes are looking straight into her own." The temptation is great: "He can make them rich with money. . . . He is so well worth making happy."

No, she must keep silence! What is it that suddenly forbids her and makes her dumb? Has she been nine years growing, and now, when the great world for the first time puts out a hand to her, must she thrust it aside for a bird's sake? The murmur of the pine's green branches is in her ears, she remembers how the white heron came flying through the golden air and how they watched the sea and the morning together, and Sylvia cannot speak; she cannot tell the heron's secret and give its life away.[19]

The "great world" of culture, of technology, of science, of money, even of heterosexuality, has "put out its hand." And Sylvia, like a nine-year-old Saint Francis, "thrusts it aside for a bird's sake." The association of birds with the soul and with spirituality are ancient.[20] The central one for Jewett's tradition was the dove as the symbol of the Holy Ghost. Others in her immediate literary tradition included Keats's nightingale and Shelley's skylark. Another source was probably Flaubert's "*Un Coeur Simple*," in which a dying peasant woman envisages the Holy Ghost in the transfiguration of her beloved pet parrot. The flight of birds, their freedom from the earth's pull, has made them the appropriate sign of human transcendence. Here, as in much of the mystical Christian tradition, spiritual transcendence is separated from the merely cultural transcendence represented by the hunter, "the great world," which could be translated into "worldly goods." In her communion with the white heron Sylvia has come into possession of a higher loyalty, which she will not sell out to the vain world. Sylvia reaffirms her original communion with nature, but she does so conscious of her choice, and her loss:

Dear loyalty, that suffered a sharp pang as the guest went away disappointed later in the day, that could have served and followed him and loved him as a dog loves! Many a night Sylvia heard the echo of his whistle haunting the pasture path as she came home from the loitering cow. She forgot even her sorrow at the sharp report of his gun and the piteous sight of thrushes and sparrows dropping silent to the ground, their songs hushed and their pretty feathers stained and wet with blood.[21]

And the choice is clear. Loyalty to the young man would bring companionship but also submission to another's lead, a taming of Sylvia's spirit and an acceptance of values not her own. Her loyalty to those values loses her the "great world," but in compensation it gives her communion with the natural world: "Were the birds better friends than their hunter might have been,—who can tell? Whatever treasures were lost to her, woodlands and summer time, remember! Bring your gifts and graces and tell your secrets to this lonely country child."[22] Like some magical fairy godmother, the narrator addresses the woodlands and summertime directly, urging them to protect Sylvia as she has protected them. But central to Sylvia's choice is the association of heterosexuality *not* with nature but with "the great world." Further, Sylvia's communion with nature does not mean that she herself is embedded in that instinctual ground but that she protects it, oversees it, loves it from above. Sylvia has escaped the pollution of undifferentiated, less-than-human fusion with nature, but she has also escaped becoming a tamed or even preserved angel in some young hunter's household. Instead, she will be an angel of the woods, presiding "like a pale star" over her kingdom of birds and beasts.

II

Although they differ markedly in other respects, recent interpretations of this story share a common thread. Elizabeth Ammons calls it an "anti-bildungsroman," a fairy tale that actually "argues against the maturation script assigned by the culture." Louis Renza emphasizes the story's "regressive or pre-fairy tale tendencies." And Carol Singley defines it as an initiation story whose core is the heroine's refusal to be initiated, "her declining the final phase of *rite of passage*."[23]

Beginning with Ammons, she sees Sylvia's ultimate silence before the hunter/prince as her trying out of the heterosexual, even male "plot," then resisting and refusing it: "To renounce matrisexual bonds for heterosexual love, this story says, is not to follow nature, as traditional fairy tales so artfully—and we should notice, nervously—insist. It is to ally oneself against nature, even against life."[24] But if heterosexuality as a patriarchal institution is represented by the hunter, the old pine tree, for Ammons, represents a more benign natural form. Thus, Sylvia's climb up its trunk does give her a glimpse of heterosexuality, a rehearsal of the masculine maturation plot. And the vision of the mated herons is wonderful, but this natural heterosexuality has little in common with its human variant. Essentially nurturant, the old tree resists the competitive, destructive qualities of the hunter. Reading the final passages against the historical background of new opportunities for women in the public sphere, Ammons sees Sylvia returning to the feminine circles of the matrisexual world: a decisive rejection of patriarchy and affirmation of female separatism in face of "the new ideology of integration, or identification with masculine values." For Ammons this rejection means arrested development, but as for Sylvia's choosing to remain in the natural and magical realm of the mother as opposed to the father, "In fairy tale terms, that is the realm of the witch and deciding to stay not only means deciding against the prince; it means deciding in favor of the witch."[25]

What Ammons sees as Sylvia's decision to choose matrisexual over heterosexual, witch over prince, Louis Renza sees in more traditional Freudian terms as the choice between preoedipal and oedipal: "Jewett's Sleeping Beauty clearly fails to respond to Prince Charming; instead, she remains silent, as if still under the spell of childhood."[26] Like Ammons, he sees the old pine tree as a masculine figure who initiates Sylvia into a form of heterosexuality. However, for Renza the tree's hidden identity is the "absent father," who literally offers Sylvia support without awakening oedipal conflict. This paternal figure "allows Sylvia to grow up in other than human terms; 'he' absolves both her and the story from the topos of 'adolescence' and therefore from the teleological function of fairy tales . . . namely to give child readers a preliminary model for arriving at social and sexual maturity."[27]

However, rather than rejecting oedipal for preoedipal, Renza sees Sylvia as remaining in a newly constructed space between: a space perhaps for the writer who wishes to retain her vision but not accept the responsibility and burden of adult female sexuality—the identity of the mother. Hence, the tree becomes an adoptive father who allows the heroine to form a sexless identity, a kind of paternal muse who quells the anxiety caused by the incest taboo: an absent/present father.[28] Thus, while Ammons argues that Sylvia stays in the world of her grandmother, Renza points out that both Sylvia's biological mother and her grandmother are allied with patriarchy. Effectively locked within her narrow sphere, the grandmother wishes that she had been allowed to see the world, the world her son has gone off to find and which Sylvia discovers from her treetop. Indeed, Sylvia's breaking out of the house at dawn and climbing the tree are unconventional female acts, acts defying traditional domesticity. Even Sylvia's decision to keep silence at the end does not meet with this particular grandmother's approval. By "fretfully rebuking" the child, she clearly allies herself with the handsome hunter.

There are aspects of both analyses that I agree with. Whereas I feel that Ammons perhaps overstates the attractions of the literal, human grandmother as witch, Renza does not seriously consider adult alternatives to heterosexuality. While Sylvia's evasion of human heterosexuality is clear, along with its oedipal implications, her return to the preoedipal, matrisexual world may also be only partial. That is, neither grandmother nor hunter solaces Sylvia's loneliness at the story's end.

While Ammons says that Sylvia rejects the vision at the top of the old pine to return to her feminine meanderings with Mistress Mooly, I see no evidence that Sylvia has lost what she has learned from that climb, nor from her communion with both male tree and heron.

This point brings me to Carol Singley's interpretation, which stresses a pattern similar to the one I have outlined. The heroine begins by confronting the masculine world of patriarchy and capitalism, which she then rejects while "appropriating . . . the phallic power of that world" for her own purposes. This appropriation is accompanied by a "compensatory spiritual insight and communion with nature as sub-stitute for human—and especially male—affection."[29] Singley does not see Sylvia as ending up at her developmental starting point but as returning to those feminine circles with a "priceless inner awareness—of herself and nature." The heroine has made "an active and autono-mous choice." She cannot go back to the unself-conscious fusion of the opening pages. However, society offers no opportunity for this heroine to integrate her newfound awareness with its patterns. Hence, she retreats to nature as a "permanent refuge," a choice that may "lock her in a child-like but strained world of innocence." Summing up her argument, Singley believes that "a rejection of patriarchal norms, an assumption of the active role reserved for males, and an infusion of natural and spiritual energy comprise a new kind of female initiation, but not a completely resolved one."[30] The heroine's social alienation is too high a price to pay.

While in basic agreement with Singley, I believe that this analysis could be deepened by considering the problematic relationship to the mother, both as human figure and as emotional "ground." An earlier interpretation that dealt with this problem comes from Pratt's "Women and Nature in Modern Fiction." Published in 1972, Pratt's essay has had an important influence on Jewett scholarship and on this study as a whole.[31]

Rather than seeing "A White Heron" as an "anti-*Bildungsroman,* an "arrested fairy tale" or "refused initiation," Pratt reconstructs a female *Bildungsroman* that she argues is essentially different from that of the male. She first links the *Bildungsroman,* and by implication the fairy tale, to the broader genre of the quest, beginning with American Indian tradition, in which a youth retreats to the desert to fast until he meets "the manifestation of his animal self." In the fictional version of this ritual, "an epiphanic vision heralding the advent of selfhood springs upon the individual in an unexpected moment and in an un-sought manifestation." Typically, the epiphany "occurs in a natural setting and is accompanied by a feeling of ecstasy, the idyllic aspect of the 'green world' with its budding trees and flowers apparently expressing the first sensual blossoming of the psyche."[32] Drawing on Simone de Beauvoir and Joseph Campbell, Pratt argues that women and men experience this naturalistic epiphany in significantly different ways. The heroine of the female genre is "more likely to view herself as coextensive with the green world and the hero of the male genre to view his heroine and the green world as coextensive parts of each other but rightfully subordinate to him."[33]

The core of her argument is a close comparison between "A White Heron" and James Joyce's *Portrait of the Artist as a Young Man*. The two works do seem to support her claim. At first the point-for-point comparisons between Stephen Daedalus's epiphany and Sylvia's make a striking fit. Both are "accompanied by a view of the ocean, a sense of soaring aloft, an apparition of a hawk or hawks, and an identification with the vehicle of the vision—bird or bird-girl—with a passage through that identity to a fuller understanding of the self."[34] Following sixteen-year-old Stephen's vision of the soaring hawks—which he connects to the mythological Daedalus, ancestor of his own artistic identity—Stephen experiences the culmination of his epiphany "through the mediation of a female apparition . . . rising like an Irish Aphrodite out of the waters, 'pure' but with a green 'sign' of incipient sensuality upon her thing."[35] This nameless girl, evanescent and evocative, "stirs the hero's masculinity and provides the catalyst for his ecstatic moment of self-discovery. Her physical concreteness is taken not for its own sake, but as portent of something besides herself." Through her Stephen finds his portal to the green world, and discovers his identity through his mastery of the moment's symbolism.

Although "A White Heron" deals with the "opposite" sex, the pattern is not simply reversed for Sylvia. Stephen is seeking self-knowledge and personal symbolism; Sylvia is seeking, according to Pratt, freedom and refuge. Stephen differentiates himself from both girl and nature, while Sylvia, although "fascinated by the stirring of her womanhood," "differentiates between boy and bird, perceiving him and nature as separate aspects of her psyche, which in some way endanger each other."[36] Thus, Sylvia confirms de Beauvoir's belief that "for the young girl, for the woman who has not fully abdicated, nature represents what woman herself represents for man: herself and her negation, a kingdom and a place of exile; the whole in the guise of the other."[37]

However, this analysis does not make entirely clear what role the young man does play in the girl's psyche. Pratt writes that the "heroine . . . worships nature as something . . . not separate from her first sexual experiences." And de Beauvoir finds that "it is when she speaks of moors and gardens that the woman novelist will reveal her experiences and her dreams to us most intimately."[38] Does this mean that the young man who "stirs" the heroine's latent sexuality also provides the "key" to her own self-awareness? If, let us say, the heron is the portal through which Sylvia discovers the green world, is the hunter the key that opens this portal? If so, why does he come to represent a separate force, one endangering the very kingdom he has revealed?

Pratt answers by placing the feminine conflict between heterosexuality and selfhood within a "specific bio-historical context, namely the lack of widespread and effective birth control." In Jewett's time a woman's sexual initiation might well mean her self-sacrifice: "an endless or at best lengthy series of childbirths and miscarriages, infants to raise, corollary illnesses, dependence upon men, waste of one's prime years, and early death."[39] Somehow the heroine must differentiate between the "indulgence of her sexual nature" and a natural kingdom "not separate from her first sexual experiences." Thus, while the heroines of various *Bildungsroman*s reject sexual love, nevertheless this initial ecstasy very often leads to a visionary naturism that becomes their salvation. Indeed, the heroine's experience of this epiphany becomes the structural center of the genre, "a touchstone by which she holds herself together in the face of the destructive roles proffered her by society."[40] This constant temptation to accept a false self is most "scathingly" represented by alternative female characters or by animal, usually canine, metaphors. For example, Sylvia follows the hunter as a "little dog follows its master" (the same metaphor that Jewett used to describe her own early relationship to her father, a problem I will discuss later). Like Carol Singley, Pratt argues that society does not offer women fully human roles to play. Thus, women, "desiring only to be human . . . turn to nature, which seems less unnatural, for solace."[41]

However, it is still not clear from Pratt's essay how this differentiation between heterosexual and naturistic ecstasies takes place. The argument might be strengthened by the addition of Nancy Chodorow's research. Revised according to Chodorow's scheme, the developmental pattern Pratt applies might look something like the following: raised by a woman, the male associates the other, the ground against which he differentiates himself, as female. "The world," especially the unstructured natural world and the inner world of the unconscious, is linked to the mother who initiated him into all relationships. Since his gender identity conflicts with his felt primary identity, he also senses a fundamental split between himself and the world associated with the mother. He cannot reenter that world by simple identification ("fusing" himself with it), since that would mean loss of his masculine gender identity. Instead, he can return through the mediation of a female figure, who takes the place of the mother.

The girl, however, has no fundamental conflict between primary identification with the mother and her gender identity. She senses that she and the green world are coextensive and finds in this fusion not a threat but an affirmation of her essential femininity. What Pratt does not account for, and Chodorow does, is the male's role in transforming this undifferentiated absorption into a communion illuminated by consciousness. The young girl cannot grow into self-awareness without the intervention of this "male." Thus, at the story's start the princess is already embedded within her kingdom but not "in possession" of it, since the two are one. From this dreamy sleep the prince's kiss awakens her.

Given the asymmetrical structure of parenting, this role is conventionally played by the father; however, it may actually be taken by any figure, male or female, who offers the daughter an image of selfhood, of difference.[42] Moreover, it is difficult to separate the girl's experience of the father figure from the experience of her developing ego, since, as Chodorow argues, she attaches herself to the father both to escape the mother and to acquire the father's independence. The girl wants to be loved by the father but also to be *like* him.

However, insofar as she associates herself fully with the male, the girl jeopardizes her own gender identity. Since the unconscious is linked to the feminine, mastery over one may lead to rejection of the other. But the girl's "masculine protest" can only be an unsatisfactory stopping point. Physically, she cannot identify completely with the father because she does not possess a penis and the father does not possess a womb. Just as critically, in a patriarchy she will not be allowed *ever* to possess the father's authority and freedom, which for the boy are only deferred. Despite the father's seductive promise, the only adult relationship to the male allowed her is neither identity nor equality but subordination. However, this is the patriarchal version of the tale. Other resolutions are possible, as we can see by looking once again at the Demeter–Persephone myth.

At this point in the myth Persephone's primordial fusion with Demeter has been broken, and union with Hades has engendered consciousness of separation. Now the daughter must find her way to reintegration. In nonpatriarchal versions of the myth, such as Annie Fields's "The Return of Persephone," two elements are crucial to the myth's resolution: Demeter's search for her daughter and Hades' transformation from father/rapist to loving husband.[43]

If Persephone in the Underworld is the nascent self associated with the ego, then Demeter is the lost stratum of the unconscious associated with the mother. Bound up with her image are feminine identity and the fertile, life-affirming power of primary love and communion. The self languishes when deprived of this power, which cries out for expression through her. This remembered relation drives Demeter to search for her daughter, defying even the Father of the Gods. Passion, love, communion will not be denied but extract their due even from Zeus. As for Hades, he is first Persephone's uncle, then her rapist. He combines the two aspects of the ego/father: the positive paternal figure who promises her freedom but also the rapist who destroys her innocence. But if Persephone's first transformation comes from the "incursion" of the masculine, so Hades' transformation comes from Persephone's reunion with the feminine. From the rigid authority who puts a boundary between the mother and daughter, Hades becomes the flexible ego, the loving husband who allows the daughter to return periodically to the mother. As we see in Annie Fields's dramatic poem, Persephone's marriage with Hades is a happy one—once the ego that Hades symbolizes has given up its isolating role for a protective one, subordinated to the love of Mother and Daughter. (Hades, remember, has Persephone only for a third of the year.)

In mythic descriptions of Persephone as Hades' wife she is portrayed as the true Queen of the Underworld, co-ruler with her husband. It is she, for example, who allows Euridyce to return to the earth with Orpheus. Thus, Erich Neumann argues that even though Persephone "becomes" Demeter and Demeter "rediscovers" Persephone, the Dual Goddess worshiped at Eleusis is greater than either. The resurrected Kore is not the Maiden but a Queen of three realms: the Underworld, the Earth, and the Heavens. In her we see expressed the harmonious relationship of all psychic elements, both male-identified and female-identified. The triangular situation in which the girl's identity was formed, with its bisexual oscillation, has been resolved. Both ties are acknowledged and the original mother-daughter bond reintegrated without sacrificing the ego that was so dearly bought.

The fruit of this resolution is the mystery revealed at Eleusis: the recognition of identity in difference, the fulfillment of the individual through communion. If the ego has been transformed from rapist to loving husband, consciousness itself has also been transformed. From awareness of separation, an abstract knowledge divorced from human emotion, it has become a "wisdom of loving participation." This wisdom is the "child" of the triangular marriage of Persephone, Hades, and Demeter. Its symbols—the seed-corn reaped in a blaze of light, the luminous child, the torches carried by the goddess herself—all testify to the transfiguration of the life force by the experience of separation, alienation, and death. Renewal now brings not simply return to life but a return illuminated by consciousness. Where once life and love were only experienced, now they are known.

"A White Heron" makes a striking fit with this paradigm but with an important difference.[44] Sylvia's society *is* a patriarchal one. The hunter in "A White Heron," like Hades, is both surrogate father and potential lover; however, this Hades will not be transformed. For Sylvia to emulate him would be to lose her sense of gender and to destroy her communion with the natural world. To become his lover would be to accept a subordinate, devalued role: to become the "little dog," perhaps the "bitch," who follows at his feet. Moreover, this grandmother is not a witch but an ally of patriarchy. She would not dare defy the hunter as Demeter defies Zeus to win her daughter back. As Carol Singley and Annis Pratt both argue, Sylvia must find her resolution in nature, not society. And as we learn from Chodorow's object-relations analysis, naturistic ecstasy, as well as sexual ecstasy, stems from the first attachment to the mother. Primary love gives us a core experience that includes, but extends beyond, heterosexual intercourse. *This* possibility the woman may possess without the male, possess as her original ability to recover her sense of communion with the "other." And that other may be found in the natural world, in other women, in children, and in friendship, as well as in husband.

Finally, despite her ultimate rejection of him, not only is the hunter necessary to Sylvia's new consciousness but something of his presence is woven into its fabric. She takes his power and fuses it with her own feminine identity. In the process both are transformed. The prince wakens Sleeping Beauty to her sexuality and her difference from the mother. But through this experience our princess rediscovers the mother and returns to her kingdom as possessor and protector, rather than as dependent and ward. Sylvia's silence is not the silence of regression but the silence of Eleusinian awareness, an awareness that can be shared but not spoken.

III

Despite Sylvia's hard-won integrity her isolation from human companionship at the story's close remains troubling. While she has found compensation in the landscape with its wild creatures, she remains outside society. In many ways she is what Renza calls her, a "nun-such, a white heroine." And yet it is important to remember that the Victorian world, Christian and pre-Freudian, had more tolerance for this contemplative choice than ours does. Jewett's friend Anna L. Dawes remarked that she favored St. Paul's advice when it came to marriage: the single state was the "better" one.[45] And, in fact, psychological maturity and conventional marriage *were* antithetical for many women in Victorian patriarchal society. However, the existence of this letter in itself confirms that Jewett had what Sylvia does not have—a confidant of her own gender, a female community of love and ritual.

These issues, suggested in "A White Heron," are more visible, more forcefully stated in *A Country Doctor*. If "A White Heron" is a *Bildungsroman* in miniature, the 1884 novel gives us the genre and its heroine, full-grown.[46] Moreover, in this longer piece, Jewett must flesh out a plausible sociocultural context for her heroine's development. Nan's resolution of the conflicts posed by this context give us a clearer sense of Jewett's world-view and ethos at this phase of her career, for, as many of her critics have pointed out, *A Country Doctor* has a strong autobiographical component. Its heroine, Nan Prince, becomes the doctor that Jewett herself might have been, had she patterned herself even more closely on her father. In telling Nan's story, Jewett seems to have offered a barely disguised *apologia pro vita sua*. But, of course, Nan is not Jewett, and her deviations from Jewett tell us a great deal about the author's reimagining and reconstruction of her actual experience. More precisely, this novel reveals the fictional world that Jewett was then capable of articulating. What is *not* said here is as important as what is.

Significantly, for a literary model Jewett seems to have turned to her childhood favorite, *Pearl of Orr's Island,* the novel that led her to see rural Maine with "new eyes." *Pearl* is also a *Bildungsroman,* and its author is what Jewett hoped to become: a successful writer. However, the differences are as important as the parallels. Jewett was acutely aware of the conflict between what Mara represented and what Stowe did. Although a promising painter of nature, Mara, as we have seen, leaves no lasting artifacts behind her, only a sainted memory. Jewett's heroine is made of sturdier stuff; through her Jewett stakes an unequivocal claim to professionalism. Again, it is the father who shows the way.

In "Looking Back on Girlhood," Jewett admitted that she had "tried to give some idea of my father's character in my story of 'The Country Doctor,' but all that is inadequate to the gifts and character of the man himself."[47] Her portrait of Dr. Leslie stresses his solitary dedication to his profession and his warmth of heart. But equally important is the doctor's quiet but firm willingness to buck convention. This unconventionality contributes to another important aspect of the doctor's character: his femininity, suggested in his androgynous name. In conversation a friend of Dr. Leslie's reflects on a doctor's highest gifts: "Do you remember how well Buckle says that the feminine intellect is the higher, and that the great geniuses of the world have possessed it? The gift of intuition reaches directly toward the truth."[48] Dr. Leslie readily remembers the Buckle passage—"it isn't a thing one easily forgets"— and then adds that he has "long believed the powers of Christ were but the higher powers of our common humanity." The Christ the two men celebrate found glory in "his usefulness and gift for helping others." This feminized Christ is very close to the deity described by Phillips Brooks, or by Horace Bushnell in his theology of Christian nurture.

Not surprisingly, the narrator compares the two ministers of Old-fields unfavorably to Dr. Leslie, the only man there "who looked far ahead or saw much or cared much for true success." Then she offers this evocative analogy of the doctor's role in the little country village: "In Titian's great Venetian picture of the Presentation of the Virgin, while the little maiden goes soberly up the steps of the temple, in the busy crowd beneath only one man is possessed by the thought that something wonderful is happening."[49] In *The Pearl of Orr's Island* the role of the Virgin was taken by Mara; here it is filled by Nan Prince.

Like Mara, the infant Nan loses her mother in the novel's opening chapter. In Stowe's novel Naomi witnesses the shipwreck that drowns her husband, then dies, having just given birth. Her final words are bitter. Adeline Prince also dies grief-stricken after her husband's death, but unlike Naomi, this mother is unworthy of her child. Dr. Leslie remembers her as "quite unbalanced and a strange, wild creature, very handsome in her girlhood, but morally undeveloped."[50] From her father's side Adeline inherited a bad genetic streak: a predisposition to alcoholism, even madness. Proud and rebellious, she used her handsome looks to rise above her class. Adeline left the simple farming stock of her mother's family to marry a young doctor, of the wealthy Prince family. But this marriage between unmatched social classes—the peasant Thachers and aristocratic Princes—was an aberration. A country neighbor comments that "'twas like setting a laylock bush to grow beside an ellum tree, and expectin' of 'em to keep together. They wa'n't mates. He'd had a different fetchin' up."[51]

After Adeline's pride and freakish temper led to a break with the Princes, the couple came upon disaster far from home. They lost their money; then the young husband lost both his health and life. Rumors circulated that the desperate widow was seen begging on the city streets. In the opening pages Adeline returns to her family's farm in the November chill. In a paroxysm of despair she heads toward the river to drown both herself and her child. She turns aside only at the last moment. At her bedside Dr. Leslie "read at a glance the shame and sorrow of the young woman who fled to the home of childhood, dying and worse than defeated, from the battlefield of life."[52] Adeline is dying not only of consumption but of alcoholism. That she is "worse than defeated" suggests other sins, possibly sexual ones. The image of the begging woman hints at prostitution.

Mara's spiritual mother is Dolores, whose Catholicism and drowning link her to fate and natural immanence. However, Adeline is a more powerful, and disturbing, image of the subversive and anomalous feminine. Her ambition is uncontrolled; her effect on society is disruptive and destructive; her sexuality and alcoholism are a kind of pollution. (In New England slang even now to be "polluted" means to be drunk.) Only the faint glimmer of some "higher" maternal instinct saves Adeline from *deliberately* drowning her child. But ultimately it is Dr. Leslie who saves Nan from this viscous femininity. On her deathbed Adeline entrusts her infant to Grandmother Thacher and Dr. Leslie: the peasant woman and the all-wise father, recurring figures in Jewett's work. Mrs. Thacher takes on the daughter first.

Josephine Donovan argues that the world of Mrs. Thacher is a "paradisical" world of women, a community of Demeters to which Adeline returns a "defeated" Persephone.[53] I would agree if we were talking about Mrs. Todd or Temperance Dent, who are unequivocally sympathetic and warmly maternal figures. Not here, however. Mrs. Thacher cannot provide the understanding that young Nan needs. Although raised on a farm, she lacks the deep sympathy with nature possessed by characters from Jewett's later fiction. In fact, Mrs. Thacher is a rather joyless woman, who "had been brought up to consider the hard work of this life." She sees the spontaneity of youth as so much wild energy "to be harnessed": "if she had known that her grand-daughter would lie down beside the anemones and watch them move in the wind . . . Mrs. Thacher would have thought it a very idle way of spending one's time."[54]

As in *Deephaven* and "A White Heron," it is the landscape that plays the part of Demeter. Like Sylvia and like Stowe's Mara, Nan is most at home in the woods. But unlike the gentle Mara, she has inherited a streak of self-reliance and stubbornness from her mother that prompts her to mischief. While she fashions a makeshift splint for a wounded squirrel, she also plays tricks on her grandmother's straitlaced neighbors. She prefers the company of the trees and birds to humans. Despairing of her ability to raise the child, Mrs. Thacher goes to Dr.

Leslie for advice. Intrigued by the "wild girl's" spirit and intelligence, he ends up taking her into his own home.

This adoption saves Nan from being broken to farm work as a young colt is broken to harness. But if Dr. Leslie saves her from the working-class woman's fate, he also saves her from genteel domesticity. He will bring her into a middle-class home, even an upper-class one, but he will not bind her roots. Instead the doctor lets the little girl who loves the woods and heals the wild animals run free. In a directly autobiographical passage, Jewett has the adult Nan remember "the first summer of her village life, when, seeing that she looked pale and drooping, the doctor, to her intense gratification, took her away from school. Presently . . . she might be seen every day by the doctor's side, as if he could not make his morning rounds without her; and in and out of the farmhouses she went, following him like a little dog.[55]

The "little dog" image, which appears negatively in "A White Heron," seems positive here, as it does in the autobiographical sketch, "Looking Back on Girlhood." I believe that the later shift in tone results in the ambiguity of the hunter in "A White Heron." As a father figure, he is partly modeled on Theodore Jewett, who led his daughter out of the home and opened up the world to her. However, unlike Theodore Jewett, the hunter does not aim to heal but to kill. Further, as a potential lover the hunter could only mean betrayal for the little girl who so admired him. He might promise freedom, but attachment to him would bring subordination. However, attachment to Dr. Leslie will become identification for Nan. No longer the little dog at the doctor's heels, the adult Nan will be the doctor herself. The nurturance Sylvia found in the masculine pine tree is analogous to Dr. Leslie's own as he "lifts" Nan to his professional height. In *A Country Doctor* the dangerous, patriarchal aspect of the male is represented by a second figure, George Gerry, who tempts Nan to give up the freedom for which Dr. Leslie prepared her. Before looking at this temptation, however, I would like to discuss Nan's rejection of domesticity.

As must be clear, *A Country Doctor* has a strong undertone of wish fulfillment. Having killed off her heroine's mother and invalidated that mother's claims for authority, Jewett gives the fictional version of herself sole possession of the beloved father. However, as Renza points out, this is still an adoptive father. A biological one would be too incestuous for comfort. Moreover, Dr. Leslie lacks the patriarchal prejudices of the absent father and incorporates the maternal care of the equally absent mother.[56] So it is just the two of them together in the old house, with the servant, Marilla, to do the cooking. And even Marilla's right to run the house along genteel lines is challenged. While the old housekeeper "had always kept the large east parlor for a sacred shrine of society, to be visited chiefly by herself as guardian priestess," Nan bypasses its ritualized formality, making it pleasant and open but using "it with a freedom which appears to the old housekeeper to lack consideration and respect."[57] The portrait of Marilla, like the portrait of Mrs. Thacher, seems at variance with Jewett's better-known writing. Ordinarily, Jewett respects the "guardian priestesses" of society's "sacred shrines," but this respect followed upon Jewett's own escape from the parlor and her ultimate liberation of its enclosed space. Other people's parlors she enters with sympathy, even reverence; her own is another matter.

However, Mrs. Jewett has not disappeared entirely. A shadow of the genteel mother now appears a convenient distance from the father-daughter dyad. Across the street is the house of Mrs. Graham, close friend of Dr. Leslie and his advisor in the raising of Nan Prince. Significantly, the widowed Mrs. Graham is presented with all the tokens of the "Root-Bound" saint. "Hopelessly lame," she is ensconced in a snug parlor, filled with geraniums, "all flourishing and green and even in bloom, unlike most treasures of their kind."[58] Warm southern sun floods the room even in the deepest winter, and a wet log on the fire sings "gently to itself, as if the sound of the summer rustlings and chirpings had somehow been stored away in its sap." Perhaps the most, or even the only, positive image of domesticity in the book, these descriptions suggest the home's transformation of natural energy into humanized warmth, a counter to the chill outside. The geraniums seem to lift their "hands" toward the fire, and outside the "trees looked naked and defenseless, if one saw them through the windows."[59]

What Mrs. Graham possesses is the power to translate undirected natural force toward social aims. Dr. Leslie has been letting Nan grow without artificial restraint, letting her self-reliance and leadership develop into the forms that nature, not convention, intended. However, as Mrs. Graham warns him, Nan is a plant that is in danger of becoming "all leaves," without the bloom of human communion. As she puts it, Nan "is like a candle that refuses to burn, and is satisfied with admiring its own candlestick. She is quite the queen of the village children in one way, and in another she is quite apart from them." Mrs. Graham suggests that Nan's strength is a gift from her mother, but if Dr. Leslie does not teach her to use it properly, she might "go adrift," as her mother did. Nan should be taught "her duty to her neighbor, . . . that she owes something to the world beside following out her own foolish plans."[60]

Like Mrs. Rush, Nan is being left to "riot in the garden." However, if Mrs. Graham represents the good side of feminine domesticity, care for others, she also represents the force of convention. She urges Dr. Leslie to impress on his charge the importance of fitting her place: "Society is a sort of close corporation, and we must know its watchwords. . . . one must feel instinctively at home with a certain class, representatives of which are likely to found everywhere."[61] In other words, Nan must be socialized. She must be made into a lady. And, we are led to understand, she possesses by birth the "Princely" nature, which needs only proper cultivation to produce a representative of its class.

Mrs. Graham, then, is as ambiguous as the hunter in "A White Heron." She brings the two aspects of domestic femininity to Dr. Leslie's attention: concern for others and restriction of natural inclinations. Acting on Nan's behalf, he accepts the first but gently rejects the second. He remarks that Mrs. Graham perhaps idealizes the "best society," which they seldom see in their country town but then adds that he believes in "turning this young woman's good instincts and uncommon powers into the proper channels instead of letting her become singular and self-centered because she does not know enough of people of her own sort."[62] The issue, of course, is whether there is any middle ground for a woman to take. Will Nan be symbolically crippled or will she be as wild and wayward as her mother? Dr. Leslie, seeing ahead to the child's future, as Jewett's own father did, feels that only a higher purpose will give Nan the freedom she needs yet preserve her from harm. Already he sees the young girl as a doctor: "When a man or woman has that sort of self-dependence and unnatural self-reliance, it shows itself very early. I believe that it is a mistake for such a woman to marry."[63] Nan, he argues, shows no interest in flirtation; her "feeling toward her boy-playmates is exactly the same as toward the girls she knows."

That Nan may be an "unnatural" woman, an anomaly set apart by God for a singular purpose, is an important theme in the novel and a key to understanding Jewett's resolution of its feminist issues. In "Tom's Husband" (1884) she offered a similar explanation for Mary Wilson's business talents; they were an inheritance from her father. Here as well, Nan receives her medical talent and "aristocratic" intelligence from her father. The story's drama is the unfolding of Nan's intrinsic, inherited identity, which, seedlike, waits to be nurtured by the wise doctor. As he tells Mrs. Graham, if "the law of her nature is that she must live alone and work alone, I shall help her to keep it instead of break it, by providing something else than the business of housekeeping and what is called a woman's natural work."[64]

Mrs. Graham, of course, is deeply shocked, but she cannot persuade the doctor to break his ward's spirit. While Dr. Leslie admits that he is not yet sure about Nan's future, he adds that "looking at her sad inheritance from her mother, and her good inheritances from other quarters, I cannot help feeling that she might be far more unhappy than to be made ready to take up my work here in Oldfields when I have to lay it down." Her vocation will save her from the mother's curse. But in many ways Nan is as much an anomaly as her mother. And part of the novel's suspense, so far as we could call it that, comes from the fear that the bad streak will break out and destroy our heroine's future. The doctor believes, however, that "she has all the good qualities of her ancestors without the bad ones."[65] And indeed, Nan has inherited from her biological father a genius for medicine. As the enlightened observer in Titian's painting had done, the good doctor senses an uncommon vocation developing in his young virgin. She is sent to boarding school but is allowed to keep her own judgment. Moreover, the doctor gives Nan open space and permission to grow into the woman she is destined to become, whatever that may be.

In direct opposition to the "Root-Bound" paradigm, *A Country Doctor* shows us the burst of bloom that follows on the widening of Nan's experience. The narrative itself seems to be structured, at least in its first half, on the progressively expanding horizons of Nan's world. Dr. Leslie, of course, is the Prince who awakens this Sleeping Beauty to the wonders outside the home—or the wise old pine who "advantages" her on the perilous journey. Upon the child's very first visit to Dr. Leslie's house she returns to the Thacher farm transformed: "Life had suddenly grown much larger, and her familiar horizon had vanished and she discovered a great distance stretching far beyond [its] limits."[66] A hundred pages later the doctor announces that they will take a trip to Boston together: "It was a more important thing than anybody understood, for a dear and familiar chapter of life was ended when the expectant pair drove out of the village on their way to the far-off railway station."[67] As for the big city, it makes an indelible impression on Nan's consciousness: "She had ceased to belong only to the village she had left; in these days she became a citizen of the world at large. Her horizon had suddenly become larger."[68]

Now Doctor Leslie is her guide, but eventually she makes these explorations outward alone, following his example. The parallel with Sylvia and the hunter is strong. The direction of this growth is not the domestic centripetal, inward and confining, but centrifugal, outward and expansive. The plant metaphor appears in connection with this outward movement: "There must be periods of repose and hibernation

like the winter of a plant, and in its springtime the living soul will both
consciously and unconsciously reach for new strength and new light.
The leaves and flowers of action and achievement are only the signs of
the vitality that works within."[69]

However, the successively widening horizons of Nan's experience are
only half the story. If the father is leading her out, Nan also returns
periodically, and unconsciously, to the mother. The novel opens with
Nan and her mother in the woods by the stream where Adeline plans
to drown them both. It is this very spot to which Nan returns at the
novel's midpoint and again at its conclusion. Even in "A White Heron"
Sylvia's climbing of the landmark pine is not a straightforward ascent
but a spiral, combining both the circular "feminine" movement and
the linear "masculine" one. Here as well we see a spiral as Nan circles
around this critical point, her conjunction with the mother. But each
time she returns to the upland stream she is at a higher level of development, though still connected to nature itself. And just as Sylvia experiences her "naturistic epiphany" from the height of the pine tree
next to the viscous swamp, so Nan discovers her vocation and essential
identity at the very place where the mother once intended to destroy
her. I would like to look at this critical moment, the turning point of
the novel, in more detail.[70]

The crisis comes in a chapter entitled "Against the Wind." Nan has
returned from boarding school a young lady, ready to take up the
domestic duties of Leslie's household. She has lost sight of her childish
ambition to be a doctor, and Dr. Leslie, thinking that she must make
her own decision, has remained silent about his own hopes for her.
Now, however, Nan begins to chafe against domestic restriction. Her
horizons have contracted; her "duties" seem merely frivolous. The private world of the home is not enough; she wants work with a public
purpose. She feels worthless, devalued, much as Tom Wilson does in
"Tom's Husband." Finally, in a fury of frustration, boredom, and confusion she "runs away," awakening the Doctor's old fears about Adeline's legacy. As she rushes toward the Thacher farm, Nan accuses
herself: "She was not good for anything after all . . . and she had been
cheating herself. This was no life at all, this fretful idleness; if only she
had been trained as boys are, to the work of their lives!" All her pent-
up hostility explodes, and "the girl savagely rebuked society in general
for her unhappiness."[71]

But as she hurries faster and faster through the underbrush and pines,
Nan still has the impulse to kneel "quickly on the soft turf or moss to
look at a little plant." Startled at first, the birds soon return to their
place "as if they had been quick to feel that this is a friend and not an

enemy, though disguised in human shape." Even as she "savagely rebukes society," Nan "looks over her shoulder to see if a favorite young
birch tree had suffered no harm." Finally, Nan reaches the Thacher
homestead and runs to the river,

where she went straight to one of the low-growing cedars, and threw herself
upon it as if it were a couch. While she sat there, breathing fast and glowing
with bright color, the river sent a fresh breeze by way of messenger, and the
old cedar held its many branches above her and around her most comfortably,
and sheltered as it had done many times before. It need not have envied other
trees the satisfaction of climbing straight upward in a single aspiration of
growth.[72]

Here is Nan's true "parlor" and true "mother": the cedar that for-
goes its upward aspiration to encircle and shelter its adoptive daughter.
This is Nan's old "playground"; in returning she was "unconscious
that she had been following in her mother's footsteps, or that fate had
again brought her here for a great decision." If femininity possesses a
polarized ambiguity, as Sherry Ortner believes, then this place is where
we see its double nature most vividly. "Poor" Adeline was polluted by
her sexuality and alcoholism, but she was also saved by her maternity.
Love for her child preserved them both from drowning. And so we see
the transformative power of maternal communion that can transcend
both natural immanence and cultural convention: "Years before, the
miserable suffering woman, who had wearily come to this place to end
their lives, had turned away that the child might make her own choice
between the good and evil things of life."[73] If the mother is the Whore,
the daughter will be the Virgin.

As Nan steps into the place vacated by her mother, "a decision
suddenly presented itself to her with a force of reason and necessity
the old dream of it had never shown. Why should it not be a reality
that she studied medicine."[74] This epiphany is the center of the entire
book: "The thought entirely possessed her, and the glow of excitement
and enthusiasm made her spring from the cedar boughs and laugh
aloud. Her whole heart went out to this work, and she wondered why
she ever lost sight of it. . . . God had directed her at last, and though
the opening of her sealed orders had been long delayed, the suspense
had only made her surer that she must hold fast this unspeakable great
motive."[75]

Like Sylvia, who temporarily loses sight of her original communion
with nature in order to come into fuller awareness of her identity, Nan
returns to her original playground, where she once merged with the
trees and squirrels, with the dangerous mother herself, but she returns
as a healer, as the overseer, the conscious protector. She will take the

energy of her natural mother and direct it toward the "good things of life." Hence, the fury that drives her to the woods is important, for we see that Nan does not decide to nurture others out of weakness or failure of selfhood but out of strength. It is undirected, latent power that threatens to overwhelm her with savagery; healing others saves her. As a doctor she can be both strong and good at once. She can reconcile the need for agency and the need for communion. But the price, as we will see, is still her sexuality—sexuality expressed through human intimacy. Hence, it is significant that Nan is reborn through auspices of two adoptive parents: Dr. Leslie replaces the young Dr. Prince, and the old cedar tree replaces Adeline Thacher. There is a curious merging of God and genes, spirit and biology in the portrait of Nan. God's "sealed orders" are Nan's genetic inheritance. She is growing like a plant into the form that God intended. But if a heavenly father made Nan, who made Adeline? Jewett is eloquent on saints but silent on sinners.

IV

The first half of the novel brings Nan to her epiphany; the second shows her coming into full possession of the identity revealed there. We see her return to society from the woods, determined to study medicine and conscious of Dr. Leslie's wise nurturance. Her actual training is sketchily treated. The real concern of the narrative now is Nan's confrontation with conventional femininity and heterosexuality. As Annis Pratt discovered in the twentieth-century female *Bildungsroman,* our heroine is presented with a series of traditional models for adult femininity; all are inadequate. She is then tempted to give up her freedom for love.

To begin with the first problem. Now grown to a proper lady, but also assured of her true vocation, Nan feels strong enough to initiate contact with her wealthy estranged aunt, Miss Anna Prince of Dunport. Her stay with this highly genteel woman brings Nan into the center of traditional New England society. Her foil in this society is Eunice Fraley, a conventional woman who has been prevented from marrying by her mother's domination. The comparison of the two women brings the "Root-Bound" imagery to the foreground. Nan appears as a beautiful young flower, "some slender, wild thing, that has sprung up fearlessly under the great sky, with only the sunshine and the wind and summer rain to teach it." Sitting beside her, "Miss Eunice, like a hindered little houseplant, took a long breath of delight . . . and felt as if somebody had set her roots free from their familiar prison."[76]

Part of Eunice Fraley's "frailty" is ascribed to the overidentification of mother and daughter. Kept closely tied to her mother all her life, she is opposed to Nan, who has been separated from her mother since earliest infancy. As Eunice complains to Miss Prince, Nan's aunt: "I know it says in the Bible that children should obey their parents, but there is no such commandment, that I can see, to women who are old enough to be grandmothers themselves."[77] But whatever rebellion this daughter might muster is quickly suppressed by guilt and dependency: "I know I ought not to say such things. I suppose I shall lie awake half the night grieving over it. You know I have the greatest respect for mother's judgment; I'm sure I don't know what in the world I would do without her." Her confidant sees the daughter's problem clearly: "'You are too yielding, Eunice,' said Miss Prince kindly. 'You try to please everybody, and that's your way of pleasing yourself; but, after all, I believe we give everybody more satisfaction when we hold fast to our own ideas of right and wrong.'"[78] Unlike the saintly Mara or her kindly Grandmother Pennel (whose innate selflessness confounded the Puritan doctrine of natural depravity), overidentification with others has cost Eunice her freedom and whatever adult life she might have had.

However, Miss Prince does not offer Nan a much better model. While she is strong and independent, she is also lonely and cold. Like Miss Sydney of "Miss Sydney's Flowers," the older woman begins to thaw only when the younger one takes the initiative. Thus, the fear and awe that Jewett remembers in her paternal grandmother finds its way into yet another portrait. And Nan, as several of Jewett's young heroines do, brings freshly cut blossoms from the garden into the aunt's forbidding parlor. But if Miss Prince is severe, Mrs. Fraley, Eunice's mother, is true guardian of the genteel tradition: "the one person whom Miss Prince recognized as a superior officer . . . [and] formerly an undisputed ruler of the highest social circles of Dunport society . . . she was still the queen of the little court that assembled in her own house."[79]

Presented at this court, Nan shocks her hostess by admitting the truth of the rumor that she is studying medicine. Mrs. Fraley, pronouncing judgment, "said again, that a woman's place was at the home, and that a strong-minded woman was out of place, and unwelcome everywhere." Nan's decision "lowers the pride of all who have any affection" for her. She is a "refined girl who bears an honorable and respected name."[80] Only knowledge of her "peculiar and unfortunate" childhood tempers the harshness of Mrs. Fraley's judgment. Nan does not accept this criticism meekly but counters with an earnest proclamation of her special vocation. She has been given her talents by God, who must have meant her to use them. Nan does not venture to argue that medicine is a proper vocation for all, or even most, women, but it is for her. Further, she adds that "it certainly cannot be the proper vocation of all women to bring up children, so many of them are dead failures at it."[81]

During this impassioned argument, "Miss Eunice grew smaller and thinner than ever, and fairly shivered with shame behind the tea-tray. She looked steadily at the big sugar-bowl, as if she were thinking whether she might creep into it and pull something over her head. She never liked an argument, even if it were a good-natured one, and always had a vague sense of personal guilt and danger."[82] Again Eunice counterpoints Nan. Her desire to hide in the sugar bowl is humorous but also significant. The tea party, with its consecrated vessels, was the central ritual of Victorian domestic life. Here we see the excessively genteel woman wishing to "creep" into its selfless sweetness, even if it means symbolic suicide.

Nan, however, has the courage of a well-nourished and firmly rooted selfhood. She stands up to the "queen," and only the entrance of Dunport's eligible young lawyer, George Gerry, puts an end to the conversation. In him the older women see the best argument for their position. And George Gerry's courtship of Nan does present the most serious threat to her vocation, at least according to the narrator. However, the scenes between them are not entirely convincing. Nan's attraction to George seems abstract, more a plot device than an intrinsic part of her character: "He was like a great magnet. . . . She liked him still, but she hated love, it was making her so miserable."[83] Even his name, as Louis Renza remarks, seems two-dimensional.

But if Nan's attraction to George does not quite ring true, her hatred of love does. In another passage the young woman feels "that the coming of Death at her life's end could not be more strange and sudden than this great barrier which had fallen between her and her girlhood." As in Jewett's unpublished poem, "The New Wife," love appears as "barrier" between the woman and "the dear old life which kept her so unpuzzled and safe." Nan can only identify it as "this fear, this change, this strange relation to another soul." Almost terrified she asks, "Who could stand now at her right hand and give her grace to hold fast the truth that her soul must ever be her own?"[84] The answer, of course, is Dr. Leslie. Significantly, Nan cannot imagine a human love that would *not* sacrifice her integrity. As Annis Pratt's analysis would suggest, Nan differentiates between the naturistic ecstasy that had revealed her innermost self and the sexual ecstasy that threatens to destroy it. And the text leaves little doubt that George Gerry *would* demand Nan's sacrifice of her vocation: "For himself he had a great prejudice against the usurpation of men's duties and prerogatives by women, and had spoken of all such assumptions with contempt."[85]

Jewett does something rather interesting with this situation. Nan, of course, rejects the young man's marriage proposal, but during their flirtation she wins both his respect and his emulation. Her professional dedication impresses on George his own dilettantism and fires a new ambition in him. The hunter had awakened Sylvia from her sleepy immersion in the woods; now Nan awakens George Gerry from his lazy socializing in a country town. She "makes a man of him," sort of. Equally important, she gently hands him over to the woman who really wants him: the conventional woman, Mary Parish, who wishes to merge her own life in his, as Nan emphatically does not.

Nan's relationship to this other woman is also interesting. Of Nan's age, Mary is her conventional double. At a summer picnic Nan and George Gerry leave their friends behind to go for a walk. As they depart, Nan is confused by Mary's mixed expression toward her, at first affectionate but then appealing. Too late to change their plans, she suddenly remembers some gossip about a possible attachment: "Nan felt a sudden sympathy, and was sorry she had not thought to share with this favorite among her new friends, the companion whom she had joined so carelessly."[86] She arranges for George to escort the other woman home at the day's end. Mary's desire for marriage is presented as being as "natural" as Nan's aversion. Moreover, the sympathy between the two women is unmarked by jealousy. Comparing this novel again to Stowe's earlier one, we see a similar love triangle. However, the roles of Sally and Mara seem reversed. Nan is more like the "tricksy," untamed Sally (the heroine Jewett said she preferred) and Mary Parish more like the demure Mara. However, this friendship is only sketched, and sketched very lightly. Although she is described as having a "crush" on a female schoolmate, Nan's intimate life, aside from her relationship to Dr. Leslie and threatened attachment to George Gerry, is essentially solitary.

If Mara's influence on Moses is feminizing, Nan's somewhat different effect on George Gerry is graphically illustrated during their walk. They come upon a homestead where a young farmer has dislocated his shoulder. After appraising the situation and overcoming a small moment of anxiety, Nan orders the patient down onto the bedroom floor and pushes George and the farmwife into the kitchen. She then strips off her right boot, "planted her foot on the damaged shoulder, and caught up the hand and gave a quick pull, the secret of which nobody understood, but there was an unpleasant cluck as the bone went back into its socket, and a yell from the sufferer, who scrambled to his feet."[87] Understandably nonplussed, George "felt weak and womanish, and somehow wished it had been he who could play the doctor."

Nan makes little of the affair, but "if possible, she looked gayer and brighter." Like Mary Wilson, who returns from the factory in a "provoking good humor," the successful professional woman seems to taunt her male admirer, who rises to the challenge: "It is in human nature to respect power; but all his manliness was at stake and his natural rights would be degraded and lost, if he could not show his power to be greater than her own." But if George Gerry now wants to dominate and control Nan, her power has also won his love: "His heart had never before been deeply touched, but life seemed now like a heap of dry wood, which had only waited for a live coal to make it flame and leap in mysterious light."[88] The "strong-mindedness" that Mrs. Fraley so deplores in a young woman is the very source of her attraction. George is drawn not only by Nan's beauty but by her sense of purpose, a purpose he himself lacks. He loses the lover but takes Nan as *his* model, a curious reversal. Like Moses, he has come to "tremble" at the measuring rod held in the hand of a woman.

Nan's rejection of George Gerry's marriage proposal is a statement of her own principles. She admits that she has been "greatly surprised and shaken" at her own inclination toward marriage. She has seen "the possibility of happiness in a quiet life that should centre itself in one man's love, and within the walls of his home." But this restriction Nan cannot accept: "something tells me all the time that I could not marry the whole of myself as most women can. There is a great share of my life which could not have its way, and could only hide itself and be sorry. I know better and better that most women are made for another sort of existence, but by and by I must do my part in my own way to make many homes happy instead of one."[89]

Although her vocation and tone differs from Mara's, Nan's speech has significant parallels with the earlier heroine's. Both argue that traditional domesticity would weaken their special powers. Both will extend their maternal strength to a larger world: Mara through death and sainted memory, Nan through medicine and personal example. And, like Mara, Nan refuses final responsibility for her vocation. She is only serving God, whose ways are mysterious: "I don't know why God should have made me a doctor, so many other things have seemed fitter for women. . . . It isn't for us to choose again, or wonder and dispute, but just to work in our places, and leave the rest to God." She backs up her invocation of this ultimate authority with an implied suicidal threat: "I know that the days would come when I should see, in a way that would make me long to die, that I had lost the true direction of my life and had misled others beside myself."[90]

When an old family friend, Captain Parish, comes to argue on George's behalf, Nan unsheaths her final weapon. She must "forbid" herself marriage "because I know the wretched inheritance I might have had from my poor mother's people. I can't speak of that to Aunt Nancy, but you must tell her not to try to change my mind."[91] Both God and the dreadful Adeline must be called in to save Nan. Only virginity and vocation can prevent her from falling back into suicidal despair and her mother's pollution. Here Jewett's failure to come to terms with the feminist issues raised by the novel shows most tellingly. Finally, Nan should be allowed to pursue her profession not because she is an ordinary, ambitious young woman exercising an inherent right to self-determination; she is a freak, who must be allowed to follow her anomalous destiny lest she wreak havoc within the structure of civilized society.[92]

The unspoken issue is reproduction. It is part of the reason that Nan cannot talk to her Aunt Nancy about her "wretched inheritance." Marriage demands heterosexual intercourse, which in turns brings children, children that the wife, not the husband, must bear and raise. Jewett never questions the necessity of bearing children. I recall Pratt's thesis that the special characteristics of the female *Bildungsroman* depend upon the lack of adequate birth control. This historical fact underlies the entire world-view of this novel, although its presence is never openly acknowledged. Jewett also never questions the asymmetrical distribution of child rearing. Women's biology forces them to bear the children; hence, this "wretched" inheritance forces women to raise them. As Dr. Leslie reflects, while man may find his professional life strengthened by domestic happiness, "the two cannot be taken together in a woman's life as in a man's. One must be made of lesser consequence, though the very nature of both domestic and professional life need all the strength which can be brought to them."[93] His terms are extreme; a woman's life must either "surrender itself wholly, or relinquish entirely the claims of such duties."

While this passage presents the conventional justification for the sexual division of labor, it is partially contradicted by Nan's own domestic experience. Earlier she had attempted to keep a genteel household for Dr. Leslie and had been thoroughly bored by the enforced idleness of the private sphere. The issue is not domesticity versus professionalism but childbearing and child rearing versus professionalism. Keeping house alone does not "need all the strength which can be brought" to it, but uncontrolled reproduction very well might. This is the danger that Adeline's undisciplined instincts present, the threat that female immanence poses to human order and transcendence. For Nan to escape, she has to deny her Terrible Mother and counter the subversive power of instinct with sublimation. She will take the higher road and extend her love to many families instead of one; her maternity will encompass many children but not her own.

Nan's only other apparent choice is to become heterosexual but crippled and subordinated to male authority. Conventional women in this novel may have their reproductive powers preserved intact but only at the price of their freedom. Their sexual power is controlled by the "irons" of "custom and circumstance."[94] Only these rigid cultural structures can keep order when sexuality is unleashed. Adeline, as the epitome of these instinctual powers, appears as the archetypal feminine who subverts the social structure by marrying above her, then destroying her husband through her defiance.

Significantly, the novel resolutely avoids Nan's bonds with other women. They have no common cause. When Dr. Leslie learns that Nan has rejected marriage, he ponders again her anomalous quality: "The simple fact that there is a majority of women in any centre of civilization means that some are set apart by nature for other uses and conditions than marriage."[95] Here again a rather idiosyncratic evolutionary philosophy intrudes as justification for Nan's freedom. It is joined by bigger guns when the doctor calls in the Deity: "It counted nothing whether God had put this soul into a man's body or a woman's." This heavenly Father "had known best, and He meant it to be a teller of new truths, a revealer of laws, and an influence for good in its capacity for teaching as well as in its example of pure and reasonable life."[96]

Nan transcends the conventional lives of both men and women. She is indeed the Virgin of Titian's painting. When George Gerry first sees her, she is dressed in white, then "a ray of sunshine touched the glass of a picture behind her and flew forward to tangle itself in her stray locks, so that altogether there was a sort of golden halo about her pretty head."[97] As Moses does when Mara announces her death, George senses a strange aura about Nan when she solemnly refuses him: "her face wore again the look he had feared to disturb the night before, and his whole soul was filled with hommage in the midst of its sorrow, because this girl . . . stood nearer to holier things than himself, and had listened to the call of God's messengers to whom his own doors had been ignorantly shut."[98]

Both the polluted and the sacred are taboo, untouchable; both are anomalous. Nan and Adeline each stand on the periphery of culture.

Adeline, on the border below, offers a life that is a "sorrow and a shame." But if Adeline transforms cultural forms into instinctual ones, producing chaos in her wake, Nan transforms human forms into spiritual ones. Standing "nearer to holier things" than George Gerry, she mediates between culture and divinity. That this transcendence is also a kind of domination is neatly revealed in the wonderful image of Nan with her unshod foot firmly planted on the shoulder of the dependent, prone farmer. But Nan's dominance heals. By refusing George, "Nan that night was a soul's physician, though she had been made to sorely hurt her patient before the new healthfulness could well begin."[99]

Like the Madonna treading Satan underfoot, Nan fuses purity and power, a maternity without spot or limit. "A great army of sick children" seem to plead that "Nan . . . not desert their cause."[100] However, the Virgin is not fully adequate as an image of Nan; like Mara, she is not the mother of a Savior but a Savior in her own right. As Dr. Leslie says, "She had come to her work as Christ came to his, not to be ministered unto but to minister."[101] And like Dr. Leslie himself, Nan cannot be typed by biological gender. It is only incidental that her soul is in a woman's body; finally, her spirit, like Christ's, transcends all such earthly confinement. Indeed, the Madonna's namesake here is not Nan but Mary Parish, the woman who will bear George Gerry's children and find her place within the parish but not the world.

So Nan finishes her training, then resists another temptation—an invitation to practice in Zurich. As Dr. Leslie had, she will come home to Oldfields. Nan returns to "the dear old town" ready not only to dispense medicines and hygienic maxims but to become herself "a tonic to mind and soul; and since she was trying to be good, go about doing good in Christ's name to the halt and maimed and blind in spiritual things."[102] In the final scenes Nan hikes back toward the farmhouses of her relatives, Jake and Martin Dyer. She has not forgotten the old people, nor her connection to the natural world that gave her birth. But now she ministers to the Dyers—those who die—as an outsider, paradoxically both loving and detached: "It pleased and amused the old people to be reminded of the days when Nan was a child and lived among them, and it was a great joy to her to be able to make their pain and discomfort less, and be their interpreter of the outside world."[103]

Completing its ascending spiral, the book brings Nan back to her mother's grave. She feels "a strange fascination about these river uplands; no place was so dear to [her], and yet she often thought with a shudder of the story of those footprints which had sought the river's brink, and then turned back."[104] But all Adeline's "evil gifts had been buried with her." Her only legacy was "some traits that had won Nan many friends." Now strong enough to sympathize, Nan sees at last the maternal love that had kept them both from drowning: "Perhaps, made pure and strong in a better world, in which some lingering love and faith had given her the true direction at last, where even her love for her child had saved her, the mother had been still taking care of little Nan and guiding her."[105] Purged finally of the biological body that betrayed her, perhaps in death Adeline had become the mother she should have been in life, ensuring in her daughter the "whiteness of soul" that she herself had lost. The not-very-hidden text here is, of course, the sexuality of the mother, whose shame may have involved not only alcoholism and begging but other horrors, perhaps prostitution.

Nan has transcended her mother but at the cost of her own children: she will never have them. Nan is not root-bound, but she will bloom only for humanity at large. Moreover, she has won her freedom by asserting her difference from other women. She has sacrificed not only marriage and family but also her place within the community of women. She will return to the female sphere not as the intimate, the recovered daughter, but as the detached healer, the new incarnation of Dr. Leslie. Thus, we see Nan reject every human mother, biological or social, who comes forward to claim her. None are adequate; all are dangerous. Having finally shed them, Nan is alone at the book's very end, virtually standing on her mother's grave. As she looks out over the river where she escaped drowning, Nan watches some eagles flying across the water; then her gaze shifts past them up into the sky itself. Her moment has come: "The soft air and the sunshine came close to her; the trees stood about and seemed to watch her; and suddenly she reached her hands upward in an ecstasy of life and strength and gladness. " 'O God,' she said, 'I thank thee for my future.' "[106] Like Athena, Nan has been reborn from the head of the Father.

V

Certainly none of the Terrible Mothers in *A Country Doctor* was modeled on Jewett's own mother, Caroline Perry Jewett. Miss Prince and Mrs. Fraley may have some traits in common with Jewett's paternal grandmother, but her mother was neither a depraved alcoholic nor an unbending authority figure. If anything, Mrs. Jewett resembled the kindly, if conventional, Mrs. Graham, or the rather timid Eunice Fraley. What is important here is that Jewett's portrait of Nan stresses the young professional woman's need to escape both biological and social femininity to find fulfillment. The price was a kind of grand isolation from the personal and particular bonds of family and friendship. The love that might have been expressed through marriage, female friendship, or motherhood must instead be sublimated into the more abstract concerns of medicine. And while the mother might be reintegrated as guiding spiritual principle—as we see in both "The Christmas Ghosts" and *A Country Doctor*—this reintegration occurs only after the mother is safely dead.

As I argued earlier, I believe Jewett felt deep ambivalence toward her own mother. Nancy Chodorow writes: "The internalized experience of self in the original mother-relation remains seductive and frightening: Unity was bliss, yet meant the loss of self and absolute dependence."[107] The mother in this novel is as ambiguous as the hunter in "A White Heron." She promises love but threatens the daughter's selfhood. Further, to identify with the mother is to accept the mother's role and, with it, subordination to the male, restriction to the domestic sphere, and finally, reproduction without control.

But ambivalence has, by definition, two sides. While Jewett may have recoiled from her mother, she also loved her deeply. Equally important, she found emotional fulfillment through her bond to Annie Fields and other female friends. However, in *A Country Doctor* Jewett could not find a way to integrate these aspects of her own experience with her fictional heroine's self-realization. The only "woman" close enough to embrace Nan is the old cedar tree. Until Jewett came to terms with her mother, around the time of Caroline Perry Jewett's final illness and death, her fiction tends to fragment the maternal figure. At the very least the mother is split in two: the bad human mother, who must be kept at a distance, and the good natural mother, a kindly cedar tree that envelops the "daughter" in a comforting but nonthreatening embrace. Only in nature can Nan recover the bliss of the original mother relationship without jeopardizing her selfhood. In "A White Heron" this naturistic ecstasy offers an alternative to the hunter; in *A Country Doctor* it offers an alternative to Adeline.

And yet, when Jewett does create a "good" human mother for her professional heroine, it will still be an adoptive one. As Nan Prince was adopted by Dr. Leslie to escape her feminine destiny, so the anonymous narrator of *The Country of the Pointed Firs* is adopted by the Bowden clan and initiated back into the feminine mysteries that Nan left behind. Moreover, Mrs. Todd and Mrs. Blackett are really the cedar tree grown to human form. Their power comes from an essential identity with the maternal landscape they cherish.

In a sense, then, *A Country Doctor* has a double plot. On the surface, Nan grows upward toward identification with Dr. Leslie. Her story appears not to be the pastoral, matriarchal one of Persephone's return but rather the patriarchal one of Christ's coming to his ministry. And yet there is that unconscious spiraling back to the mother. Mara in the *Pearl of Orr's Island* is finally buried beside Dolores, while her soul journeys up to join, perhaps to complete, Christ's own. Nan herself, by standing on her mother's grave, acknowledges this source of her being. Sublimation of communion into her medical profession is finally not enough. Deep in the ground, the earlier connection still holds.

In her analysis of "A White Heron" Elizabeth Ammons argues that Sylvia's adventure, particularly her linear climbing of the masculine tree, represents her experimental assumption of the masculine maturation plot: a hierarchical plot stressing conflict over cooperation. And yet Sylvia's experiment convinces her that this pattern, "the shape of violence," is not her own. Not only does Sylvia resume "her circles of earthbound meanders with the cow," but so does Jewett. As Ammons puts it, "having perfectly reproduced male-defined narrative structure she writes against it in her ultra feminine last paragraph, full of flowery, personal invocations and hovering apostrophes."[108] In the earlier *A Country Doctor,* however, the return to the "mother" is much more ambivalent, indeed much more repressed, and the narrative structure consequently more linear, more conventionally masculine. If we correlate this structure with Jewett's own development, a significant analogy emerges.

When Freud probed the substrata of woman's personality, he was startled to find the relics of the earlier matrisexual attachment lying "beneath" the heterosexual structures of her oedipal complex. Fascinated by archeology, Freud turned there for an explanatory image: "Our insight into this early, pre-Oedipus, phase in girls comes to us as a surprise, like the discovery in another field, of the Minoan-Mycenaean civilization behind the civilization of Greece."[109] Freud sounds very much like Bachofen, who was puzzled by the anomalous survivals of matriarchal rituals. And like Bachofen, Freud reconstructed from these fragments the patterns of a "lost" stage of development, destroyed and hidden behind the civilization of the Father: "Everything in the sphere of this attachment to the mother seemed to me so difficult to grasp in analysis—so grey with age and shadowy and almost impossible to revivify—that it was as if it had succumbed to an especially inexorable repression."[110] Just as the matriarchal world lay hidden in ruins beneath the Hellenic city, the mother's plot literally lies beneath Nan's feet as she looks up into the sky to thank her Father for the future. But the matrisexual world, as the Demeter–Persephone myth itself affirms, *can* be revivified. Although it seems to die, to grow "grey with age and shadowy," its heart is eternally young.

Chapter Eight

The Return

Like Nan and Sylvia, Jewett left home to gain "wide views on life."
And like them she returned to heal, preserve, and instruct. Jewett no
more accepted the role of passive princess than her heroines did. In an
undated letter to Annie Fields she playfully adapted the fairy tale motif
to her own anomalous role: "Every time I come back to South Berwick
I am so so eager to know what I can do for it—but the little town is
so unconscious of possible betterments and goes on with its cooking
stoves so comfortably in spite of Aladdin Cookers that it is like sleeping
beauty in its wood well. Perhaps I am the prince to wake it up but I
never know how."[1] On another occasion Jewett again found herself
playing the prince, this time to a "pale-faced, dark-haired girl, who
was just home from a seminary." Jewett noticed how tired she seemed
and how narrow her life had been. The closer they became, the more
Jewett wished that her friend "would read novels all her summer va-
cation; good-tempered well-bred English society novels, and no matter
if some of them were naughty, for she could only see how much better
it is to be good. I wished her to know another sort of people beside
the teacher and scholars she was always with, and I wished to make
her world a little larger, I liked her so very much."[2]

As I have shown earlier, her father and Annie Fields had played this
role for Jewett herself. However, the woods and fields, beaches and
streams of coastal Maine also gave Jewett a refuge from genteel conventions and a companionship that lasted all of her life. As a very small
child Jewett discovered an exhilarating freedom within the fenced yard
of the Berwick house. When older, she explored the countryside on
horseback, provoking the stares and comments of country people un-
used to seeing women riding alone in out-of-the-way places. As Sylvia
and Nan discover, nature could offer a young woman her first taste of
freedom, a place to test her powers.

The tension between the open spaces of nature and the demands of
conventional femininity is expressed clearly in "Was This a Little Ancestress," an unpublished Jewett poem now in the Houghton Library.

"One who likes to play," Martha Pratt is an older girl forced to sew samplers among the little five- and six-year-olds. She can manage only "the simplest stitch." "The little *f* she tried to lose" becomes identified with Martha herself and is "brought back a prisoner" to the domestic design. Contrasted with the bright summer landscape full of birds and flowers, women's work seems imprisonment, and the stern grand-mother a jailer:

"No needlewoman!" Grandmother says
"Nor one who perseveres—
I see the dropping yellow head
I count the falling tears[3]

Significantly, Martha Pratt is presented as a possible ancestress of the poem's speaker. The maternal legacy includes more than decorous submission. In Martha's "crooked stitches" can be read the "sorrows" of a rebellious female spirit. The poem seems a precursor of Adrienne Rich's "Aunt Jennifer's Tigers." Rich's speaker also "reads" a female relative's needlework and finds that the "bright topaz" tigers embroi-dered there "do not fear the men beneath the tree." Aunt Jennifer expresses all of her power and defiance in this domestic "screen." However, the expression is necessarily covert; sublimated, not direct. She finds "the ivory needle hard to pull" for "the massive weight of Uncle's wedding band / Sits heavily upon Aunt Jennifer's hand." De-spite oppression, Aunt Jennifer's spirit wins through to independence in art, if not in life:

When Aunt is dead, her terrified hands will lie
Still ringed with ordeals she was mastered by.
The tigers in the panel that she made
Will go on prancing, proud and unafraid.[4]

Poor Martha Pratt can neither roam the summer woods "proud and unafraid" nor sublimate her energy into imagery. She has neither free-dom nor art; Jewett wanted both.

While sympathizing with her "little ancestress," Jewett found her own way to transmute the tools of domesticity into symbols of inde-pendence. In the unpublished essay, "Outgrown Friends," she offers the following "lesson from sewing": "If you haven't sufficient purpose and determination and only do things that are not worth your while, you are sewing the seam of life . . . as if you had your needle un-threaded." A woman's life should not be marked by the wide, loose stitches of a child but should show "the close firm even seam of the long practised work."[5] In another unpublished fragment, entitled "Thoughts about Housekeeping," Jewett stresses the importance of possessing one's domestic kingdom, rather than being possessed by it. The first rule of housekeeping is "that your house shall never keep you. . . . To follow the spirit of that often forgotten rebuke of our great Master of Right Living—the Sabbath is made for man. We must often remind ourselves that the house is made for the ~~women~~ [Jewett's deletion] dwellers in it."⁶

Jewett brought the freedom of the woods back home. In *A Country Doctor* Nan pointedly opens the stuffy parlor to light and air. She brings garden flowers inside the formal space of her genteel aunt's house and places them in vases without permission. Intent on blurring the boundaries between nature and culture—"spiritualized" nature and culture—Nan domesticates the forest itself. The woods become her "playground" and the cedar tree her "sofa." The autobiographical sources for these passages appears in "A Bit of Shore Life," in which Jewett describes the great pines she had played under as a child. That winter her well-loved woods had all been cut down: "There never will be such trees for me any more in the world. I knew where the flowers grew under them, and where the ferns were greenest, and it was as much home to me as my own house."⁷

For Nan the woods are not only a home but a family. She is both sheltered and nurtured by the cedar tree that circles down to enfold her. The great pine that Sylvia climbs at first resists but then helps her on her quest. It steadies its branches for her and holds the winds at bay. Jewett, like her characters, nurtured and protected nature because she felt a mystical communion with its spirit. As a child she felt kin to the squirrels, flowers, and even bushes. Mothered by nature, she grew up to become nature's mother. Her empathy appears in this quiet passage: "I shall remember as long as I remember anything a small seedling appletree that stood by a wall in a high wild pasture at the White Hills,—standing proudly over its first small crop of yellow apples all fallen into a little almost hollow of the soft turf below."⁸ Part of this description's power—and the scene's original impact—comes from its muted sexuality. The very feminine tree has given birth to this "small crop" of apples that nestle in a nest of "soft turf." Like many Victorian women Jewett responded strongly to feminine sensuality expressed as maternity, not as heterosexuality.

In a different mood, Jewett memorialized a dying elm, "the dearest tree of my childhood and all my days," which was then in danger of crashing against the South Berwick house: "I begin to feel as if it were holding itself up just as long as it could, in a kind of misery of apprehension, poor old tree! It seems as if it must know all about us."⁹ However, Jewett also admitted that, while she had some acute griefs at the loss of a few familiar trees, "it was years before she could extend this sympathy beyond her "family": "now I have a heart-ache at the sight of a new clearing, and I follow sadly along the road behind a great pine log as if I were its next of kin and chief mourner at its funeral." Her description of this stately pine echoes the vision of Sylvia's *axis mundi*: "A live tree that holds its head so high in the air that it watches the country for miles around,—that has sheltered a thousand birds and families of squirrels and little wild creatures."[10]

Jewett apparently did not see these ideas as mere fancy but speculated on the possibility of consciousness in the plant world: "How low down in the scale of existence we may find the first glimmer of self-consciousness nobody can tell, but it is as easy to be certain of it in the higher orders of vegetable life as in the lower orders of animals."[11] One spirit pulsed through the great chain of being. To commune with the great trees was to find one's own essence mirrored in leafy form. However, Jewett always keeps a sense of incarnation. She recalls the mythic hamadryads and wonders if they were not a dim recognition of consciousness within the trees themselves. And yet these ancient stories ignored the trees' individuality. The imaginary creatures "accounted for things that could not otherwise be explained, but they were too much like people, the true nature and life of a tree could not be exactly personified."[12] All life might be the embodiment of one spirit, but the boundaries of individuals must be respected.

Here as elsewhere in her work Jewett confronted the problem of the one and the many and resolved it through the paradox of incarnation: "There was an old doctrine called Hylozoism, which appeals to my far from pagan sympathies, the theory of the soul of the world, of a life residing in nature, and that all matter lives; the doctrine that life and matter are inseparable."[13] Jewett's aim was not to transcend matter— the immanence of biological, physical life—but to celebrate the life embedded, incarnated there. Each tree is reverenced in itself, for itself, a unique and irreducible identity. God exists only in detail and can only be known through loving communion with the created world. Each is a part of the whole, but the whole is known only through the part: glimpsed in the face of a friend, of a parent, of a flower, even a friendly hop toad:

The relationship of untamed nature to what is tamed and cultivated is a very curious and subtle thing to me; I do not know if every one feels it so intensely. In the darkness of an early autumn evening I sometimes find myself whistling a queer tune that chimes in with the crickets piping and the cries of the little creatures in the garden. I have no thought of the rest of the world. I wonder where I am; there is a strange self-consciousness, but I am only a part of great existence which is called nature. The life in me is a bit of all life, and where I am happiest is where I find that which is next of kin to me, in friends, or in trees, or hills, or seas, or beside a flower, when I turn back more than once to look in its face.[14]

These epiphanies illuminated Jewett's life and gave it meaning: "The true importance of life is not our misery or despair, however crushing, but the *one good moment which outweighs it all*."[15] I believe this one good moment has its origin in the primary love between mother and child; its power is the recovery of that love. In the blissful fusion of infancy, personal boundaries seem magically erased; the mother's identity extends downward to the child, while the child's reaches upward through the mother to generations before. Now the mother, who was the ground of the child's being, has been rediscovered in nature, the ground of human life: "I believe that there are few persons who cannot remember some trees which are as much connected with their own lives as people are. When they stand beside them there is at once a feeling of very great affection. It seems as if the tree remembered what we remember; it is something more than the fact of its having been associated with our past."[16]

And yet if nature is often portrayed as an adoptive mother in Jewett's fiction, it was her father who took her out of the house and into the country when she was a small girl "drooping" over her schoolbooks like an uprooted wildflower. Many years later Jewett described a "forgotten" place they had visited together: "We followed a woods road into an old farm where I used to go with father years and years ago (the first time I ever knew anemones was there, I remember). It is high on a great rocky hillside and deep in the woods, and what I had completely forgotten was the most exquisite of glens. I am not going to try and describe it except to say I have never seen a more exquisite spot, and I must certainly take you to see it."[17]

Earlier I quoted de Beauvoir's remark that women revealed themselves most fully when speaking of landscapes. While it may be too speculative, nevertheless we may pick up a suggestion of Jewett's relationship to her father. The two of them had discovered this "most exquisite of glens," isolated and hidden from all others. The memory of these visits, which had been frequent, had been forgotten by Jewett, but now it is Annie Fields with whom she wishes to return to this special precinct, where she had "first known anemones." Here we sense the sweet and innocently sensuous quality of her relationship to her father: their conspiracy of exploration and communion. And consistent throughout Jewett's writing is her own identification with landscape to be explored. Kin to the tree, the bird, the land itself, she is "co-extensive" with the green world that her father unlocks and brings to her awareness.[18]

However, the male who "unlocks" may become the male who violates. While Jewett idealized her nurturant father, she dreaded the men who exploited and destroyed the landscape. As Josephine Donovan demonstrates, Jewett saw before many others did the gradual spoiling of the natural environment by industrialization. In "The White Rose Road" she concludes, "Man has done his best to ruin the world he lives in."[19] The polluted Piscataqua River mutely supported her claims. The devastated clearings gave Jewett "such a hunted feeling, like the last wild thing that is left in the fields."[20] In "A Neighbor's Landmark" she excoriated the village capitalist who bought up the woodlots of hard-pressed farmers, then "stripped the land to its bare skin . . . he left nothing to grow: no sapling-oak or pine stood where his hand had been."[21] Jewett's language again reveals her visceral identification with the landscape, which is "stripped" to its "skin" and left barren by a brutal male hand. This rape leads to sterility; even maternity cannot counter the violation. But Jewett, like Sylvia, sees the danger and sets out to preserve the wild creatures with which she identifies. In this case, she actually bought a stand of South Berwick's timber pines and prevented them from being cleared for new houses and roads. The tree's daughter had become its mother.

Thus, as Jewett became aware of her identification with the green world unlocked by her father, she came finally to that deeper stratum in the psyche that was her mother. And this stratum, which was always there, could not be easily spoken. How much easier to talk of maternal trees and loving birds, sympathetic flowers and confiding hop-toads than of human beings. Only when Jewett was strong enough to love without loss of self could she articulate the very deep bond that she had to her mother. Until then these feelings tended to be expressed through descriptions of landscapes rather than of women. Although her mother, sisters, and friends were central in Jewett's life, she did not put these ties at the center of her fiction until the late 1880s.

Jewett's awareness of her own reticence and ambivalence may have motivated a remark in a letter to Willa Cather: "It is always hard to write about the things near to your heart, from a kind of instinct of self-preservation you distort them and disguise them."[22] Earlier I quoted a letter to Thomas Bailey Aldrich in which Jewett mentioned the "bars of shyness . . . difference . . . [and] carelessness" in her relationship with her mother. These were all swept away in the final years of Caroline Jewett's illness while her daughter sat with her through the long afternoons in the upstairs bedroom. Their new intimacy prepared the way for Jewett's best writing, writing that no longer shied away from the "things near to her heart."

However, Jewett's best later work still did not deal with women of her mother's class and background. She turned instead to those preindustrial countrywomen she had known in childhood: women close to nature, kin to the great pines and soaring birds. Jewett preferred to create characters past childbearing age, either single or widowed. These women may be mothers, but they are no longer "polluted" by heterosexuality nor subordinated by patriarchal marriage. While they may be richly domestic, they are rarely crippled. They sustain themselves through their own work and through bonds of mutual affections and sympathy. Their sturdy figures balance love and strength. This is the matrifocal society that Chodorow found flourishing in Morocco, despite that culture's extreme patriarchalism. It is a female sphere in which mutual support and productive work grant mothers and daughters self-respect and love singularly free from ambivalence. As Marjorie Pryse writes, "the lost world in *The Country of the Pointed Firs* is not the world of shipping, but a world in which women were once united with their mothers and inherited their mothers' powers."[23]

Written during her mother's illness, stories such as "The Town Poor" (1890) and "Miss Tempy's Watchers" (1888) reveal Jewett's growing sensitivity to the muted power of these women's rituals. "Miss Tempy's Watchers," for example, shows Jewett's longstanding concern with memory and the dead. Clearly, there is a close relationship between this story and "The Christmas Ghosts," in which another "watcher" finds peace through fusion with a loving female spirit. However, not until *The Country of the Pointed Firs* does Jewett bring a literate, professional heroine into relationship with these powerfully maternal figures. Unlike Nan Prince, the *Pointed Firs* narrator "returns" to Mrs. Todd's cottage, not as a detached savior but as a friend, ultimately as an adoptive sister and daughter. As a child Jewett had trailed her physician father from house to house like "a little dog," an action that Nan Prince repeats. Now the narrator walks the Dunnet Landing paths behind Mrs. Todd, who initiates her into the mysteries of country life. Her landlady's herbal potions seem the remedy not only for "the common ails of humanity" but also for "love and hate and jealousy and adverse winds at sea." By the end of her summer's stay the narrator admits, "She was a great soul, was Mrs. Todd, and I her humble follower."[24] Jewett's art still aims to heal, but now her model comes from women's domestic traditions: the quiet art that draws individual selves into communion and transforms raw nature into sacrament.

I

Placed within the context of Jewett's own development, the heroines of *Deephaven, A Country Doctor,* and *Pointed Firs* reflect a gradual progression toward integration. Confirming Erich Neumann's thesis on archetypal imagery, the maternal figures in Jewett's fiction also grow from the eccentrics and grotesques in *Deephaven* to the alcoholic mother and forbidding aunt in *A Country Doctor* toward the clear, numinous outlines of Mrs. Todd and Mrs. Blackett in *Pointed Firs.* We see in this transformation the distance Jewett traveled from her own adolescence, with its ambivalence and fits of blues, to the new serenity she found following the death of her mother.[25]

Thus, *Pointed Firs* begins with "The Return." The title fits on many levels, but its richest meaning appears in relation to Annie Fields's "The Return of Persephone." While the narrator's story begins the mythic return to the Mother, so does her vision. She has the eyes of the returned Persephone: conscious of separation but full of love. Without this love, consciousness is dangerous; Demeter commands the restored Persephone not to look at her. The Medusa myth is inverted: it is not the sight of the mother that threatens the daughter but the eyes of the daughter that frighten the mother—for good reason. Consciousness is first won by "killing off" the mother, perhaps as the hunter of "A White Heron" kills and preserves his birds. To use the language of Martin Buber, the daughter struggling to free herself turns the mother into an "other," into "it." Only later can she see the mother as "thou." The narrator of "A White Heron" warns Sylvia not to look at the sacred bird with "arrows" of consciousness. The right way is to look *with*, not at, the heron: they watch the dawn together.

This communion is only "a moment." Persephone will die every autumn and return every spring. This inevitable rhythm gives the pastoral its poignancy. The narrator of *Pointed Firs* must leave for the city at the summer's end. Her loyalty is divided between Mrs. Todd's Dunnet Landing and the anonymous city where her other shadowy life waits for her. But like the Persephone of Annie Fields's poem, the narrator does not speak of that other life during her pastoral reunion. Her departure is always in the air but never spoken. And no matter how deeply attached the narrator might become to her landlady, she has no pretense of taking her place or making Mrs. Todd's cottage her own. Further, the narrator's very distance from this setting is the "light" that allows her to describe its value to us—to place it in relation to those ancient myths that can give these muted rituals a name. In this sense the narrator is also "married" to her solitude, to the work that must be done in silence, all alone. She combines allegiance to the male-identified ego and female-identified heart.

By contrast Kate Brandon and Helen Denis in *Deephaven* evade separation: the solitude necessary to independence and vocation. Not fully differentiated, they cannot fully return to the mother but must ward off maternal figures with overt praise and covert subversion. Their friendship, with its mirror-like quality, helps them keep their distance while protecting them from loneliness. This psychological situation is reflected in their ethos, which denies the reality of suffering, separation, and loss.

In *A Country Doctor* Nan Prince stands alone but does so by unequivocally rejecting the mother or mothers: Adeline Prince, Grandmother Thacher, and Anna Prince. The father becomes her way out, and Nan returns to Oldfields as its androgynous savior. She has discovered the value of independence and agency and has kept her communion with the maternal landscape. But she has lost even the ambivalent communion with the mother that Kate and Helen retain. Further, she has lost female friendship. She has consolidated her identity through the guidance of the father, but this has drawn her boundaries so sharply that a twinlike friendship such as we see in *Deephaven* seems hardly possible.

By the time of *Pointed Firs* Jewett's heroine has achieved this differentiation; her vocation is secure. Now she can embrace the community of women. And yet she is even less rooted than Helen Denis. The narrator lacks a history or even a name to place her in time and space. Virtually all we know is that she is a writer, that she lives in the city during the winter, that she occasionally travels to Europe. Most of what we know about this woman comes from the quality of her vision. What she sees tells us who she is. She can recognize the goddess in Mrs. Todd and knows her name.

Not only does Jewett's relationship to her mother shape the internal structure of these three books, it shapes the relationship of each one to the "mother texts" analyzed earlier. *Deephaven, A Country Doctor,* and *Pointed Firs* all adapt Stowe's *Pearl* and Annie Fields's "Return of Persephone," "misreading" or "swerving" from their patterns in new ways. In this literary tradition the family romance between mothers and daughters guides the strategic innovations of the younger artist.[26] These influences were particularly important in the writing of *Pointed Firs.*

Jewett returned to her mother texts in the early 1890s for several reasons. First there was a general resurgence of interest in the Demeter–Persephone myth. Pater's essay "The Myth of Demeter and Persephone" reappeared as part of his 1894 *Greek Studies*. Annie Fields included "The Mysteries of Eleusis" in her new collection of poems, *The Singing Shephard* (1895). Then there was Tennyson, one of Jewett's heroes, whom she visited in England in 1892. He had recently published his own adaptation of the myth in *Demeter and Other Poems* (1889). In 1889 Jewett also reread *Pearl* with renewed appreciation. Her awareness of its lifelong influence may have been heightened by Stowe's death in 1896. The death of this literary mother echoed the death of her actual mother in 1891. Jewett's letter to Georgina Halliburton stressed a daughter's need to "stand on her own ground"; only then could she "flow into the lives of others with all the greater power." In "The Christmas Ghosts" the solitary writer confronts her mother's spirit, the tall white flame whose core is love. This flame she makes her own.[27]

Equally significant, Jewett's greatest work is a revision of her first. Houghton Mifflin brought out a new edition of *Deephaven* in 1893. Preparing to write a new preface, Jewett reread the book closely. Although she said that she felt like her characters' "grandmother," in a curious sense *Deephaven* is also one of Jewett's "mother texts." As Richard Cary points out, and as Jewett herself acknowledged, these early sketches present in dim outline the settings, characters, and themes that were handled so successfully in *Pointed Firs*. Contrasted with the ambiguities of the immature work, the integrity of the later one emerges clearly.[28] For example, in a 1904 *Atlantic* article Charles Miner Thompson complained that *Deephaven*'s narrator sounded like a genteel tourist. Although pained by his criticism, Jewett admitted it might have a grain of truth: "It was hard for this person (made of Berwick dust) to think of herself as a "summer visitor," but I quite understand your point of view; one may be away from one's neighborhood long enough to see it quite or almost from the outside, though as I make this concession I remember that it was hardly true at the time of 'Deephaven.'"[29]

However, the problem with *Deephaven,* as Jewett implies, was not that its young author was too detached from her setting, but that she was not detached enough. In a well-known letter to Willa Cather in 1908, Jewett explained the importance of this separation to the beginning writer:

I want you to be surer of your backgrounds,—you have your Nebraska life,— a child's Virginia, and now an intimate knowledge of what we are pleased to call the "Bohemia" of newspaper and magazine-office life. These are uncommon equipment, but you don't see them yet quite enough from the outside,— you stand right in the middle of each of them when you write, without having the standpoint of the looker-on who takes them each in their relation to letters, to the world.[30]

Only when she saw her material from the outside could a writer express its value to the world and to herself. Only then could she return to her own experience and do it justice. As Jewett's letter to Cather continues:

> . . . you must find your own quiet center of life, and write from that to the world which holds offices, and all society, all Bohemia; the city, the country— in short, you must write to the human heart, the great consciousness that all humanity goes to make up. Otherwise what might be strength in a writer is only crudeness; and what might be insight is only observation; sentiment falls to sentimentality—you can write about life but never write life itself.[31]

This sentimentality and crudeness are particularly apparent in the *Deephaven* characters that prefigure Mrs. Todd and Mrs. Blackett. For example, in Mrs. Kew we have the kernel of Mrs. Blackett but only the kernel. Mrs. Kew is Helen's first acquaintance in Deephaven. Along with her husband she keeps the Deephaven light. The lighthouse itself is a powerful image of pastoral balance, flashing its light over earth, sea, and sky. And yet the woman who lives within the lighthouse brings no comparable illumination. The following sums up her characterization:

> . . . knowing Mrs. Kew was one of the pleasantest things which happened to us in that delightful summer. . . . When we went out to the lighthouse for the last time to say good-by, we were very sorry girls indeed. We had no idea until then how much she cared for us, and her affection touched us very much. She told us that she loved us as if we belonged to her, and begged us not to forget her,—as if we could!—and to remember that there was always a home and warm heart for us if she were alive. Kate and I have often agreed that few of our acquaintances were half so entertaining.[32]

Mrs. Kew, to whom the reader has barely been introduced (we are at the close of the second chapter), suddenly says good-bye to Kate and Helen with all of the fervor of Miss Roxy unburdening her hidden love for Mara. She loves them as if they "belonged to her," as if they were her own daughters. But while Mara gives her own love in return, Kate and Helen accept the countrywoman's affection as their due. They are sorry to leave, but they are touched by *her* affections, not by their own. She is an "entertaining acquaintance." And their explanation for why they value her seems superficial, as if the woman were a kind of picturesque attraction: "Her comparisons were most striking and amusing, and her comments upon the books she read—for she was a great reader—were very shrewd and clever, and always to the point. She was never out of temper, even when barrels of oil were being rolled across her kitchen floor. And she was such a wise woman!"[33] The flavor of this wisdom we are never given; indeed we are never *shown* much of anything about Mrs. Kew. We are told things about her from a safely detached perspective. Somehow the spirituality evoked so lyrically in the Deephaven landscape and Mrs. Kew's own lighthouse could not be seen in the woman herself.

Another precursor is the Widow Jim Patton. She "had no equal in sickness, and knew how to brew every old-fashioned dose and to make every variety of herb tea, and when her nursing was put to an end by the patient's death, she was commander-in-chief at the funeral." Kate and Helen visit the Widow Jim at home where "we were much entertained; we always liked to see our friends in their own houses. Her house was a little way down the road, unpainted and gambrel roofed, but so low that the old lilac bushes which clustered around it were as tall as the eaves."[34] In the best parlor, preserved with the same ceremonious dignity as Mrs. Blackett's, the Widow Jim invites her visitors to sit in her grandest rocking chair. However, this is not her own chair, as Mrs. Blackett's will be, but a chair for important visitors. It is obviously uncomfortable, and the young women decline. But then they do enjoy listening to her stories: "Mrs. Patton knew everybody's secrets, but she told them judiciously if at all. She chattered all day to you as a sparrow twitters, and you did not tire of her; and Kate and I were never more agreeably entertained than when she told us of old times and of Kate's ancestors and contemporaries."[35]

The stress is again on "entertainment." There is a strongly voyeuristic aspect to Kate and Helen's treatment of their country neighbors. They seem almost exploitive, as if savoring from a distance perceptions they dimly understand and affectionate pledges they cannot return. In this scene the Widow Patton, like Mrs. Kew, suddenly announces her love for the girls:

> "I come home and had a good cry yesterday after I was over to see you," said Mrs. Patton, and I could not help wondering if she really could cry, for she looked so perfectly dried up, so dry that she might rustle in the wind. "Your aunt had been failin' so long that just after she died it was a relief, but I've got so's to forget all about that, and I miss her as she used to be; it seemed as if you had stepped into her place, and you look some as she used to when she was young."
>
> "You must miss her," said Kate, "and I know how much she used to depend upon you."[36]

Kate is sympathetic to the old woman who had been her late aunt's housekeeper, but she is distanced. *She* will not cry for the widow, who is in fact not crying for Kate but for the woman she resembles. The two young women, it is clear, will never penetrate to the bedroom of this house, nor will they sit in the Widow Jim's favorite chair and look through a window with her eyes.

This chapter closes with the startling revelation that the queer dent on Widow Jim's head is the mark of a stone bottle thrown by her shiftless husband. Earlier the two girls had heard about the Widow Jim's marital woes, for "she did not mind talking about the troubles of her married life any more than a soldier minds telling the story of his campaigns and dwells with pride on the worst battle of all." Even so, the two young women are "very much shocked," and they gain another insight into Deephaven life. However, the tone still has a kind of gentle humor and curiosity. Helen displays her quaint character almost as a curator might show off the finest specimen of a collection, or a novice writer her best material.

The danger that observation will descend to voyeurism appears in "The Denby Circus." There Kate and Helen encounter Marilly, perhaps the most interesting of "Almiry" Todd's precursors. The outlines of this maternal figure are not numinous but grotesque. Erich Neumann comments that for the eye unprepared to see, divinity is monstrous. The undeveloped psyche perceives the mother not as transforming but as overwhelming, threatening. In this scene Kate and Helen use their friendship and artistic detachment as a shield. The author, herself undeveloped, further protects them by creating a woman who seems to possess horrifying power but is revealed to be pitifully impotent.

The confrontation is initiated by Mrs. Kew. Her curiosity roused by a brilliant poster advertising "the Kentucky Giantess," she persuades Kate and Helen to enter the sideshow tent with her. Inside, the giantess is sitting on two chairs, next to a "large cage of monkeys." "Ashamed of [themselves] for being there," Kate and Helen head straight for the monkeys, thereby averting their gaze from the main attraction: "No matter if she had consented to be carried round for a show, it must have been horrible to be stared at and joked about day after day."[37] To their surprise, however, Mrs. Kew recognizes this human mountain and is gathering the sad story of how her old friend came to this dreadful pass.

Marilly's father had taken to drink and died, leaving her penniless. Unable to earn a living and growing fatter by the day, she began to charge gawkers ten cents apiece to see her. Eventually she was taken up by a huckster whose former "giantess . . . had begun to fall away consider'ble." Now Marilly herself is so depressed that she has lost her appetite and fears she also will lose her livelihood. Her son's wife does not want her, and Marilly wishes she had a daughter who would care for her. Then, confiding to Mrs. Kew how her job depends upon her bulk,

the poor giantess lost her professional look and tone as she said, "I believe I'd rather die than grow any bigger. I do lose heart sometimes, and wish I was a smart woman and could keep house. . . . Is Tom along with you?"
    "No I came with these ladies, Miss Lancaster and Miss Denis who are stopping over to Deephaven for the summer."[38]

This entire conversation has been overheard by Kate and Helen, who have been "gravely" observing the monkeys. Now they turn as they hear themselves introduced: "I never saw Kate treat anyone more politely than she did that absurd, pitiful creature with the gilt crown and many bracelets. It was not that she said much, but there was such an exquisite courtesy in her manner, and an apparent unconsciousness of there being anything in the least surprising or uncommon about the giantess."[39]
    It is not too much, I think, to say that Mrs. Todd is a "far descended shadow" of this giantess with her gilt crown and many bracelets. Marilly also personifies her setting: New England as the tourist attraction deserted by her menfolk. Like Mrs. Todd, Marilly is grief-stricken by this desertion, but unlike Mrs. Todd she is helpless and dependent. The passage implies that her enormous size results from her grief: a kind of symptomatic inflation, as if the female domination of the region were a kind of monstrous distortion, picturesque but "absurd." Whereas Mrs. Todd's sorrow infuses her figure with a dignity akin to the ancient goddesses, Marilly seems "pitiful," a "creature," barely woman and far from a goddess. Her gilt crown is a cheap masquerade, not the halo of a revealed spirituality. Further, Marilly's size engulfs her personality; she is defined by her enormous body. Although Mrs. Kew considers bringing her out to the lighthouse, she quickly realizes that the poor woman would sink the boat in a moment. Marilly is drowning in her own flesh, the viscous grip of the biological world. She's chthonic, all right, but a chthonian unredeemed by divinity. Thus, we have a recognition scene here, but unlike the communicant who "sees" the expanding outlines of a numinous goddess, the onlookers confront a monstrous figure that shrinks to human size as they speak. Marilly is a graphic image of that "absurd" side of the pastoral character that blinds Helen and Kate at times, preventing them from seeing the "other side," which they are coming to "reverence." Marilly mediates between nature and culture but only because she has more flash

than Kate and Helen; she is closer to the monkeys than Kate and Helen are.

Significantly, Marilly, unlike Mrs. Todd, has been uprooted from her home and family. A native New Englander, she is being touted as the "Kentucky giantess." Moreover, she is pathetically dominated by the man who displays her. Mrs. Todd's large body may link her to the ancient fertility goddesses, but she is in command of this body. She steers her small boat skillfully and moves majestically across the landscape, "mateless and appealing." Although loving, she is also self-sufficient. Marilly's body, however, condemns her to dependency. Further, this image of a distended female figure, uncontrollably distorted, suggested a kind of grotesque pregnancy—biology run amok. But this is a false pregnancy, of course. Marilly is "mother" without the "divine child." She has no daughter to care for her, and her son's wife has refused her. Finally, she must earn her keep by exhibiting the very body that weighed her down—a suggestion of prostitution. No wonder Kate and Helen avert their eyes for "shame." Marilly is a pathetic Medusa, her terror diminished to a sideshow thrill.

II

Compared to *Deephaven*, *Pointed Firs* sets up a very different relationship between the narrator and her subject. The opening chapter is very brief, less than a page in some editions. The speaker not only has no name but does not yet possess the first-person pronoun. In the first paragraph she appears only as the implied member of a generalization: "When one really knows a village like this and its surroundings, it is like becoming acquainted with a single person." In the next paragraph she appears as "a lover of Dunnet Landing," "a single passenger" who has arrived on a June evening. The tone is subdued but expectant. It is, in a curious sense, the opening of a love story, a courtship. She had fallen in love with Dunnet Landing two or three summers before and has returned to it, aware that "the process of falling in love at first sight is as final as it is swift in such a case, but the growth of true friendship may be a lifelong affair." That's all. But it is a great deal. Her subject is the place and her relationship to that place. We will come to know *her* only through her relation to this other, a place that is also a person.

Significantly, she comes to this place alone. Unlike Helen, she is not accompanied by a friend of her own age and background. She cannot withdraw to a house over which she has control. She is dependent on Dunnet Landing for companionship. But if she is in some ways more vulnerable than Kate and Helen, in other ways she is more defined. She is, for example, a writer with a purpose. She has work to do. There is a reason for her being there besides "digging in the sand" or playing at being six years old. To return to Nancy Chodorow's definition of "mature dependence," the narrator is able to stand alone and able to acknowledge her need for support.

The opening chapter thus sets up the tensions that will propel the sketches. The narrator finds "all that mixture of remoteness, and child-ish certainty of being the centre of civilization of which her affectionate dreams had told." But is this certainty truly childish? Where is a true center, and compared to what? And what will the writer's relationship to this place be? She is the outsider, the foreigner. If she wants to be happy in Dunnet Landing, she must achieve connection. If she wants to write, she must achieve separation. Moreover, if she wants to write about Dunnet landing, she must achieve both. To truly know that place, the writer will need love—the growth of a true friendship, a lifetime's affair.

These implicit tensions become explicit in the second chapter. If knowing a place is like knowing a single person, that person would be Mrs. Todd. The narrator introduces her with a complaint about her house and its "complete lack of seclusion." Her landlady is in the midst of her busiest season for gathering herbs and selling spruce beer. De-spite the house's apparently private location, the narrator finds herself at a crossroads of neighborly activity. Glad to please and eager to be accepted, she answers the door for Mrs. Todd's customers while the herbalist gathers her wild plants. Before long the narrator's original intention has been submerged: "I remembered a long piece of writing, sadly belated now, which I was bound to do."[40]

The choice is a painful one. She fears that she will have to sacrifice friendship and community for achievement: "To have been patted kindly on the shoulder and called 'darlin'," to have been offered a surprise of early mushrooms for supper, to have had all the glory of making two dollars and twenty-seven cents in a single day, and then renounce it all and withdraw from these pleasant successes, needed much resolution." With conscience loud in her ears, the narrator mus-ters the strength to say her "unkind words of withdrawal" to Mrs. Todd, who "only became more wistfully affectionate than ever in her expressions, and looked as disappointed as I expected."[41]

Mrs. Todd had in some ways begun to make the narrator her ap-prentice. She remarks "sorrowfully" that she had never had "nobody I could so trust." With characteristic frankness she adds, "All you lack is a few qualities, but with time you'd gain judgement an' experience, an' be very able in the business." It may seem as if Jewett is recalling her own rejection of domesticity for literature, and yet we actually have a rejection of one business for another. Mrs. Todd offers companionship in work and the approval of a female mentor. But the narrator's commitment is to writing. She has her own business to watch.

Significantly, the narrator's honesty and resolute withdrawal to further her own purposes do not estrange the two women, "on the contrary a deeper intimacy seemed to begin." Rather than genteel guest, aspiring apprentice, or surrogate daughter, the narrator assumes a new equality with her landlady. As Jewett noted after her mother's death, a woman who stood on her own ground could "flow" into the lives of others with all the greater force. The narrator's assertion of her own will and need for solitude prepares the way for the beautiful moment when Mrs. Todd reveals "all that lays deepest in her heart."

Numerous critics have noticed the alternating pattern of society and solitude in *Pointed Firs*. Josephine Donovan's analysis seems similar to mine:

This work presents a series of solitaries who are seen as lonely, shipwrecked souls who long for companionship and communion. These include William, Joanna, and Captain Littlepage. On the other hand, the work also provides high emotional points and these come when people are engaged in relationships, in visits, in conversations, at reunions, in social rituals. These are the only thing that give human life significance, that enable a measure of transcendence.[42]

I agree with Donovan about the central importance of communion; however, I would also stress the importance of solitude and the narrator's dedication to her vocation. The isolation necessary for her art is not rejected, nor is individuality and self-consciousness. What is important is that these "masculine" traits are kept in proper relation to the heart. Jewett's advice to Cather is worth recalling: "To work in silence and with all one's heart, that is the writer's lot; he is the only artist who must be a solitary, and yet needs the widest outlook upon the world."[43]

In her letter to Cather, Jewett also stressed the psychological sources of vision. There is observation; then there is insight. The sources of insight are complex, and they lie in the relationship between the writer and her subject. In *Deephaven* Kate and Helen retell the myth of Demeter and Persephone and apply its patterns to village life. However, they are unable to see the present incarnation of Demeter in the countrywomen they encounter. The name alone is not enough. The narrator also comes to Dunnet Landing well prepared with analogies from classical myth and history. But like an anthropologist on her first field assignment, she quickly discovers that the distance between theory and experience is enormous. Names disconnected from life are dead forms; names attached to the moment are filled with power.

Mrs. Todd's herbalism is perhaps the most important case in point. At first the narrator sees only fragments of what she believes to be a lost tradition. In a corner of the garden are curious plants, survivors of an ancient pharmacopoeia whose "strange and pungent odors . . . roused a sense of something in the forgotten past." She speculates that "some of these might once have belonged to sacred and mystic rites, and have had some occult knowledge handed with them down the centuries." But then she assures herself that "now they pertained only to humble compounds brewed at intervals with molasses or vinegar or spirits in a small caldron on Mrs. Todd's kitchen stove."[44] Through her reference to the caldron the narrator links Mrs. Todd to the tradition of witchcraft, which Elizabeth Cady Stanton, among others, believed to be the remnants of ancient matriarchal cults. While the original consciousness of the mysteries may have been obscured by time, the narrator notices that a vague memory lingers, for "some of Mrs. Todd's medicinal potions had to be accompanied on their healing way as far as the gate, while she muttered long chapters of directions, and kept up an air of secrecy and importance to the last."

The notion that New England herbalists might be the survivors of some such ancient cult was widely accepted. In 1872 Wilson Flagg presented his views on the matter in the *Atlantic Monthly*. According to his article, when the medical profession became centered on scientific chemistry, the ancient practices of the medieval doctors and alchemists "fell into the hands of certain individuals of the female sex. They became the conservators of ancient medical notions which science had rejected, and gradually introduced a sort of domestic practice which is not yet entirely discontinued."[45] Thus, Flagg explains, herbs raised in New England gardens "were formerly dedicated to the Virgin or some worshipful saint, and were considered holy." In fact, their curative power may stem more from their spiritual associations than their chemical properties. Indeed, Flagg links the Roman Catholic saints to their pagan precursors. Like many others writing in the *Atlantic,* and in Jewett's literary circle, Flagg recognized that much Christian symbolism was simply the more ancient religion disguised.

Among the herbs in the ancient pharmacopoeia, "the mints were held in great esteem by these charitable dames," particularly spearmint, "the mint of mints." Its smell was "believed to 'corroborate the brain and increase and preserve the memory.'" Mrs. Todd's association with mint therefore seems especially apt, considering how much of her community's history she preserves in her conversation and tales. Equally

important, however, is her association with the Greek sibyl, an association the narrator stresses. Here Flagg's article is especially interesting, for he links the New England herbalists back through the
generations to a prophetic ancestress. He describes the "Pythian oracles" and how "the priestess who delivered them was made drunk with
an infusion of laurel-leaves before she prophesied."[46] The potion was
used in the temple of Apollo, god of music, poetry, and the arts. Ultimately, the laurel wreath became the poet's crown.

While the narrator can name the origins of Mrs. Todd's practice, at
first she does not seem to know what to make of this association. She
assumes that the matriarchal tradition is in ruins. She is seeing only
survivals, like those that Tylor found in the English nursery rhymes or
Bachofen in ancient mythology. But these fragments, as she will discover, are not the tradition itself, only its outward signs. The tradition
is living in Mrs. Todd herself. Finally, it is not fragments of archaic
science that give Mrs. Todd her power but her own link to the natural
world. Like Miss Tempy, who possessed the secret of bringing her aged
quince tree into bloom and preserving its sweetness, Mrs. Todd's medicine gathers the strength of the "wild-looking plants" and transforms
their essence into power. She is the "far descended shadow" of the
Demeter who "cooked" Demophon on Metaneira's hearth and so purified his spirit. The transformational energy is love. As sorrow and
sympathy, its flame transfigures.

Erich Neumann's description of the matriarchal seeress, although
written long after Jewett's book, confirms her portrait of Mrs. Todd.
He finds the source of female prophecy, as did Bachofen and Pater, not
in chemical intoxicants or pseudoscience but in woman's mystical participation in the natural world:

> . . . the woman is the original seeress, the lady of the wisdom-bringing waters
> of the depths, of murmuring springs and fountains, for the "original utterance
> of seerdom is the language of water." But the woman also understands the
> rustling of the trees and all the signs of nature, with whose life she is so closely
> bound up. The murmuring of the waters in the depths is only the "outside"
> of the speech of her own unconscious, which rises up in her like the water of
> a geyser.[47]

Mrs. Todd is directly descended from this seeress. On the way to the
Bowden Reunion she stops briefly to commune with a young ash tree.
Reining in her horse, she bows to the sapling, then remarks to the
narrator, "Last time I was up this way that tree was kind of drooping
and discouraged. Grown trees act that way sometimes, same's folks."
Such caring leads to insight and to healing: "There's sometimes a good
hearty tree growin' right out of the bare rock, out o' some crack that

just holds the root . . . right on the pitch o' one of them bare stony hills . . . but that tree'll keep a green top in the driest summer. You lay your ear down to the ground an' you'll hear a little stream runnin'. Every such tree has got its own livin' spring; there's folks made to match 'em."[48] Mrs. Todd's stories and pronouncements flow from her own "living spring," her deep sympathy with trees, plants, and people. As the narrator of *Pointed Firs* listens to this landlady (a wonderfully appropriate title), she reflects that "Mrs. Todd's wisdom was an intimation of truth itself. She might belong to any age, like an idyl of Theocritus."[49]

The ancient feminine mysteries centered on ecstatic possession. Although the Bacchic dance and other rites of intoxication might seem far removed from Jewett's decorous country ladies, Mrs. Todd's blackened vessel with its pungent scents draws the herb gatherer into the sibylline company, for "over and over again we find this mantic woman connected with the symbols of caldron and cave, of night and moon."[50] In this chapter's loveliest passage the narrator places Mrs. Todd at the center of these symbols. I have analyzed this scene at length earlier, but it is worth looking at again from this angle. In it Jewett not only evokes the myth of Demeter's revelation to Metaneira but the traditions that link Mrs. Todd to the visionary origins of the goddess herself:

> I do not know what herb of the night it was that used sometimes to send out a penetrating odor late in the evening after the dew had fallen, and the moon was high, and the cool air came up from the sea. Then Mrs. Todd would feel that she must talk to somebody, and I was only too glad to listen. We both fell under the spell, and she either stood outside the window or made an errand to my sittingroom, and told, it might be very commonplace news of the day, or, as happened one misty summer night, all that lay deepest in her heart.[51]

Here we see the sense of possession overtaking Mrs. Todd, who "felt she *must* talk" (emphasis mine). This impression is strengthened by the narrator's invocation of the "spell" that impels the two women into their roles of speaker and audience, the one to open her heart to its depths, the other to be taught, initiated into "a deeper intimacy."[52] After Mrs. Todd's tale has been told, and the narrator has glimpsed these depths, she grasps the significance of Mrs. Todd for the first time; she senses the other woman's closeness to the heart and to the sources of life: "[Mrs. Todd] stood in the center of the braided rug, and its rings of black and gray seemed to circle about her feet in the dim light. Her height and massiveness in the low room gave her the look of a huge sibyl, while the strange fragrance of the mysterious herb blew in from the little garden."[53]

Observation has deepened to insight. The narrator is learning to see with a visionary eye. Significantly, Neumann finds the sibyl at "the center of magic, of magical song, and finally, of poetry." In this aspect she becomes the Muse, the Graces, the nymphs, or even—in her darker form—the Fates. These and "innumerable corresponding figures . . . are the singing, dancing, and prophetic forces of inspired and inspiring woman to whom, in time of need, the male, farther removed as he is from the origin, appeals for wisdom."[54] Although in this case the artist is female, she too will turn to this prophetic woman for inspiration. It is an apprenticeship not in business but in wisdom. And its first step is the narrator's "unkind words of withdrawal."

III

Retreating from Mrs. Todd's cottage to the schoolhouse above Dunnet Landing, the narrator finds that "selfish as it may appear, the retired situation seemed to possess great advantages, and I spent many days there quite undisturbed."[55] High above Dunnet Landing, she can see the whole town and its relation to sea beyond. Captain Littlepage portrays it with a quotation from Milton: "A happy rural sea of various views." It is a poet's perspective, from on high. The schoolhouse itself suits her. She describes how she hangs her hat and lunch basket in the entry as if she were "a small scholar" but then sits at the teacher's desk as if she were "that great authority." The distinctions are amusing but significant. In a letter to Annie Fields, Jewett once wrote how strange it seemed that "Fuffy," playmate of "Pinny," and Mrs. Fields, author of *Under the Olive,* were one and the same.[56] Child and authority, lover and poet, inhabit the same body; the needs of both must be met.

Thus, one afternoon solitude loses its pleasure. Earlier in the day the narrator attended a funeral service for Mrs. Begg, a childhood friend of Mrs. Todd. Heeding her "conscience," she left before the burial and retreated to the schoolhouse to write. In *Deephaven* Kate and Helen recognize that they do not belong in a funeral party, and they watch it from a nearby hillside. Here, however, the narrator's loyalty is uncertain: she has compromised between work and friendship. Now she also watches from above as the funeral procession winds its way across the landscape. The "sorrowful, large figure of Mrs. Todd" stands out among the mourners, and the narrator knows, "with a pang of sympathy, that hers was not an affected grief. . . . Watching the funeral gave one a sort of pain. I began to wonder if I ought not to have walked with the rest, instead of hurrying away at the end of the services. . . . I had now made myself and my friends remember that I did not really belong to Dunnet Landing."[57] The solitude of the schoolhouse begins to seem more like alienation, and the narrator's writing cannot compensate for her loneliness: "The sentences failed to catch these lovely summer cadences. For the first time I began to wish for a companion and for news from the outer world, which had been, half consciously, forgotten."

The description of the funeral procession juxtaposed against the pastoral landscape returns Jewett to the issues raised by the *Deephaven* chapter "In Shadow." The link can be seen in the *Pointed Firs* passage:

The bay-sheltered islands and the great sea beyond stretched away to the far horizon southward and eastward; the little procession in the foreground looked futile and helpless on the edge of the rocky shore. It was a glorious day early in July, with a clear, high sky; there were no clouds, there was no noise of the sea. The song sparrows sang and sang, as if with joyous knowledge of immortality, and contempt for those who could so pettily concern themselves with death. I stood watching until the funeral procession had crept round of a shoulder of the slope below and disappeared from the great landscape as if it had gone into a cave.[58]

The funeral procession with its burden is juxtaposed with a "glorious" summer landscape; the birds sing in "contemptuous" awareness of immortality. In *Deephaven* the birds beat against the cold winds of oncoming autumn, and a "strange shadow" falls across the scene. It seems to Kate and Helen as if they and all the world are waiting on the boundary between this world and the next; all spirit has withdrawn from the grayed landscape, which must be renewed in the world to come. Here only the funeral procession seems "in shadow." The mourners with their burden retreat from the vital landscape as if "into a cave." Perhaps the mysterious boundary is presented in a different way. Mrs. Todd, as we have seen earlier, is associated with the ancient goddesses of vegetation and fertility. Her large sorrowful shape echoes those of Demeter, Rhea, and Hecate herself, goddess of the caves and the moon. But these are also goddesses of renewal. From the retreat to the cave will come new life. Grief is a passage. Death is acknowledged, but out of sorrow comes strength and reaffirmation.

In *Pointed Firs* there is much less attention to the aristocratic survivors of New England's prosperity. The world of Dunnet Landing is primarily the world of the classic pastoral. However, there is Captain Littlepage, who plays a role similar to that of Miss Chauncy in *Deephaven*. Both represent the decadent pastoral. His values are those of otherworldly spirituality, the patriarchal Protestantism that looks for redemption in the world to come, after release from the cycles of birth and death. Looking at him the narrator wonders "if he had sprung from a line of ministers; he had the refinement of look and air of command which are the heritage of the old ecclesiastical families of

New England. But as Darwin says in his autobiography, 'There is no such king as a sea-captain; he is greater even than a king or school-master!' "[59]

But if Captain Littlepage had that authority once, he has lost it now. He resembles the disenfranchised ministers Ann Douglas describes. Earlier the narrator describes him as "an aged grasshopper of some strange human variety." The comparison is telling, for it recalls the fable of the grasshopper and the ant. In the funeral procession, which appears so small against the landscape, Captain Littlepage stands out as if among the tiny dark-clothed ants themselves. But in that fable it is the grasshopper who dies when the winter comes, for he fails to make provision for the inevitable change of seasons. The ants, on the other hand, work with knowledge of winter always shadowing them and so survive for another season.

In an unpublished essay, "The Decay of Churches," Jewett commented that the failure of the Protestant ministry stemmed from its isolation, its alienation from the everyday lives of its parishioners. Otherworldly theology did not take into account the personal and particular needs of the people and so lost its root in their lives.[60] Captain Littlepage's madness has a similar source, as does Miss Chauncy's, his *Deephaven* counterpart. Both have lost their contact with the earth; they have no source of earthly renewal. The decadent pastoral is close to nature only because of its physical and social degeneration. Its psyche is associated with the past and looks forward to its reward in the other world to come. If they are the grasshoppers, perhaps the Bowdens, as we shall see at their reunion, are less a colony of ants than a swarm of bees, transforming raw nature into sustaining honey.

As the narrator is feeling her own isolation from the funeral procession most keenly, Captain Littlepage appears at the schoolhouse. His conversation clearly reveals his despair over the decline of his authority and the economy that supported it: "I see a change for the worse even in our town here; full of loafers now, small and poor as 't is, who once would have followed the sea, every lazy soul of 'em. . . . Yes, they lived more dignified, and their houses were better within an' without. Shipping's a terrible loss to this part o' New England from a social point o' view, ma'am."[61] Indeed there is nothing to take the place of the old occupations. The world of the patriarchs is gone forever and nothing but decline lies ahead:

"There's no large-minded way of thinking now: the worst have got to be best and rule everything; we're all turned upside down and going back year by year."

"Oh no, Captain Littlepage, I hope not."[62]

In the silence that follows they hear the noise of the sea, which "sounded like the strange warning wave that gives notice of the turn the tide." However, this image is countered by another: "A late golden robin, in the most joyful and eager of voices, was singing close by in a thicket of wild roses." In her 1893 Preface to *Deephaven*, Jewett had carefully disengaged herself from Captain Littlepage's despair: "That all the individuality and quaint personal characteristics of rural New England were so easily swept away, or are even now dying out, we can refuse to believe. It appears, even, that they are better nourished and shine brighter by contrast than in former years." Jewett came to believe, as Walter Pater also did, that the classic pastoral world would remain vital and fresh as long as its people remained close to the earth: "Human nature is the same the world over, provincial and rustic influences must ever produce much the same effects upon character."[63] As Jewett admits in the *Deephaven* Preface, she did not see the pastoral world's vitality when she wrote that book.

In this case the distance between the two books can be measured in the portrait of Captain Littlepage. The story he tells is of the "waiting place" between this world and the next. He had taken passage north on a ship named the *Minerva*. The name may be significant: knowledge born of the head of the Father. Littlepage's poet is Milton, whom he admires for his "lofty" spirit. And his story concerns the spirit divorced from the body. Littlepage has from the old man, Gaffert, the tale of the strange region way up north beyond the charts:

> . . . It appeared . . . like a place where there was neither living nor dead. They could see the place when they were approaching it by sea pretty near like any town, and thick with habitations; but all at once they lost sight of it altogether, and when they got close inshore they could see the shapes of folks, but they never could get near them,—all blowing gray figures that would pass along alone, or sometimes gathered in companies as if they were watching.[64]

According to Gaffert, these spirit-people do not seem to see but only sense them. One of them appears to be a figure out of Bunyan's *Pilgrim's Progress*: a "fog-shaped" man that "was going along slow with the look of a pack on his back among the rocks, an' they chased him; but, Lord! he flittered away out o' sight like a leaf the wind takes." As the sailors get ready to leave shore, the shadowy figures "stood thick at the edge o' the water like the ridges o' grim war." This "waiting place" between this world and the next seems much like purgatory, Hades, or the Underworld described in Virgil's *Aeneid*. Ghostlike and lonely, caught between immortality and incarnation, Captain Littlepage and Miss Chauncy have much in common with these flittering figures beyond the touch or call of the living.

Captain Littlepage, like Miss Chauncy, seems sane only when returned to this otherworldly sphere. In *Deephaven* Miss Chauncy has a sudden moment of clarity as she sees her mother's features in Kate Lancaster, but then her confusion resumes when she turns to see her mother's portrait and discovers instead the blank space on the wall. The disparity between imagination and reality dislocates her. Thus, the narrator notices, as Littlepage tells the story of the "waiting place," "that dulled look in his eyes had gone, and there was instead a clear intentness that made them seem dark and piercing."[65] However, this clarity is only momentary. As his tale closes, "the old, pathetic, scholarly look returned. Behind me hung a map of North America . . . his eyes were fixed upon the northernmost regions and their careful recent outlines with a look of bewilderment."

Josephine Donovan remarks that the Green Island section "presents images of community that contrast with the half-mad isolation of Captain Littlepage."[66] She notes the later description of him as a man who feels as if "the world were a great mistake and he had nobody with whom to speak his own language or find companionship." It also seems to me that Captain Littlepage cannot find consolation for the loss of his authority. His vision is dimmed and blurred, fixed on the past and on the beyond. Hence, he is not able to recognize the sources of renewal that his own world offers. Following their conversation the narrator returns to the village, where she meets Mrs. Todd, who quickly surmises that the captain has been sharing his tales. Then the two friends look out over the Dunnet Landing landscape together. The "waiting place" image of cobwebbed spirits descending to the shore like the "ridges o' grim war" seems to be repeated—but with a difference: "There was a fine view of the harbor and its long stretches of shore all covered by the great army of the pointed firs, darkly cloaked and standing as if they waited to embark. As we looked far seaward among the outer islands, the trees seem to march seaward still, going steadily over the heights and down to the water's edge."[67]

In Jewett's reflections on the natural world and the "great trees," she often remarked on their possible sentience. Earlier I discussed her belief that all that lives possessed its own soul, its own share in the spirit that circulates through the material world. Here we do not see the spirits disembodied but cloaked in their physical form, incarnated and embedded in the material world. Then, as the narrator and Mrs. Todd watch, the significance of this vision is revealed:

It had been growing gray and cloudy, like the first evening of autumn, and a shadow had fallen on the darkening shore. Suddenly, as we looked, a gleam of golden sunshine struck the outer island, and one of them shone out clear in the light, and revealed itself in a compelling way to our eyes. Mrs. Todd was looking off across the bay with a face full of affection and interest. The sunburst upon that outermost island made it seem like a sudden revelation of the world beyond this which some believe to be so near.[68]

The island, of course, is Green Island: " 'That's where mother lives,' said Mrs. Todd. 'Can't we see it plain? I was brought up out there on Green Island. I know every rock an' bush on it.' "

In the myth that Kate and Helen retell in *Deephaven*, mortal life is a mixture of matter and spirit: the two deeply interfused. Humanity has a special grace because once a goddess "held us in her arms." The "world beyond this" is mysteriously *within* this one: it is the potential sweetness interfused in life itself, the gift of love and communion. In an 1884 letter to John Greenleaf Whittier, Jewett described another pastoral haven, a Moravian settlement. According to John Eldridge Frost, "Jewett found the sisters' cloistered world 'so small that you could have walked around it in an afternoon if one side of it wasn't bounded by heaven.' "[69] In an 1894 letter to Annie Fields, following the death of Celia Thaxter, Jewett took up the theme once more: "All this new idea of Tesla's: must it not, like everything else, have its spiritual side, and yet where imagination stops and consciousness of the unseen begins, who can settle that even to one's self?"[70] There is no rigid boundary between this world and the next. The spiritual world is within this one, but we must have the vision necessary to recognize the moment when it "reveals itself in a compelling way to our eyes."

After the landscape has been illuminated and Green Island presented to the narrator, Mrs. Todd prepares a special drink for the narrator, a mug of her special beer, with a bit of camomile: "I heard her going down into the cool little cellar, and then there was a considerable delay. When she returned, mug in hand, I noticed the taste of camomile, in spite of my protest; but its flavor was disguised by some other herb that I did not know, and she stood over me until I drank it all and said that I liked it."[71]

Brought up virtually from the Underworld, this herbal potion is the mark of Mrs. Todd's special esteem, one she "doesn't give to everybody." Drinking it down with a slight hesitation, the narrator feels "for a moment as if it were part of a spell and incantation." She wonders if she will now see Gaffert's "cobweb shapes." Despite this playful evocation of the visionary sibyl and her laurel tea, nothing mysterious happens "but a quiet evening and some delightful plans that we made about going to Green Island." And yet the narrator's tone is sly. Green Island is itself that "world beyond this which some believe so near." Revelation need not be a melodramatic voyage to unexplored regions. It might be a silent moment of communion in another woman's room, a peaceful landscape seen from a curtained window. Indeed the special potion her "enchantress" prepares does have a mysterious flavor, a flavor the narrator cannot name. Perhaps this active ingredient is love, a love that Mrs. Todd "doesn't give to everybody." And this love does grant visionary powers, for when the narrator steps foot on Green Island, she is prepared to see. Sympathy is the only "eye" to which this world is revealed.

IV

As Mrs. Todd's boat nears Green Island, she points out the distant flash of her mother's apron. The narrator "looked, and could see a tiny flutter in the doorway, but a quicker signal had made its way from the heart on shore to the heart on the sea."[72] In just this way Captain Sands of Deephaven described those hidden faculties that communicate without words, defying time and space, even death itself. This intuition also links William Blackett and his mother. Fishing with aging, shy William, the narrator is at first uneasy about his habitual silence, but then she reflects on his Green Island life: "For him there were long days of silence in a sea-going boat, and I could believe that he and his mother usually spoke very little because they so perfectly understood each other. There was something peculiarly unresponding about their quiet island in the sea, solidly fixed into the still foundations of the world, against whose rocky shores the sea beats and calls and is unanswered."[73]

These images of Mrs. Blackett living in serene silence with her androgynous son recall not only the Divine Persephone with her androgynous child but also the matriarchal figures of Bachofen's *Mother-Right*. His reconstruction of the mother-age stressed its "aura of Saturnian innocence." He found its fullest literary portrayal in the pastoral poets, and his description fits Green Island well: "How natural we find Hesiod's silver age, with its dominant mother lavishing eternal loving care upon an ever dependent son who, growing more physically than spiritually, lives beside his mother to ripe old age; how close it is to the pictures of a lost happiness which always center round the dominance of motherhood, and to [that primordial race of women] with whom all peace vanished from the earth."[74]

Green Island, the "tiny continent," is a pastoral center on the periphery of the civilized world. When William guides the narrator to the height of the island, she looks out at the larger world from his perspective, one that has an organic integrity all its own: "Through this rough piece of pasturage ran a huge shape of stone like the great backbone of an enormous creature. At the end, near the wood, we could climb up on it and walk along to the highest point; there above the circle of pointed firs we could look down over all the island, and could see the ocean that circled this and a hundred other bits of island-ground, the mainland shore and all the far horizons."[75]

For William, a native, this island *is* the center of the world. And indeed, as in Emerson's "Circles," his eye determines the horizon. The narrator recognizes that William's vision is limited by his inexperience; he has no other center for contrast. At the same time she reverences his innocent perception. "'There ain't no such view in the world, I expect,' said William proudly, and I hastened to speak my heartfelt tribute of praise; it was impossible not to feel as if an untraveled boy had spoken, and yet one loved to have him value his native heath."[76]

The link between pastoral and Emersonian romanticism is clear, but there is also a distinct movement away from the domestic romanticism of "Root-Bound." Freedom and movement in space are stressed, not enclosure. This is a horizon that opens outward, not a circumference that restricts: "It gave a sudden sense of space, for nothing stopped the eye or hedged one in,—that sense of liberty in space and time which great prospects always give." William himself is rooted, chthonic; he shares the spirit of that "creature" whose great backbone seems to rise up through the fields. However, he is not root-bound, for his instincts— like his mother's and Mrs. Todd's—penetrate deep into the earth, unlimited by the walls of a genteel house.

This brings us to the image of the house itself. When the narrator and Mrs. Todd land on Green Island, they "could see the small white house, standing high like a beacon, where Mrs. Todd was born and her mother lived." Like the Deephaven lighthouse, it seems "deep-rooted in the ground, as if . . . two-thirds below the surface, like [an] ice-berg." And like Mrs. Todd's house, it is penetrable by the natural world. The front door is hospitably open; the path to the kitchen is marked by flowers, "portulacas along under the lower step and strag-gling off into the grass, and clustering mallows that crept as near as they dared, like poor relations."[77] Within this house there is no genteel restriction of female action. One of Mrs. Blackett's triumphs is turning a heavy carpet unassisted. Glorying in her strength, she is far from being crippled and far from disdaining manual labor. As in Mrs. Kew's lighthouse, work is preindustrial, and gender roles are not rigidly dif-ferentiated. Mrs. Blackett tells the narrator that William has been both a son and daughter to her since Mrs. Todd left for the mainland.

The pastoral ethos itself is revealed through Mrs. Blackett, as it was earlier revealed in Mrs. Todd. For if Mrs. Todd seems the type of the

Mater Dolorosa, with shadows of the earliest chthonian goddesses still clinging to her, her mother seems the type of the Sophia, the Dual Goddess. Paradoxically, Mrs. Blackett suggests the Maiden rather than the Mother. She is much smaller and lighter than her daughter, more mobile and more ethereal. Further, she has a youthful freshness of heart, "an affectionate air of expectation like a child on a holiday." Not only does her island open up its horizons, but she opens both her house and her heart to visitors. Her boundaries are penetrable not only to the natural world but to the presence and spirit of other people. She possesses "that final, that highest gift of heaven, a perfect self-forget-fulness": "Her hospitality was something exquisite; she had the gift which many women lack, of being able to make themselves and their house belong entirely to a guest's pleasure,—that charming surrender for the moment of themselves and whatever belongs to them, so they make a part of one's own life that can never be forgotten."[78]

As with her recognition of Mrs. Todd, the narrator's awareness of Mrs. Blackett's shining sweetness comes from her own receptivity: "Sympathy is of the mind as well as the heart, and Mrs. Blackett's world and mine were one from the moment we met." The communion of the two women is completed when the narrator is shown Mrs. Black-ett's bedroom and seats herself in the older woman's favorite chair, "drawn to the window with the prettiest view in the house":

There was a worn red Bible on the lightstand, and Mrs. Blackett's heavy silver-bowed glasses; her thimble was on the narrow window-ledge, and folded carefully on the table was a thick striped-cotton shirt she was making for her son. Those dear old fingers and their loving stitches, that heart which had made the most of everything that had need of love! Here was the real home, the heart of the old house on Green Island![79]

In this bedroom, seated on the thronelike rocking chair, the narrator sees through Mrs. Blackett's eyes:

I sat in the rocking chair, and felt it was a place of peace, the little brown bedroom, and the quiet outlook upon field and sea and sky.
I looked, and we understood each other without speaking. "I shall like to think of your settin' here today," said Mrs. Blackett. "I want you to come again."[80]

A source for the narrator's moment of sympathetic recognition in the tiny bedroom appears in another pastoral cottage, Miss Roxy Toothacre's in *Pearl of Orr's Island.* After Miss Roxy breaks down and confesses her love for the dying Mara, "she opened the door of a little room, whose white fringy window-curtains were blown inward by breezes from the blue sea, and laid the child to rest on a clean sweet-smelling bed with as deft and tender care as if she were not a bony, hard-visaged, angular female."[81] Mara recognizes the beautiful soul within this hard-visaged woman, a recognition expressed not only through tears but also through direct touch.

But another, more personal source may be the moment described in "The Christmas Ghosts" when the narrator and her mother share a golden moment of content in the quiet bedroom overlooking the garden. That Jewett felt the power of the scene on Green Island especially strongly is shown in her unusual use of two exclamation marks. In "The Christmas Ghosts" she tried hard to control her feelings. The second draft of that story shows she toned down its original excess.[82] In this passage as well her style cannot quite restrain her emotions.

Earlier I used Northrop Frye to argue that the pastoral mediation between nature and culture may be expressed in the landscape, in the domestic settings, and in the women themselves. *Deephaven* offers this mediation most powerfully in its final image. In its closing lines the Deephaven lighthouse sweeps its beam over the sea, as if to bring its dreamy speech to consciousness. The power that Kate and Helen could not see in Mrs. Kew emanates quite literally from her "place" between earth, sea, and sky. It may not be surprising then that when a numinous figure does emerge in *Pointed Firs* she emerges from the "ground" of the earlier book. This is nowhere more graphically demonstrated than in the transformation of the *Deephaven* lighthouse into Mrs. Blackett's shining face: "Sometimes, as I watched her eager, sweet old face, I wondered why she had been set on this lonely island of the northern coast. It must have been to keep the balance true, and make up to all her scattered and dependent neighbors for other things which they may have lacked."[83]

The final lines of the quotation are less obscure when placed against Stowe's description of the hidden saints, usually feminine, who "are the priests and priestesses of the spiritual life, ordained of God to keep the balance between the rude but absolute necessities of physical life and the higher sphere to which they must at length give place."[84] As pastoral priestess on her "complete and tiny continent and home of fisherfolk," Mrs. Blackett mediates between heaven and earth, keeping the "balance true." From the figure of the lighthouse rooted in the earth, surrounded by the sea, and rising through the sky, we now have a shining vision. From her cottage, high on its hill like a beacon, Mrs. Blackett's eye encompasses a "quiet outlook upon field and sea and sky." She has taken the role of the Dual Goddess, the risen Persephone whose torch illuminates the three realms: underworld, earth, and Olympian sky. Her presence is recognized because the narrator herself can enter this vision, can hear the words that are not spoken but leap from heart to heart.

V

The narrator's initiation into this pastoral world reaches a kind of climax, if not a conclusion, with the Bowden Reunion. The date of the reunion, with its "great expedition," is August 15. Ordinarily, Mrs. Todd says, the reunion is held in mid-September. While September was the time of the Eleusinian Mysteries, originally a harvest festival, August 15 is equally sacred, the Feast of the Virgin's Assumption. But primarily, it is the day of the Bowden Reunion. As the narrator travels inland toward the Bowden homestead with Mrs. Todd and her mother, she discovers the true faith of these country people: "I had often noticed how warmly Mrs. Todd was greeted by her friends, but it was hardly to be compared to the feeling now shown toward Mrs. Blackett. A look of delight came to the face of those who recognized the plain, dear old figure beside me; one revelation after another was made of the constant interest and intercourse that had linked the far island and these scattered farms into a golden chain of love and dependence."[85] Stopping at houses as they go, Mrs. Todd remarks how people all along the road offer them fresh doughnuts. At least one commentator has noticed that there could hardly be a better image of this "golden chain of love and dependence." Each household presents its own golden circle, a token of love, a part of a sacramental chain. Mrs. Todd herself carries a basket of homemade "hearts and rounds."

As they arrive at the reunion, the narrator gets her first sight of the Bowden homestead. In this ritual, the domestic center, not a church, will be the proper setting. The house itself appears as a pastoral matriarch: "The old Bowden house stood, low-storied and broad-roofed, in its green fields as if it were a motherly brown hen waiting for the flock that came straying toward it from every direction. The first Bowden settler had made his home there, and it was still the Bowden farm; five generations of sailors and farmers and soldiers had been its children."[86] But in the Bowden graveyard the narrator notices far more women buried there; so many men died far from home, at sea or in the West.

As these children come flocking back to the mother hen, there is an echo of Bunyan's imagery: "We could see now that there were different footpaths from along shore and across country. In all these there were straggling processions walking in single file, like old illustrations of the Pilgrim's Progress. There was a crowd about the house as if huge bees were swarming in the lilac bushes."[87] Captain Littlepage's tale of the "waiting-place" also evoked *Pilgrim's Progress*. However, nothing could be more different from those shadowy, fog-shaped people than this vital swarm of human bees seeking their matriarchal hive. And if these are a swarm, then Mrs. Blackett is their queen. As people catch sight of her, they break out in lovely exclamations of surprise, "as if it were pleasure enough for one day to have a sight of her":

An elderly man who wore the look of a prosperous sea-captain put up both arms and lifted Mrs. Blackett down from the high wagon like a child, and kissed her with hearty affection. "I was master afraid she wouldn't be here," he said, looking at Mrs. Todd with a face like a happy sunburnt schoolboy, while everybody crowded round to give her their welcome.
    "Mother's always the queen" said Mrs. Todd.[88]

As for the narrator herself: "I already knew some of Mrs. Todd's friends and kindred, and felt like an adopted Bowden in this happy moment. It seemed to be enough for any one to have arrived by the same conveyance as Mrs. Blackett." Now the narrator's commitment to this ritual is wholehearted. Whereas she turned aside from the funeral of Mrs. Begg, here she gives herself to the "happy moment" with full consciousness of its significance.

In her description of the reunion's importance, the pastoral synthesis of matter and spirit is revealed once more: "Such is the hidden fire of enthusiasm in the New England nature that, once given an outlet, it shines forth with almost volcanic light and heat . . . when . . . the altars to patriotism, to friendship, to the ties of kindred are reared in our familiar fields, then the fires glow, the flames come up as if from the inexhaustible heart of the earth; the primal fires break through the granite dust in which our souls are set."[89] As in the pastoral landscapes of *Deephaven,* the "dust" of the material world is lit from within by a "primal fire," a flame from the "inexhaustible heart of the earth." This fire the cobwebbed, ashy shapes of the "waiting-place" lack; they are poor ghosts lost and drifting far from the earth's warmth and love. Here "each heart is warm and every face shines with the ancient light." Again the strange image of cooking appears, as those who are cold, raw, and unformed in their feelings are brought to new wholeness and completion: "Such a day as this has transfiguring powers, and easily makes friends of those who have been cold-hearted, and gives to those who are dumb their chance to speak, and lends some beauty to the plainest faces."[90]

Even Mrs. Todd is awakened and illuminated: "She was not so much reminiscent now as expectant, and as alert and gay as a girl. We who were her neighbors were full of gayety, which was but the reflected light from her beaming countenance." The narrator's recognition of her friend's renewed joy makes her reflect on "the waste of human ability in this world." She realizes that "sometimes when Mrs. Todd had seemed limited and heavily domestic, she had simply grown sluggish for lack of proper surroundings." Indeed, "more than one face among the Bowdens showed that only opportunity and stimulus were lacking,—a narrow set of circumstances had caged a fine character and held it captive."[91] In *Deephaven* Kate and Helen try to gloss over the "hard fate" that condemns country people to poverty, suffering, and despair. Now the narrator acknowledges the power of circumstances. She does not offer the otherworldly consolation of a life to come, nor counsel a free choice based on nonexistent economic power. While she sees plainly that fate is not to be escaped by money or denial, she also sees that love is stronger than fate.

It is love that renews, that counters death itself. Jewett affirmed her faith in this lovely letter to Sarah Whitman, written in 1898:

Even for me things go cross wise, which one cannot bear to say, and I won't say, after all, but send you love and beg to hold on fast to the only certainty in this world, which is the certainty of Love and Care. I can't help feeling that Mary Darmesteter speaks true, out of great pain and the deep places of life, when she ends that last book, "The true importance of life is not misery or despair, however crushing, but that one good moment which outweighs it all." I cannot say how often I have remembered this in the last month. The only thing that really helps any of us is love and doing things for love's sake.[92]

But this wisdom came "out of great pain and the deep places of life." I recall again Jewett's letter to Cather, from late in her life, "It is always hard to write about the things that are near to your heart, from a kind of self-preservation you distort them and disguise them."[93] It was only when Jewett had gone down into these "deep places of life" that she could write the things near to her heart. Although the narrator of *Pointed Firs* is an adopted daughter and sister, Jewett's own love for her mother, family, and friends illuminates these simple scenes of love and recognition.

As the Bowdens march across their fields to the grove where their ceremony will be held, the suggestion of ancient myth and ritual is strong. Jewett drew these images from the *Idylls* of Theocritus, from a passage describing shepherds on their way to Demeter's yearly festival:

There was a wide path mowed for us across the field, and, as we moved along, the birds flew up out of the thick second crop of clover, and the bees hummed as if it were still June. . . . The splash of water could be heard faintly, yet still be heard; we might have been a company of ancient Greeks going to celebrate a victory, or to worship the god of harvests in the grove above. It was strangely moving to see this and to make a part of it.[94]

Now the narrator does "make a part" of the procession, as well as observe it. She participates in this family, but she is also conscious of her participation and its meaning. Thus, she notes the "strange" quality of her emotions and sees herself returned to the flow of generations. These are the Eleusinian emotions: clearing away "obstacles" to the life flow, linking the individual to generations before and after: "The sky, the sea, have watched poor humanity at its rites so long; we were no more a New England family celebrating its own existence and simple progress; we carried tokens and inheritance of all such households from which this had descended, and were only the latest in our line. We possessed the instincts of a far, forgotten childhood; I found myself thinking that we ought to be carrying green branches and singing as we went."[95]

This "far, forgotten childhood" is perhaps the same "forgotten past" evoked by the "strange and pungent odors" of Mrs. Todd's herbs: "Some of these might have once belonged to sacred and mystic rites." What these rites might have been is shadowy and lost, but the source is still fresh. Here, as well as in the "forgotten childhood," the heart is eternally young. Wherever people are close to the earth, they may hear its voice and celebrate its mysteries. And these mysteries are more than the biological facts of reproduction, the repetition of species life. They are the mysteries of spiritual transformation: the love that links all life in an unbroken chain, the single spirit circulating in all Being. In Pater's description of the Eleusinian Mysteries he felt that the story of Demeter and Persephone represented the pastoral people's faith in the continuity of life despite inevitable death. Thus, "Demeter cannot but seem the type of divine grief. Persephone is the goddess of death, yet with a promise of life to come."[96] In "The Return of Persephone," Annie Fields quotes Pater's description of the Eleusinian goddess: "the goddess of summer and the goddess of death—Kore and Persephone, that strange dual being . . . whose latent capabilities the poets afterwards developed . . . full of purpose for the chastened intelligence. *Awake and sing, ye that dwell in the dust.*"[97]

And so the marchers come to the Bowdens' sacred grove "still silent, and were set in our places by the straight trees that swayed together and let sunshine through here and there like a single golden leaf that flickered down, vanishing in the cool shade."[98] We have seen earlier how central the figures of trees and forests were in Jewett's writing. In *Deephaven* Kate and Helen pass through a similar cathedral-like grove on the way to Mrs. Bonny's. There they saw the "exquisite contrast" of the new and dying leaves. In "An October Ride" Jewett wrote:

> ... yet there can be no such thing as a life that is lost. The tree falls and decays, in the dampness of the woods, and is part of the earth underfoot, but another tree is growing out of it; perhaps it is part of its own life that is springing again from the part of it that died. God must always be putting again to some use the life that is withdrawn; it must live, because it is Life. There can be no confusion to God in this wonderful world, the new birth of the immortal, the new forms of the life that is from everlasting to everlasting, or the new way in which it comes.[99]

Although the God Jewett names here is male, the sense of transcendence found through immanence, a spirit circulating through all of the incarnate world and never separate from it, is not Protestant but pastoral. As the procession assembles in the grove, it seems like a great room: a cathedral or a cave. From it they look back across the fields to their home as if, like the couple in "A Modern Idyll," to review their life and its meaning:

> ... there was thick growth of dark pines and firs with an occasional maple or oak that gave a gleam of color like a bright window in the great roof. On three sides we could see the water shining behind the tree-trunks, and feel the cool salt breeze that began to come up with the tide just as the day reached its highest point of heat. We could see the green sunlit field we had just crossed as if we looked at it from a dark room, and the old house and its lilacs standing placidly in the sun.[100]

Now Mrs. Todd is the "picture of content." She has always wanted the narrator to share this place but "never looked for such a beautiful opportunity . . . I don't ask no more." Then she asks if the narrator has seen Mrs. Blackett walking at the head of the procession: "'It choked me right up to see mother at the head, walkin' with the ministers,' and Mrs. Todd turned away to hide the feeling she could not instantly control."[101] As we have seen before in Jewett's work, she preserves the dignity of her sentiment through restraint. Her characters may be transfigured by love, but their attachments preserve a subtle sense of individual boundaries. Their emotions seem all the more powerful for their confinement and quiet expression. Mrs. Blackett may possess the gift of "perfect self-forgetfulness," making her the queen of this pastoral world, but Mrs. Todd's large figure has a mysterious self-possession that places her at the center of the narrator's text.

In the feast that follows, the Bowdens affirm their vision by celebrating a domestic communion. The tables are garlanded with fresh leaves and graced with early-apple pies. However, "the most renowned essay in cookery . . . was a model of the old Bowden house made of durable gingerbread, with all the windows and doors in the right places, and sprigs of genuine lilacs set at the front." When this monument falls "into ruin at the feast's end . . . it was shared by a great part of the assembly, not without seriousness, and as if it were a pledge and token of loyalty."[102]

Erich Neumann describes how the feminine mysteries take place always in relation to the realities of everyday life. The boundaries between sacred and profane are subtle. In many ways the sacred is a heightening of the potential "fire" and "sweetness" at the core of profane life. Here the sacrament is the very image of the family and of the home, the very image of everyday life. Its fall into ruins is only appropriate, for this ceremony does not celebrate escape from the cycles of birth and death but a loyalty that endures despite them. The image of the ruined gingerbread house, whose pieces are ritually consumed, evokes the fallen trees of the sacred grove, whose branches and leaves feed another generation. The fire at the earth's heart brings honey out of ashes. The Bowdens, like the bees that swarm in their lilacs, distill an ineffable sweetness from life.

Chapter Nine

Sympathy Is of the Mind As Well As the Heart

In *Pointed Firs* the narrator introduces the reader to a succession of Dunnet Landing's citizens. The sketches form a kind of portrait gallery through which we move at a leisurely pace. However, these portraits are not fixed or objective. We see the writer's "material" but always in the context of her coming to know it. Her portraits are of individuals in relation. Each is present not as an "other" but as a "thou." There are always two perceiving subjects: the narrator and the person with whom she is engaged. What the narrator knows, or can know, is determined by that dialogue. Thus, there are always two subjects in another sense: the story of each character and the story of how she came to know that story. The first is always embedded in the second.

The creation of the sketches depends fundamentally on the narrator's ability to enter into these dialogues. Faced with each person, she must bring herself into connection through an imaginative leap. Her ability to make this leap comes from her own history. That history is kept from us by the narrator's resolute anonymity. But this anonymity does not mean that she is a kind of "transparent eyeball," purged of subjectivity, perfectly void of identity. No, the narrator's life before and beyond Dunnet Landing is more like the submerged seven-eighths of the iceberg that Hemingway said gave a story its substance. It is the thing left out. She comes to these people with a history, just as we do. Her capacity to interpret them has been developed through living a human life.

But what of our capacity? In the midst of "William's Wedding," the last in the *Pointed Firs* series, the narrator turns aside from her story and addresses the reader directly on the problems of her art: "It is difficult to report the great events of New England; expression is so slight, and those few words which escape us in moments of deep feeling look but meagre on the printed page."[1] As a participant in these scenes she has had to read between the lines of New England speech. Her interpretive skills are considerable, but she herself is a New Englander, as she admits when she uses the first person plural, "those few words which escape *us*." The reader must come to her text prepared with the same skills she has brought to Dunnet Landing, and perhaps that is asking more than is fair: "One has to assume too much of the dramatic fervor as one reads." Finally, the success of these sketches depends on that assumption. To see what she would show us, we must reenact her process of interpretation. We must read these human texts as she has read them, with a sympathy of the mind as well as the heart.

I

The interdependence of love and knowledge appears in the portrait of Joanna Todd. As Josephine Donovan points out, Joanna's story is placed after the Green Island sketches and before the Bowden Reunion, thus reinforcing the theme of isolation versus community seen in the juxtaposition of Captain Littlepage and Green Island.

On Green Island the narrator is taken into the heart of Mrs. Todd's family. When she returns to Dunnet Landing with Mrs. Todd, they are so comfortable with each other that they live in the little white cottage "with as much comfort and unconsciousness, as if it were a larger body, or a double shell . . . until some wandering hermit crab of a visitor marked the little spare room for her own."[2] A wandering hermit crab *is* due to arrive, however, and the narrator hears "of Mrs. Fosdick for the first time with a selfish sense of objection." Accepted by Mrs. Todd's family, the narrator now is challenged to be accepted by Mrs. Todd's friends, to become a part of the feminine community.

Mrs. Fosdick's prestige within this community is large. A visit from her is an honor, and she seems as grand a personage as Queen Elizabeth traveling through her dominions. The narrator describes her own apprehensions with amusement. She "inconsiderately" worries about sharing her supper, and after being formally presented, she sits alone in the front room while the two friends proceed to the warmer kitchen. Looking out the front window, she has "an unreasonable feeling of being left, like the child who stood at the gate in Hans Andersen's story."[3] She is lonely and jealous of Mrs. Todd's attentions. Perhaps after all she is only a visitor, a foreigner.

But then Mrs. Todd comes to the rescue. She gives a "ceremonious knock" on the door, then "reached behind her and took Mrs. Fosdick's hand as if she were young and bashful, and gave her a gentle pull forward." Mrs. Fosdick may seem as grand as a queen, but she too has a child's vulnerability. In her essay "For Country Girls" Jewett advised her shy readers that the enemy is as afraid of you as you are of him.[4] Mrs. Todd, who takes friendships seriously, brings the two women together carefully, knowing the risks of failure. She gives them something to talk about and "a refuge in case of incompatability." When Mrs. Fosdick and the narrator rejoin their hostess, they are "sincere friends."

Now commences the telling of stories. As the narrator notes, "the gathering of herbs was nearly over, but the time of syrups and cordials had begun." These tales, which distill the healing powers of experience, bring the women together. Mrs. Fosdick comments that " 'conversation's got to have some root in the past, or else you've got to explain every remark you make, an' it wears a person out.' " This analysis seems to foreclose the possibility of new bonds, but "Mrs. Todd gave a funny little laugh. 'Yes'm, old friends is always best, 'less you can catch a new one that's fit to make an old one out of.' "[5] Although the narrator does not share the same past, her powers of sympathy are such that she can reconstruct the history that binds these women together. One story in particular heals old differences and reaffirms their friendship. This is the story of Joanna, the woman who could not find solace in such friendship, who chose to live on "Shell-heap Island," outside the warmth of home and community.

Joanna's story highlights a major theme of *Pointed Firs,* the humanizing of the grotesque through sympathy. She is first introduced in a conversation about the "strange, strayin' creatur's that used to rove the country." Mrs. Fosdick says that they don't see such characters much anymore. The narrator, however, cannot help thinking of Captain Littlepage and William Blackett, although she has the tact not to mention them. When Joanna, Mrs. Todd's cousin by marriage, is described as one of these "peculiar people," a kind of "nun or hermit person," Mrs. Todd is "confused by sudden affectionate feeling and unmistakeable desire for reticence." Anxiously, she says, "I never want to hear Joanna laughed about." In the give-and-take that follows we see them comparing their interpretation of this text, comparing their judgment and experience of life. At one point, the narrator senses that the two women had once disagreed. Now, through their double narrative, they discover that time has brought a "happy harmony." With this reassurance, Mrs. Todd's speech gains a "new openness and freedom." The origins of this tale were bitter, but the tale itself is healing.

Like Captain Littlepage, Joanna is associated with patriarchal Protestantism. Deserted by her lover, she believed that she had committed the unpardonable sin by cursing God. In her reminiscences Mrs. Todd recalls her visit to Shell-heap Island to visit Joanna—her husband's cousin—who had voluntarily retreated from human society. When

Mrs. Todd entreated her to come to Green Island to live with Mrs. Blackett, "she looked the same way, sad an' remote through it all. . . . 'I haven't got no right to live with folks no more,' she said. 'I feel a great comfort in your kindness, but I don't deserve it. I have committed the unpardonable sin. . . . I was in great wrath and trouble, and my thoughts was so wicked toward God that I can't expect ever to be forgiven.' "[6]

While there is no true accounting for Joanna, Mrs. Todd and Mrs. Fosdick reflect on the lonely woman's character. Mrs. Todd remembers how the first sight of the simple cabin brought tears to her eyes: "I said to myself, I must get mother to come over an' see Joanna; the love in mother's heart would warm her, an' she might be able to advise."[7] But Mrs. Fosdick, hearing the story afresh, interjects, "Oh no, Joanna was dreadful stern." Although Joanna told Mrs. Todd that in time of sickness she wished Mrs. Blackett to come for her, she would not turn to maternal sympathy for consolation, perhaps because her own mother was as stern as she was. Joanna is presented as attached to her father. As Mrs. Todd remembers, Joanna had spent the best of her girlhood on Shell-heap Island with him: "He was one o' the pleasantest men in the world, but Joanna's mother had the grim streak, and never knew what 't was to be happy. The first minute my eyes fell upon Joanna's face that day I saw how she had grown to look like Mis' Todd. 'Twas the mother right over again."[8] Betrayed by one man, Joanna returns to where she was happiest with her father on Shell-heap Island: " 'T was the same little house her father had built him when he was a bachelor, with one livin' room, and a little mite of a bedroom out of it where she slept, but 't was as neat as a ship's cabin."[9]

In a curious way Joanna, like Miss Chauncy, has retreated to the mansion of the Father. However, Miss Chauncy dealt with her suffering and injustice not by turning against her Father in the sky but by denying the reality of her life. Madness is the result. Caught in the same agonizing position, Joanna turns on God in wrath and denounces him. But having rejected the heavenly father, she cannot find forgiveness within herself: "I have come to know what it is to have patience, but I have lost my hope." The comfort of human sympathy is alien to her, and the sentiment of tears seems to threaten her integrity. Mrs. Fosdick explains that Joanna retreated not because she felt too little but because she felt too much: "No, I never went to work to blame Joanna, as some did. She was full o' feeling, and her troubles hurt her more than she could bear."[10]

As a solitary sinner Joanna has a forbidding strength, a powerful independence: "I've done the only thing I could do, and I've made my choice."[11] When Mrs. Todd sees Joanna, she is moved to tears and runs to embrace her, but consolation is not for Joanna, who prefers loneliness to vulnerability. Even Mrs. Blackett could not warm her heart. Joanna's resistance is a kind of blindness. As Mrs. Todd says, "'T is like bad eyesight, the mind of such a person: if your eyes don't see right there may be a remedy, but there's no kind of glasses to remedy the mind."[12] The link between poor Joanna's failure of vision and the Calvinism that she believed condemned her is seen in the Reverend Dimmick, whose very name suggests his own "bad eyesight."

Dimmick is a living illustration of the faults Jewett had condemned in her essay "The Decay of Churches." Mrs. Fosdick comments that another minister "would have been a great help to [Joanna],—one that preached self-forgetfulness and doin' for others to cure our own ills; but Parson Dimmick was a vague person, well meanin', but very numb in his feelin's."[13] The vagueness of abstract theology and the numbness of the man's human sympathies are scathingly revealed in Mrs. Todd's tale of their visit to Joanna.

Reverend Dimmick's failure is prefigured on their sail out. He is afraid to cut his hand on the rope and insists on tying it, against Mrs. Todd's better judgment. Then, as he sits "talking rather high flown," "all of a sudden there come up a gust, and he give a screech and stood right up and called for help, way out there to sea." Never at a loss, Mrs. Todd knocks him down and sets things right. "He wasn't but a little man."

Confronted with Joanna's forbidding if gentle resistance, the minister prefers to avoid direct contact and pain. He again puts his behavior on a kind of automatic pilot and assumes his "high flown" speech:

> . . . he got embarrassed, an' when he put on his authority and asked her if she felt to enjoy religion in her present situation, an' she replied that she must be excused from answerin', I thought I should fly. She might have made it easier for him; after all, he was the minister and had taken some trouble to come out, though 't was kind of cold an' unfeelin' the way he inquired. I thought he might have seen the little ole Bible a-layin' on the shelf close to him, an' I wished he knew enough to just lay his hand on it an' read somethin' kind an' fatherly 'stead o' accusin' her, an' then given poor Joanna his blessin' with the hope she might be led to comfort.[14]

Instead of giving forgiveness and comfort, Reverend Dimmick joins with the accusations of Joanna's own rigid conscience. He fails to see the depth of Joanna's pain, just as he does not understand the significance of the Bible lying right in front of him. Instead of mercy he offers a prayer, "all about hearin' the voice o' God out o' the whirlwind; and I thought while he was goin' on that anybody that had spent the long winter all alone out on Shell-heap Island knew a good deal more about those things than he did. I got so provoked I opened my eyes and stared right at him."

However, Joanna herself does not seem to hear; nothing could be louder than her own wrathful deity. She calmly brushes the ineffectual minister aside, just as Mrs. Todd had done "way out to sea." When he finishes his harangue, Joanna takes some Indian relics from her shelves and "showed them to him same's as if he was a boy." Quietly put in his place once more, Reverend Dimmick is unusually silent on the way home. Mrs. Todd remembers: "He preached next Sabbath as usual, somethin' high soundin'. about the creation, and I couldn't help thinkin' he might never get no further; he seemed to know no remedies, but he had a great use of words."[15] The characteristic word associated with Reverend Dimmick is "high": "high flown" and "high soundin'." But the way to wisdom is down, not up. He has not got past the creation: experience has not touched him nor sorrow educated him. He has a "great use of words," but he is spiritually undeveloped: "numb" and "dim."

While Mrs. Todd and Mrs. Fosdick agree that Joanna's retreat grew out of her overwhelming sorrow and her fright at her feelings, they also feel that "self-forgetfulness" might have been the remedy. The nurture of others can help heal one's own pain, as they themselves have discovered. Grief can deepen character and educate the heart, as we saw in *Pearl of Orr's Island*. In Francis Fike's fine essay on *Pointed Firs* he comments that "Mrs. Todd's own grief-stricken life is the living testimony of the resourcefulness of human nature."[16] He draws attention to the scene on Green Island when Mrs. Todd tells the narrator of her own lost love. Her sorrow "is revealed precisely while she is standing in a patch of pennyroyal, as if to emphasize those healing resources which come from within the very source of grief."[17]

Mrs. Todd's compassion for Joanna comes from her own experience: she shares in the other woman's pain. With trembling voice, Mrs. Todd recalls that as soon as she saw the minister's "stupid back" leave the cabin that long ago day,

> . . . I just ran to her an' caught her in my arms. I wasn't so big as I be now, and she was older than me, but I hugged her tight, just as if she was a child. "Oh, Joanna dear," I says, "won't you come ashore an' live 'long o' me at the Landin', or go over to Green Island to mother's when winter comes? Nobody shall trouble you, an' mother finds it hard bein' alone. I can't bear to leave you here"—and I burst right out crying. I'd had my own trials, young as I was, an' she knew it. Oh, I did entreat her; yes, I entreated Joanna.[18]

Mrs. Todd offers Joanna the remedy of women's love and community. She need not feel her pain alone; others will help her bear it. But this renewal Joanna cannot accept. She puts Mrs. Todd from her gently. Rather than become a child in Mrs. Todd's arms, she takes Mrs. Todd's hand "as if she turned round an' made a child of me." The reversal parallels the earlier scene with the minister, whom Joanna treats "same's if he was a boy." She has found identity in despair; hers is a separate and lonely knowledge, bereft of a child's hope. In parting Mrs. Todd gives Joanna a coral pin, a present from Nathan, Mrs. Todd's husband and Joanna's cousin. For the first time Joanna "lights up." But then she returns the pin to Mrs. Todd as a token of the deep love she feels but to which she cannot yield.

While this sketch clearly reveals the limits of Joanna's vision, it also underlines her dignity and strength. When the narrator makes her own visit to the now deserted island, she finds it "touching . . . that this lonely spot was not without its pilgrims." She reflects that "there are paths trodden to the shrines of solitude the world over,—the world cannot forget them, try as it may."[19] These pilgrims are drawn through their own sense of solitude; their own awareness of that inner self, bounded and alone: "In the life of each of us, I said to myself, there is a place remote and islanded, and given to endless regret or secret happiness; we are each the uncompanioned hermit or recluse of an hour or a day; we understand our fellow of the cell to whatever age of history they may belong."[20]

The writer alone in her schoolhouse watching the funeral procession below has much in common with Joanna, who watched the summer boating parties pass by her lonely island. The moment she spent lonely and jealous in the front room, while Mrs. Fosdick and Mrs. Todd talked cheerfully in the kitchen, is fresh in her memory. The narrator's own solitude teaches her to sympathize with Joanna's experience. As she hears voices from a pleasure boat sailing by, she "knew as if she had told me, that poor Joanna must have heard the like on many a summer afternoon, and must have welcomed the good cheer in spite of hopelessness and winter weather, and all the sorrow and disappointment in the world."[21] Although the narrator originally had no root in the same past as Joanna, never knew or even saw her, nevertheless she can imaginatively reconstruct the other's experience. She stands in Joanna's place just as she sat in Mrs. Blackett's rocking chair, and she gazes out at the world through the other woman's eyes. This loneliness is human, as is this loss. Here too there is communion.

II

The Bowden Reunion is followed by "Along Shore," a sketch echoing several in *Deephaven,* particularly "Danny," which describes the initial steps of a friendship between Kate, Helen, and an old fisherman, "an odd-looking, silent sort of man, more sunburnt and weatherbeaten than any of the others."[22] Kate and Helen first see only a strange, silent figure; then through sympathetic listening they come to recognize a deeply affectionate but lonely man. Like Danny, Elijah Tilley in "Along Shore" belongs to a group of old fishermen, "ancient seafarers," who have a "secret companionship." Unlike Mrs. Todd's circle, however, this is a silent group: "As you came to know them you wondered more and more that they should talk at all." If a member should make a remark, "you felt almost as if a landmark pine should suddenly address you in regard to the weather, or a lofty-minded old camel."[23]

The narrator's friendship with such an unpromising character begins when she sights an old lobster smack, the *Miranda*, wandering aimlessly off Burnt Island: "Her vagaries offered such an exciting subject for conversation that my heart rejoiced at the sound of a hoarse voice behind me." Just then she sees a large object thrown overboard with a splash. " 'Boy got kind o' drowsy sterrin' of her; Monroe he hove him right overboard; 'wake now fast enough,' " explained Mr. Tilley, and we laughed together."[24] The incident seems simple enough, but its pattern fits others in the book. The two are looking at a mystery, a humorous text whose interpretation they share.

Later that day she calls on Tilley. His little cottage is warm and immaculately clean. Surprised, she discovers that Tilley himself is the housekeeper. The cottage is just as his late wife had left it eight years before. Relatives had offered help, but he refused it: " 'I wa'n't goin' to have my house turned upsi' down an' all changed about; no, not to please nobody. I was the only one knew just how she liked to have things set, poor dear." The old man's grief has not lessened since the day his wife died. He cannot get over her loss, and he stares at her rocking chair thinking " 'how strange 't is a creatur' like her should be gone an' that chair be right here in its old place."[25] But the things in their places, the "careful housekeeping, and the clean bright room which had once enshrined his wife . . . now enshrined her memory." His grief and his tribute touch the narrator deeply.

Trusting her understanding, Tilley ventures to show the narrator his wife's pride and joy, their parlor and its treasures. At first the aspiring parlor seems "a much sadder and more empty place than the kitchen; its conventionalities lacked the simple perfection of the humbler room." We sense that class differences between the writer and the fisherman might break the thread of their understanding. To her educated eye, the more primitive kitchen fulfills an aesthetic, perhaps romantic vision, while the parlor "failed on the side of poor ambition." But then the narrator's imagination comes to her aid. She begins to place the ugly, cold space within its human context: "I could imagine the great day of certain purchases, the bewildering shops of the next large town, the aspiring woman, the clumsy sea-tanned man in his best clothes." Finally, she looks at the parlor's carpet and its glass vases filled with dusty arrangements of dried flowers, and she sees not a set of banal conventions but a text within which she "could read the history of Mrs. Tilley's best room from its very beginning."[26]

The theme of interpretation is deepened in the next passage. Elijah shows the narrator his wife's best tea things, a complete set of "real chiny" bought in Bordeaux when they were first married. "With its gay sprigs of pink and blue," the china had become a symbol of their marriage, complete, treasured. After Sarah Tilley died, the women who came to help discovered a teacup broken and wrapped in paper, hidden in the back of the shallow cupboard. For Tilley, the teacup in pieces revealed the only secret that ever lay between him and his wife, a secret disclosed by a moment of imaginative reconstruction: "I knowed in one minute how 't was. We got so used to sayin' 't was all there just's I fetched it home, an' so when she broke that cup somehow or 'nother she couldn't frame words to come an' tell me."[27] His flash of sympathy for his wife was so intense he "had to put right o' the house" lest the watching women see his grief. Like the narrator, Tilley read a "whole history" in this simple object and recovered his wife's presence from its fragments.

Thus, sorrow began for Elijah her educating task, as it did for Moses in *Pearl of Orr's Island*. Alone, he looks back on his life with Sarah and begins to see it with new eyes: "'I used to laugh at her, poor dear,' said Elijah. . . . 'I used to make light of her timid notions. She used to be fearful when I was out in bad weather or baffled about gettin' ashore. She used to say the time seemed long to her, but I've found out all about it now. I used to be dreadful thoughtless as a young man. . . . Lord, how I think o' all them little things!'"[28] Sorrow teaches him to see from the other's point of view. It also teaches compassion. The narrator hints that Elijah has indeed "learned all about it now." These hints come through Elijah's oblique comments about the fish he kills. In the opening scene, after the narrator asks about the haddock he is bringing home, Elijah says simply, "must eat to live." Then in response to her question about the day's catch he answers, "Well, I don't expect they feel like bitin' every day; we l'arn to humor 'em a little, an' let 'em have their way 'bout it. These plaguey dog-fish kind of worry 'em."[29] The narrator notices something odd about this, for she says that "Mr. Tilley pronounced the last sentence with much sympathy, as if he looked upon himself as a true friend of all the haddock and codfish that lived on the fishing grounds." And yet perhaps Elijah *is* their true friend, for he has come to sympathize with these fish, to imagine their watery lives, plagued by enemies, including himself. No longer "dreadful thoughtless," Elijah describes his own death as a relief to the creatures he must eat to live: "No, I sha'n't trouble the fish a great sight more."

This compassion contributes to Elijah's oddly feminized quality. When he greets the narrator at home, he is "knitting a blue yarn stocking without looking on." This knitting continues throughout the sketch. He learned it from his mother during a childhood illness. However, Elijah won't learn any "womanish tricks" such as rug making (evidently he does not consider his knitting womanish). For the narrator, the knitting becomes especially evocative. When Elijah explains that his grief won't last much longer, because "I shall be done afore a great while," her vision of him assumes mythic overtones: "The old widower sat with his head bowed over his knitting, as if he were hastily shortening the very thread of time."[30] Curiously androgynous, the grieving man seems one of the Fates, as did Miss Roxy in that moment when she saw Mara's fatal illness. Seeing Miss Roxy's tears start from such a hardened, impassive face, Mara is startled, as if one of the Fates had thrown down her "fatal distaff to cry."

Sorrow has taught Elijah Tilley that love brings loss and that life is inextricably linked to death. The narrator quietly points out these links. When death claims a man like Elijah Tilley, she says, it will have to use a "good servicable harpoon."[31] Perhaps Tilley is but a larger fish in the great "mackerel-crowded sea." And yet, if Elijah has been educated by grief, he has not found solace. His home has become a shrine to the dead, not a place of living communion. This may be why the sketch ends with Mrs. Todd's final comment: "I do esteem 'Lijah, but he's a ploddin' man." Unlike Mrs. Todd, who also carries a great grief, Elijah has not found the sources of renewal. The old fishermen who sit with him in their "secret companionship" are pointedly silent. What sustains Elijah is the memory of the only relationship that gave him love, acceptance, and freedom of expression: "Her an' me was always havin' our jokes together same 's a boy and girl. Outsiders never'd know nothin' about it."[32]

Mrs. Todd does not want to hasten the thread of time but to savor time, knowing it brings death with it. She and the narrator devour the gingerbread house and devour it happily, without saving the pieces. The Eleusinian chain is also a food chain—big fish eat little fish, dust comes to dust—yet love endures for all that. Elijah, however, feels himself in an earthly wilderness. He cannot find within himself or others the forces to transform his grief. The other fishermen are silent, but it is not a silence that implies intimacy. As Tilley says, he had that kind of closeness only with his wife; only with her did he have access to love and wholeness. In their studies of the quest Joseph Campbell and Annis Pratt agree that, for man, woman is the portal to the green world. For Elijah that door has closed.

III

The following three sketches, as well as "William's Wedding," were published after the 1896 edition of *Pointed Firs*. Scholars have long debated whether they should be added to the text or appended to it as related works. According to Warner Berthoff and Marcos Portales, in a posthumous 1909 edition "A Dunnet Shepherdess" and "William's Wedding" followed "A Backward Glance," originally the last sketch. In 1919 the two sketches, along with "The Queen's Twin," were interpolated into the text just before "A Backward Glance." Finally, in what became a standard arrangement, Willa Cather reversed "William's Wedding" and "The Queen's Twin" in 1925.[33]

Numerous critics—including Berthoff, Mary Ellen Chase, and Marjorie Pryse—have argued for the integrity of the original 1896 version. In many ways I agree with them. However, since this study deals with the pastoral genre and form, as well as the narrator's development, I have chosen to work with the sketches according to the seasonal pattern that they reflect and that Jewett gave them. That is, my sequence follows the sketches' implicit chronology and the narrator's progress within the Dunnet Landing community. "A Backward Glance," set in the fall, closes one pastoral cycle, while "William's Wedding," set in the spring, opens another.[34] And although some critics see the various episodes as interchangeable, I do not. For example, the narrator's vision of the Bowden Reunion depends on her previous visit to Green Island and her intimacy with Mrs. Blackett.

The pastoral tradition is especially evident in "A Dunnet Shepherdess," first published in 1899. The quiet leafy scenes of fishing for trout in the clear (but empty) stream recall the "piscatory" pastoral of Izaak Walton. Esther Hight, standing on her hill "like a figure of Millet's high against the sky," recalls the French painters and writers that Jewett loved, George Sand among them. And the love story between the shepherdess and the fisherman takes us back to the very beginnings of the genre, to Theocritus and Virgil themselves. In "Along Shore" we had a story of loneliness and grief over a marriage ended. Here we have a frustrated romance, the enduring hope for a marriage as complete as the one Elijah Tilley lost.

William, like Elijah, is a silent man. He deliberately avoids the social gatherings that sustain Almira and her mother. While he conscientiously sails Mrs. Blackett to Dunnet Landing in time for the Bowden Reunion, he himself does not attend. Almira often complains of her brother's passivity: "William *is* thoughtful; if he only had a spark o' ambition, there be few could match him." Mrs. Blackett comments that William had "been 'most too satisfied to stop at home 'long his old mother, but I always tell 'em I'm the gainer." The "them" in this passage may be those neighbors who comment on William's shyness, his withdrawal from society. But Mrs. Blackett adds, as Almira also does, that "William has very deep affections."[35]

As the sketch opens, Mrs. Todd orders William to undergo one of her treatments and smears his face with an unattractive green lotion concocted from pennyroyal. It will keep off the mosquitoes. As she applies it, she teases him sharply about his annual trout fishing. You would think he would have had enough fishing on Green Island. William merely blushes and squirms. His behavior in this scene, as in many others, is curiously childlike. Although he is about sixty when the narrator first meets him, she feels as if she must "make the occasion easy for one who was young and new to the affairs of social life."[36] Now, as the two of them head inland to fish, "he looked more boyish than ever, and kept a more remote and juvenile sort of silence. Once I wondered how he had come to be so curiously wrinkled, forgetting, absent-mindedly, to recognize the effects of time."[37]

The narrator is describing a kind of arrested development; socially, emotionally, William *is* a boy. The sources of this situation are complex and sketched ever so lightly. A clue appears when the narrator discovers the romance between Esther and William. They have had their happy afternoon together, their one afternoon a year. As William and Esther enter the Hight house, "William looked almost bold, and oddly like a happy young man rather than an ancient boy."[38] The frustration of this romance has meant the frustration of his own development. He is waiting patiently, as is Esther. The reason they are waiting is their mothers.

A stroke has left Mrs. Hight partially deaf and nearly completely helpless. Widowed, she is dependent on Esther's care. Although Mrs. Blackett seems at times to have the freshness and movement of youth, she too is dependent on the care of her remaining child. William's "stayin' long side" his mother allows Almira the freedom and scope of her ambition on the mainland and allows Mrs. Blackett to remain rooted on the island she loves so much. So too, Esther's willingness to shoulder the economic burdens of her dead father allows her mother to remain in her home, cared for and secure. Esther's determination to raise her sheep in spite of local skepticism has paid the mortgage on their house and put money in the bank. Duty to their mothers has come first, but it is primarily duty toward Mrs. Hight, who seems unwilling and unable to move.

The narrator's first impression of Mrs. Hight is of a strong, domineering, even tyrannical presence: "In a large chair facing the window there sat a masterful-looking old woman with the features of a warlike Roman emperor, emphasized by a bonnet-like black cap with a band of green ribbon. Her sceptre was a palm-leaf fan."[39] The narrator is at first intimidated; her hostess "was more than disapproving, she was forbidding." There is an awkward introduction, then William "lingered for a moment like a timid boy. I could see that he wore a look of resolve, but he did not ask the permission for which he evidently waited." After a long, "anxious" pause, the ruler of this little world relents: "'You can go search for Esther' . . . and William in his pale nankeens disappeared with one light step and was off."[40]

In the mothers of Esther and William, Jewett seems to have recreated the good and bad sides of her own mother. We have seen how, in the bedroom scene on Green Island, Jewett recreated her own moment of loving understanding with Caroline Jewett. In Mrs. Thankful Hight she recreates another side and another moment: the bedridden, helpless woman who prevented her from joining Annie Fields in Boston on the day that left "a little crack in her heart." Jewett then compared herself to Odysseus, tied to the mast by duty but still hearing the siren song of romance. But this sketch was written after that struggle was long over, and its author could look back with understanding. Thus, left to cope with her stern hostess, the narrator "was not long in suspecting that she felt the natural resentment of a strong energy that has been defeated by illness and made the spoil of captivity."[41] Unlike the crippled woman of Rose Terry Cooke's "Root-Bound," captivity has not made Mrs. Hight a saint but a tyrant. Although her manner is that of a ruler, she is the defeated, the "spoil" and not the victor, an object of pity, not resentment. Significantly, her strength is presented in masculine terms. If Mrs. Blackett is "always the queen," Mrs. Hight is the "Roman emperor," but such dominance grows out of weakness, not strength.

The narrator's role in this romantic episode is especially interesting. She is challenged with entertaining the lonely old woman. That she does so shows not only her powers of invention but also how far she has come as an adopted member of this small society. The visit begins auspiciously because, as the narrator notes, she "was happily furnished with the particulars of a sudden death, and an engagement of marriage between a Caplin, a seafaring widower home from his voyage, and one of the younger Harrises."[42] The narrator soon passes this formidable social test as she has passed others: "We came at last upon such terms of friendship that she unbent her majestic port and complained to me as any poor old woman might of the hardships of her illness."

At first the narrator does not suspect the romance between William and Esther, and as she talks with Mrs. Hight, she expects them to return soon. But the time lengthens, and the conversation goes into such particulars that the two women "had pretty nearly circumnavigated the globe and reached Dunnet Landing from an opposite direction to that in which we had started."[43] Mrs. Hight becomes suspicious, and the narrator suddenly intuits "with quick leap of amusement and delight" that she has "fallen upon a serious chapter of romance." Now a conspirator on the side of thwarted love, she soothes the old woman and "doubles her diligences." Like Scheherazade's, her storytelling prolongs the lovers' freedom. But at last both she and her hostess are worn out, and the narrator is sent to find the pair, only a stone's throw from the house. She has given the gift of a "lovely afternoon" but, like a "messenger of Fate," must bring it to a close.

In the hands of another writer these characters might assume very different qualities. A post-Freudian might question their patience and serenity and ask if repression could take such a gentle form and so little toll. A Sherwood Anderson, for example, might see in William the twisted spirit of another grotesque. And it might be fair to ask if this sketch shows Jewett at her most Victorian, celebrating restraint and duty, unaware of sexuality and its drives. The narrator herself stresses the innocence of both Esther and William: "I am not sure that they acknowledged even to themselves that they had always been lovers; they could not consent to anything so definite or pronounced but they were happy in being together in the world."[44]

And yet the narrator quietly points out the price that both have paid for their waiting. There is not only the diminution of William's manhood, so long put off, but also Esther's loneliness and the loss of her potential motherhood. As the narrator says good-bye, Esther gives her "a smile of noble patience, of uncomprehended sacrifice, which I can never forget. There was all the remembrance of disappointed hopes, the hardships of winter, the loneliness of single-handedness in her look, but I understood, and I love to remember her worn face and her young blue eyes."[45] The "young blue eyes" are quintessential Jewett, the Jewett who refused to believe that people could not rise above their circumstances. This character has lived "in the sunshine and rain among her silly sheep, and been refined instead of coarsened." Even the domineering mother does not destroy Esther's spirit but has "given back a lovely self-possession, and a habit of sweet temper." Then, by way of acknowledging difficulties, the narrator must add, "I had seen enough of old Mrs. Hight to know that nothing a sheep might do could vex a person who was used to the uncertainties and severities of her companionship."[46]

Again, the narrator's insight has brought her within the frame of these lives and allowed her to see them whole. Her reading of their subtle gestures has allowed her to discover a "little chapter of romance." Her interpretation of this chapter presents her fishing companion in a new light. In the final passage she steals a glance at William Blackett, whose name she writes in its entirety, formally: "We had not seen a single mosquito, but there was a dark stripe across his mild face, which might have been an old scar won long ago in battle."[47] This warlike imagery permeates the sketch. Mrs. Hight is a Roman general, then a beaten captive. "As for Esther, she might have been Jeanne d'Arc returned to her sheep, touched with age and gray with the ashes of a great remembrance." Now William with his scar. Mild and passive as he seems, he has struggled. The old scar has been "won," not inflicted. It is a badge of strength, not weakness.

IV

The stories of Joanna Todd and Elijah Tilley do not shy away from loneliness and grief, but their pain is individual, apart from the larger community. In "The Foreigner," published in 1900 and rediscovered only relatively recently, Jewett turned her attention to a darker side of Dunnet Landing. This story does not celebrate community but reflects on its failure. With the exception of Mrs. Blackett, the people of Dunnet Landing cannot sympathize with the story's central figure, the lonely foreigner, Mrs. Captain Tolland. Even Mrs. Todd confesses that she never gave this woman the kiss of friendship until she was in her coffin. One of Jewett's most complex stories, technically as well as thematically, "The Foreigner" gives her Dunnet Landing portraits new shadows and new depth.[48]

She sets the sketch on a stormy late August night. Mrs. Todd now feels close to the narrator, enough to confess an uncharacteristic timidity about the roaring sea and wind. Her apparent fear is for her mother. She cannot help imagining disaster, perhaps even a tidal wave, overtaking Mrs. Blackett's tiny island. The narrator sees freshly the

anxiety that seafaring families must bear. Partly to distract her landlady, she asks for a ghost story. Although its identity is not revealed
until its end, Mrs. Tolland's history is that story. But in a narrative so
artfully structured on opposites, this ghost does not appall but comfort.

Mrs. Todd's narrative begins long ago in Jamaica. Four Dunnet
Landing sea captains, Mrs. Todd's father among them, encounter a
pretty widow playing her guitar in a public house. Before they know
it, they are rescuing her from the clutches of some wasteful high rollers.
Although Mrs. Todd hastens to explain that all four were respectable
men, she admits that the captains themselves were "three sheets in the
wind." In this susceptible mood they cast lots for the widow's passage
to America. After some arranging, Captain John Tolland takes her on
and returns to Dunnet Landing a married man.

Unlike the narrator, Mrs. Tolland cannot overcome her difference to
make a part of this tiny Maine village. "She come a foreigner and she
went a foreigner," says Mrs. Todd, "and never was anything but a
stranger amongst our folks."[49] Mrs. Tolland's English is no better than
a child's; her Catholicism remains suspect to the end. This story is
about community, but more seriously it is about culture. Seeing itself
as center, the pastoral world risks seeing all else as periphery. At Mrs.
Tolland's funeral the minister gently suggests, "there might be roads
leadin' up to the New Jerusalem from various points."[50] But even
though Mrs. Todd herself "guessed quite a number must ha' reached
there what wa'n't able to set out from Dunnet Landin'," many in that
village aren't so sure.

The incident which underscores Mrs. Tolland's difference also un-
covers the sources of Mrs. Todd's long-standing enmity toward Mari
Harris. Mrs. Blackett brings the new Mrs. Tolland to a social circle in
the meetinghouse vestry. But "social circle" is a misnomer. At first all
seems well. Then Mari Harris and one of the Caplin girls begin a duet.
When their singing goes flat, Mrs. Tolland "put her hands right up to
her ears, give a little squeal, an' went quick as could be an' give 'em
the right notes."[51] Although the singers try the piece again, Mrs. Tolland makes faces when they get it wrong. The atmosphere becomes
perceptibly colder; the company looks "prim as dishes." Then Mrs.
Blackett, "that never expects ill feelin'," invites Mrs. Tolland to sing.
Up she gets, beginning a little round, a song with "something gay about
it that kept a-repeatin'." In the joy of the moment she begins to dance,
drumming on a pie plate instead of a tambourine. Although the crowd
catches her delight and Mrs. Blackett pats the dancer's hand after her
performance, the next day the parish is scandalized. Mari Harris re-
proaches Mrs. Blackett publicly. When Mrs. Todd ventures that even

David danced before the Lord, Mari Harris retorts, "such a man as David would never have thought 'o dancin' right there in the Orthodox vestry."[52]

In Mari Harris and Mrs. Blackett we have two poles of Dunnet Landing's culture. The first is ethnocentric. Mari Harris cannot imagine other roads to the New Jerusalem besides her own. The rules of the Orthodox vestry cannot be bent, even for King David. But in Mrs. Blackett there is a tolerance born of the seafarer's life. In the opening of "The Queen's Twin" the narrator celebrates the sea captains and their wives who "knew something of the wide world, and never mistook their native parishes for the whole instead of a part thereof."[53] Only Mrs. Blackett knows enough to send for the Catholic priest when Mrs. Tolland lies dying.

However, the sources of Mrs. Tolland's difference go even deeper. Language and religion are both barriers, but so is her open display of emotion in a society where feelings are often hidden. When the captain sets out for sea, on what will be his last voyage, Mrs. Tolland is inconsolable. Her open tears embarrass her husband. Her dancing in the vestry is another example of her spontaneity. Bypassing language, her music touches her listeners directly. But the next day they mistrust their hearts' response. According to Dunnet Landing mores, pleasure, perhaps even more than grief, should be restrained.

The scandal points up another important aspect of Mrs. Tolland's difference. She is an artist, moreover, a woman artist. Her offense to Mari Harris comes of artistic integrity: between musical and social harmony her choice is clear. There are two scenes in which Mrs. Tolland retreats from social situations. The first is in Jamaica. The captains see her running from the tavern out into the street, having evidently been mistreated by the drunken young men inside. The second is in the Dunnet Landing meetinghouse. Mrs. Todd remembers Mrs. Tolland getting up proudly and leaving after the morning sermon, a sermon that probably reflected Mari Harris's condemnation. In both cultures Mrs. Tolland's art is misinterpreted. In the first she is exploited for her sexuality; in the second she is condemned for it. In neither is her art valued as a "dancing before the Lord," an expression of pleasure and celebration of life. (Significantly, the story begins with those four tipsy sea captains. For them, a double standard allows some leeway.) In the end perhaps Mrs. Todd inherits not only Mrs. Tolland's house and healing knowledge but also sympathy for another woman artist, the foreigner whose text she inhabits.

However, "The Foreigner" is not only about Mrs. Tolland but also about how Mrs. Todd came to know Mrs. Tolland's story. In this sketch Mrs. Todd's role is more ambiguous than in many of the others. She stresses that she was younger then, younger than she "be now." At times she speaks of herself as if in the third person. Her assessment of this earlier self is mixed. She cannot help seeing how she failed Mrs. Tolland. She couldn't "get to no affectionateness" with her. After Captain Tolland sailed, Mrs. Blackett did what she could to comfort his distraught wife. Afterward she reproached her daughter: "I want you to neighbor with that poor lonesome creatur'." But Mrs. Todd is torn between Mari Harris's provincialism and her mother's compassion: "Why, since she flaunted out o' meetin', folks have felt she liked other ways better'n our'n." Then she scolds Mrs. Blackett for letting their supper get cold. Her mother's reply is withering: "What consequence is my supper? . . . or your comfort or mine, beside letting a foreign person an' a stranger feel so desolate; she's done the best a woman could do in her lonesome place, and she asks nothing of anybody except a little common kindness. Think if 'twas you in a foreign land!"[54] Mari Harris's apparently Christian decorum is merely cultural prejudice. Mrs. Blackett follows the golden rule; like the good Samaritan, she neighbors with the stranger.

Her chastened daughter tries to make amends, "if 'twas only for mother's sake." When she visits Mrs. Tolland, she notices, "'twas the same as with me at home, there was only one plate." Mrs. Todd, newly widowed, can interpret this text. In that lonely supper she tries to find grounds for sympathy and friendship. But only when she mentions Mrs. Blackett and sees the tears in Mrs. Tolland's eyes is it "all right" between them. Even so, the two women never share the intimacy that flowers in the earlier chapters of Pointed Firs. Almira Todd never tells the Frenchwoman "all that lies deepest in her heart." To her Mrs. Tolland always wears a "very singular expression . . . a fixed smile that wa'n't a smile: there wa'n't no light behind, same's a lamp can't shine if it ain't lit."[55] When Mrs. Todd discovers that she is the inheritor of Mrs. Tolland's estate, she bursts into tears, "I wished I had her back again to do somethin' for, an' to make her know I felt sisterly to her more'n I'd ever showed, an' it come over me 'twas all too late, an' I cried the more, till uncle showed impatience."[56]

But if Mrs. Todd recalls her guilt, she also shows a curious forgiveness toward her failure. When she says, "I used to blame me sometimes," she uses the past tense. Remembering Mrs. Tolland getting up to dance, she sighs, "It all seems so different to me now." And after Mrs. Tolland's funeral she describes herself feeling much as usual: "You can't be sorry for a poor creature that's come to the end o' all her troubles; my only discomfort was I thought I'd ought to feel worse at losin' her than I did; I was younger then than I be now."[57] Perhaps, Mrs. Todd suggests, such failures are part of being human. Regrettable, painful, but inevitable. She looks back on the foreigner *and* herself from outside the frame of culture and, understanding, can forgive. But for Mari Harris, who has not suffered remorse, she has no mercy.

These barriers of language and pride recall the Tower of Babel and humanity's fall into disparate cultures. Like the sea and wind that rage throughout the story, human life can appear an uproar of blind loyalties and bewildered emotion. Mrs. Todd's narrative is full of repetitions, and among the phrases she repeats most often are "poor creatur'" and "poor human natur'." In the midst of this uproar Mrs. Blackett appears, as always, like a beacon of light. Her home is a refuge of prelapsarian innocence. As Mrs. Todd says, "Nothing ain't ever happened out to Green Island since the world began."[58] Mrs. Blackett's intuitive kindness makes her an "angel" to the lost Mrs. Tolland. Able to cross the boundaries of culture, the mistress of Green Island resembles the mythic figures Sherry Ortner saw mediating between culture and heaven. She offers a higher vision of the human family. In this story, as in "The Christmas Ghosts," the daughter vows to do good, not for Christ's sake but for mother's. And here as well we have not only a figurative angel but a literal one.

As Mrs. Todd comes to tell of Mrs. Tolland's death, she pauses; "'I ain't told you all . . . no, I haven't spoken of all to but very few. The way it came was this,' she said solemnly, and then stopped to listen to the wind, and sat for a moment in deferential silence, as if she waited for the wind, to speak first."[59] From the very beginning the wind has seemed alive, at times "like a distressed creature" trying to enter the house for shelter. At first this human quality disturbs Mrs. Todd, but now, looking like an "old prophetess," as "unconscious and as mysterious as any sibyl of the Sistine Chapel," Mrs. Todd announces, "There, that's the last struggle o' the gale." She speaks confidently but quietly, as if they might be overheard. That this should be the last struggle of the storm is appropriate, for it ushers in the final turn of the narrative, the ending of Mrs. Tolland's own struggle. But it is also the end of another, more subtle struggle, the struggle to get that story told. For it is only now that Mrs. Todd can bring herself to tell the core story to the narrator, the story she has only told to a "very few."

On that far-off stormy night Mrs. Todd watches by Mrs. Tolland's bedside. As the light shines on the sick woman's face, it wears "a look that made her seem a stranger you'd never set eyes on before."[60] At once detached and compassionate, Mrs. Todd thinks "what a world it was that her an' me should have come together so, and she have nobody but Dunnet Landin' folks about her in her extremity. 'You're one o' the stray ones, poor creatur'.' I said." In *Pearl of Orr's Island,* on the night that Mara Lincoln dies, Captain Kittridge dreams he sees Christ the Shepherd coming to lead Mara "home." In the opening of "The Foreigner" Mrs. Todd recalls the old folk saying that "these gales only blew when somebody's a-dyin', or the devil was a-comin' for his own." But then she adds, meditatively, "The worst man I ever knew died a real pretty mornin' in June." The reversal is significant, for on this worst night of all the devil is not coming for his own, but a mother's ghost is coming for her child.

As Mrs. Todd holds the lamp, its beam suddenly strikes out across the room to reveal "a woman's dark face lookin' right at us. . . . I felt dreadful cold, and my head begun to swim; I thought the light went out; 'twa'nt but an instant . . . an' when my sight come back I couldn't see nothing there."[61] What Mrs. Todd sees makes "poor human natur' quail." The face itself is "pleasant enough . . . shaped somethin' like Mrs. Tolland's, and a kind of expectin' look." Like the Eleusinians overwhelmed by Demeter's unveiling, Mrs. Todd sees "all that she could bear," but finally her sight fails. This vision blinds. It is, she admits, a moment she "couldn't live under." Shaking and "overcome," Mrs. Todd turns to the dying woman who, quiet and "perfectly reasonable," asks simply, "You saw her, didn't you? . . . 'tis my mother." Mrs. Todd then knows that "her change was comin'," but rather than make an "uproar," she too faces death with a new acceptance: "I felt calm then, an' lifted to somethin' different as I never was since." Asked again if she had seen the "other watcher," Mrs. Todd replies at last, "*Yes, dear, I did: you ain't never goin' to feel strange an' lonesome no more.*" The stormy passage through life is done. "An' in a few quiet moments 'twas all over. I felt they'd gone away together."[62]

In this story it is not death but life—with its emotional poverty and human alienation—that is the source of terror. That pain is now forever healed. It is the ghost that consoles, that soothes the child into death, restoring harmony and curing loneliness. Like the dying woman in "Root-Bound," Mrs. Tolland falls into death like a child into sleep. The preoedipal union, with its trustful bond between mother and child, becomes a source of faith, a green island despite the inevitable "foreignness" of existence. The one who ushered her daughter into life leads her out again, as the ends of life circle back upon each other. As Mrs. Todd says, "You know plain enough there's somethin' beyond this world; the doors stand wide open. There's somethin' of us must still live on; we've got to join both worlds together an' live in one but for the other."[63]

The tale is closed. Mrs. Todd and the narrator sit "together in silence in the warm little room: the rain dropped heavily from the eaves, and the sea still roared, but the high wind had done blowing." The silent intimacy in the womblike room mirrors the greater peace and intimacy of Mrs. Tolland's death. Mrs. Todd returns to her everyday tone. Her fear for her mother is over; she too is soothed and restored to wholeness. "Sometimes these late August storms'll sound a good deal worse than they really are." But then she adds, "I do hate to hear the poor steamers callin' when they're bewildered in thick nights in winter, comin' on the coast."[64] These final words recall Mrs. Todd's own anxiety and the bewilderment of the "stray one" whose story she has just told. But her satisfied voice also reveals her faith, albeit sometimes shaken, that there is a calm and safety beyond death itself. Out of human ignorance comes pride and fear. The mother's revelation, though fearful, testifies to a love enduring beyond death itself. Here lies true shelter: "They'll find it rough at sea, but the storm's all over."

In her fine work on Jewett, Marjorie Pryse cites "The Foreigner" for the complex relationship between this narrative frame and the core story. Not only is Mrs. Todd calmed by the story's end, so is the narrator. Initially, her landlady's unaccustomed anxiety unsettles her. She wonders if she will be told a tale that will haunt her all her days. But Mrs. Todd's sharing of this particular tale is proof of the "affectionateness" between them. Reassured, the narrator is brought within the fold. This relationship between storyteller and listener, Pryse writes, "resembles the ties that link mother and daughter." Moreover, "the device of tale-within-a-tale creates a hierarchy of listeners. The narrator's own listener has nothing to contribute to the telling of the tale but provides the essential link between 'generations' of storytellers. Just as a granddaughter feels the ties, through her mother, to earlier generations of grandmothers and great-grandmothers."[65]

If the context of Mrs. Todd's narrative evokes Eleusinian imagery, so does its structure. Its progress is not linear but spiral. Like the rings of gray and black that once circled beneath her feet, Mrs. Todd's story spirals in upon itself, reaching for its center—the moment of the mother's revelation.[66] The momentum of that progress depends on the narrator: her interest and sensitivity. Mrs. Todd begins her story again and again. Each time she comes to an end with Mrs. Tolland's death. Each time the narrator's eager listening prompts her to begin once more. Each cycle starts from a different point; each comes closer to the story's deepest meaning. With its constant refrain, "'Twas such a gale as this the night Mis' Tolland died," the narrative becomes a solemn analogue to that other song, the song Mrs. Tolland sang that

day in the meetinghouse vestry, the one with something gay about it
that "kept a-repeatin'." I think of the "old crone," the sea, in Whitman's "Out of the Cradle Endlessly Rocking." "Death death death
death," she sings, "the strong and delicious word," "the word of the
sweetest song and all songs." In Jewett's work, as in Whitman's, death
is different from what you might suppose, and luckier.

V

Jewett set "The Queen's Twin," published in 1899, in late summer.
It is September, time for blackberries and witch hazel. The timing is
key. While the themes are muted in "The Foreigner," this sketch deals
explicitly with women's spirituality and religious traditions. It is important that the narrator be experienced enough in Dunnet Landing
ways to see what Mrs. Todd now has to show her.

There is a "cool freshness" in the morning air when Mrs. Todd and
the narrator set out along the old Indian footpath to visit Abby Martin,
the gentle old lady who is, Mrs. Todd reveals, "The Queen's Twin."
The two women were born the same day, and Abby believes their lives
are linked in a mysterious fashion, what she calls a "birthright": "Her
royal majesty and I opened our eyes upon this world together; say what
you may, 't is a bond between us."[67] The link extends to the actual
patterning of their lives, which mystically mirror each other: "And I
married a man by the name of Albert, just the same as she did, and all
by chance." After her first son and "the little Prince o' Wales had been
christened just the same," Abby "made excuse to wait till I knew what
she'd named her children. I didn't want to break the chain."

The relationship to Victoria has sustained Abby Martin through a
life of hard struggling, of poverty and loneliness. While Abby never
complains about her late husband, Mrs. Todd speaks of him with
contempt and puts her finger, as she usually does, right on the spot:
"She'd been patient an' hardworkin' all her life, and always high above
makin' mean complaints of other folks. I expect all this business about
the Queen has buoyed her over many a shoal place in life. Yes, you
might say that Abby'd been a slave, but there ain't any slave but that
has some freedom."[68]

Abby Martin's house stands on top of a small hill, "a dreadful out-
o'-the-way place." All alone since her husband died, she lives far from
the female community that sustains Mrs. Todd. Her own mother is
dead, and her children have left. Her rough-mannered daughter-in-law
complains that "she'd much rather have the Queen to spend the day if
she could choose between the two." Only one granddaughter seems to
offer comfort, but she can visit only occasionally. Though she promises

someday to "come an' stay quiet 'long o' grandma," Abby suspects she will marry instead. While Abby cannot help wishing she had "a dear daughter to stay at home with," even here Victoria comes first, "if only one of us could have a little Beatrice, I'm glad 't was the Queen."[69] When Mrs. Todd first made the trek to the isolated cottage, she had not visited Abby for three years: "There, she really cried, she was so glad to see anybody comin'."

Now Mrs. Todd leads the narrator to Abby Martin. The road is too far for horse and wagon; they must walk the old trail through the heron swamp. That this should be an Indian trail is appropriate, for the narrator is going deeper into wilderness, farther away from the pastoral settlements. The setting resembles "In Shadow" in *Deephaven*. The land is "always hungry," and most of the families that once farmed it have died and scattered. Mrs. Todd herself knew three families whose hopes were beaten by one farm alone, a farm now deserted: "Seems sometimes as if wild Natur' got jealous over a certain spot, and wanted to do just as she'd a mind to." For once the trees seem savage, even alien: "One felt a sudden pity for the men and women who had been worsted after a long fight in that lonely place; one felt a sudden fear of the unconquerable, immediate forces of Nature, as in the irresistible moment of a thunderstorm."[70]

Sensing the narrator's thought, Mrs. Todd tells of lingering fears about the woods they have just passed through. People are apt to get "bewildered" or lost there. The fears are primitive, going back to the Indian days or the witchcraft scares. But they are still potent. One group of women lost in the woods overnight became so frightened that even though they were "not half a mile from home" they panicked. One of them never quite recovered: "'T was like them victims that drowns in a foot o' water; but their minds did suffer dreadful."[71] The story sets up an important theme: the psychological construction of reality. It also highlights the varieties of response to the natural world: a primitive fear but also a primitive bond; for immediately after describing this "groundless" panic, Mrs. Todd continues: "Some folks is born afraid of the woods and all wild places, but I must say they've always been like home to me." Even her favorite pennyroyal is one that "objects" to garden ground.

It is now that the narrator sees the lineaments of Demeter in Mrs. Todd: "I glanced at the resolute, confident face of my companion. Life was very strong in her, as if some force of Nature were personified in this simple-hearted woman and gave her cousinship with the ancient deities." The narrator's imagination has already taken hold of Abby Martin's story and begun to play with its significance. On her way to visit the Queen's Twin, she begins to see Mrs. Todd as herself a divine twin, moving in synchrony with the goddess of ancient Greece: "She might have walked the primeval fields of Sicily; her strong gingham skirts might at that very moment bend the slender stalks of asphodel and be fragrant with trodden thyme, instead of the brown, wind-brushed grass of New England and frost-bitten goldenrod."[72]

But Mrs. Todd is unconscious of her twinship; she carries her divinity within herself, integrated as a part of her own being, rooted in the very forces that she personifies. In the earliest passages of the book, as the narrator sees her outlines expand, Mrs. Todd's numinous power is her own. The next lines affirm this self-possession: "She was a great soul, was Mrs. Todd, and I her humble follower, as we went our way to visit the Queen's Twin." The poignance of Abby Martin is that she has had to find her dignity through Victoria. But as Mrs. Todd helps the narrator to see, this twinship is not madness but religion, home-made.

The slave's religion, Nietzsche said, was Christianity. And one might expect that it would be to Christianity that Abby Martin would turn. Her situation is similar to that of the lonely man whose funeral Kate and Helen encounter in *Deephaven*. Impoverished, widowed, he turned to drink and died embittered. Kate and Helen reflect that if he had only led a Christian life, found a friend in Jesus, he might not have gone beneath the waves of his despair. But as Jewett's essay "The Decay of Churches" recognized, Christianity often failed its followers. Its doctrines did not meet their human needs for comfort and understanding. Moreover, as Thomas Wentworth Higginson and so many other Victorian writers complained, Christianity especially failed women. Protestant churches gave women few or no models for their own lives, few "ideal" images to guide them. In *Little Women* the lonely Amy put up a portrait of the Madonna and, Protestant though she was, found solace in the motherly face. To the Calvinist such worship is idolatry, but as the mother's spirit says in "The Christmas Ghosts," "We made us many idols in the old life, but they were only the signs of love." This "old way" was "but to find a shape and body for the soul of love."[73]

Abby Martin has found that way through Victoria, whose images are her greatest treasures: "She's been collectin' 'em an' cuttin' 'em out o' newspapers an' magazines time out o' mind, and if she heard of anybody sailin' for an English port she'd contrive to get a little money to 'em and ask to have the last likeness there was." The walls of her best room are now almost covered, and "she keeps that room shut up sacred as a meetin' house!"[74] Deprived of a religious tradition that would give her life value and dignity, equally deprived of the friendship that could give her sympathy and love, Abby Martin has constructed her own mythos. Like the young James Gatz, who created a God out of magazine advertisements and pulp novels, she has found her materials in the illustrated weeklies: "'I won't say but I have my favorites amongst 'em,' she told me t' other day, 'but they're all beautiful to me as they can be!'"

Within the context of her imagination, these pictures assume a meaning far greater than any they originally possessed. Significantly, Mrs. Martin's tributes to her queen are the "pretty little frames" around each picture. As Mrs. Todd explains, Abby carefully follows the latest fashion; only the best will do: "first 'twas shell-work, and then 'twas pine-cones, and bead-work's had its day." Mrs. Todd herself is bringing an offering, some pink silk and gold thread. Like the anonymous artists who created Notre Dame and Chartres, Abby Martin labors not for her own glory but her queen's.

If the sacred space of the church has been reconstructed in Mrs. Martin's best room, other aspects of religious life also appear in new guise. Like Mara in *The Pearl of Orr's Island,* who feels that God is always a dear mother to her, Abby confides, "I've often walked out in the woods alone and told her what my troubles was, and it always seemed as if she told me 't was all right, an' we must have patience." Through Mrs. Todd's help she has even found a substitute for Scripture: "I've got her beautiful book about the Highlands; 't was dear Mis' Todd here that found out about her printing it and got a copy for me, and it's been a treasure to my heart, just as if 't was written right to me. I always read it Sundays now, for my Sunday treat." Victoria is clearly more than royal; she is divine: "She's been the great lesson I've had to live by. She's been everything to me. An' when she had her Jubilee, oh, how my heart was with her!"[75]

Perhaps Abby Martin *is* an idolator, a pagan, like the Indians whose ancient trail leads to her house. But Mrs. Todd can follow this trail. Through her mediation the sketch presents Abby's paganism within a sympathetic context. It is a context rooted in the liberal, Romantic Protestantism represented by Friedrich Schleiermacher, the German theologian who believed that religious symbols, Christian and pagan both, were ways of naming the ineffable, gestures toward the *experience* of religious dependence on powers greater than ourselves. The liberal Protestantism of Schleiermacher and others leads directly to ministers like Phillips Brooks, whom Jewett so admired, and includes sentimentalists such as Stowe and Lydia Maria Child. Child herself wrote that all religious traditions have some kind of mother goddess, an intermediary who brings the divine closer to human needs. Refined and secularized, the tradition extends to the twentieth century by way of Jewett's friend and reader, William James. James knew that in a skeptical age human beings still needed faith, still had a will to believe. In *The Varieties of Religious Experience* he acknowledged the psychological sources of that need.[76]

A twentieth-century inheritor of this hermeneutical line is Mircea Eliade. His classic study, *The Sacred and the Profane: The Nature of Religion,* puts Abby Martin's "birthright" in a new light. According to Eliade, the religious person *always* sees himself as a "twin" of his god: "He does not consider himself to be *truly man* except in so far as he imitates the gods, the culture heroes, or the mythical ancestors."[77] As Eliade explains, the separation of the sacred from the profane is the essential ordering principle of the religious mind. Life as it is in itself, apart from the sacralizing power of myth or paradigm, is meaningless and chaotic. Only insofar as life mirrors myth can it be real: "When a captain [in New Guinea] goes to sea he personifies the mythic hero Aori. 'He wears the costume which Aori is supposed to have worn, with blackened face . . . [and] the same kind of *love* in his hair which Aori plucked from Iviri's head. He dances on the platform and extends his arms like Aori's wings.'"[78] Like the New Guinean sea captain extending his arms like Aori's wings, Abby Martin models her life on Victoria's. Transcending the poverty of her outer circumstances she has found a kind of inner greatness.

Thus, as the two guests approach their hostess, the narrator senses the presence of a woman who might well be Victoria herself, greeting them with an air of "unmistakeable dignity." There is "something distinctly formal in the occasion," and the narrator becomes anxious to rise to it: "On the way I had torn my dress in an unexpected encounter with a little thornbush, and I could now imagine how it felt to be going to Court and forgetting one's feather or her Court train."[79] However, in truly regal fashion, Mrs. Martin is "oblivious of such trifles" and welcomes them with "calm look" and "kind hand." Identification with the queen has not produced self-aggrandizement but self-respect: "She was a beautiful old woman, with clear eyes and a lovely quietness and genuineness of manner; there was not a trace of anything pretentious about her, or high-flown, as Mrs. Todd would say, comprehensively."[80]

In this sketch, as in all of them, there are two stories unfolding at once. The first is the story of the central characters: Mrs. Todd, Elijah Tilley, Poor Joanna, and now Abby Martin. The second is the story of the narrator's coming to know them. In a sense each sketch is structured as an initiation in which the narrator must make an imaginative leap of identification and interpretation. In this sketch the initiatory structure is especially obvious. The testing and instruction begin early. When Mrs. Todd first tells the narrator about Abby Martin, "there was a serious silence" before she formally announces: "She is the Queen's Twin." She then looks at the narrator "steadily to see how I might bear the great surprise."[81] The narrator bears the surprise well. She accepts Mrs. Todd on faith and readies herself for the journey.

As she guides the narrator through the wilderness to Abby Martin's little house, Mrs. Todd prepares the outsider: "I do hope Mis' Martin'll ask you into her best room where she keeps all the Queen's pictures. Yes, I think it likely she will ask you; but 't ain't everybody she deems worthy to visit 'em, I can tell you!" The meeting of the two women is delicate and must be negotiated carefully. As Mrs. Todd explains, "you mustn't look for anything elegant. . . . Mis' Martin's always been in very poor, strugglin' circumstances."[82] The countrywoman risks exposing her lonely friend to misunderstanding or even ridicule. She trusts the narrator's sympathy but not enough to leave it uninstructed.

Once seated in Abby Martin's kitchen, the narrator is tested again. The conversation is following the "slow current of neighborhood talk" when their hostess turns to the narrator and asks if she has ever been to London. When the narrator says she has, it is a chance for Mrs. Martin to broach the subject of her one trip there long ago: "In those days they didn't object to a woman's being aboard to wash and mend, and voyages were sometimes very long. And that was the way I come to see the Queen." Suddenly the narrator finds "Mrs. Martin was looking straight into my eyes to see if I showed any genuine interest in the most interesting person in the world."[83] Abby is like an evangelist looking for signs of possible conversion, or a priestess questioning a potential initiate. The narrator, however, is prepared: " 'Oh, I am very glad you saw the Queen,' I hastened to say. 'Mrs. Todd had told that you and she were born on the very same day.' " Mrs. Martin "leaned back comfortably and smiled as she had not smiled before." The narrator's guide and sponsor "gave a satisfied nod and glance, as if to say that things were going on as well as possible in this anxious moment."

Now Abby Martin begins to open her heart. She tells her new audience all about her twin and the chain of coincidence that binds them. Then Mrs. Todd prompts Abby to return to her story of how she came to see the queen. When their ship anchored in the Thames, she heard that Victoria was riding out from Buckingham Palace that very morning. Abby begged her husband Albert and her brother Horace to take her, but they laughed at her, then got impatient with her seriousness until she was "most broken-hearted." She "gave way," broke down:

" 'They'd acted sort of ashamed of me when I pled so to go ashore, an' that hurt my feelin's most of all.' " To be laughed at, treated as frivolous or even insane—these do hurt most of all. It is no wonder Mrs. Martin keeps her best room closed up "sacred as a meetin' house"; she knows all are not worthy.

But this story has a happy ending. Her husband, frightened by the intensity of her feelings, "treated me gentle just as he did when we was goin' to be married." He arranged for the ship's carpenter to take her ashore:

'T was a great day, with sights 'o folks everywhere, but 't was just as if they were nothin' but wax images to me, I kep' askin' my way an' runnin' on . . . and just as I worked to the front o' the crowd by the palace, the gates was flung open and out she came; all prancin' horses and shinin' gold, and in a beautiful carriage there she sat; 't was a moment o' heaven to me. I saw her plain, and she looked right at me so pleasant and happy, just as if she knew there was somethin' different between us from other folks.[84]

As the eyes of the two women met, Abby Martin's love flowered and took its final form. It was "a moment of heaven," sacred and out of profane time. Ordinary people, who did not understand the meaning of these events, were "like wax images," unreal and lifeless. As with the mother's revelation in "The Foreigner," telling the story of communion creates communion: "There was a moment when the Queen's Twin could not go on and neither of her listeners could ask a question."[85] When she can continue, Abby recalls how after seeing the queen that day she sat on the quarterdeck in the sun mending her husband Albert's coat, "and 't was all as if I was livin' in a lovely dream. I don't know how to explain it, but there hasn't been no friend I've felt so near to me ever since."

As Mrs. Martin talks, her eyes grow brighter. The narrator admits that "one could not say much—only listen." But it is how they listen. Abby Martin trusts them. She admits that she does not play a role in the queen's life, but she thinks that "now she's older, she might like to know about us." Old people lose their friends, Abby explains, and it may be the same with Victoria as it is with herself. And although Victoria "don't know nothin' yet about me, except she may feel my love stayin' her heart sometimes an' not know just where it comes from."[86] Usually we think of the higher power "stayin' the heart" of the lower. And yet it is Abby's love that sustains the queen. One of the poignant qualities of Abby's love is her recognition that the queen *is* human, could be lonely and troubled. Victoria is not omnipotent, nor even omniscient, but suffers as all incarnate creatures do. And this image of the suffering Victoria ushers in the final phase of the conversation.

Abby would dream about the two of them "being together out in some pretty fields, young as ever we was, and holdin' hands as we walk along." Sometimes she would make believe that Victoria, tired and lonely, had that dream too and was coming to see her. She would plan their day together, their meals and quiet socializing with Mrs. Todd or maybe Mrs. Blackett (Mrs. Todd cannot help chiming in with an invitation for the queen to visit Green Island). Strengthened by the faith of her audience, feeling they'll understand, Abby Martin is moved to tell them something she has never told "a livin' soul before."

One day she was "livin' so in her thoughts" that she got the house all ready just as if her queen were really coming. Fresh flowers all around, the best sheets and blankets that she wove herself on the bed, a beautiful supper. All day Abby works, "sort of telling myself a story all along." Finally, at nightfall, she finds herself still alone, "the dream left me, an' I sat down on the doorstep an' felt all foolish an' tired." [87] Bereft of the fiction that has sustained her, she is about to give way to despair. But then something happens.

A cousin, an old woman, even more impoverished than Abby herself, appears: "She wasn't all there, as folks used to say, but harmless enough and a kind of poor old talking body. And I went right to meet her, when I first heard her call, 'stead o' hidin' as I sometimes did." Instead of shunning this half-mad cousin, Abby Martin invites her to share her meal. It is a supper made for a queen but one Abby "had no heart to eat alone." The poor woman, as surprised as if Victoria herself offered the invitation, "come in dreadful willin'."

Mrs. Todd "compassionately" remembers the cousin: "I don't believe she ever had such a splendid time in her life as she did then. I heard her tell about it afterwards." Then, with her strange wisdom, Mrs. Todd adds, "There, now I hear all this it seems most as if the Queen might have known and couldn't come herself, so she sent that poor old creatur' that was always in need!" The comment sheds new light on the story, which becomes a kind of parable. The meal set for the highest is given to the lowest, for as Christ admonished, "Inasmuch as ye did it not to one of the least of these my brethren, ye did it not to me."

But the parable also reveals something else. If Abby is the twin of the queen, she is also twin to the impoverished, half-mad cousin. In a real sense, Abby too is "not all there." These are the sides of her own life: a shining divinity and an impoverished near-madness. Mrs. Todd's compassion lets her see this truth, and she tells Abby that the divinity

within her bids her love what she has been "shy of." She need no longer
hide from loneliness and pain. The poor woman who deserves to be
loved like a queen is Abby Martin herself.

After Mrs. Todd speaks, we sense a new vulnerability in Abby. Given
love and acceptance, she is able to acknowledge her fear: "Mrs. Martin
looked timidly at Mrs. Todd and then at me. ''T was childish o' me
to go an' get supper,' she confessed." Mrs. Todd's answer confers on
her neither nobility nor madness but simple humanity: "'I guess you
wa'n't the first one to do that,' said Mrs. Todd. 'No, I guess you wa'n't
the first one who's got supper that way, Abby,' and then for a moment
she could say no more."[88] Mrs. Todd is a great healer, and she heals
through sympathy, a sympathy that is of the mind as well as the heart.
This sympathy is hard-won. In the moment she cannot speak we
sense Mrs. Todd's own grief. Her own loneliness allows her to see
another's.

The narrator is keenly aware of the sensitivity of this moment. She
describes their positions carefully, so we can see the intensity of their
communication: "Mrs. Todd and Mrs. Martin had moved their chairs
a little so that they faced each other, and I, at one side, could see them
both." "'No, you never told me o' that before, Abby,' said Mrs. Todd
gently. 'Don't it show that for folks that have any fancy in 'em, such
beautiful dreams is the real part o' life? But to most folks the common
things that happens outside 'em is all in all."

Mrs. Martin's beautiful dream may be all a-livin' in her mind, a
story she is telling herself all the time. And yet, Mrs. Todd assures her,
such fictions are the "real part of life." We make our worlds; we con-
struct our own realities. The "common things" that happen "outside"
us are not "all in all." Abby Martin's spiritual poverty is great, and in
her hunger for meaning she is teetering between a kind of homemade
fundamentalism and madness. Mrs. Todd heals through acceptance of
the imagination. Although a skeptic might think she is encouraging
insanity, Mrs. Todd's interpretation is a curiously modernist one, as if
Harriet Beecher Stowe were crossed with Wallace Stevens. Abby Martin's salvation is to believe in a supreme fiction, knowing it is a fiction.
A story to live by. A will to believe.

The articulation of this idea offers Abby a chance for self-acceptance,
a way to accept, perhaps even to integrate, the two sides of her life:
"Mrs. Martin did not appear to understand at first, strange to say,
when the secret of her heart was put into words; then a glow of pleasure
and comprehension shone upon her face. 'Why I believe you're right,
Almira!' she said, and turned to me."[89] The final test has been passed.
The moment Mrs. Todd had hoped for has come: "'Wouldn't you like

to look at my pictures of the Queen?' she asked, and we rose and went into the best room."

The narrator has been deemed worthy. She has been taken in to the shrine. Because she is worthy, she does not describe what she sees there. The best room remains closed to profane eyes. To enter, we must use our imaginations.

Like her cousin, like us all, Abby Martin is a "poor talking body." Out of existential poverty she has invented her own goddess. And yet, as the opening description of Mrs. Todd suggests, everyone carries such a force within them, a shining divinity mated to an impoverished mortality. The penny(royal) is humanity's sign. Thus, the Homeric hymn describes the child Demophoon who was fated to die but had always an inscrutable grace because once a goddess held him in her arms. In that first blissful union, child and mother are one. Like the scent of Demeter's mint, the unconscious memory of that identification survives. It is the source of our well-being, of our capacity to love ourselves and each other. These sketches center themselves repeatedly around this recognition. Finally, *The Country of the Pointed Firs* seems itself a version of Abby Martin's best room, a true meeting house whose walls are lined with portraits, each carefully framed to evoke the same "shining face," the ghost of a love linking generation to generation. Perhaps in our hearts we are all a queen's twin.

Chapter Ten

Writing Life

I

As the family prepared to leave the Bowden Reunion, what began
with joyful greetings ended with partings and promises: "I heard the
words 'next summer' repeated many times, though summer was still
ours and all the leaves were green." Finally, the narrator must come to
her own time of parting and promises: "At last I had to say good-bye
to all my Dunnet Landing friends, and my homelike place in the little
house, and return to the world in which I feared to find myself a
foreigner." The season is ending; all the quiet signs are there: "every
bush of bay and every fir-top, gained a deeper color and a sharper
clearness. There was something shining in the air,—a northern look."[1]
The decision that was made at the beginning of the summer must
be made again. Then she separated herself reluctantly from Mrs. Todd
and retreated to the schoolhouse to write. Now she separates again,
to return to the city, where she will, we can only suppose, write the
sketches we have just read. But her adoption in this little world has
made a difference. Perhaps she will be unfitted for the urban world she
has left; perhaps she is now a foreigner in both worlds, loyal to each
but unable to accept the limitations of either.
The narrator's departure evokes the Persephone who returned to
Demeter knowing that with the autumn the chariot would come for
her. The Persephone of Annie Fields's poem does not resist Hades'
coming but recognizes its inevitability—values the insight that her separation has given her. Now, however, it is not an Underworld chariot
that comes to take the "daughter" but "the small unpunctual steamer
that went down the bay in the afternoon." And, like Demeter herself,
Mrs. Todd's sorrow makes her impatient with the daughter's willingness to leave: "Mrs. Todd had hardly spoken all day except in the
briefest and most disapproving way; it was as if we were on the verge
of a quarrel. It seemed impossible to take my departure with anything
like composure."[2]
However, Mrs. Todd's apparent coldness is only an attempt to hide

her feelings, as the narrator soon sees: "I glanced at my friend's face, and saw a look that touched me to the heart. I had been sorry enough before to go away." Before her vulnerability is more exposed, Mrs. Todd, "still trying to be gruff," seems to remember some task forgotten and quickly turns away to leave: "I could not part so; I ran after her to say good-bye, but she shook her head and waved her hand without looking back when she heard my hurrying steps, and so went down the street." In the now silent house the narrator sees her empty bedroom as Mrs. Todd will find it on her return: "I and all my belongings had died out of it, and I knew how it would seem when Mrs. Todd came back and found her lodger gone. So we die before our own eyes; so we see some chapters of our lives come to their natural end."[3]

Death is evoked again as the narrator waits for the steamer that will carry her back toward winter and the city. She sees Mrs. Todd walking along the shore. From "a distance" the narrator can feel "the large, positive qualities that control a character." Now the deeper significance of Mrs. Todd's numinous figure stands out against the landscape: "Close at hand, Mrs. Todd seemed able and warmhearted and quite absorbed in her bustling industries, but her distant figure looked mateless and appealing, with something about it that was strangely self-possessed and mysterious."[4] Stooping occasionally to "pick something—it might have been her favorite pennyroyal," Mrs. Todd seems to emerge from the landscape and then to mysteriously melt back into it: "at last I lost sight of her as she slowly crossed an open space on one of the higher points of land, and disappeared again behind a dark clump of juniper and the pointed firs." As the narrator gazes back over the bay from the steamer, "the little town, with the tall masts of its disabled schooners in the inner bay, stood high above the flat sea for a few minutes, then it sank back into the uniformity of the coast, and became indistinguishable from the other towns that looked as if they were crumbled on the furzy-green stoniness of the shore."[5] Like trees sinking back into mold or a gingerbread house falling down to ruin, the setting itself dissolves down to its crumbling elements: "Presently the wind began to blow, and we struck out seaward . . . when I looked back again, the islands and the headland had run together and Dunnet Landing and all its coast were lost to sight."

If the narrator has seen her own death, she brings a token and pledge of loyalty back with her to the city. All that Mrs. Todd could not say was expressed in her parting gifts left on the kitchen table: a prized West Indian basket, a "seafaring supper, with a neatly tied bunch of southernwood and a twig of bay, and a little old leather box which held the coral pin that Nathan Todd had brought home to give to poor

Joanna." The gifts are curiously ambiguous. Expressing Mrs. Todd's love for the narrator, the pin is the sign of her adoption into the Bowden family. But it is also Joanna's pin, and the parallel between that woman's self-exile and the narrator's departure cannot be missed. And yet there is that twig of bay—a gift of laurel, the poet's inspiration and crown.

At the end of *Deephaven* Kate and Helen acknowledge to themselves that they will probably never return to Deephaven, despite their promises to their friends. The narrator makes no such promises. In this perhaps she is more honest than her precursors. She is a writer with work to do, and she returns to her old life to do it. So Jewett left her, until she began "William's Wedding," unfinished at her death in 1909. In all of the other *Pointed Firs* sketches she stayed within the frame of one summer. But now she began a new cycle. In Jewett's own life there had been the disappointment of *The Tory Lover*, whose reception had been only lukewarm. Literary colleagues such as Alice Brown urged her to return to Dunnet Landing, to the pastoral world and style she knew so well. As "William's Wedding" opens, Jewett's narrator finds that "the hurry of life in a large town, the constant putting aside of preference to yield to a most unsatisfactory activity, began to vex me, and one day I took the train, and only left it for the eastward-bound boat."[6]

Dunnet Landing is a return to balance: "the first salt wind from the east, the first sight of a lighthouse set boldly on its outer rock, the flash of a gull . . . made me feel solid and definite again, instead of a poor, incoherent being." The narrator had thought her parting the previous autumn had been final. That chapter was complete; she had died out of those lives. But now her heart has revived with the spring, like Mrs. Todd's memories of her lost lover or Persephone's blooms of purple and white. As the Maine coast comes into sight, "life was resumed, and anxious living blew away as if it had not been. I could not breathe deep enough or long enough. It was a return to happiness."[7]

But the return is also painful. Like T. S. Eliot's April, this northern May is a cruel month. It too mixes lilacs out of a dead land, and the first stirrings bring guilt and apprehension. Although the little houses seem to climb down their hill to greet her, the narrator cannot help seeing that "all the shore looked cold and sterile." She is met at the Landing by Johnny Bowden. This first emissary raises unanticipated fears: "Johnny's expression did not change as we greeted each other, but I suddenly felt that I had shown indifference and inconvenient delay by not coming sooner."[8]

In "The Backward View" the narrator worried that she might find herself a foreigner in the city, but now perhaps she will find herself a foreigner everywhere. Perhaps she is to be the perpetual outsider, the alienated artist, sympathetic but uncommitted, a figure well known in American literature as far back as Washington Irving's Geoffrey Crayon, that other sketcher of charming, picturesque scenes. Her response to the wintry face of the landscape shows a certain bewilderment, as if she had not expected change, as if that world had ceased to exist when it was "lost to sight." But now she discovers, with a kind of pang, that it has gone on without her: "it had never occurred to me the summer before that Johnny was likely . . . to grow into a young man; he was such a well-framed and well-settled chunk of a boy that nature seemed to have set him aside as something finished, quite satisfactory, and entirely completed."[9]

Johnny Bowden's changing shape is analogous to the narrator's own book, which had reached a satisfying and conventionally pastoral conclusion with "The Backward View," then found resources for further growth. Closure is a kind of death, and the characters of *Pointed Firs* came dangerously close to being transfixed within the magical glass of genre, properly and aesthetically placed, once and for all. The narrator now sees that her acquaintances are not types, Platonic ideas, but living creatures who must grow and change, must move from birth toward death. To be alive is to be "in the middest," to be unfinished. Her book will imitate immanent life—incomplete, collaborative, evocative of mackerel-crowded seas.

As the narrator approaches Mrs. Todd's house, her mixed feelings intensify. All seems strange, the "wonderful little green garden had been enchanted away by winter." Only a few twigs and scraggly shrubs adorn what now seems "a most unpromising piece of ground." Heart "beating like a lover's," she comes to the house, which suddenly seems smaller and then emptier. Just on the doorstep she is overcome with anxiety: perhaps Mrs. Todd has gone away; everything seems so diminished. "Then on my homesick heart fell the voice of Mrs. Todd. She stopped, through what I knew to be excess of feeling, to rebuke Johnny for bringing in so much mud, and I dallied without for one moment during the ceremony, then we met again face to face."[10]

If this moment of silent meeting seems reminiscent of those we have seen before—in "A Queen's Twin," for example—the text does not bear this out. We do not see the look that passes between them, but as soon as Mrs. Todd "could say anything," she says, "I dare say you can advise what shapes they are goin' to wear. My meetin'-bunnit ain't goin' to do me again this year; no! I can't expect 't would do me forever." Not exactly a warm greeting, even allowing for Mrs. Todd's

usual repression of feeling. The narrator can make herself useful by
bringing news of the outside world and its fashions. Mrs. Todd's remark underlines the opening theme: the shapes of hats and boys both
change with time.

Mrs. Todd apparently is testy, in the full meaning of the word. She
treats her guest as a city person, commenting that they are "prone to
run themselves to death," and advises the narrator to rest up now that
she "taken the trouble to come." The narrator quickly understands the
situation. Mrs. Todd has no way of knowing "how long I had been
homesick for the conditions of life at the Landing the autumn before."
Given the break in their community, the narrator concludes, realisti-
cally, that her lukewarm reception is justified, although "it was natural
enough to feel a little unsupported by compelling incidents on my
return."

There is big news, however. A wedding. As Mrs. Todd explains, "the
Lord's seen reason at last an' removed Mis' Cap'n Hight up to the
farm, an' I don't know but that the weddin's goin' to be this week."
She then goes into the details—Esther's business, the sheep and the
property—in such a headlong rush that the narrator, amazed, must
interrupt to make certain of the central fact: " 'William's going to be
married?' . . . whereat Mrs. Todd gave me a searching look that was
not without scorn."[11] Her hostess repeats simply that Mrs. Hight was
buried the week before, as if that fact alone would explain everything.
" 'Poor thing!' said I, with a sudden vision of her helplessness and angry
battle against the fate of illness; 'it was very hard for her.' " But Mrs.
Todd replies crisply, "I thought it was hard for Esther!"

The scornful look is ominous. Somehow the narrator has misread
some signs. Perhaps she has seen William and Esther, like Johnny Bowden, as crystallized types, locked in a world without change. Perhaps
she has sentimentalized their long wait and worked too hard to sympathize with the "masterly" woman who thwarted them. Mrs. Todd,
who speaks "without sentiment," gave a comfortable laugh when she
announced Mrs. Hight's death. That night the narrator "had an odd
feeling of strangeness; I missed the garden, and the little room, to which
I had added a few things of my own the summer before, seemed oddly
unfamiliar." Gone is the happy sense of belonging, the feeling of companionship so close that she and Mrs. Todd seemed two creatures in
the same shell. Now she compares herself to "the hermit crab in a cold
new shell,—and with the windows shut against the raw May air, and
a strange silence and grayness of the sea all that first night and day of
my visit, I felt as if I had after all lost my hold of that quiet life."[12]

But overnight another change comes. The ground is thawing, loosening. In the morning the "bright May sun was streaming in," and the narrator begins to feel that she has really arrived. "There was the first golden robin singing somewhere close to the house." Life and death work together, and now it is life's turn. In that "warm night" some of the garden's "treasures had grown a hand's breadth; the determined spike of yellow daffies stood against the doorsteps and the bloodroot was unfolding leaf and flower." As she comes out of her room, she meets Mrs. Todd face to face: "This weather'll bring William in after her; 't is their happy day!" Hearing these words, the narrator feels "something take possession of me which ought to communicate itself to the least sympathetic reader of this cold page. It is written for those who have a Dunnet Landing of their own: who either kindly share this with the writer, or possess another."[13]

As always, there are two stories here. What is expressed in these compressed lines is not only Mrs. Todd's joy in William's happy day but her reacceptance of the narrator, her recognition of their friendship. The narrator has been taken back into the fold. As for the narrator, she deliberately reaches out of the text, acknowledging the limitations of words and print, demanding our collaboration. We too can share, can be brought into the fold, but we must draw on our own experience, our own sympathy. The page is cold; like a frostbitten garden it needs our warmth to live.

The hours that pass waiting for William to fetch his bride are solemn with suppressed emotion: "to be expectant of life or expectant of death gives one the same feeling." All day the grass seems to grow greener and greener as the spring sunlight pours down. Mrs. Todd is in her "highest mood." She "beckons" the narrator "as if she were a sibyl." It is time to be direct: "I thought you comprehended everything that day you was up there." She speaks with "a little more patience" than the evening before, but the narrator still feels that Mrs. Todd "thought I had lost instead of gained since we parted the autumn before."[14] Then Mrs. Todd triumphantly explains "William's made this pretext o' goin' fishin' for the last time. 'T wouldn't have done to take notice, 't would 'a scared him to death!" With a shock of admiration the narrator realizes that Mrs. Todd had known about this forty-year courtship all along. Then she remembers "that under pretext of mosquitos she had besmeared the poor lover in an awful way—why it was outrageous! Medea could not have been more conscious of high ultimate purposes." But now we see that the narrator has not always been able to read between the lines:

"Darlin'," said Mrs. Todd, in the excitement of my arrival and the great concerns of marriage, "he's got a beautiful shaped face, and they pison him very unusual—you wouldn't have had him present himself to his lady all lop-sided with mosquito-bite. . . ." She stood before me reproachfully, and I was conscious of a deserved rebuke. "Yes, you've come just in the nick of time to advise me about a bunnit. They say large bows on top is liable to be worn."[15]

The rebuke is deserved; the narrator's vision failed her, and she had to be shown the whole picture. Her indignation suggested a criticism and distrust of Mrs. Todd's own motives. She missed the slight expression of strong emotions and confused texts with pretexts. Rather than sabotaging William's romance, Mrs. Todd has been furthering it as skillfully as she could, watching near-helpless as her brother struggled to find his place. Her impatience with his shyness, her curtness with his shortcomings were expressions of a deep but baffled sympathy. And when she sights William sailing in for his bride, we see how deep that sympathy runs:

> I could see her eye follow the gray shores to and fro, and then a bright light spread over her calm face. "There he comes, and he's strikin' right in across the open bay like a man!" she said with splendid approval. . . .
> I looked too, and saw the fleck of white no larger than a gull's wing, but present to her eager vision.[16]

But if the narrator is conscious of a deserved rebuke, it is a loving one, unaccompanied by any scornful looks. Indeed, Mrs. Todd has even let drop her true fondness for the narrator, whom she addresses, in the emotion of the moment, as "Darlin'." Moreover, she softens her reproach by again acknowledging the narrator's citified authority. At least she can advise on "bunnits."

The long afternoon of waiting has its lulls and its commonplace cares. Some people from Black Island whom Mrs. Todd dislikes bring a sick child for attention. The little girl is failing for lack of care: "She needed feedin' up, and I don't expect she gets milk enough; they're great butter-makers down to Black Island, 't is excellent pasturage, but they use no milk themselves."[17] When they have left, Mrs. Todd is both "indignant and wistful about the little girl." She had wanted to keep her, "I kind of advised it, and her eyes was so wishful in that pinched face when she heard me, so that I could see what was the matter with her, but they said she wa'n't prepared. Prepared!" This scene might seem incidental, but it introduces an important issue. Mrs. Todd has no daughter of her own, no children to raise and nurture, and neither will Esther. We can sense that Mrs. Todd's own face mirrors the little girl's, with its "wishful look." To be pulled apart by the uncomprehending and selfish family is enough to make her "snuff like an offended war-horse." The narrator "could hear her still grumbling and talking to herself in high dudgeon an hour afterward."[18]

Now enters a parade of neighbors hungry for details about the possible wedding. Mrs. Todd routs them all with noncommittal remarks and resolute lack of information. After the last visitor she is highly amused and comments that only one of the bunch showed "real interest" rather than "cheap curiosity." When the narrator ventures that the one person might be "Miss Maria Harris," Mrs. Todd laughs and gives her a measure of reinstatement: " 'Certain, dear,' she agreed, 'how you do understand poor human natur'!' "

Finally the moment arrives:

A short distance down the hilly street stood a narrow house that was newly painted white. It blinded one's eyes to catch the reflection of the sun. It was the house of the minister, and a wagon had just stopped before it; a man was helping a woman to alight, and they stood side by side for a moment, while Johnny Bowden appeared as if by magic, and climbed to the wagon-seat. Then they went into the house and shut the door.[19]

Like the best room in "The Queen's Twin," the marriage remains sacred, undescribed, within a house so purely white it blinds the eyes with dazzling light. Jewett outlines just the shapes of a man and a woman. Expression is slight; she deliberately withholds information, presents us with silhouettes whose significance we must supply. Only Johnny Bowden is named. These events are far away, like the speck of a sail no bigger than a gull's wing. But a loving eye can interpret the signs: "Mrs. Todd and I stood close together and watched; the tears were running down her cheeks."

Finally, the couple emerges, and bride and groom come up the hill to Mrs. Todd's little house. They first shake hands in silence with Mrs. Todd and then with the narrator. In the quiet the narrator hears "a plaintive little cry from time to time." As the wagon waited by the minister's house, they had seen Johnny Bowden bend over "as if there was something very precious left in his charge." Now Esther goes to the wagon and returns carrying a little white lamb. Its mother had died that very morning, and Esther could not bear to leave it behind. The death of Esther's own mother allowed her to marry. Now another mother's death has given her a kind of child: "She gave a shy glance at William as she fondled it and held it to her heart, and then, still silent, we went into the house together. It was lovely to see Esther carry it in her arms."[20]

Safely in the house, away from public gaze, "all the repression of Mrs. Todd's usual manner was swept away by her flood of feeling." New Englander or no, "she took Esther's thin figure, lamb and all, to her heart and held her there, kissing her as she might have kissed a child, and then held out her hand to William and they gave each other the kiss of peace." The marriage has freed more than the bride and groom. This kiss of peace between brother and sister "was so moving, so tender, so free from their usual fetters of self-consciousness, that Esther and I could not help giving each other a happy glance of comprehension."[21]

After the death of Jewett's own mother, she wrote that such a loss brought something "new and sweet" despite the pain. The sense of late blooming, a blooming withheld far into May itself, is close to Jewett's own. Significantly, the prolonged waiting has developed traits in each lover usually associated with the opposite gender. Sleeping outside at night alone to protect her sheep, Esther has become strong and self-reliant. She has assumed the role of her dead father and paid the mortgage on their land. William, living alongside his mother, has become feminized. Deeply private, with strong affections, he lends his voice to Mrs. Blackett's on the high notes of "Home, Sweet, Home." Possessed of these virtues, they will find a new balance. William strikes across the bay "like a man" and walks up the hill "like a king." Esther holds her lamb as tenderly as any mother with a newborn child.

The lamb itself is a pastoral image but also a Christian one. Its presence suggests a love sanctified by discipline and virtue. In the celebration that follows, the narrator quietly recalls the marriage feast at Cana, Christ's first miracle and his blessing on love, marriage, and family: "We took the cake and wine of the marriage feast together, always in silence, like a true sacrament."[22] This sacrament is within the home, not the church. Its food expresses a human history: a rare plum cake from Mrs. Todd's best recipe, and wine, one of two bottles presented by old Captain Denton on Mrs. Todd's own wedding day: "one we had and one we saved, and I've never touched it till now. He said there wa'n't one like it in the State O' Maine."

It is a solemn moment that the narrator shares. Not even the minister is there. But when it is over, the neighbors must play their part. As they appear with congratulations, the narrator shrinks "from the thought of William's possible sufferings, but he welcomed both the first group of neighbors and the last with heartiness." He has truly changed. As Mrs. Todd and the narrator walk the couple down to their boat at the landing, William shakes hands with the narrator, then "looked me full in the face to be sure I understood how happy he was."[23]

The final scenes suggest the new life that has opened: "I watched him make a nest for the lamb out of an old sea-cloak at Esther's feet, and then he wrapped her own shawl around her shoulders, and finding a pin in the lapel of his Sunday coat he pinned it for her." These are a husband's gestures. The expression is slight but sweetly sexual: he has made their symbolic child a nest and dressed his wife, enclosing her with a pin from his own coat. Esther looks "at him fondly while he did this, and then glanced up at us, a pretty, girlish color brightening her cheeks." She is blushing.

As Mrs. Todd and the narrator watch them sail away up the bay, we are suddenly reminded of another who has been waiting through the long May morning and afternoon: "'Mother'll be watching for them,' said Mrs. Todd. 'Yes, mother'll be watching all day, and waiting. She'll be so happy to have Esther come.'"[24] If the Lord has finally seen reason and removed the bad mother, the good mother still reigns on her island of peace. The image of William and Esther united under the loving gaze of Mrs. Blackett recalls the marriage of Moses and Sally, educated by a great sorrow and blessed by Mara's motherly ghost.

The ending of "William's Wedding" provides a different kind of closure than that of "The Backward View." This is the closure of a love story, of a romance: "and they lived happily ever after." Like the fairy tale's ending, this marriage represents a kind of psychic wholeness, an integration achieved after struggle and risk. But there are always two stories in these sketches, and this conclusion gives us two images of integration. The two friends watch the bride and groom sail out to sea. Then, the final lines explain, "We went home together up the hill, and Mrs. Todd said nothing more; but we held each other's hands all the way."

As her steamer left the bay the autumn before, the narrator watched Mrs. Todd's large, determined shape climbing the hill. From a distance it seemed "mateless and appealing." The term "mate" is key. In "The Foreigner" Mrs. Todd remembered Mrs. Blackett's grief at the loss of her "mate," a dear friend who had died young. The word's connotations are complex. It suggests friendship but also a kind of twinship: one shoe in a pair is mate to the other. It also suggests marriage: a spouse is one's mate. Finally, it suggests the companionship of those who share the same labor: mates on the same voyage. The term is rich and genderless, suggesting commonalities of work and love, marriage and friendship. The myth that sustains Abby Martin is not the conventional tale of rescue by a charming prince but the fantasy of a visit by a tired queen from a faroff city. In Abby's dream she and her mate walk hand in hand through "some pretty field." For Mrs. Todd and the narrator that dream has come true.

II

Despite their power, neither ending of *Pointed Firs*, neither "The Backward View" nor "William's Wedding," suggests that the narrator will remain in Dunnet Landing for good and all. What, finally, is her relationship to this place and these people? In *Deephaven* Kate and Helen retreat from the country and its women almost out of fear. In *A Country Doctor* Nan Prince returns to her village but only after having rejected the conventional feminine roles it offers. This literate woman may also seem to reject the roles played by Mrs. Blackett and Mrs. Todd. After all, she is not biologically a Bowden; she will not bear children to join these generations. She does not keep her own house on Green Island, nor will she ever become Mrs. Todd's literal apprentice and inherit the herbal mysteries.

But if the narrator does turn away from this pastoral world to seek her quiet center of solitude in the city, it is only to recreate these mysteries through her art. Nan Prince expressed maternal care through her "masculine" profession, thereby transforming its skills through the "feminine intellect," those "higher powers" of human insight and intuition. In "A White Heron" Sylvia's ambitions were awakened by the hunter, but her communal sympathies transformed the domination of nature to a wise nurturance. Once fused with the leaves and shadows, Sylvia became an overseeing angel.

Thus, the narrator of *Pointed Firs* retreats to her own ground, but the result is an art that flows into the lives of her characters with all the greater power. Nameless through the sketches, she ministers to them with the "perfect self-forgetfulness" that she celebrates in Mrs. Blackett. Her forbearance grants them the freedom of self-revelation. The adopted daughter of the Bowdens becomes their mother, reproducing and nurturing them through her art. Edward Garnett, one of Jewett's earliest critics, saw this maternal quality as Jewett's own: "Perhaps we shall touch near to the secret of Miss Jewett's power and the secret of her limitations if we say that her art is exceedingly feminine in the sense that she has that characteristically feminine patience with human nature which is intimately enrooted in a mother's feeling."[25]

Like the ideal mother described by Nancy Chodorow—the mother who merges sympathetically with her child yet recognizes the child's "difference"—Jewett and her narrator see their characters merge with the pastoral landscape and with each other, but they also respect each character's individuality, the strength of their specific speech and movement, history and choices. As Garnett observed, "Just as a woman's criticism of people near and dear to her is modified by her instinctive understanding . . . that nothing will ever change them radically, so Miss Jewett's artistic attitude shows a completely sympathetic patience with the human nature she has watched and carefully scrutinized."[26] Thus, Barton St. Armand argues that while Jewett's art "yields an oceanic sense of the hidden significance of all things," her sharp eye for the particular keeps it from blurred confusion or sentimental excess: "so Jewett's landscapes blur, decompose, disappear entirely, and then reassert themselves through a sudden glimpse of the strong color of the pines or a spur of distinct headland."[27]

She is writing life, not about life. While Jewett's artistic goal is often described as preservation of the past, her 1893 preface to *Deephaven* argues that the pastoral world's spirit is still present. Unlike the hunter in "A White Heron," who preserved his birds stuffed and classified, Jewett wishes to evoke a living spirit from her written landscapes. Like Sylvia, who watches the dawn with the heron and preserves its life by setting it free, the narrator of *Pointed Firs* joins her characters and watches their lives with them.

But writing life is also a collaboration between writer and reader. Here too there is a continuity between Dunnet Landing and the art that celebrates it. While the narrator turns the maternal love of Mrs. Blackett to the creation of her characters, she turns the chthonic wisdom of Mrs. Todd to the healing of her readers. Jewett's own youthful ambition was to make the people of a state "acquainted with each other." She emulated the art of her father, a physician. Now that emulation is deepened by the addition of a feminine model. Though her medium is decidedly different, her narrator does become Mrs. Todd's apprentice, even her mate. The parallel between the two women's arts brings this study full circle, back to the issues with which it opened.

According to Simone de Beauvoir, Man, writ large, transcends the meaningless repetition of biological life through the creation of cultural forms, lasting objects that express the human project of self-creation. While our bodies age, die, and decay, these imperishable objects give form and meaning to individual lives. In this sense all fine art is a memorial to its maker, a triumph of self-expression, of Existence over the everlasting round of birth, death, and decay. However, on the symbolic continuum marking the transformation of raw to cooked, women's domestic art is only a middle or mediating term. She cooks, but what she cooks is consumed; it disappears back into the hungry chain of being that she serves. The clothing wears away, the dinner disappears, the children age and die. When men transform nature into culture, as the cliché goes, the organic dross is purged, and only everlasting form remains. As Sherry Ortner puts it, "He creates relatively lasting, eternal, transcendent objects, while the woman creates only perishables—human beings." Hence, "in most cultural symbolic concordances" woman is not associated with life, "let alone life everlasting, but with death."[28]

But in works such as *Pointed Firs* the repetition of biological life is not death to the individual, but solace; not a negation of meaning, but a source. Identity is not achieved through monumental assertion of will but through reconciliation of self and other, a position that maintains connection without losing center. Jewett's countrywomen turn their art to the expression of this insight. Their work acknowledges, even celebrates, its origins in nature. Rather than transforming raw to cooked, these creators aim for both at once. Like Lévi-Strauss's honey, their artifacts are "natural" but mysteriously preserved from decay. Although these monuments are sometimes literally perishable, they preserve the memory of their makers. But they do so through the transformation of living beings, through awakening memory, engendering awareness. This art does not, like Yeats's mechanical bird, escape the mackerel-crowded seas and dying generations. Rather it becomes a pledge between those generations, a sign connecting the individual to the chain of being.

In "Miss Tempy's Watchers," for example, the two women watching over Temperance Dent's dead body are drawn together by memories of her. They overcome an old antipathy and, to celebrate their new understanding, they open a jar of Tempy's best quince preserves. As they share them, they muse on Tempy's gift for love: perhaps it was love that brought her aged tree into bloom each spring and gave its fruit a distinctive sweetness. By the story's end all of the celebrated preserves have, ironically, been consumed. However, the two women have repeated Tempy's own act: they have found communion. In a mysterious way the dead woman's spirit is preserved in the living friends. Despite her evocative name, Tempy has transcended time by working within and through it.

In the Bowden Reunion the simple ceremonies of "Miss Tempy's Watchers" are raised to new power. Even the pies and cakes testify to the importance of the moment with "dates and names . . . wrought in lines of pastry at [their] tops." The narrator's sharp eye catches how word has become flesh; these pastries celebrate the Bowdens' incarnate spirit: "There was even more elaborate reading matter on an excellent early-apple pie which we began to share and eat, precept upon precept. Mrs. Todd helped me generously to the whole word *Bowden,* and consumed *Reunion* herself, save an undecipherable fragment."[29] What a wonderful moment. There's Mrs. Todd, with her death-signifying name, happily consuming the "Reunion" itself; while the author, with no name at all, polishes off the whole of "Bowden." Conventional values are set on their heads. Since *this* memorial aims at mimesis of immanent life, death is its ultimate realization. Mrs. Todd and the narrator select carefully. At the feast's end only the "undecipherable" fragment is preserved; all of the signs are eaten.

How then might the narrator imitate her landlady's art? A clue appears in a passage from George Sand, whose work Jewett rediscovered in 1888, the year she published "Miss Tempy's Watchers."[30] In the preface to *Little Fadette*, Sand's narrator and a friend are listening to a plowman's recitative, punctuated by long silences: "I admired the infinite variety which the solemn pulse of his improvisation imposed on the old sacramental theme. It was like a reverie of nature itself, or like a mysterious formula whereby the earth proclaimed each phase of the union between her power and the labour of mankind."[31] Drawn into the plowman's song, the narrator begins to dream herself. Poetry, she says, transcends the poet: "It does not even have to be much; the song of a bird, the hum of an insect, the murmur of a breeze, the very silence of nature, constantly interrupted by mysterious sounds of an indescribable eloquence. If this furtive language can reach your ear, be it only for an instant, you escape in thought from man's cruel yoke, and your soul soars free through creation." These are the voices that the country people in *Deephaven* hear when other ears are deaf. The friends in *Little Fadette* speculate that the charm of this poetry, distilled from the mysterious voice of nature itself, can heal the suffering of the poor, the "distressed and unhappy." They resolve to "gently celebrate this poetry that is so sweet. Let us express it, like the sap of some healing plant, on to the wounds of humanity."[32]

Mrs. Todd also knows how to express the power of these pastoral herbs. The narrator even suggests that "love and hate and jealousy and adverse winds at sea might . . . find their proper remedies . . . in Mrs. Todd's garden."[33] Like the infusions of laurel drunk by the Greek prophetess, her potions open the spiritual eye. And as in the plowman's song, the formula lies in a mysterious harmony between nature and human labor. Mrs. Todd's voice is healing; her speech distilled from experience. Listening to the countrywoman's tales, the narrator concludes: "Mrs. Todd's wisdom was an intimation of truth itself. She might belong to any age, like an idyl of Theocritus."[34] As Mrs. Todd's "humble follower," the narrator learns to preserve the essence of this pastoral world. Her stories aim to open her readers' eyes and guide their vision. The revelation itself is ineffable. It cannot be named, only suggested. Thus, the language of *The Country of the Pointed Firs*—like the plowman's recitative, like Almira Todd's tales—encloses a moment of silence, of communion. This moment is the source of its healing power and the core of Jewett's artistic innovation.

As Josephine Donovan points out, the technique had deep roots. In her 1871 diary Jewett remembered her father telling her: "A story should be managed so that it should *suggest* interesting things to the *reader* instead of the author's doing all the thinking for him, and setting it before him in black and white. The best compliment is for the reader to say 'Why didn't he put in "this" or "that."'"[35] Following his advice, "Jewett . . . extended her conception of authorial restraint to the point where she allowed the reader a creative role in the process." Rather than controlling the reader's thoughts, she tried "to communicate images that 'open seed' in the reader's mind, that allow the reader to intuit meanings beyond the literal."[36]

Later in life Jewett pinned this quote from Flaubert above her writing desk: "Ce n'est pas de faire rire—mais d'agir à la façon de la nature, c'est à dire de faire rêver."[37] Writing to make us dream, writing to recall the hidden language of nature—this is the silence that is speech. Jewett's stories offer her readers a way of seeing, a code suggesting "those unwritable things which the story holds in its heart, if it has any." But to read these unwritable things we must bring "something to the reading of a story that the story would go very lame without." According to Louis Renza, such dependence on a reader's response reveals the author's failure to become an "author-ity." The narrator's confession that her page is "written for those who have a Dunnet Landing of their own" concedes the text's "possible contingency" while trying to "foreclose the possible consequence of this contingency—failure to become a narrative with universally apprehensible significance."[38] However, she may not want to escape the text's contingency or its consequences. As the loneliness of Mrs. Captain Tolland testifies, interpretation is a social act. For Jewett, who resisted elevation to Olympian authority, meaning cannot exist independent of context, of human connection. To acknowledge such dependence is not weakness but wisdom.

Thus, if the narrator's efforts to connect sometimes fail, it may be because, as her quotation from Saint Theresa suggests, "true proficiency of soul is not in much thinking but in much loving." To read her text demands love's visionary power. Foreigners at first, to enter the world of Dunnet Landing we must draw on our own history, our own experiences of love and communion: "The happiness of life is in its recognitions. It seems we are not ignorant of these truths, and even that we believe them; but we are so little accustomed to think of them, they are so strange to us."[39] The passage might seem less obscure placed within the context of the Persephone myth itself. We are not accustomed to value love consciously, to turn back and look at this simple ground of our being. And yet, recognizing the feelings of others, we come to recognize our own. Dreaming of others, we awaken ourselves.

This is the lesson the narrator learns in Dunnet Landing. As she was initiated into this mystery, so she initiates her readers. While the narrator had never "found love in its simplicity as I had found it at Dunnet Landing in the various hearts of Mrs. Blackett and Mrs. Todd and William," she assures her readers that their "counterparts are in every village in the world, thank heaven, and the gift to one's life is only in its discernment."[40] The narrator turns her readers back to their own villages, but first she offers them a healing poetry, a poetry with a mysterious flavor.

It is a flavor informing the entire text: form and content are expressions of the same difference. In *Pointed Firs* Elizabeth Ammons finds "a book that locates itself formally outside the masculine mainstream. Patterns of concentricity, net-work, web, and oscillation mold a narrative that does not know how to march and scale. Rather, it rocks, circles, ebbs, and swells."[41] Rather than "conventional inherited forms, at which she was not very good anyway," Jewett fitted innovative form to innovative vision. The result, Josephine Donovan writes, is "an essentially feminine literary mode expressing a contextual, inductive sensitivity, one that 'gives in' to the events in question, rather than imposing upon them an artificial, prefabricated 'plot.'"[42]

Perhaps this mode would be best described as lyric rather than dramatic or narrative. According to Joanna Russ, "A writer who employs the lyric structure is setting various images, events, scenes or memories to circling around an unspoken, invisible center. The invisible center is what the novel or poem is about; it is also unsaying in available dramatic or narrative terms."[43] Russ argues that the lyric mode is particularly appropriate for women writers—Virginia Woolf, for example, wrote in it—because there is so little that their heroines can do in a patriarchal society: "Hence the lack of 'plot,' the repetitiousness, the gathering-up of the novels into moments of epiphany, the denseness of the writing, the indirection. There is nothing the female characters can *do*—except exist, except think, except feel." Not surprisingly, this literary mode encounters the same devaluation as women's cultural mode. Russ finds critics using "the usual vocabulary of denigration: these novels lack important events; they are hermetically sealed; they are too full of sensibility; they are trivial; they lack action; they are feminine."[44]

Very early in her career Jewett realized her vulnerability to such criticism. In 1873 she wrote to Horace Scudder at the *Atlantic*:

I don't believe I could write a long story as [Howells] suggested. In the first place, I have no dramatic talent. The story would have no plot. I should have to fill it out with descriptions of character meditations. It seems to me that I can furnish the theatre, and show the actors, and the scenery, and the audience, but there never is any play! I could write you some entertaining letters perhaps from some desirable house where I was in most charming company, but I couldn't make a story about it.[45]

Deephaven, of course, seems very much like those "entertaining letters." Richard Cary quotes a passage from Howells's *A Chance Acquaintance* that suggests the literary aim of the young *Atlantic* author: "I'll tell you a book after my own heart: *Details,*—just the history of a week in the life of some young people who happen together in an old New England country-house, nothing extraordinary, little, everyday things told so exquisitely, and all fading naturally away without any particular result, only the full meaning of everything brought out."[46] Thus, Kate and Helen spend long hours studying epitaphs in the Deephaven graveyard. These beautiful phrases reveal "that tenderness for the friends who had died, that longing to do them justice . . . which is so touching and unmistakable." Their patient attention to these lines, usually observed "carelessly by the tearless eyes of a stranger," reveals an unsuspected depth of romance and tragedy in the quiet town; but to see it one must "have an instinctive, delicious interest in what to other eyes is unflavored dullness."[47] The phrasing is significant; to find flavor, the interest itself must be "delicious."

It is this delicious interest on which *Pointed Firs* still depends. In an 1890 letter to Annie Fields, Jewett humorously compared herself to those writers, like Mary N. Murfee, who could write a "good big Harper's story." Then there is "S.O.J., whose French ancestry comes to the fore and makes her nibble all around her stories like a mouse." As she comes nearer their core, her stories assume new forms: "They used to be long as yardsticks, they are now as long as spools, and they will soon be the size of old-fashioned peppermints, and have neither beginning or end, but shape and flavor may still be left to them, and a kind public may still accept them when there is nothing else."[48] In this passage Jewett perversely seems to welcome "the usual vocabulary of denigration." According to Louis Renza, "in a nonserious, nonhonorifically critical manner, Jewett here records a diachronic diminution in her works that virtually outlines her hidden agenda for producing minor literature . . . who but a child or a *minor* could hope to appreciate such written 'peppermints'?" Jewett again fails to assume "author-ity": "she here produces a text which she can never quite read because she has never quite written it—and which she can never quite write because it promises to disappear like a small piece of candy in the hands of a child."[49] But there is another way of looking at that strange progression of images.

In terms of plot, we see that the first is an abstract, rigid measurement, linear and applied to experience from the outside. It is the image of "masculine" logic: the scale applied by the scientific hunter in "A White Heron" and perhaps the calibration by which Jewett measured Nan Prince's growth in that carefully plotted *Bildungsroman*. Next Jewett substitutes a spool of thread for the abstract measure. The rectilinear form has received a circular orientation. The plot now seems like the trunk of Sylvia's tree: a cylinder around which the story's thread will spiral. The metaphor now comes from the domestic arts, not from the masculine world of construction and abstraction.

The movement toward the circle is completed with the image of the peppermint. Now we have the art of cooking: the creation of a perfect round without beginning or ending, only "shape" and "flavor." At the center is the self-sufficient epiphany, radiating outward. Crucially, the peppermint is meant to be eaten. It is created to be consumed. Jewett playfully makes her art into a domestic communion wafer: a sweet designed to disappear into the substance of the reader, *not* to remain outside experience like a yardstick. This art should melt into the reader and impart directly, sensuously, the flavor of life. While this flavor may be "natural," Jewett does not present the green leaf raw but transforms it into a cultural object. She gives it shape as well as flavor. Those who criticize a Jewett story for lack of plot may fail to recognize the center that gives it form. To amend Joanna Russ, "being" may be a way of "doing."

If literary fictions cannot really be consumed as peppermints can, or die as all children eventually do, nevertheless these are stories that respect the world of immanence, even seek transcendence through its mimesis. But writing life presents Jewett with a problem curiously similar to those faced by later modernist writers. In *The Sense of an Ending* Frank Kermode discusses Sartre's discovery in *Nausea* that "there is an irreducible minimum of geometry—of humanly-given shape or structure—which finally limits our ability to accept the mimesis of pure contingency."[50] Sartre and Jewett must deal with the same paradox.

Notice, however, how the valuation of the terms shifts. For Sartre and Kermode: "Contingency is nauseous and viscous; it has been suggested that the figure is ultimately sexual. This is unformed matter, *materia, matrix*; Roquentin's is ultimately the form-giving male role. He experiences reality in all its contingency, without benefit of human fiction; he resolves to make a fiction. Between his experience and his

fiction lies Sartre's book."⁵¹ The experience Jewett wishes to acknowledge may be a matrix but not an inhuman one. For her the imposition
of geometry is not necessarily redemptive, and form-giving can too
easily become life-emptying. Rather than becoming a verbal icon, a
self-reflexive and self-sufficient fiction, her text gently but resolutely
returns its readers to the rough ground.

Thus, like Sartre's book, *The Country of the Pointed Firs* lies somewhere between "experience and fiction." However, like the women
interviewed by Carol Gilligan, Jewett's text speaks in a different voice.
It acknowledges that it is a sign, not a sign that refers to itself alone
but to itself in connection—to the reader, to the writer. For completion
it depends on our collaboration: our experience, our vision, finally our
memory of our own connections. Form cannot die, but only those who
die can make it live.

At the last, Jewett approached her literary materials much as Temperance Dent approached her one quince tree. As Mrs. Crowe remembers, Tempy would "go out in the spring and tend to it, and look at it
so pleasant, and kind of expect the old thorny thing into bloomin'."
Sarah Ann Binson recalls that Miss Tempy "was just the same with
folks. . . . And she'd never git more'n a little apernful o' quinces, but
she'd have every mite o' goodness out o' those, and set the glasses up
onto the best-room closet shelf, *so* pleased."⁵² While New England was
a very thorny old tree, Jewett's secret, as Edward Garnett intuited, was
this maternal power of transformation: the nurturance, release, and
preservation of a sweetness at the core. Jewett's art offers a vision of
transcendence so embedded in everyday use, so incarnate in the particular, that our sense of its power comes upon us suddenly, rising out
of its ground, then just as suddenly fading back. She is kin to the
anonymous artist who reproduced the Bowden homestead in gingerbread. Like that "renowned essay in cookery," sacramentally shared at
the feast's end, Jewett's landscapes, houses, and people fall into ruins
at her story's end. But if Jewett's fiction carefully acknowledges death's
power, it also affirms love's endurance. Like Miss Tempy's watchers,
Jewett's readers may find these preserves still sweet though their maker
lie in "ceaseless rosemary." And that, of course, is the mystery.

Notes

PREFACE

1. Willa Cather, Preface to *The Best Short Stories of Sarah Orne Jewett*, 2 vols. (Boston: Houghton Mifflin, 1925).

2. Nina Baym, "Melodramas of Beset Manhood: How Theories of American Fiction Exclude Women Authors," *American Quarterly* 33:2 (Summer 1981): 123–39. See also Elizabeth Ammons, "Stowe's Dream of the Mother-Savior: *Uncle Tom's Cabin* and American Women Writers before the 1920s," in *New Essays on Uncle Tom's Cabin*, ed. Eric J. Sundquist (Cambridge, London, and New York: Cambridge University Press, 1986), pp. 155–95; and Martin Green, *The Great American Adventure* (Boston: Beacon, 1984).

3. Carroll Smith-Rosenberg, "The Female World of Love and Ritual: Relations Between Women in Nineteenth-Century America," *Signs* 1:1 (1975): 1–29.

4. Ralph Waldo Emerson, "The Poet," in *Selections from Ralph Waldo Emerson*, ed. Stephen E. Wicher (1843; rpt. Boston: Houghton Mifflin, 1957), p. 224. Sarah Orne Jewett, *The Country of the Pointed Firs and Other Stories*, selected and introduced by Mary Ellen Chase, with an introduction by Marjorie Pryse (1896; rpt. New York: W. W. Norton, 1982). I will refer to this edition hereafter as *Firs*.

Studies that discuss the "matriarchal" or mythic qualities of Jewett's work include Josephine Donovan, *Sarah Orne Jewett* (New York: Frederick Ungar, 1981); Donovan, "A Woman's Vision of Transcendence: A New Interpretation of the Works of Sarah Orne Jewett," *Massachusetts Review* 21:2 (Summer 1980), 365–80; Elizabeth Ammons, "Going in Circles: The Female Geography of *The Country of the Pointed Firs*," *Studies in the Literary Imagination* 16 (Autumn 1983): 83–92; Ammons, "Jewett's Witches," in *Critical Essays on Sarah Orne Jewett*, ed. Gwen Nagel (Boston: G. K. Hall, 1984); Marjorie Pryse, "Introduction to the Norton Edition," in *The Country of the Pointed Firs and Other Stories*, by Sarah Orne Jewett (New York: W. W. Norton, 1982), pp. v–xix; Robin Magowan, "The Outer Island Sequence in *Pointed Firs*," *Colby Library Quarterly* 6 (June 1964): 418–24; Annis Pratt, "Women and Nature in Modern Fiction," *Contemporary Literature* 13 (Autumn 1972): 476–90; Barton L. St. Armand, "Jewett and Marin: The Inner Vision," *Colby Library Quarterly* 9 (December 1972): 632–43. Excellent discussions can also be found in Joseph Allen Boone's *Tradition Counter Tradition: Love and the Form of Fiction* (Chicago: University of Chicago Press, 1987), pp. 304–11; and Sandra Zagarell's "Narrative of Community: The Identification of a Genre," *Signs* 13:31 (Spring 1988): 498–527. Both appeared after this study was essentially completed.

CHAPTER 1

1. Sarah Orne Jewett to Sarah Whitman, South Berwick, Maine, Thursday morning [1894 or 1895], in *The Letters of Sarah Orne Jewett,* ed. Annie Fields (Boston: Houghton-Mifflin, 1911), p. 112.

2. Clifford Geertz, "Thick Description: Toward an Interpretive Theory of Culture," in *The Interpretation of Cultures* (New York: Basic Books, 1973), p. 14.

3. Roland Barthes, *Writing Degree Zero* (New York: Hill and Wang, 1968), 86–87; quoted in Marcia Landy, "The Silent Women: Toward a Feminist Critique," in *The Authority of Experience: Essays in Feminist Criticism,* ed. Arlyn Diamond and Lee R. Edwards (Amherst, MA: University of Massachusetts Press, 1977), p. 24. Landy's article helped me to formulate my approach. See also Tillie Olsen, *Silences* (New York: Delacorte, 1978); Helene Cixous, "The Laugh of Medusa," *Signs* 1:4 (Summer 1976): 875–94; and *New French Feminisms,* ed. Elaine Marks and Isabelle de Courtivron (Amherst, MA: University of Massachusetts Press, 1979).

4. Elaine Marks, "Women with Women: Community among Women in Fiction," paper presented at Midwest Modern Language Association Convention, Women and Literature Section, Minneapolis, Fall 1978.

5. Nina Auerbach, *Communities of Women: An Idea in Fiction* (Cambridge, MA: Harvard University Press, 1978).

6. Sherry Ortner, "Is Female to Male As Nature Is to Culture?," *Feminist Studies* 1:2 (Fall 1972): 5–31; rpt. in *Women, Culture, and Society,* ed. Louise Lamphere and Michelle Z. Rosaldo (Stanford, CA: Stanford University Press, 1974). The beautifully dovetailed research of Ortner, Michelle Z. Rosaldo, and Nancy Chodorow underlies a large part of this study. See Michelle Z. Rosaldo, "Women, Culture and Society: A Theoretical Overview," and Nancy Chodorow, "Family Structure and Feminine Personality," also in *Women, Culture and Society.* A more detailed discussion of Chodorow's theory appears in her *The Reproduction of Mothering: Psychoanalysis and the Sociology of Gender* (Berkeley, CA: University of California Press, 1978).

Elaine Showalter's article, "Feminist Criticism in the Wilderness," *Critical Inquiry* 8:2 (Winter 1981): 179–205, discusses work by Chodorow and Geertz as possible directions for feminist criticism.

7. Ortner, p. 10. Contemporary discussion of this link between women and nature begins, of course, with Simone de Beauvoir, *The Second Sex,* trans. H. M. Parshley (New York: Knopf, 1952). Some other texts include Mary Ellman, *Thinking About Women* (New York, 1968); Mary Daly, *Beyond God the Father: Toward a Philosophy of Women's Liberation* (Boston: Beacon, 1973); Mary Daly, *Gyn/Ecology: The Metaethics of Radical Feminism* (Boston: Beacon, 1978); Rosemary Reuther, *New Women/New Earth: Sexist Ideologies and Human Liberation* (New York: Seabury, 1975); Adrienne Rich *Of Woman Born: Motherhood as Experience and Institution* (New York: W. W. Norton, 1976).

For the structuralist background of Ortner's argument see Claude Lévi-Strauss, *The Elementary Structures of Kinship,* trans. J. H. Bell and J. R. von Sturmer (Boston: Beacon, 1969); also *The Raw and the Cooked: Introduction to a Science of Mythology,* vol. 1 (New York: Harper and Row, 1964, 1969).

8. Ortner, p. 11. See also Frank Kermode, *The Sense of an Ending* (New

York: Oxford University Press, 1966, 1967); and Mary Douglas, *Purity and Danger: An Analysis of the Concepts of Pollution and Taboo* (Baltimore: Penguin, 1966, 1970). For a critique of cultural attitudes toward the "feminine" and the "viscous": Margery Collins and Christine Pierce, "Holes and Slime: Sexism in Sartre's Psychoanalysis" in *Women and Philosophy*, ed. Carol C. Gould and Mary W. Wartofsky (New York: Capricorn Books, 1976).

As support for her position on semantic universals, Ortner cites Stephen Ullman, "Semantic Universals," in *Universals of Language*, ed. Joseph H. Greenberg (Cambridge, MA: MIT Press, 1963). For a discussion of feminist universalism and its critics, see Louise Lamphere, "Beyond Dichotomies," review of *Gender and Kinship: Essays Toward a Unified Analysis*, ed. Jane Fishburne Collier and Sylvia Junko Yanagisako, *Women's Review of Books*, 5:5 (February 1988), 17–18.

9. Ortner, p. 12.

10. Ortner, p. 12.

11. Chodorow, "Family Structure," p. 65. Elaine Showalter's "Feminist Criticism in the Wilderness" acknowledges "the enormous influence" of Chodorow's work on women's studies (p. 194). Chodorow's object-relations approach differs sharply from Freud's, as she explains on pp. 57–76 in *Reproduction of Mothering*. Among the authorities she cites are Alice and Michael Balint, represented by *Primary Love and Psycho-Analytic Technique*, ed. Michael Balint (London: Tavistock; New York: Liveright, 1956) and Alice Balint, *The Early Years of Life: A Psycho-Analytic Study* (New York: Basic Books, 1954); John Bowlby, *Attachment and Loss*, vol. 1: *Attachment* (London: Penguin, 1969); W. E. D. Fairbairn, *An Object-Relations Theory of the Personality* (New York: Basic Books, 1952). A special issue of *Feminist Studies*, 4:2 (June 1978), devoted to mothers and daughters, includes a related and particularly helpful article by Jane Flax, "The Conflict Between Nurturance and Autonomy in Mother-Daughter Relationships Within Feminism" (pp. 171–89).

See also David Bakan, *The Duality of Human Experience: Isolation and Communion in Western Man* (Boston: Beacon, 1966); Juliet Mitchell, *Psycho-Analysis and Feminism: Freud, Reich, Laing, and Women* (New York: Random House-Vintage, 1975); Dorothy Dinnerstein, *The Mermaid and the Minotaur: Sexual Arrangements and Human Malaise* (New York: Harper and Row, 1976).

12. Chodorow, *Reproduction of Mothering*, p. 180.

13. Ortner, p. 23. The ethical implications of women's communal style are examined at length in Carol Gilligan's *In a Different Voice* (Cambridge, MA: Harvard University Press, 1982) and Nel Nodding's *Caring: A Feminine Approach to Ethics and Moral Education* (Berkeley, CA: University of California Press, 1984).

14. Ortner, p. 26. See Edmund Leach, "Genesis as Myth," in *Interpretations of Cultures: Myth and Cosmos*, ed. John Middleton (Garden City, NY: The Natural History Press, 1967).

15. Edwards and Diamond, eds., *The Authority of Experience*; and Showalter, "Feminist Criticism in the Wilderness" (both cited above). Ironically, this definition of "minority" can be expanded to include those who might conventionally be associated with cultural authority. For as Marcia Landy points out, all writers (including white male Protestant ones) may experience language as silence. The burden of renovating language is not borne by fem-

inists alone. For example, in "Melodramas of Beset Manhood" Nina Baym describes "classic" American male novelists as a group producing a "consensus criticism of the consensus" (p. 129).

16. For social background, see Nancy F. Cott, *The Bonds of Womanhood: "Woman's Sphere" in New England, 1780–1835* (New Haven, CT: Yale University Press, 1977); Carl Degler, *At Odds: Women and Family in America from the Revolution to Present* (New York: Oxford University Press, 1980); Ann D. Gordon and Mari Jo Buhle, "Sex and Class in Colonial and Nineteenth-Century America," in *Liberating Women's History,* ed. Berenice A. Carroll (Urbana, IL: University of Illinois Press, 1976), pp. 278–300; Gerda Lerner, "The Lady and the Mill Girl: Changes in the Status of Women in the Age of Jackson, 1790–1840," in *A Heritage of Her Own,* ed. Nancy F. Cott and Elizabeth H. Pleck (New York: Simon and Schuster, 1979), pp. 182–96; Barbara Welter, "The Cult of True Womanhood," *American Quarterly,* 18 (Summer 1966): 151–74.

17. Margaret Coxe, *The Young Lady's Companion: In a Series of Letters* (Columbus, OH: I. N. Whiting, 1839), pp. 14, 15.

18. Welter, p. 152.

19. Carroll Smith-Rosenberg, "The Female World of Love and Ritual." See *At Odds* by Carl Degler for a discussion of how Victorian physicians perceived women's sexuality and marital satisfaction; also Nancy F. Cott, "Passionlessness: An Interpretation of Victorian Sexual Ideology, 1790–1850," in *A Heritage of Her Own,* ed. Nancy F. Cott and Elizabeth H. Pleck (New York: Simon and Schuster, 1979), pp. 162–81 originally in *Signs* 4 (1978): 219–36; Daniel Scott Smith, "Family Limitation, Sexual Control, and Domestic Feminism in Victorian America," *Feminist Studies* 1 (Winter-Spring 1973): 40–57; Ruth H. Bloch, "American Feminine Ideals in Transition: The Rise of the Moral Mother, 1785–1815," *Feminist Studies* 4 (June 1978): 101–26. As several historians point out, this ideology arose during a time of unprecedented opportunities for women in the public sphere.

20. Smith-Rosenberg, p. 14. See also Ann Douglas, *The Feminization of American Culture* (New York: Knopf, 1977); Kathryn Kish Sklar, *Catherine Beecher: A Study in American Domesticity* (New Haven, CT: Yale University Press, 1973); William L. O'Neill, *Everyone Was Brave: The Rise and Fall of Feminism in America* (Chicago: Quadrangle, 1969).

21. While describing this homosocial world as a subculture may help us locate its boundaries and rituals, it is important not to forget the very real and inescapable connection this domestic world has to the masculine one outside it. The two are indissolubly linked, since changes in the economic, public sphere—industrialization, for example—shape the structure of the family. Conversely, the relationship of a mother to her male child effectively shapes his consciousness and attitude toward the world outside. See Chodorow, *Reproduction of Mothering, passim.* For studies of domestic, "matrifocal" society, see Louise Lamphere, "Strategies, Cooperation, and Conflict among Women in Domestic Groups," and Nancy Tanner, "Matrifocality in Indonesia and Africa and among Black Americans," both in *Women, Culture, and Society,* ed. Michelle Z. Rosaldo and Louise Lamphere (Stanford, CA: Stanford University Press, 1974).

22. Ann Douglas, *passim*; Gail Parker, Introduction to *The Oven Birds: American Women on Womanhood, 1820–1920* (Garden City, NY: Doubleday-

Anchor, 1972); Mary Kelley, *Private Woman, Public Stage: Literary Domes-ticity in Nineteenth-Century America* (New York and London: Oxford University Press, 1984). See also Barbara Welter, "The Feminization of American Religion: 1800–1860," in *Dimity Convictions* (Athens, OH: Ohio University Press, 1976).

Other important studies of sentimentalism and the domestic novel include Nina Baym, *Women's Fiction: A Guide to Novels by and about Women in America, 1820–1870* (Ithaca, NY: Cornell University Press, 1978); Herbert Ross Brown, *The Sentimental Novel in America, 1789–1860* (Durham, NC: Duke University Press, 1940); Fred Lewis Pattee, *The Feminine Fifties* (New York: D. Appleton, 1940); and Helen Papashvily, *All the Happy Endings: A Study of the Domestic Novel in America, the Women Who Wrote It, the Women Who Read It, in the Nineteenth Century* (New York: Harper and Brothers, 1956). See also Lucy Freibert and Barbara White, eds., *Hidden Hands: An Anthology of American Women Writers, 1790–1870* (New Brunswick, NJ: Rutgers University Press, 1985); Judith Fetterley, ed., *Provisions: A Reader from 19th-Century American Women* (Bloomington, IN: Indiana University Press, 1985).

The meaning of "sentimentalism" shifted over the nineteenth century. According to the *Oxford English Dictionary*, its earliest meanings, in the eighteenth century, were not disparaging: "Of persons, their dispositions and actions: Characterized by sentiment. Originally in a favorable sense: Characterized by or exhibiting refined and elevated feeling. In later use: addicted to indulgence in superficial emotion; apt to be swayed by sentiment." [*The Compact Edition of the Oxford English Dictionary*, vol. 2 (New York: Oxford University Press, 1971), p. 2730]. This earlier meaning is especially appropriate for the work of writers like Stowe because they emphasized feeling as the source of ethical and religious values. However, as the *OED* makes clear, later generations of writers tried to disassociate themselves from the excesses of this earlier school, a trend exacerbated after World War I when modernists rejected their Victorian precursors. Despite the term's complex history, I have retained it because it links the religious trend toward Christian nurture—sentimental education—and women's fiction.

23. Ammons, "Stowe's Dream," p. 176. Although their perspectives are radically different, Josephine Donovan, *New England Local Color Literature: A Women's Tradition* (New York: Ungar, 1983) and Ann Douglas (Wood), "The Literature of Impoverishment: The Women Local Colorists in America 1865–1914," *Women's Studies*, 1 (1972): 3–45, both discuss the relationship between the sentimentalists and the later generation that included Jewett. Significantly, Jewett seems to have used the term "sentimentalism" in its disparaging sense, a use that reflects her ambivalence toward the tradition that Stowe represented. According to Willa Cather's biographer, Sharon O'Brien, "Although she drew on the 'power of loving' which Cather thought the woman writer's particular strength, Jewett was determined to control sentimentality. Jewett's training in nineteenth-century Continental fiction taught her the virtues of simplicity, control, and understatement. . . . As she warned Cather in 1908, one had to be careful not to let 'sentiment' degenerate into 'sentimentality'—a code word for the excesses of the female pen" [Sharon O'Brien, *Willa Cather: The Emerging Voice* (New York: Oxford University Press, 1987), p. 342].

24. Elizabeth Ammons, Introduction to *"How Celia Changed Her Mind"*

and Selected Stories by Rose Terry Cooke (New Brunswick, NJ: Rutgers University Press, 1986), pp. xxiii, xxxv.

25. Judith Fetterley, Introduction to "Miss Lucinda," in *Provisions*, p. 346.

26. Jean Downey, "A Biographical and Critical Study of Rose Terry Cooke," Ph.D. diss., University of Ottawa, 1956. See also Susan Allen Toth, "Character Studies in Rose Terry Cooke: New Faces for the Short Story," *Kate Chopin Newsletter* 2 (1976): 19–26; Jay Martin, *Harvests of Change: American Literature, 1865–1914* (Princeton, NJ: Princeton University Press, 1967, pp. 139–42; Donovan, *New England Local Color Literature*, pp. 68–81; Perry D. Westbrook, *Acres of Flint: Sarah Orne Jewett and Her Contemporaries* (Metuchen, NJ: Scarecrow Press, 1951; rev. ed., 1981), pp. 78–85.

27. Fetterley, p. 346.

28. Rose Terry Cooke, *Root-Bound, and Other Sketches* (Boston: Congregational Sunday School and Publishing Society, 1885). "Root-Bound" may be from an earlier period. According to Ammons, "date of publication is not always a reliable reflection of composition for Cooke, and she herself mixed early and later stories when she compiled for anthologies" (Ammons, p. xxxix).

29. Cooke, p. 12.   30. Cooke, p. 15.
31. Cooke, pp. 17–18.   32. Cooke, p. 6.
33. Cooke, p. 10.   34. Cooke, pp. 10–11.
35. Cooke, pp. 13–14.   36. Cooke, p. 20.

37. See Parker, Introduction to *The Oven-Birds*; and O'Neill, *Everyone Was Brave*.

38. *The Gates Ajar* by Elizabeth Stuart Phelps (Ward) (Boston: Fields, Osgood, 1868) is a particularly good example of this genre. For a discussion of the "continuity" between this world and the next, see Barton Levi St. Armand, "Paradise Deferred: The Image of Heaven in the Work of Emily Dickinson and Elizabeth Stuart Phelps," *American Quarterly*, 29 (Spring 1977): 55–78.

39. For discussions of feminized religion and the female savior, see Douglas, *The Feminization of American Culture*; Welter, "The Feminization of American Religion," and Ammons, "Stowe's Dream."

CHAPTER 2

1. Henry Adams, *The Education of Henry Adams* (1907; rpt. Boston: Houghton Mifflin, 1961), pp. 385–88. See also Henry Adams, *Mont-Saint-Michel and Chartres* (1904; rpt. Garden City: Doubleday-Anchor, 1959). Leslie Fiedler is one contemporary literary critic who accepted Adams's analysis. See his *Love and Death in the American Novel* (New York: Stein and Day, 1966).

2. Caroline Healy Dall, *Margaret and Her Friends, or Ten Conversations upon the Mythology of the Greeks and Its Expression in Art* (Boston: Roberts Brothers, 1895; the conversations themselves were transcribed in 1841), p. 41.

3. Thomas Wentworth Higginson, "The Greek Goddesses," *The Atlantic Monthly*, 24 (July 1869): 97. I choose the *The Atlantic Monthly* for several reasons. First, it was perhaps the most influential magazine for New England, if not American, writers. Second, it regularly published Jewett's work. Third, through her relationship to Annie Fields, wife and then widow of the *Atlantic*'s publisher, Jewett was closely acquainted with its editors and regular contributors. Annie Fields's own poems, which occasionally appeared in the magazine,

were also an important source, especially since she adapted mythic themes from both Greek and Latin sources.

In addition to the *Atlantic* articles cited below, the magazine published virtually the entire text of John Fiske's *Myths and Mythmakers* (1872, rpt. Boston: Houghton Mifflin, 1900), a book dedicated to William Dean Howells, then an *Atlantic* editor (indeed, Jewett's editor). See, for example, John Fiske, "The Origins of Folk-Lore," *The Atlantic Monthly*, 27 (February 1871). The magazine also regularly reviewed works on mythology and the "higher criticism" of the Bible. See review of Conway's *Sacred Anthology*, 35 (January 1875): 113; review of Strauss's *Der Alte und der nere Glaube*, 31 (March 1978): 367.

4. Higginson, "Greek Goddesses," p. 108. See also Thomas Wentworth Higginson, "Sappho," *The Atlantic Monthly*, 28 (July 1871).

5. Hamilton Wright Mabie, "My Search for the Godddess," in *Liber Scriptorum*, ed. Rossiter Johnson, John Denison Champlin, and George Cary Eggleston (New York: Authors Club, 1893), pp. 381–85. This book is a limited edition of 251 copies; the one I saw was in the Berg Collection of English and American Literature, New York Public Library. For the Twain story, see Justin Kaplan, *Mr. Clemens and Mark Twain: A Biography* (New York: Simon and Schuster, 1966); for more on Isabella Beecher Hooker's matriarchal millennialism, see Forrest Wilson, *Crusader in Crinoline: The Life of Harriet Beecher Stowe* (Philadelphia: J. B. Lippincott, 1941).

6. As an editor of the *Atlantic* and friend of James T. Fields (as well as of Annie Fields), Higginson had great literary influence, particularly in New England. Moreover, he supported the moderate branch of the woman's rights movement and enthusiastically promoted women writers (despite his prolonged myopia regarding Emily Dickinson). Influential, but rather conventional, Higginson is a good example of the context within which Jewett wrote. For the midwestern grange story, see Mari Jo Buhle, *Women and American Socialism, 1870–1920* (Urbana, IL: University of Illinois Press, 1981), p. 82.

7. Higginson, "Greek Goddesses," p. 97.

8. Higginson, "Greek Goddesses," p. 103.

9. Higginson, "Greek Goddesses," p. 97. For contemporary discussion of this issue, see Mary Daly, *Beyond God the Father*, and *The Church and the Second Sex, with a New Feminist Post-Christian Introduction by the Author* (New York: Harper and Row–Colophon, 1975); Ann Barstow Driver, "Review Essay: Religion," *Signs* 2:2 (Winter 1976): 434–42; Giovanni Mieggi, *Virgin Mary* (Philadelphia: Westminster, 1955); Rosemary Reuther, *Religion and Sexism: Images of Women in the Jewish and Christian Tradition* (New York: Simon and Schuster, 1974); Ann B. Ulanov, *The Feminine in Jungian Psychology and Christian Theology* (Evanston, IL: Northwestern University Press, 1971). A number of pertinent essays are collected in Judith Plaskow and Joan Arnold Romero, eds., *Women and Religion*, rev. ed. (Missoula, MT: Scholar's Press and the American Academy of Religion, 1974).

10. Higginson, "Greek Goddesses," p. 107.

11. Nathaniel Hawthorne, *The Marble Faun, or, The Romance of Monte Beni* (1860; rpt. New York: New American Library, 1960). Louisa May Alcott, *Little Women* (1868; rpt. New York: Modern Library, 1983), pp. 239–40; Henry James, *The Bostonians: A Novel* (1886; rpt. New York: Crowell, 1974), p. 356.

12. Adams, *Education*, pp. 385, 388.

13. Higginson, "Greek Goddesses," pp. 107, 104.

14. Kate Chopin, *The Awakening* (1899; rpt. New York: W. W. Norton, 1976). For a discussion of its mythic imagery, see Grace Stewart, *A New Mythos: The Novel of the Artist as Heroine, 1877–1977* (St. Albans, VT: Eden, 1979).

15. Alcott, pp. 311, 600–603. Pre-Freudian Victorians were unlikely to analyze the Demeter–Persephone myth as an interior drama played by the splintered-off pieces of a single psyche. They did, however, see this story as symbolizing the experience of an individual woman.

16. Erich Neumann, *The Great Mother: An Analysis of the Archetype*, trans. Ralph Manheim (Princeton, NJ: Bollingen Foundation, Princeton University Press, 1955). While I will refer to Neumann's work on female symbolism throughout this study, I prefer to use it as the explication of an iconographical tradition—i.e., a tradition shaped by historical and cultural forces. Insofar as the members of a culture are shaped by similar structures—such as the asymmetrical distribution of parenting—they can be said to share a "collective unconscious." They respond in similar ways to similar symbols. Whether or not these symbols are universal or the product of a collective *memory* is beyond the scope of this study.

For other psychological studies of the Demeter–Persephone myth, see Carl Jung, "Psychological Aspects of the Kore," in *Essays on a Science of Mythology: The Myths of the Divine Child and the Divine Maiden*, rev. ed., trans. R. F. C. Hull (New York: Harper and Row, 1963); Károly Kerényi, *Eleusis: Archetypal Image of Mother and Daughter*, trans. Ralph Manheim (New York: Bollingen Foundation, Pantheon, 1967); Nor Hall, *Mothers and Daughters: Reflections on the Archetypal Feminine* (Minneapolis, MN: Rusoff, 1976). For information on the Eleusinian rituals, see George E. Mylonas, *Eleusis and the Eleusinian Mysteries* (Princeton, NJ: Princeton University Press, 1969); Walter F. Otto, "The Meaning of the Eleusinian Mysteries," in *The Mysteries, Papers from the Eranos Yearbooks*, vol. 2 (New York and London: Pantheon, 1955). For critiques of archetypal theory, see Naomi Goldenberg, "A Feminist Critique of Jung," *Signs* 2:2 (1976): 444–49; Lillian S. Robinson, "Dwelling in Decencies: Radical Criticism and the Feminist Perspective," *College English* 32 (May 1971): 879–89.

17. Nathaniel Hawthorne, *A Wonder-Book for Girls and Boys* (Boston: Ticknor, Reed, and Fields, 1852; London, 1851) and *Tanglewood Tales for Boys and Girls: Being a Second Wonder-Book* (Boston: Ticknor, Reed, and Fields, 1853).

18. Higginson, "Greek Goddesses," p. 108.

19. Coxe, p. 15. See also Elizabeth Ammons, "Stowe's Dream"; Barbara Welter, "The Feminization of American Religion"; and Dorothy Berkson, "Millennial Politics and the Feminine Fiction of Harriet Beecher Stowe," in *Critical Essays on Harriet Beecher Stowe*, ed. Elizabeth Ammons (Boston: G. K. Hall, 1980), pp. 244–58.

20. Johann Jakob Bachofen, "Das Mutterrecht" (1861), in *Myth, Religion, and Mother Right*, trans. Ralph Manheim (Princeton, NJ: Bollingen Foundation, Princeton University Press, 1967).

Contemporary versions of Bachofen's theory include Elizabeth Gould Davis, *The First Sex* (Baltimore: Penguin, 1971); Helen Diner, *Mothers and Amazons* (New York: Julian, 1965); Evelyn Reed, *Woman's Evolution: From Matriarchal*

Clan to Matriarchal Society (New York: Pathfinder, 1975); Merlin Stone, *When God Was a Woman* (New York: Dial, 1976).

For background on the popularity of Bachofen's theories, see George Boas, Preface to *Myth, Religion, and Mother Right*; Joseph Campbell, Introduction to *Myth, Religion, and Mother Right* (see note 20 above); Joan Bamberger, "The Myth of Matriarchy: Why Men Rule in Primitive Society," in *Woman, Culture, and Society,* ed. Michelle Zimbalist Rosaldo and Louise Lamphere (Stanford, CA: Stanford University Press, 1974), pp. 263–80; Elizabeth Fee, "The Sexual Politics of Victorian Anthropology," *Feminist Studies* 1 (1973): 23–29; Jill Conway, "Stereotypes of Femininity in a Theory of Sexual Evolution," *Victorian Studies* 14 (September 1970): 47–62; Elizabeth Fee, "Science and the Woman Problem: Historical Perspectives," in *Sex Differences,* ed. Michael Tietelbaum (New York: Doubleday-Anchor, 1976); Janice Law Trecker, "Sex, Science, and Education," *American Quarterly* 26 (October 1974): 352–66.

Critics of the matriarchal theory include Sarah B. Pomeroy, "A Classical Scholar's Perspective on Matriarchy," in *Liberating Women's History: Theoretical and Critical Essays,* ed. Berenice A. Carroll (Urbana, IL: University of Illinois Press, 1976), pp. 217–23; Harriet Whitehead, "Review: *Woman's Evolution: From Matriarchal Clan to Matriarchal Society* by Evelyn Reed," *Signs* 2:2 (1976): 746–48. For an overview of the issue, see Paula Webster, "Matriarchy: A Vision of Power," in *Toward an Anthropology of Women,* ed. Rayna R. Reiter (New York: Monthly Review Press, 1975).

21. Margaret Fuller (Ossoli), in Dall, *Margaret and Her Friends,* pp. 42–43.

22. H. M. Alden, "The Eleusinia," pt. 2, *Atlantic* 6 (August 1860): 157–68. See also H. M. Alden, "The Eleusinia," pt. 1, *Atlantic* 4 (September 1859): 295–303.

23. Lydia Maria Child, "The Intermingling of Religions," *Atlantic* 28 (October 1871): 391.

24. Child, p. 392.

25. B. W. Ball, "Woman's Rights in Ancient Athens," *Atlantic,* 27 (March 1871): 286.

26. G. E. Woodberry, review of *Demeter and Other Poems* by Alfred Lord Tennyson, *Atlantic* 65 (March 1890): 421.

27. Woodberry, p. 421.

28. Sir James George Frazer, *The Golden Bough: A Study in Magic and Religion,* vol. 1, abridged (1922, rpt. New York: Macmillan, 1963).

29. Elizabeth Cady Stanton, "The Matriarchate, or Mother-Age," published in the *Transactions of the National Council of Women of the United States* (Philadelphia, 1891); reprinted in *Up from the Pedestal,* ed. Aileen S. Kraditor (Chicago: Quadrangle, 1968), p. 147. See also Stanton, *The Woman's Bible* (1895; rpt. New York: Arno, 1972); Mathilda Joslyn Gage, *Woman, Church, and the State* (1900; rpt. New York: Arno, 1972); Charlotte Perkins Gilman, *Herland* (1915; rpt. New York: Pantheon, 1979).

30. Ball, p. 276. See also John Fiske, "Athenian and American Life," *Atlantic* (November 1974): 551–67.

31. Walter Pater, "The Myth of Demeter and Persephone," *Greek Studies* (New York: Macmillan, 1894), pp. 81, 102. Pater's essay was first published in *Fortnightly Review* (January and February 1876). *Atlantic* readers were

apparently so barraged with descriptions of Demeter's mysteries that H. M. Alden opens his 1859 article, "The Eleusinia," with yet another elaborate apology for the familiarity of his subject: "What did the Eleusinia mean? Perhaps, reader, you think the question of little interest. 'The Eleusinia! Why, Lobeck made that little matter clear long ago; and there was Prophryr, who told us the whole thing was only an illustration of the Platonic philosophy. St. Croix too—he made the affair as clear as day!' [But] the question is not so easily settled, my friend, and I insist . . . that you *have* an interest in it" (Alden, "The Eleusinia," pt. 1, p. 295).

32. Ann Douglas, *Feminization*, p. 128.

33. Ann Douglas, *Feminization*, p. 128.

34. Neumann, p. 331. The Sophia represents the apex of Neumann's developmental scheme, which begins with the "elementary feminine," uroboric and featureless, with a negative side as the Terrible Mother; ascends through the "transformative feminine" comprising the Lady of the Plants and the Animals, represented by Demeter and other totemic goddesses; then reaches its height with Sophia, represented by the Virgin or the resurrected Persephone who, united with her mother as the Dual Goddesses, is greater than Demeter or her maiden self.

35. Neumann, p. 325.

36. Ann Douglas, p. 195.

37. Harriet Beecher Stowe, *The Pearl of Orr's Island* (1862; rpt. Hartford, CT: The Stowe-Day Foundation, 1979).

38. See Chapter 7 for a discussion of the *Bildungsroman*.

39. For a fine study of "matrifocal" Christianity in Stowe's work, see Dorothy Berkson, "Millenial Politics in the Feminine Fiction of Harriet Beecher Stowe." According to Berkson, "*The Minister's Wooing* (1859), *The Pearl of Orr's Island* (1862), *Oldtown Folks* (1869), and *Poganuc People* (1878) are all connected by the common symbol of matriarchy as the ideal form for the millenial society" (p. 245). Elizabeth Ammons has dealt extensively with these issues; in addition to "Stowe's Dream of the Mother-Savior," see "Heroines in Uncle Tom's Cabin," *American Literature* 49 (May 1977): 116–79; rpt. in Ammons, *Critical Essays on Harriet Beecher Stowe*. See also Laurie Crumpacker, "Harriet Beecher Stowe: A Study of Nineteenth-Century Androgyny," in *American Novelists Revisited: Essays in Feminist Criticism,* ed. Fritz Fleischman (Boston: G. K. Hall, 1982), pp. 78–106; and Alice Crozier, *The Novels of Harriet Beecher Stowe* (New York: Oxford University Press, 1969).

40. Alden, pt. 2, p. 158.   41. Alden, pt. 2, p. 158.

42. Alden, pt. 2, p. 164.   43. Alden, pt. 2, p. 168.

44. Alden, pt. 2, p. 158.

45. For a discussion of Jewett's response to Stowe and her tradition see Ammons, "Stowe's Dream"; Ann Douglas (Wood), "The Literature of Impoverishment"; Donovan, *New England Local Color Literature*; and Parker, Introduction to *The Oven-Birds*.

46. Stowe, p. 15.   47. Stowe, p. 131.

48. Stowe, p. 109.   49. Stowe, pp. 52–53.

50. Stowe, pp. 56–57.   51. Stowe, pp. 57–58.

52. Stowe, p. 222.   53. Stowe, p. 178.

54. Stowe, p. 175.   55. Stowe, p. 371.

56. Stowe, p. 60.   57. Stowe, pp. 178–79.

58. Stowe, pp. 38–39.
59. Stowe, p. 81.
60. Stowe, pp. 320–21.
61. Stowe, p. 348.
62. Stowe, pp. 348–49.
63. Stowe, p. 134.
64. Stowe, p. 134.
65. Frazer, *The Golden Bough,* pt. 2, p. 18.
66. Stowe, p. 176.
67. Stowe, p. 178.
68. Stowe, p. 337.
69. Stowe, p. 306.
70. Stowe, p. 339.
71. Stowe, p. 371.
72. Stowe, p. 394.
73. Stowe, p. 382.
74. Alden, pt. 2, p. 166.
75. Stowe, p. 401.
76. Stowe, p. 414.
77. Stowe, p. 417.
78. Stowe, p. 416.
79. Stowe, p. 423.
80. Stowe, p. 423.
81. Stowe, p. 424.
82. Stowe, p. 407.
83. Stowe, p. 424 (emphasis Stowe's).
84. Stowe, p. 399.
85. Stowe, p. 431.
86. Stowe, pp. 431–32.
87. Stowe, p. 434.
88. Stowe, p. 436.
89. Stowe, p. 437.
90. Stowe, p. 414.

91. Homerus, *The Homeric Hymns: A New Prose Translation and Essays, Literary and Mythological,* ed. and trans. Andrew Lang (New York: Longmans, Green, 1899; London: G. Allen, 1899), p. 198.

92. Henry James, *The Wings of the Dove* (1902; rpt. New York: Modern Library, 1937).

93. Hawthorne, *The Marble Faun.*

94. Jewett to Annie Fields, 5 July [1889], in *The Letters of Sarah Orne Jewett,* ed. Annie Fields (Boston: Houghton Mifflin, 1911), pp. 46–47.

95. Jewett to Annie Fields, Saturday morning, n.d., n.p. [folder 117 (2)], Jewett Collection, Houghton Library, Harvard University.

96. Sarah Orne Jewett, "The Christmas Ghosts," drafts 1 and 2, MS. 1743.22 (15), Houghton Library, Harvard University. This story is discussed in Chapter 3.

97. Stowe, p. 21.
98. Stowe, p. 379.
99. Stowe, p. 379.
100. Stowe, p. 372.
101. Stowe, pp. 372–73.
102. Stowe, p. 376.
103. Stowe, p. 420.
104. Stowe, pp. 420–21.
105. Stowe, p. 380.

CHAPTER 3

1. Sarah Orne Jewett, "River Driftwood," in *Deephaven and Other Stories,* ed. Richard Cary (1881; rpt. New Haven, CT: College and University Press, 1966), p. 16. For the history of the Jewett house, see Marie Donahue, "Sarah Orne Jewett's 'Dear Old House and Home,'" *Downeast Magazine,* August 1977, 62–67.

The available biographies are John Eldridge Frost, *Sarah Orne Jewett* (Kittery Point, ME: The Gundalow Club, 1960); and F. O. Matthiessen, *Sarah Orne Jewett* (Boston and New York: Houghton Mifflin, 1929). Published letters include *Sarah Orne Jewett Letters,* rev. and enl. ed.; ed. Richard Cary (Waterville, ME: Colby College Press, 1967); *The Letters of Sarah Orne Jewett,* ed.

Annie Fields (Boston: Houghton Mifflin, 1911); and *Letters of Sarah Orne Jewett in the Colby College Library,* ed. Carl Weber (Waterville, ME: Colby College Library, 1947). Among the few full-length critical studies are Richard Cary, *Sarah Orne Jewett* (New York: Twayne, 1962); Donovan, *Sarah Orne Jewett*; Jean Sougnac, *Sarah Orne Jewett* (Paris: Jouve et Cie., 1937); Margaret F. Thorp, *Sarah Orne Jewett,* University of Minnesota Pamphlets on American Writers, No. 61 (Minneapolis, MN: University of Minnesota Press, 1966).

   Much of the best criticism on Jewett is collected in *Appreciation of Sarah Orne Jewett: Twenty-Nine Interpretive Essays,* ed. Richard Cary (Waterville, ME: Colby College Press, 1973) (hereafter abbreviated as *Appreciation*) and in Gwen Nagel's excellent *Critical Essays on Sarah Orne Jewett* (Boston: G. K. Hall, 1984 (hereafter cited as Nagel). Further information on both primary and secondary sources may be found in Clara Carter Weber and Carl J. Weber, comps., *A Bibliography of the Published Writings of Sarah Orne Jewett* (Waterville, ME: Colby College Press, 1949) and Gwen L. Nagel and James Nagel, comps., *Sarah Orne Jewett: A Reference Guide* (Boston: G. K. Hall, 1978).

   2. Jewett, "River Driftwood," p. 10.
   3. Sarah Orne Jewett, "From a Mournful Villager," in *Country By-Ways* (Boston: Houghton Mifflin, 1881), p. 127. On the implications of these traditions in Jewett's fiction, see Gwen Nagel's richly detailed "'This Prim Corner of Land Where She Was Queen': Sarah Orne Jewett's New England Gardens," *Colby Library Quarterly* 22:1 (March 1986): 43–62.
   4. See Ann Douglas, "The Literature of Impoverishment."
   5. Sarah Orne Jewett, "*Deephaven,*" in *Deephaven and Other Stories,* ed. Richard Cary (1877; rpt. New Haven, CT: College and University Press, 1966), p. 71.
   6. Elizabeth Cleghorn Gaskell (Stevenson), *Cranford* (New York: Harper, 1864), p. 1. For discussions of the relationship between preindustrial and feminine culture, as well as connections between Gaskell and Jewett, see Zagarell, *passim*; and Boone, pp. 285–304, 304–308. Also Clarice Short, "Studies in Gentleness," *Western Humanities Review* 11 (Autumn 1957): 387–93; reprinted in *Appreciation*.
   7. See Mitchell, pp. 382–406; Chodorow, *Reproduction of Mothering, passim.*
   8. Sarah Orne Jewett, "Looking Back on Girlhood," in *The Uncollected Short Stories of Sarah Orne Jewett,* ed. Richard Cary (Waterville, ME: Colby College Press, 1971), p. 7.
   Evidently Dr. Jewett's personality and profession impressed themselves on his daughter so much that she considered becoming a doctor herself. In a letter to Annie Fields, which Fields dated as 1882, Jewett wrote that she had been reading an anatomy handbook, which she found extremely interesting. "Sometimes," she continued, "I think I should like to give up the f— and the d— [*sic*] and be a doctor, though very likely I am enough of one already to get the best of it for myself and perhaps I have done as much as I ever could for other people" (Jewett to Annie Fields, Tuesday [1882], in Fields, *Letters,* p. 14).
   9. Jewett, "Looking Back," p. 7.
   10. Jewett, "Looking Back," p. 6. Richard Cary discusses the literary influence of Jewett's family and community, including Theodore Jewett, in "The Literary Rubrics of Sarah Orne Jewett," Nagel, pp. 198–211.

11. Jewett to Annie Fields, 12 October 1890, in Fields, *Letters,* p. 82.

12. Jewett, "Looking Back," p. 7.

13. Jewett, "Looking Back," p. 6.

14. This translation from Flaubert is quoted in Frost, p. 114.

15. Jewett, "Looking Back," p. 6.

16. Sarah Orne Jewett, "The White Rose Road," in *Strangers and Wayfarers* (Boston and New York: Houghton Mifflin, 1890). The letter describing her actual expedition with her mother was written to Annie Fields, Wednesday morning, n.d. [1889?] in Fields, *Letters,* pp. 64–66. After their deaths Jewett wrote eulogies for both her father and maternal grandfather but not for her mother: "Dr. Theodore Herman Jewett," MS. Am 1743.22 (28), Houghton Library, Harvard University; "Recollections of Dr. William Perry of Exeter," MS. Am 1743.22 (102), Houghton Library, Harvard University.

17. Sarah Orne Jewett, "The Christmas Ghosts," drafts 1 and 2, MS. 1743.22 (15), Houghton Library, Harvard University.

18. Jewett to Georgina Halliburton, London, 22 April [1892], Houghton Library, Harvard University.

19. Jewett to Thomas Bailey Aldrich, n.p., n.d., quoted in Matthiessen, pp. 94–95.

20. Theophilus Parsons to Sarah Orne Jewett, Cambridge, 22 September 1878, Houghton Library, Harvard University.

21. Edward Eastman to Mrs. Abby O. Eastman, South Berwick, 23 September 1878, Columbia University Library.

22. Jewett to Sara Norton, South Berwick, 3 September 1897, in Fields, *Letters,* p. 126. See also Ann Douglas, "Literature of Impoverishment"; and Eugene Hillhouse Pool, "The Child in Sarah Orne Jewett," *Colby Library Quarterly* 7 (September 1967): 503–9; reprinted in *Appreciation.*

23. Lily Munger was a younger friend from Farmington, Maine (and originally from South Berwick), with whom Jewett corresponded in the late 1870s. See Marti Hohmann, "Sarah Orne Jewett to Lily Munger: Twenty-Three Letters," *Colby Library Quarterly* 22:1 (March 1986): 28–35.

24. Sarah Orne Jewett, "Confessions of a Housebreaker," in *The Mate of the Daylight, and Friends Ashore* (Boston: Houghton Mifflin, 1884).

25. Jewett to Lily Munger, South Berwick, 8 January 1878, Barrett Coll., University of Virginia.

26. Jewett to Caroline Perry Jewett, At Sea, 1 June 1882, Houghton Library, Harvard University.

27. Caroline Perry Jewett to Sarah Orne Jewett, n.p., n.d. [1888], Houghton Library, Harvard University. Jewett family letters in the archives of the Society for the Preservation of New England Antiquities also reveal Mrs. Jewett's intense concern over Sarah's health.

28. Jewett to Annie Fields, Saturday afternoon, March 1882, n.p., Houghton Library, Harvard University.

29. Jewett to Annie Fields, Saturday afternoon, March 1882, n.p., Houghton Library, Harvard University.

30. Jewett to Annie Fields, August 1891, n.p., Houghton Library, Harvard University.

31. Jewett to Annie Fields, Wednesday night, 1891, Houghton Library, Harvard University.

32. Jewett to Annie Fields, Sunday night, August 1891, Houghton Library, Harvard University.

33. Jewett to Annie Fields, 10 September 1891, Houghton Library, Harvard University.

34. Jewett to Loulie [Louisa] Dresel, South Berwick, 10 January [1891], Special Coll., University of New Hampshire.

35. Jewett to "Cousin Caroline" [Gilman], 148 Charles Street, Thursday, n.d., Barrett Coll., University of Virginia.

36. Jewett to Annie Fields, 24 March 1882, in Fields, *Letters,* p. 16.

37. Josephine Donovan discusses Celia Thaxter's effort to reach her mother through a séance. She cites Rosamond Thaxter's *Sandpiper, The Life of Celia Thaxter* (Sanbornville, NH: Wake-Brook House, 1962), p. 237. See Donovan, *Jewett,* p. 116.

38. Several of Professor Parsons's letters to Jewett from the early 1870s are found in the Houghton Library collection, along with his study of Swedenborgian philosophy, *The Finite and the Infinite* (Boston: Roberts Brothers, 1872), a gift from him to Jewett.

39. Jewett, "Christmas Ghosts," draft 2, p. 1. The language of "The Christmas Ghosts" is very close to the letters Jewett wrote after her mother's death. However, the "watcher" recalls "Miss Tempy's Watchers," where two women are transfigured by the memories of a loved and loving friend, over whose dead body they keep watch. "Miss Tempy" was published in 1888, well before Caroline Jewett's death. However, hers was a long and difficult dying, and her daughter may well have begun to reflect on its meaning before the event.

40. Jewett, "Christmas Ghosts," draft 2, pp. 3–4.

41. Jewett, "Christmas Ghosts," draft 2, p. 4.

42. Jewett, "Christmas Ghosts," draft 2, pp. 4–5.

43. Jewett, "Christmas Ghosts," draft 2, p. 6.

44. Jewett, "Christmas Ghosts," draft 1, p. 11.

45. Jewett, "Christmas Ghosts," draft 1, pp. 15–16. These deletions are especially interesting in the context of letter to Jewett from fellow writer Elizabeth Stuart Phelps: "You have often been told what a quiet and finished touch you have. I need not repeat the story. Shall I tell you one thing I would like to see you do? When you brought Mrs. Fields the roses, there was a red one hidden among the protecting white. *Once*—the day I met you—I saw the flash of the red rose in your quiet face. Now god [*sic*] makes both kinds, and many people love the white better—learn its lesson better—if the other is there contrasting—Give us sometime 'the red, red rose' " [Elizabeth Stuart Phelps to Sarah Orne Jewett, Andover, 10 December (1879, dated from internal evidence), Houghton Library, Jewett collection]. This letter was brought to my attention by Susan Coultrap McQuin. What we see in Jewett's first draft *is* a "red, red rose," but one being carefully pruned back for the sake of "the protecting white," the aesthetic quality Phelps herself acknowledges as "high, and calm, and fine."

46. Jewett, "Christmas Ghosts," draft 1, p. 17.

47. Jewett, "Christmas Ghosts," draft 1, p. 17.

48. Jung, p. 162.

49. Jung, p. 162.

50. Neumann, p. 319.

51. Jewett to Sarah Whitman, Tuesday, [1894–5, dated by another hand],

Houghton Library, Harvard University. See also Susan Allen Toth, "The Value of Age in the Fiction of Sarah Orne Jewett," *Studies in Short Fiction* 8 (Summer 1971): 433–41; reprinted in *Appreciation*. While Jewett's sentiments clearly reflect her criticism of the age, I do not think that this passage reveals, as Ann Douglas and Eugene Hillhouse Pool have argued, Jewett's failure to "grow up" and form attachments with people of her own age. She had many close younger friends.

52. Jewett to Sara Norton, South Berwick, Maine, 28 October 1897, in Fields, *Letters,* p. 133.

53. Jewett to Grace Norton, Saturday morning, 1898, Houghton Library, Harvard University.

54. Jewett, *Firs,* p. 35.

55. Jewett, "Mournful Villager," p. 134. Mary Jewett, however, was Captain Jewett's third wife and not Sarah Jewett's biological grandmother, who was Sarah (Sally) Orne of Portsmouth, New Hampshire.

56. Jewett, "Mournful Villager," p. 134.

57. Jewett, "Mournful Villager," p. 137.

58. Jewett, "Mournful Villager," pp. 137–38.

59. Jewett, "Mournful Villager," p. 138.

60. Jewett, "Mournful Villager," p. 138.

61. Sarah Orne Jewett, "An Autumn Holiday," in *Country By-Ways* (Boston: Houghton Mifflin, 1881), p. 146.

62. Jewett, "Autumn Holiday," p. 148. These models for characters such as Mrs. Todd might well have been midwives, or at least attended at childbirth when necessary. During the latter nineteenth century, midwives were being forced out of practice by the growing specialization of obstetrics and gynecology. Jewett's father would have been closely involved with this process since he served at the Maine General Hospital as Professor of Obstetrics and of Women's and Children's Diseases. Jewett is careful to describe the relations between Mrs. Todd and the Dunnet Landing physician as professional and friendly, implying that such was not often the case in similar towns. See Dierdre English and Barbara Ehrenreich, *Witches, Midwives, and Nurses: A History of Women Healers* (Old Westbury, NY: Feminist Press, 1972); Gerda Lerner, "The Lady and the Mill Girl."

CHAPTER 4

1. Willa Cather, "Miss Jewett," in *Not Under Forty* (New York: Knopf, 1953), p. 85. For a discussion of women's friendships, see Janice Raymond, *A Passion for Friends: Towards a Philosophy of Female Affection* (Boston: Beacon, 1986). On nineteenth-century women's communities, see Carroll Smith-Rosenberg, "The Female World of Love and Ritual"; Nancy Cott, *The Bonds of Womanhood*; Carl Degler, *At Odds*; William R. Taylor and Christopher Lasch, "Two 'Kindred Spirits': Sorority and Family in New England, 1836–1846," *New England Quarterly* 36:1 (March 1963): 23–41; Lillian Faderman, *Surpassing the Love of Men: Romantic Friendship between Women from the Renaissance to the Present* (New York: William Morrow, 1981); Susan Allen Toth, "Sarah Orne Jewett and Friends: A Community of Interest," *Studies in Short Fiction* 9 (Summer 1972): 223–41.

2. According to Lillian Faderman, "Jewett's most assiduous biographers

have been unable to find a trace in her life of even the slightest interest in a heterosexual love affair or marriage" (Faderman, pp. 197–98). That Jewett did not feel any especial call to heterosexuality is confirmed by her exchange with her friend, the poet John Greenleaf Whittier. According to F. O. Matthiessen, "One day Mr. Whittier asked her: 'Sarah, was thee ever in love?' She answered, with a rush of color, 'No! Whatever made you think that?' and again she laughingly explained that she had more need of a wife than a husband" (Matthiessen, *Sarah Orne Jewett*, p. 72).

3. Sarah Orne Jewett, 1867 Diary, MS. Am 1743.26 (3), Houghton Library, Harvard University.

4. Jewett, 1867 Diary, n.p.

5. Jewett, 1867 Diary, entry for 7 September 1867, four days after Jewett's eighteenth birthday.

6. Donovan, *Jewett*, p. 33.

7. Anna L. Dawes to Sarah Orne Jewett, Washington, D.C., 26 May 1876, Bancroft Coll., Columbia University.

8. Dawes to Sarah Orne Jewett, Washington, D.C., 23 December 1876, Bancroft Coll., Columbia University.

9. Sarah Orne Jewett, "The New Wife," MS. Am 1743.25 (83), Houghton Library, Harvard University.

10. Jewett to Sara Norton, South Berwick, 3 September 1897 [dated by another hand], Houghton Library, Harvard University; reprinted in Fields, *Letters*, p. 126.

11. Jewett, *Firs*, pp. 1–2.

12. Jewett to Sarah Whitman, n.p., Friday night, *late* [Jewett's emphasis], n.d., Houghton Library, Harvard University.

13. Jewett, letter quoted in Frost, pp. 128–29. Full text published in Cary, *Letters*, p. 102.

14. Jewett to Lily Munger, 9 May 1876, Barrett Coll., University of Virginia. For more information on this relationship, see Hohmann, "Sarah Orne Jewett to Lily Munger: Twenty-Three Letters."

15. Sarah Orne Jewett, Manuscript Diary 1871–72, entry for 3 October 1872, Houghton Library, Harvard University; quoted in Donovan, *Jewett*, p. 7.

16. See Frost, pp. 53–54.

17. For a discussion of "pure and passionate" friendship in Jewett's life and work, with particular attention to the story "Martha's Lady" (1897), see Glenda Hobbs, "Pure and Passionate: Female Friendship in Sarah Orne Jewett's 'Martha's Lady,'" in Nagel, pp. 99–107; reprinted from *Studies in Short Fiction* 17 (1980): 21–29.

18. Faderman, p. 190.

19. Indeed, Smith-Rosenberg believes that our modern tendency to rate human love and sexuality according to the polarities of "deviance and normality, genitality and platonic love, is alien to the emotions and attitudes of the nineteenth century and fundamentally distorts the nature of these women's emotional interaction" (Smith-Rosenberg, "Female World," p. 8).

20. Faderman, pp. 190, 203.

21. Frost, p. 118.

22. Sarah Orne Jewett, "Outgrown Friends," MS. Am 1743.22 (87), Houghton Library, Harvard University, pp. 4–5.

23. I am indebted to Josephine Donovan's *Sarah Orne Jewett* for these

references from the manuscript diary for 1871–72 in the Houghton Library. Donovan also comments on Jewett's refusal to deal with these emotions in her portrayal of "leisure-class adolescents": "What remains is a rose-colored version of their lives" (p. 12).

24. Sarah Orne Jewett, "For Country Girls," MS. Am 1743.22 (38), Houghton Library, Harvard University, n.p.

25. Jewett to Annie Fields, Little Compton, RI, 8 September 1880, Houghton Library, Harvard University.

26. Jewett, "Outgrown Friends," pp. 17–18.

27. Jewett, "For Country Girls."

28. W. S. Tryon, "Annie Adams Fields," in *Notable American Women, 1607–1950: A Biographical Dictionary*, vol. 1, ed. Edward T. James and Janet W. James (Cambridge, MA: Harvard University Press, 1971), p. 616. See also Judith Roman, "A Closer Look at the Jewett-Fields Relationship," in Nagel, pp. 119–34; Josephine Donovan, "The Unpublished Love Poems of Sarah Orne Jewett," in Nagel, pp. 107–17; reprinted from *Frontiers: A Journal of Women Studies* 4:3 (1979): 26–31; Rita K. Gollin, "Annie Adams Fields, 1834–1915," *Legacy: A Journal of Nineteenth-Century American Women Writers* 4:1 (Spring 1987): 27–33.

29. Matthiessen, p. 70.

30. Willa Cather, "148 Charles Street," *Not Under Forty, passim*.

31. Roman, p. 127; she cites as evidence Annie Fields's personal diaries in the collection of the Massachusetts Historical Society.

32. Tryon, p. 616. Much of the information in this summary of Annie Fields's life comes from Tryon's essay in *Notable American Women*.

33. Harriet Prescott Spofford, *A Little Book of Friends* (Boston: Little, Brown, 1916), p. 18.

34. Henry James, "Mr. and Mrs. James T. Fields," *Atlantic Monthly* 116 (July 1915): 30.

35. Jewett to Annie Fields, Little Compton, RI, 8 September 1880, Houghton Library, Harvard University.

36. Jewett to Annie Fields, South Berwick, 12 January 1881, Houghton Library, Harvard University.

37. Jewett's nickname, "Pinny Lawson," remained with her all of her life. It apparently had two sources. One was "pinhead," a reference to her disproportionately small head, and the other was "Sam Lawson," a country storyteller who narrates some of Harriet Beecher Stowe's dialect sketches.

38. Jewett to Annie Fields, Thursday afternoon, June 1882, Houghton Library, Harvard University.

39. Sarah Orne Jewett, "The Friendship of Women," MS. Am 1743.22 (41), Houghton Library, Harvard University, n.p.

40. Jewett, "Friendship," n.p.

41. Roman, p. 127.

42. Henry James, *The Bostonians* (1886; rpt. New York: Penguin, 1974). See also Lillian Faderman, "Female Same-Sex Relationships in Novels by Longfellow, Holmes, and James," *New England Quarterly* 51:3 (September 1978), 309–22. In "The Unpublished Love Poems of Sarah Orne Jewett," Josephine Donovan argues that Henry James was "unnerved" by the Jewett/Fields relationship and suggests that he may have partially based the Chancellor/Tarrant one on it.

43. Henry James, "Mr. and Mrs. James T. Fields," *The Atlantic* 116 (July 1915): 30.

44. In her essay on the Ladies of Langollen, the French writer Colette reflected on the similar "innocence" of these celebrated female lovers. See Colette, *The Pure and the Impure* (New York: Farrar, Straus, and Giroux, 1966), pp. 109–29.

45. Faderman, p. 201.

46. Annie Fields, Introduction to Fields, *Letters*, p. 6; quoted in Roman, p. 126.

47. Jewett to Annie Fields, Thursday afternoon, June 1882, Houghton Library, Harvard University.

48. See Neumann, *passim*.

49. Jewett to Annie Fields, Thursday morning [1882 or 1883], Houghton Library, Harvard University.

50. Jewett to Annie Fields, 5 June [1883], Houghton Library, Harvard University.

51. Jewett to Annie Fields, n.d., Houghton Library, Harvard University.

52. Annie Fields to Sarah Orne Jewett, Saturday, n.d., Houghton Library, Harvard University.

53. Roman, p. 123.

54. O'Brien, p. 332.

55. John Greenleaf Whittier, "Godspeed," in *The Complete Poetical Works of John Greenleaf Whitter*, ed. Horace Scudder (Boston: Houghton Mifflin, 1894), p. 294.

56. Spofford, pp. 9–13.

57. Annie Fields, "The Return of Persephone" (Boston: privately printed, 1877). This poem was later collected in Annie Fields, *Under the Olive* (Boston: Houghton Mifflin, 1881).

58. Fields, "The Return," p. 144.

59. Fields, "The Return," p. 150.

60. Fields, "The Return," p. 152.

61. Fields, "The Return," pp. 172–73.

62. Fields, "The Return," p. 170.

63. Fields, "The Return," p. 177.

64. Fields, "The Return," p. 178.

65. Fields, "The Return," p. 178.

66. Fields, "The Return," p. 180.

67. Fields, "The Return," pp. 181–82.

68. Fields, "The Return," p. 182.

69. Fields, "The Return," p. 185.

70. Margaret Fuller (Ossoli), *Woman in the Nineteenth Century* (1845), quoted in Annie Fields, *Under the Olive*, p. 309.

71. Pater, "The Myth of Demeter and Persephone," pp. 155–56; quoted in Fields, *Under the Olive*, p. 315.

72. Annie Fields, "The Mysteries of Eleusis," in *The Singing Shepherd* (Boston and New York: Houghton Mifflin, 1895), p. 137.

73. Fields, "The Mysteries," p. 137. The reference to Demeter as "Mother of the shadowed sphere" fuses the Mother and Daughter into one figure, a practice supported by Pater's analysis of the Dual Goddess. "Where we dwell

and suffer now" suggests that our human, living world is a type of Underworld, which the poet sees illuminated by the revelation of the Goddess.

CHAPTER 5

1. Jewett to Sara Norton, Hotel Bristol, Naples, 18 March 1900, p. 170; Jewett to Sarah Whitman, Athens, 27 March 1900, pp. 172–73; in Fields, *Letters.* While Jewett did not explain just what the myth meant to her, Annie Fields's poem *Orpheus: A Masque* was published just that year, after several years of writing. Jewett apparently discussed Annie Fields's project with Whittier as early as 1897, as mentioned in a letter from Jewett to Annie Fields, Amesbury, Mass., Wednesday afternoon 1897, Houghton Library, Harvard University.

Jewett's interest in mythology was furthered by Annie Fields, but it did not begin with her. Emily Beaufort's *Egyptian Sepulchres and Syrian Shrines* (1874) is still on the bookshelves in the South Berwick parlor; chapter 7 is entitled "Where Homer Lived and Sappho Sang," and the book is inscribed "Sarah O. Jewett, July 1877." The parlor collection also includes Plato's *Apology and Crito,* Benjamin Jowett's *Tollemache, Chamber's Encyclopedia,* T. G. Appleton's *A Nile Journey* (1876), and the Vicomtess Strangeford's *Egyptian Sepulchres.* Upstairs, by Jewett's bedside, may be found *An Introduction to the Making of Latin,* flanked by a Bible, an edition of Fenelon, an English dictionary, a French grammar, and *Goldsmith's England.* For an inventory of the family library, see Mrs. Ernest Bowditch, "The Jewett Library," *Colby Library Quarterly* 5 (December 1961): 357–65.

2. Jewett to Sarah Whitman, Athens, 27 March 1900, in Fields, *Letters,* p. 173.

3. Sarah Orne Jewett, "A Modern Idyll," MS. Am 1743.22 (70), Houghton Library, Harvard University, n.p.

I will not discuss the influence of the classic pastoral tradition in great detail since it has been treated at length in several fine studies. See Robin Magowan, "Fromentin and Jewett: Pastoral Narrative in the Nineteenth Century," *Comparative Literature* 16 (Fall 1964): 331–37; Robin Magowan, "The Outer Island Sequence in *Pointed Firs,*" pp. 418–24; Robin Magowan, "Pastoral and the Art of Landscape in *The Country of the Pointed Firs,*" *New England Quarterly* 36 (June 1963): 229–40, reprinted in *Appreciation;* David Stouck, "*The Country of the Pointed Firs*: A Pastoral of Innocence," *Colby Library Quarterly* 9 (December 1970): 213–20, reprinted in *Appreciation.* Also, Louis Renza, "'A White Heron As a Rare Bird of Pastoral,'" in *"A White Heron" and the Question of Minor Literature* (Madison, WI: University of Wisconsin Press, 1984), pp. 116–41.

Three published dissertations are particularly important here: Robert L. Horn, "Universality in the Fiction of Sarah Orne Jewett," Ph.D. diss., University of Wisconsin, 1968; Robin Magowan, "The Art of Pastoral Narrative: Sand, Fromentin, Jewett," Ph.D. diss., Yale University, 1964; Sister Mary Williams C.S.J., "The Pastoral in New England Local Color: Celia Thaxter, Sarah Orne Jewett, and Alice Brown," Ph.D. diss., Stanford University, 1972.

4. Jewett, "A Modern Idyll," n.p.

5. In addition to Donovan's sensitive work on these issues, see Ammons, "Going in Circles," *passim;* Boone, pp. 304–11; Zagarell, *passim.* Richard

Cary's Introduction to *Deephaven and Other Stories* does an excellent job of assessing this first book and comparing it with Jewett's later work, including *Pointed Firs* (pp. 7–23). The following were also particularly helpful: Fermin Bishop, "The Sense of the Past in Sarah Orne Jewett," *University of Wichita Bulletin*, University Studies No. 41 (February 1959), pp. 3–10, reprinted in *Appreciation*; Paul Eakin, "Sarah Orne Jewett and the Meaning of Country Life," *American Literature* 38 (January 1967): 508–31, reprinted in *Appreciation*; Francis Fike, "An Interpretation of *Pointed Firs*," *New England Quarterly* 34 (December 1961): 478–91, reprinted in *Appreciation*; David Bonnell Green, "The World of Dunnet Landing," *New England Quarterly* 34 (December 1961): 514–17; Robert L. Horn, "The Power of Jewett's *Deephaven*," *Colby Library Quarterly* 9 (December 1972): 617–31; Paul D. Voelker, "*The Country of the Pointed Firs*: A Novel by Sarah Orne Jewett," *Colby Library Quarterly* 9:4 (December 1970): 201–13, reprinted in *Appreciation*.

6. Pater, p. 104.

7. Pater, p. 104.

8. Sarah Orne Jewett, "The Queen's Twin," in *The Country of the Pointed Firs and Other Stories* (1899; rpt. New York: W. W. Norton, 1982), p. 199.

9. Pater, p. 91. This primitive philosophy Pater sees as a "systematized form of that poetry ... [which] we may study in either Shelley or Wordsworth," for a "spirit" or "personal intelligence" abiding in the earth or the clouds is "assumed in every suggestion which poetry makes to us of a sympathy between the ways and aspects of outward nature and the mood of men" (p. 92).

Further, all mythology derives from this initial reverie, a half-conscious stage in which oral traditions, rituals, and local observances express "certain primitive impressions of the phenomena of the natural world." As opposed to modern science, this "older, unmechanical, or spiritual or Platonic philosophy envisages nature rather as the unity of a living spirit or person, revealing itself in various degrees to the kindred spirit of the observer" (p. 96).

10. Pater, p. 92.   11. Pater, p. 100.

12. Pater, p. 100.   13. Pater, p. 120.

14. Pater, p. 120.

15. Pater, p. 150. For information on the shrine of Demeter uncovered at Cnidus, Pater cites Sir Charles Thomas Newton, *A History of Discoveries at Halicarnassus, Cnidus, and Branchidae* (London: Day and Sons, 1862).

16. Pater, p. 92.

17. Pater, pp. 155–56; quoted in Fields, *Under the Olive*, p. 315.

18. Compare, for example, this passage from Pater: "Then Demeter manifested herself openly. She put away the mask of old age ... and the spirit of beauty breathed about her ... the long yellow hair descended waving over her shoulders, and the great house was filled as with the brightness of lightning" (Pater, *Greek Studies*, p. 88). Here is *Deephaven*: "'I always thought that part of the story beautiful where Demeter throws off her disguise and is no longer an old woman, and the great house is filled with brightness like lightening, and she rushes out through the halls with her yellow hair waving over her shoulders ...'" (Jewett, *Deephaven*, p. 130).

Annie Fields's poem, "The Return of Persephone," was published privately in 1877. It was also included in *Under the Olive* (1880) where it was footnoted with lengthy extracts from Pater's essay, which had appeared in *Fortnightly Review* (January and February 1876). Jewett certainly read Annie Fields's poem, with the Pater commentary, since she wrote Annie Fields, "I have been reading Under the Olive a good deal . . . I can't begin to tell you how beautiful it is to me and how helpful. I long to hear you read from it again." (Sarah Orne Jewett, ALS to Annie Fields, Thursday afternoon, June 1882, n.p., Houghton Library, Harvard University). While this letter confirms an 1882 reading of the poem, Jewett may have known "The Return of Persephone" earlier, and the Pater essay, since she mentions having heard Annie Fields read some of her work aloud, and this piece was published during the time the two women were becoming friends.

19. Jewett, *Deephaven*, p. 121.
20. Jewett, *Deephaven*, p. 85.
21. Jewett, *Deephaven*, p. 124.
22. Jewett, *Deephaven*, p. 124.
23. Jewett, *Deephaven*, pp. 129–31.
24. Jewett, *Deephaven*, p. 166.
25. Erich Neumann, pp. 28, 71.
26. In the next chapter I will present the evidence and analysis supporting this rather harsh judgment.
27. Pater, p. 149.
28. Pater, p. 150.
29. Jewett, *Firs*, p. 49.
30. Jewett, *Firs*, p. 131.
31. Jewett, "Queen's Twin," p. 199.
32. Pater, p. 100.
33. Pater, p. 100. See also Neumann, p. 296.
34. "The Homeric Hymn to Demeter," in Lang, *The Homeric Hymns: A New Prose Translation*, p. 196.
35. Pater, p. 100.
36. "Homeric Hymn," pp. 193–94.
37. "Homeric Hymn," p. 199.
38. Jewett, *Firs*, p. 7.
39. Jewett, *Firs*, pp. 7–8.
40. Jewett, *Firs*, p. 8.
41. Jewett, *Firs*, pp. 1–2.
42. Jewett, *Deephaven*, p. 84. See also Robert D. Rhode, "Sarah Orne Jewett and 'The Palpable Present Intimate,'" *Colby Library Quarterly* 8 (September 1968): 146–155, reprinted in *Appreciation*; also Rhode, *Setting in the American Short Story of Local Color, 1885–1900* (The Hague: Mouton, 1975).
43. Joseph Boone and Sandra Zagarell also emphasize this association between preindustrial and feminine communities in Jewett's, as well as Gaskell's, work. Although written independently, my analysis of these communities and Jewett's narrative technique has much in common with theirs. See Boone, pp. 295–304, 304–308; Zagarell, pp. 503–11.
44. Jewett, *Deephaven*, p. 161.
45. Sarah Orne Jewett, "Preface to the 1893 Edition," in Cary, *Deephaven*, p. 32.
46. Jewett, "1893 Preface," p. 33.
47. Leo Marx, *The Machine in the Garden: Technology and the Pastoral Ideal in America* (New York: Oxford University Press, 1964). Marx on Virgil's *Ecologues:* "This ideal pasture has two vulnerable borders: one separates it

from Rome, the other from the encroaching marshland. It is a place where Tityrus is spared the deprivations and anxieties associated with both the city and the wilderness. Although he is free of the repressions entailed by a complex civilization, he is not prey to the violent uncertainties of nature. His mind is cultivated and his instincts are gratified. Living in an oasis of rural pleasure, he enjoys the best of both worlds—the sophisticated order of art and the simple spontaneity of nature" (p. 22). He sees "the pastoral ideal as an embodiment of what Lovejoy calls 'semi-primitivism'; it is located in a middle ground somewhere 'between,' yet in transcendent relation to, the opposing forces of civilization and nature" (p. 23).

See also Arthur O. Lovejoy, Gilbert Chinard, George Boas, and Ronald Crane, *A Documentary History of Primitivism and Related Ideas* (Baltimore, 1935), p. 369. Annette Kolodny's fine study, *The Lay of the Land: Metaphor as Experience and History in American Life and Letters* (Chapel Hill, NC: University of North Carolina Press, 1975) examines the association of the "middle landscape" with the feminine. Her work was extremely helpful in formulating my ideas for this section of the study.

48. Here the structuralist idea that the individual elements of a semantic system are defined by their position within the system as a whole, synchronically rather than diachronically, applies directly. Thus, while there are some constraints on the range of meanings assigned to a particular setting—or signifier—within this range the meanings are "arbitrary." My title for this chapter is adapted from the title of Clause Lévi-Strauss's structuralist study, *From Honey to Ashes: Introduction to a Science of Mythology*, vol. 2 (New York: Harper and Row, 1966). Vol. 1 in the series is *The Raw and the Cooked* (New York: Harper and Row, 1964, 1969).

49. Jewett, *Deephaven*, p. 150.

50. Jewett, *Firs*, p. 50.

51. Jewett, *Deephaven*, p. 151.

52. Jewett, *Deephaven*, p. 153.

53. Jewett, *Deephaven*, p. 134.

54. Jewett, *Deephaven*, p. 140.

55. Jewett, *Deephaven*, p. 165.

56. Jewett, *Deephaven*, pp. 52–53.

CHAPTER 6

1. Jewett, *Firs*, p. 55. See Northrop Frye, *The Anatomy of Criticism: Four Essays* (Princeton, NJ: Princeton University Press, 1957), esp. pp. 119, 136.

2. Erich Neumann, *passim*.

3. How these different phases are interpreted is, of course, open. Nan Prince "returns" to Adeline at the end of her quest, but it is to Adeline's grave, and her reincorporation of her mother's identity is severely limited: she accepts only that shred of Adeline's maternal instinct that saved them both from drowning.

4. Jewett, *Deephaven*, p. 34. Two essays on *Deephaven* are Robert L. Horn, "The Power of Jewett's *Deephaven*"; and Ann Romines, "In *Deephaven*: Skirmishes Near the Swamp," in Nagel, pp. 43–57. My analysis, written independently of Romines, has much in common with it. She also compares the

young heroines unfavorably to the narrator of *Firs* and stresses their ambivalence toward the community and its rituals.

5. Judith Kegan Gardiner, "On Female Identity and Writing by Women," *Critical Inquiry* 8:2 (Winter 1982): 357. See also Judith Kegan Gardiner, "The Heroine as Her Author's Daughter," in *Feminist Criticism: Essays on Theory, Poetry and Prose,* ed. Cheryl L. Brown and Karen Olson (Metuchen, NJ: Scarecrow, 1978), pp. 344–53; Elizabeth Abel, "(E)Merging Identities: The Dynamics of Female Friendships in Contemporary Fiction by Women," *Signs* 6 (Spring 1981): 413–35.

6. Gardiner, "The Heroine," *passim.*

7. Jewett, "1893 Preface," p. 34.

8. Jewett, "1893 Preface," p. 34.

9. Jewett, *Deephaven,* pp. 41, 54.

10. Sarah Orne Jewett, "Preface to the 1877 Edition," in *Deephaven,* p. 29.

11. Jewett, *Deephaven,* p. 54.

12. Jewett, *Deephaven,* p. 55.

13. Chodorow, *Reproduction of Mothering,* p. 137.

14. Chodorow, *Reproduction of Mothering,* p. 137.

15. Chodorow, *Reproduction of Mothering,* p. 137.

16. Chodorow, *Reproduction of Mothering,* pp. 137–38.

17. Jewett, *Deephaven,* p. 37. For a discussion of Jewett's "fits of blues" in adolescence, see Chapter 4.

18. Jewett, *Deephaven,* pp. 37–38.

19. Jewett, *Deephaven,* p. 38.

20. Jewett, *Deephaven,* p. 38.

21. Jewett, *Deephaven,* p. 54.

22. Jewett, *Deephaven,* p. 164.

23. Jewett, *Deephaven,* p. 53.

24. Jewett, *Deephaven,* p. 41. Josephine Donovan's studies of Jewett handle this matrilineal aspect of Jewett's work very nicely.

25. Jewett, *Deephaven,* p. 45.

26. Jewett, *Deephaven,* p. 45.

27. Jewett, *Deephaven,* p. 45.

28. Jewett, *Deephaven,* p. 45.

29. Jewett, *Deephaven,* p. 46.

30. Jewett, *Deephaven,* p. 47.

31. Jewett, *Deephaven,* p. 49.

32. Jewett, *Deephaven,* p. 60.

33. Jewett, *Deephaven,* p. 60.

34. Jewett, *Deephaven,* p. 161.

35. Jewett, *Deephaven,* p. 162.

36. See Ann Douglas (Wood), "The Literature of Impoverishment," for a discussion of Jewett's ambivalence toward the domestic house and New England itself.

37. Jewett, *Deephaven,* pp. 55–56.

38. Jewett, *Deephaven,* p. 76.

39. Jewett, *Deephaven,* p. 70.

40. Jewett, *Deephaven,* p. 76.

41. Jewett, *Deephaven,* p. 77.

42. Jewett, *Deephaven,* p. 164.

43. Jewett, *Deephaven,* p. 132.
44. Jewett, *Deephaven,* p. 84.
45. Jewett, *Deephaven,* p. 78.
46. Jewett, *Deephaven,* p. 104.
47. Ann Douglas (Wood), "Literature of Impoverishment," p. 30.
48. Jewett, *Deephaven,* p. 71.
49. Jewett, *Deephaven,* p. 51.
50. Jewett, *Deephaven,* p. 51.
51. Jewett, *Deephaven,* pp. 51–52.
52. Jewett, *Deephaven,* p. 52.
53. Jewett, *Deephaven,* p. 52.
54. Jewett, *Deephaven,* p. 140.
55. Jewett, *Deephaven,* pp. 56, 139.
56. Jewett, *Deephaven,* p. 135.
57. Jewett, *Deephaven,* p. 138.
58. Jewett, *Deephaven,* p. 138.
59. Jewett, *Deephaven,* p. 136.
60. Jewett, *Deephaven,* p. 138.
61. Jewett, *Deephaven,* p. 133.
62. Jewett, *Deephaven,* p. 133.
63. Jewett, *Deephaven,* p. 133.
64. Jewett, *Deephaven,* p. 141.
65. Jewett, *Deephaven,* p. 144.
66. Jewett, *Deephaven,* pp. 145–46.
67. Jewett, *Deephaven,* p. 146.
68. Jewett, *Deephaven,* p. 146.
69. Jewett, *Deephaven,* p. 147.
70. Jewett, *Deephaven,* p. 145, 148.
71. Jewett, *Deephaven,* p. 149.
72. Jewett, *Deephaven,* p. 151.
73. Jewett, *Deephaven,* p. 152.
74. Jewett, *Deephaven,* p. 152.
75. Jewett, *Deephaven,* p. 153.
76. Jewett, *Deephaven,* p. 153.
77. Jewett, *Deephaven,* pp. 153–54.
78. Jewett, *Deephaven,* p. 154.
79. Jewett, *Deephaven,* p. 154.
80. Jewett, *Deephaven,* p. 154.
81. Jewett, *Deephaven,* p. 156.
82. Jewett, *Deephaven,* p. 158.
83. Jewett, *Deephaven,* p. 157.
84. Jewett, *Deephaven,* p. 155.
85. Jung, p. 162.
86. Jung, p. 162.
87. Neumann, p. 309.
88. Jewett, *Deephaven,* p. 155.
89. Jewett, *Deephaven,* p. 155.
90. Jewett, *Deephaven,* pp. 155–56.
91. Jewett, *Deephaven,* p. 76.
92. Jewett, *Deephaven,* p. 48.

93. Jewett, *Deephaven*, p. 46.
94. Jewett, *Deephaven*, p. 160.
95. Jewett, *Deephaven*, p. 160.
96. Jewett, *Deephaven*, p. 160.
97. Jewett, *Deephaven*, p. 161.
98. Jewett, *Deephaven*, p. 159.
99. Jewett, *Deephaven*, pp. 164–65.
100. Jewett, *Deephaven*, p. 165.

CHAPTER 7

1. Elizabeth Ammons, "The Shape of Violence," pp. 6–16. Sarah Orne Jewett, "A White Heron," in *The Country of the Pointed Firs and Other Stories* (1886; rpt. Garden City, NY: Doubleday-Anchor, 1956); Sarah Orne Jewett, *A Country Doctor* (Boston and New York: Houghton Mifflin, 1884). Since "A White Heron" has received much more scholarly attention, I have reversed the chronological order so as to use some of those critical tools in my discussion of the longer work.
2. Louis Renza, *"A White Heron" and the Question of Minor Literature* (Madison, WI: University of Wisconsin Press, 1984).
3. Jewett, "White Heron," p. 205.
4. Jewett, "White Heron," pp. 203–4.
5. Jewett, "White Heron," pp. 205–6.
6. Jewett, "White Heron," pp. 206–7.
7. Jewett, "White Heron," p. 207.
8. Jewett, "White Heron," p. 207.
9. The figure of the "house breaker" who breaks *out* of the domestic house rather than into it is an important one for Jewett; see my earlier discussion in Chapter 3.
10. Jewett, "White Heron," p. 208.
11. Jewett, "White Heron," p. 209.
12. Jewett, "White Heron," p. 209.
13. Jewett, "White Heron," p. 209.
14. Jewett, "White Heron," p. 209.
15. Jewett, "White Heron," pp. 209–10.
16. Jewett, "White Heron," p. 210.
17. Although Renza argues that the narrator in the story is male and paternal, I do not find any textual evidence for this and tend to see the narrator's voice as female, perhaps Jewett's own. See Renza, p. 98; Ammons, "The Shape of Violence," p. 16, n. 15.
18. Jewett, "White Heron," pp. 210–11.
19. Jewett, "White Heron," p. 211.
20. For a discussion of this iconographical tradition, see Joseph Campbell, *The Flight of the Wild Gander: Explorations in the Mythological Dimension* (New York: Viking, 1951). See also Renza, p. 202, n. 93.
21. Jewett, "White Heron," pp. 211–12.
22. Jewett, "White Heron," p. 212.
23. Ammons, "The Shape of Violence," p. 14; Renza, p. 138; Carol Singley, "Reaching Lonely Heights: Sarah Orne Jewett, Emily Dickinson, and Female Initiation," *Colby Library Quarterly* 22:1 (March 1986): 75–82. Also Theo-

dore Hovet, "'Once Upon a Time': Sarah Orne Jewett's 'A White Heron,'" *Studies in Short Fiction* 15:1 (Winter 1978): 63–68.

For a discussion of the psychosocial dimension of fairy tales, see Bruno Bettelheim, *The Uses of Enchantment: The Meaning and Importance of Fairy Tales* (New York: Vintage, 1977); also Sandra Gilbert and Susan Gubar, *The Madwoman in the Attic: The Woman Writer and the Nineteenth-Century Literary Imagination* (New Haven, CT: Yale University Press, 1979) for their feminist analysis of "Snow White." Renza focuses on the story's affinities with the Grimms' "Little Briar-rose" and Charles Perrault's "La belle au bois dormant": Charles Perrault, *Popular Tales* (Oxford: Clarendon Press, 1878) and *The Complete Grimms' Fairy Tales* (New York: Pantheon Books, 1972).

24. Ammons, "The Shape of Violence," p. 14.

25. Ammons, "The Shape of Violence, pp. 9, 16.

26. Renza, pp. 137–38.

27. Renza, p. 139.

28. "If Sylvia's tree climbing surrealistically outlines climbing the father from a child daughter's point of view, it outlines a would-be daughterly writer's writing in terms of metonymical proximity of an absent paternal figure 'who' will allow her to grow up—just as Sylvia literally grows up when climbing the tree—in a way that quells any adult definitions of sexual self-identity" (Renza, p. 113).

29. Singley, p. 76.

30. Singley, p. 82.

31. Pratt, "Women and Nature in Modern Fiction"; Annis Pratt, *Archetypal Patterns in Women's Fiction* (Bloomington, IN: University of Indiana Press, 1981.

32. Pratt, "Women," pp. 476–77.

33. Pratt, "Women," p. 477. Joseph Campbell, *The Hero with a Thousand Faces* (Princeton, NJ: Princeton University Press, Bollingen, 1949); Simone de Beauvoir, *The Second Sex,* trans. Helen Parshley (New York: Knopf, 1953).

34. Pratt, "Women," p. 478.

35. Pratt, "Women," p. 480.

36. Pratt, "Women," p. 479.

37. de Beauvoir, pp. 710–11; quoted in Pratt, "Women," p. 477.

38. Pratt, "Women," p. 477; de Beauvoir, p. 711; quoted in Pratt, "Women," p. 477.

39. Pratt, "Women," p. 490.

40. Pratt, "Women," p. 488.

41. Pratt, "Women," p. 488.

42. I stress this point because otherwise Chodorow's framework can be seen as enforcing what Adrienne Rich has called "compulsory heterosexuality."

43. See Chapter 4 for a discussion of this poem.

44. Although Renza does not deal with Jewett's conscious use of mythological tradition, he does note the possible link between Sylvia and Artemis, as well as Demeter: "As W. K. C. Guthrie notes in his *The Greeks and Their Gods,* rpt. ed. (Boston: Beacon Press, 1955), 101, the Greek Goddess Demeter . . . was assumed to be the mother of and sometimes Artemis herself, 'an earth goddess, associated essentially and chiefly with wild life and growth of the fields, and with human birth'" (Renza, p. 196).

45. Dawes to Sarah Orne Jewett, Washington, D.C., 26 May 1876, Bancroft Collection, Columbia University.

46. Studies of *A Country Doctor* include Marie Thérèse Blanc-Bentzon, "Le Roman de la femme-medecin," *Revue des Deux Mondes* 67 (1 Feburary 1885): 598–632 (a translation is reprinted in *Appreciation*); Ellen Morgan, "The Atypical Woman: Nan Prince in the Literary Transition to Feminism," *The Kate Chopin Newsletter* 2 (Fall 1976): 33–37; Jean Carwile Masteller, "The Women Doctors of Howells, Phelps, and Jewett: The Conflict of Marriage and Career," in Nagel, pp. 135–47; Josephine Donovan, "Nan Prince and the Golden Apples," *Colby Library Quarterly* 22:1 (March 1986): 17–27.

47. Jewett, "Looking Back," p. 6.

48. Jewett, *Country Doctor,* p. 113.

49. Jewett, *Country Doctor,* pp. 121–22.

50. Jewett, *Country Doctor,* p. 99.

51. Jewett, *Country Doctor,* p. 27.

52. Jewett, *Country Doctor,* p. 33.

53. Josephine Donovan describes the opening setting as a "paradisiacal women's community" and Adeline as a "defeated" Persephone who is "returning, dying, to the land of her mother's garden" ("Nan Prince," p. 17).

54. Jewett, *Country Doctor,* pp. 50–51.

55. Jewett, *Country Doctor,* p. 85.

56. Renza comes up with an intriguing phrase to describe this relationship: "the elliptically androgynous neoFreudian father who represents, even as he displaces, the preoedipal mother for the little girl" (p. 103).

57. Jewett, *Country Doctor,* p. 157.

58. Jewett, *Country Doctor,* pp. 127–28. See Renza, p. 98; Cary, *Sarah Orne Jewett,* p. 138.

59. Jewett, *Country Doctor,* p. 131.

60. Jewett, *Country Doctor,* p. 134.

61. Jewett, *Country Doctor,* p. 134.

62. Jewett, *Country Doctor,* p. 135.

63. Jewett, *Country Doctor,* p. 137.

64. Jewett, *Country Doctor,* p. 137. In her well-researched article on these issues Josephine Donovan proposes that "*A Country Doctor* may have been one of the earliest feminist repudiations of Krafft-Ebbing and other theorists who saw women's choice of masculine vocations as unnatural, indeed pathological" ("Nan Prince," p. 23).

65. Jewett, *Country Doctor,* p. 102.

66. Jewett, *Country Doctor,* p. 54.

67. Jewett, *Country Doctor,* p. 153.

68. Jewett, *Country Doctor,* pp. 153–54.

69. Jewett, *Country Doctor,* p. 154.

70. Josephine Donovan sees Nan's relationship to the feminine community more positively than I do: "Unlike her mother, a Persephone, Nan returns from her other-world journey unscathed. Nor is she required to abandon or to silence feminine traditions. What is achieved is a synthesis, or what Hegel called *Aufhebung*; in the dialectical process those traditions and Nan herself have been elevated to a higher plane" ("Nan Prince," p. 27). For a discussion of "circular," feminine plot structures in Jewett's work, see Elizabeth Ammons's two

fine articles, "Going in Circles" and "The Shape of Violence in Jewett's 'A White Heron.'"

71. Jewett, *Country Doctor,* p. 164.
72. Jewett, *Country Doctor,* p. 165 (all quotations in this paragraph).
73. Jewett, *Country Doctor,* p. 166.
74. Jewett, *Country Doctor,* p. 166.
75. Jewett, *Country Doctor,* p. 167.
76. Jewett, *Country Doctor,* p. 303.
77. Jewett, *Country Doctor,* p. 205.
78. Jewett, *Country Doctor,* pp. 205–6.
79. Jewett, *Country Doctor,* p. 272.
80. Jewett, *Country Doctor,* pp. 279, 281.
81. Jewett, *Country Doctor,* p. 284.
82. Jewett, *Country Doctor,* p. 278.
83. Jewett, *Country Doctor,* p. 313.
84. Jewett, *Country Doctor,* p. 304. See also Jewett, "The New Wife."
85. Jewett, *Country Doctor,* pp. 294–95.
86. Jewett, *Country Doctor,* p. 262.
87. Jewett, *Country Doctor,* p. 265.
88. Jewett, *Country Doctor,* p. 296.
89. Jewett, *Country Doctor,* p. 327.
90. Jewett, *Country Doctor,* p. 326.
91. Jewett, *Country Doctor,* p. 317.
92. See Donovan, "Nan Prince," for a discussion of Nan's "unnatural" personality.
93. Jewett, *Country Doctor,* p. 335.
94. Jewett, *Country Doctor,* p. 138. The equation of convention with "irons" echoes Dr. Leslie's conversation with his friend Dr. Ferris, in which he explains his educational theory: allowing the child to grow into her vocation naturally. As Ferris comments, "most of us are grown into the shapes that society and family preferences fasten us into." (p. 106).
95. Jewett, *Country Doctor,* p. 337.
96. Jewett, *Country Doctor,* p. 334.
97. Jewett, *Country Doctor,* p. 242.
98. Jewett, *Country Doctor,* p. 328.
99. Jewett, *Country Doctor,* p. 328. Eunice Fraley demonstrates the unrealistic sense of responsibility that Nancy Chodorow diagnosed as the affliction of women with confused ego boundaries.
100. Jewett, *Country Doctor,* p. 338.
101. Jewett, *Country Doctor,* p. 340.
102. Jewett, *Country Doctor,* p. 342.
103. Jewett, *Country Doctor,* p. 344.
104. Jewett, *Country Doctor,* p. 350.
105. Jewett, *Country Doctor,* p. 350.
106. Jewett, *Country Doctor,* p. 351.
107. Nancy Chodorow, *Reproduction of Mothering,* p. 194.
108. Ammons, "The Shape of Violence," p. 16.
109. Sigmund Freud, "Female Sexuality" (1929, 1931), in *Complete Psychological Works of Sigmund Freud* (Standard Edition), vol. 21 (1927–31), ed. and trans. James Strachey (London: Hogarth, 1961), p. 226. This passage is

discussed in Mitchell, pp. 56, 119. Studies that discuss the "mythmaking" aspect of Freud's work include Nina Auerbach, "Magi and Maidens: The Romance of the Victorian Freud," *Critical Inquiry* 8:2 (Winter 1981), 281–300; Norman A. Etherington, "Rider Haggard, Imperialism, and the Layered Personality," *Victorian Studies* 22 (Autumn 1978): 71–87; and Frank J. Sulloway, *Freud: Biologist of the Mind* (New York, 1979).

110. Freud, p. 226.

CHAPTER 8

1. Jewett to Annie Fields, n.p., n.d., Houghton Library, Harvard University. Quoted in Frost, p. 89.

2. Sarah Orne Jewett, "Good Luck: A Girl's Story," in *Country By-Ways* (Boston: Houghton Mifflin, 1881), p. 198.

3. Sarah Orne Jewett, "A Little Ancestress," MS 1743.25 (134), Houghton Library, Harvard University.

4. Adrienne Rich, "Aunt Jennifer's Tigers," in *The Fact of a Doorframe: Poems Selected and New, 1950–1984*. New York: W. W. Norton, 1984).

5. Jewett, "Outgrown Friends," n.p.

6. Sarah Orne Jewett, "Thoughts about Housekeeping," MS 1743.22 (115), Houghton Library, Harvard University, p. 1.

7. Sarah Orne Jewett, "A Bit of Shore Life," in *Old Friends and New* (Boston: Houghton, Osgood, 1879), p. 263.

8. Sarah Orne Jewett, quoted in Spofford, p. 35.

9. Jewett to Annie Fields, Monday [1889 or 1890], in Fields, *Letters*, p. 56.

10. Sarah Orne Jewett, "A Winter Drive," in *Country By-Ways* (Boston: Houghton Mifflin, 1881), p. 163.

11. Jewett, "Winter Drive," p. 170.

12. Jewett, "Winter Drive," p. 170.

13. Jewett, "Winter Drive," p. 168.

14. Sarah Orne Jewett, "An October Ride," in *Country By-Ways* (Boston: Houghton Mifflin, 1881), p. 101.

15. Jewett to Sarah Whitman, Friday night, *late* (Jewett's emphasis), n.d., Houghton Library, Harvard University.

16. Jewett, "Winter Drive," p. 163.

17. Jewett to Annie Fields, Thursday morning, Decoration Day, 1889, in Fields, *Letters*, pp. 60–61.

18. Louis Renza also discusses the shift from the preoedipal relationship between father and daughter. Although Renza uses Nancy Chodorow's theory, my interpretation seems weighted more toward the object-relations approach than his does. Renza, pp. 96–113.

19. Jewett, "White Rose Road," p. 87.

20. Jewett to Annie Fields, Saturday afternoon, 1892, in Fields, *Letters*, p. 90.

21. Sarah Orne Jewett, "A Neighbor's Landmark," *The Life of Nancy* (Boston: Houghton Mifflin, 1894), p. 152.

22. Jewett to Willa Cather, quoted in Donovan, *Jewett*, p. 136. See also Josephine Donovan, "A Woman's Vision,."

23. Marjorie Pryse, "Introduction to the Norton Edition," p. xiii.

24. Jewett, *Firs*, p. 4; "Queen's Twin," p. 199. Josephine Donovan's article

on *A Country Doctor* has an illuminating discussion of Nan's decision *not* to follow the path of that novel's herbalist/healer, Eliza Dyer. Dr. Leslie, Donovan argues, is the only way that Nan (and vicariously Jewett herself) can achieve professional status in the larger world. I would add to this analysis a consideration of social class. It is important that Nan be accepted by the higher social classes represented by the Princes and Dr. Leslie himself. Eliza Dyer represents a working-class, preindustrial tradition that would mean a drop in social status, as well as professional status, for Nan.

25. See Neumann, *passim*. In her study of Jewett's career Josephine Donovan sees a pattern similar to the one I have outlined. Donovan identifies three stages. In the first, Jewett's writing focuses on independent or even professional women. By the mid-1880s she becomes more concerned with women's communities. Then, in the late 1880s, a new emotional intensity and "a kind of matriarchal Christianity" emerge (Donovan, *Jewett*, p. 367).

26. On the connection between Stowe and Jewett, see Chapter 2, note 45; also Katherine T. Jobes, "From Stowe's Eagle Island to Jewett's 'A White Heron,'" *Colby Library Quarterly* 10 (December 1974): 515–21.

On literary tradition and influence, see Harold Bloom, *The Anxiety of Influence* (New York: Oxford University Press, 1973); Ellen Moers, *Literary Women: The Great Writers* (Garden City, NY: Doubleday-Anchor, 1977); Elaine Showalter, *A Literature of Their Own: Women Novelists from Brontë to Lessing* (Princeton, NJ: Princeton University Press, 1977). Studies adapting Chodorow to the study of literary influence include Elizabeth Abel, "(E)Merging Identities: The Dynamics of Female Friendships in Contemporary Fiction by Women" and Judith Kegan Gardiner, "On Female Identity and Writing by Women."

27. Alfred (Lord) Tennyson, "Demeter and Persephone," in *Demeter and Other Poems* (New York and London, 1889). In a letter to Sarah Whitman, dated London, 20 August 1892, Jewett describes her feelings visiting Tennyson: "I know exactly what I should have felt a thousand years ago if I were paying a visit to my king." Fields, *Letters*, p. 125).

28. Richard Cary, Introduction to Sarah Orne Jewett, *Deephaven and Other Stories* (New Haven, CT: College and University Press, 1966), pp. 7–23. Jewett writes in an unpublished letter, "Thank you all for the kind words about the Pointed Firs which seems to me like a later Deephaven in a sort of way though I did not think about that when I was writing" [Jewett, Letter to Kate ——, 11 January, n.y., Barret Coll., University of Virginia]. See also Ann Romines, "In *Deephaven*: Skirmishes Near the Swamp"; Marilyn Mobley, "Rituals of Flight and Return: The Ironic Journeys of Sarah Orne Jewett's Female Characters," in *Colby Library Quarterly* 22:1 (March 1986): 36–42.

29. Jewett to Charles Miner Thompson, South Berwick, Maine, 13 October 1904, in Fields, *Letters*, pp. 194–97. The letter is in response to Thompson's "The Art of Miss Jewett," *Atlantic Monthly* 94 (October 1904): 485–97, reprinted in *Appreciation*.

30. Jewett to Willa Cather, 148 Charles Street, Boston, Mass., Sunday 13 December [1908], in Fields, *Letters*, p. 248.

31. Jewett to Willa Cather, p. 249.

32. Jewett, *Deephaven*, p. 42.

33. Jewett, *Deephaven*, p. 42.

34. Jewett, *Deephaven*, p. 61.

35. Jewett, *Deephaven,* p. 61.

36. Jewett, *Deephaven,* p. 63.

37. Jewett, *Deephaven,* p. 106.

38. Jewett, *Deephaven,* p. 107.

39. Jewett, *Deephaven,* p. 107.

40. Jewett, *Firs,* p. 6.

41. Jewett, *Firs,* pp. 6–7.

42. Donovan, *Jewett,* p. 376.

43. Jewett to Willa Cather, 148 Charles Street, Boston, Mass., Sunday, 13 December [1908], in Fields, *Letters,* p. 250.

44. Jewett, *Firs,* pp. 3–4.

45. Wilson Flagg, "Simples and Simplers," *Atlantic Monthly* 29 (June 1872): 743. See also Sylvia Gray Noyes, "Mrs. Almira Todd, Herbalist-Conjurer," *Colby Library Quarterly* 9 (December 1972): 643–49. Elizabeth Ammons has a wonderful essay on these patterns: "Jewett's Witches," in Nagel.

46. Flagg, p. 749. "Among the early Romans, plants were supposed to derive their virtues from some rural deity to whom they were dedicated; and the curative powers of mineral waters were attributed to the nymph who presided at the spring, and those who drank at the fountain worshipped the beautiful goddess from whose divine qualities these virtues emanated. When the heathen world was converted to the religion of Christ, these superstitions changed their character, but were not cast aside" (p. 744).

47. Neumann, p. 296. The internal quotation is from Martin Hermann Ninck, *Wodan und germanischer Schicksalsgleube* (Jena: E. Diederichs, 1935), p. 305.

48. Jewett, *Firs,* p. 92.

49. Jewett, *Firs,* p. 59.

50. Neumann, p. 297.

51. Jewett, *Firs,* p. 7.

52. Jewett, *Firs,* p. 7.

53. Jewett, *Firs,* p. 8.

54. Neumann, p. 296.

55. Jewett, *Firs,* p. 9.

56. Jewett to Annie Fields, Thursday afternoon, June 1882, Houghton Library, Harvard University.

57. Jewett, *Firs,* p. 15.

58. Jewett, *Firs,* p. 14.

59. Jewett, *Firs,* pp. 17–18.

60. Sarah Orne Jewett, "The Decay of Churches," MS 1743.22 (25), Houghton Library, Harvard University.

61. Jewett, *Firs,* p. 20.

62. Jewett, *Firs,* p. 21.

63. Jewett, "1893 Preface," p. 33.

64. Jewett, *Firs,* p. 25.

65. Jewett, *Firs,* p. 22.

66. Donovan, *Jewett,* p. 105.

67. Jewett, *Firs,* p. 29.

68. Jewett, *Firs,* pp. 29–30.

69. Frost, p. 70. The internal quotation is from Sarah Orne Jewett to John Greenleaf Whittier, 22 April 1884, Houghton Library, Harvard University.

70. Jewett to Annie Fields, Spring House, Richfield Springs, New York [1894], in Fields, *Letters,* pp. 110–11.

71. Jewett, *Firs,* pp. 30–31.

72. Jewett, *Firs,* p. 35.

73. Jewett, "A Dunnet Shepherdess," in *The Country of the Pointed Firs and Other Stories* (1899; rpt. New York: W. W. Norton, 1982), p. 145.

74. Johann Jakob Bachofen, *Das Mutterrecht*, p. 81.

75. Jewett, *Firs*, p. 45.   76. Jewett, *Firs*, p. 45.

77. Jewett, *Firs*, p. 39.   78. Jewett, *Firs*, p. 46.

79. Jewett, *Firs*, p. 54.   80. Jewett, *Firs*, p. 54.

81. Stowe, *Pearl*, p. 376.

82. For discussion of "The Christmas Ghosts" and Jewett's revisions, see Chapter 3.

83. Jewett, *Firs*, pp. 46-47.   84. Stowe, *Pearl*, p. 164.

85. Jewett, *Firs*, p. 90.   86. Jewett, *Firs*, p. 97.

87. Jewett, *Firs*, p. 98.   88. Jewett, *Firs*, p. 98.

89. Jewett, *Firs*, pp. 95-96.   90. Jewett, *Firs*, p. 96.

91. Jewett, *Firs*, p. 105.

92. Jewett to Sarah Whitman, South Berwick, Maine, Friday night [n.d.] in Fields, *Letters*, pp. 129-30. The internal quotation is from Agnes Mary Frances Duclaux (Robinson), *The Life of Ernest Renan* (Boston: Houghton Mifflin, 1898). Annie Fields places this letter among those written in 1897. However, I believe that it is from 1898, since the Renan book was published that year and this letter is so similar, even to the same quotation, to a letter Jewett wrote Grace Norton after Jewett's sister, Caroline Jewett Eastman, died in 1898 (Jewett to Grace Norton, Saturday morning 1898, Houghton Library, Harvard University). For the text of the Norton letter see Chapter 3.

93. Jewett to Willa Cather, quoted in Donovan, *Jewett*, p. 126.

94. Jewett, *Firs*, pp. 99-100. Here is Pater's translation of a passage from Theocritus's *Idylls* describing two shepherds on their way to Demeter's "homely feast": "Many poplars and elm-trees were waving over our heads, and not far off the running of the sacred water from the cave of the nymphs warbled to us; in the shimmering branches the sun-burnt grasshoppers were busy with their talk, and from afar the little owl cried softly. . . . the bees flew round and round the fountains softly; the scent of late summer and of the fall of the year were everywhere" (Pater, pp. 126-27).

95. Jewett, *Firs*, p. 100.

96. Pater, pp. 92-93.

97. Pater, p. 155; quoted in Fields, *Under the Olive*, p. 315.

98. Jewett, *Firs*, p. 100.

99. Sarah Orne Jewett, "An October Ride," pp. 102-103.

100. Jewett, *Firs*, p. 100.

101. Jewett, *Firs*, pp. 100-101.

102. Jewett, *Firs*, p. 108.

CHAPTER 9

1. Jewett, "William's Wedding," in *The Country of the Pointed Firs and Other Stories* (1910; rpt. New York: W. W. Norton, 1982), p. 217. My approach in this chapter has much in common with Marcia McClintock Folsom's sensitive " 'Tact Is a Kind of Mind-Reading': Empathic Style in Sarah Orne Jewett's *The Country of the Pointed Firs*," *Colby Library Quarterly* 18 (1982): 66-78; reprinted in Nagel. Folsom argues that "since 'empathy' does not carry the suggestions of compassion for another's sorrow that 'sympathy' does, it

seems the more general term" (Nagel, p. 89). However, since "sympathy" is the term that Jewett and her contemporaries (as well as her sentimentalist precursors) used, I have kept it. Also, "sorrow" in these works often develops more awareness: the capacity to see and "feel with" another human being. Elizabeth Ammons, Sandra Zagarell, and Joseph Boone also offer excellent studies of women's "ways of knowing," narrative form, and literary tradition.

2. Jewett, *Firs*, p. 55.

3. Jewett, *Firs*, p. 57.

4. Jewett, "For Country Girls."

5. Jewett, *Firs*, p. 62.

6. Jewett, *Firs*, p. 76.

7. Jewett, *Firs*, p. 74.

8. Jewett, *Firs*, p. 74.

9. Jewett, *Firs*, p. 73.

10. Jewett, *Firs*, p. 69.

11. Jewett, *Firs*, p. 76.

12. Jewett, *Firs*, pp. 77–78.

13. Jewett, *Firs*, p. 69. Among the numerous essays that have addressed Jewett's attitude toward the clergy are Ann Douglas (Wood), "The Literature of Impoverishment"; John Paul Eakin, "Sarah Orne Jewett and the Meaning of Country Life"; and Francis Fike, "An Interpretation of *Pointed Firs*." Josephine Donovan's studies offer the most thorough assessment of the issue. Richard Cary's *Sarah Orne Jewett* offers a sympathetic overview of Jewett's philosophical and theological themes.

14. Jewett, *Firs*, pp. 74–75.

15. Jewett, *Firs*, p. 77.

16. Fike, p. 176.

17. Fike, p. 176.

18. Jewett, *Firs*, p. 75.

19. Jewett, *Firs*, pp. 81–82.

20. Jewett, *Firs*, p. 82.

21. Jewett, *Firs*, p. 82.

22. Jewett, *Deephaven*, p. 86.

23. Jewett, *Firs*, p. 115.

24. Jewett, *Firs*, pp. 113–14.

25. Jewett, *Firs*, p. 122.

26. Jewett, *Firs*, p. 124.

27. Jewett, *Firs*, pp. 124–25.

28. Jewett, *Firs*, pp. 122–23.

29. Jewett, *Firs*, pp. 118–19.

30. Jewett, *Firs*, p. 122.

31. Jewett, *Firs*, p. 115.

32. Jewett, *Firs*, p. 126.

33. Warner Berthoff, "The Art of Jewett's *Pointed Firs*," *New England Quarterly* 32 (March 1959): 31–53; Marco A. Portales, "History of a Text: Jewett's *The Country of the Pointed Firs*," *New England Quarterly* 55:4 (December 1982): 586–92.

34. See Pryse, "Introduction to the Norton Edition," pp. vi–vii; also David Bonnell Green, "Bibliographical Note," *The World of Dunnet Landing: A Sarah Orne Jewett Collection* (Lincoln, NE: University of Nebraska Press, 1962). The text's integrity is also discussed in Hyatt Waggoner's "The Unity of *The Country of the Pointed Firs*," *Twentieth Century Literature* 5 (July 1959): 67–73; reprinted in *Appreciation*; and Paul Voelker, "*The Country of the Pointed Firs*: A Novel by Sarah Orne Jewett," Colby Library Quarterly 9:4 (December 1970): 201–13; reprinted in *Appreciation*.

35. Jewett, *Firs*, p. 42.

36. Jewett, *Firs*, p. 44.

37. Jewett, "Dunnet Shepherdess," p. 143.

38. Jewett, "Dunnet Shepherdess," p. 154.

39. Jewett, "Dunnet Shepherdess," p. 148.

40. Jewett, "Dunnet Shepherdess," p. 149.

41. Jewett, "Dunnet Shepherdess," p. 148.

42. Jewett, "Dunnet Shepherdess," p. 149.

43. Jewett, "Dunnet Shepherdess," p. 151.
44. Jewett, "Dunnet Shepherdess," p. 154.
45. Jewett, "Dunnet Shepherdess," p. 155.
46. Jewett, "Dunnet Shepherdess," p. 154.
47. Jewett, "Dunnet Shepherdess," p. 156.
48. Sarah Orne Jewett, "The Foreigner" in *The Country of the Pointed Firs and Other Stories* (1900; rpt. New York: W. W. Norton, 1982). For discussion of the story, see Pryse, "Introduction to the Norton Edition" and "Women 'at Sea': Feminist Realism in Sarah Orne Jewett's 'The Foreigner,'" *American Literary Realism* 15 (1982): 244–52); reprinted in Nagel, pp. 89–98. See also Donovan, *New England Local Literature*, pp. 117–18.
49. Jewett, "The Foreigner," p. 170.
50. Jewett, "The Foreigner," p. 175.
51. Jewett, "The Foreigner," p. 166.
52. Jewett, "The Foreigner," p. 167.
53. Jewett, "The Foreigner," pp. 189–90.
54. Jewett, "The Foreigner," p. 169.
55. Jewett, "The Foreigner," p. 171.
56. Jewett, "The Foreigner," p. 180.
57. Jewett, "The Foreigner," p. 176.
58. Jewett, "The Foreigner," p. 158.
59. Jewett, "The Foreigner," p. 182.
60. Jewett, "The Foreigner," p. 183.
61. Jewett, "The Foreigner," p. 184.
62. Jewett, "The Foreigner," p. 184.
63. Jewett, "The Foreigner," p. 187.
64. Jewett, "The Foreigner," p. 187.
65. Pryse, "Introduction to the Norton Edition," pp. x–xi.
66. I am indebted to Melody Graulich for this analogy between Mrs. Todd's braided rug and "The Foreigner"'s narrative structure.
67. Jewett, "Queen's Twin," p. 203.
68. Jewett, "Queen's Twin," p. 200.
69. Jewett, "Queen's Twin," p. 203.
70. Jewett, "Queen's Twin," p. 198.
71. Jewett, "Queen's Twin," p. 199.
72. Jewett, "Queen's Twin," p. 199.
73. Jewett, "The Christmas Ghosts," draft 2, pp. 3, 5.
74. Jewett, "Queen's Twin," p. 200.
75. Jewett, "Queen's Twin," pp. 206–7.
76. Friedrich Schleiermacher, *The Christian Faith* 1 (1821, rev. ed. 1830; rpt. New York: Harper and Row, 1963) and *On Religion: Speeches to Its Cultured Despisers* (1799; rpt. New York: Harper and Row, 1958). William James, *"The Will to Believe" and Other Essays on Popular Philosophy* (New York: Longmans, Green, 1896); *The Varieties of Religious Experience* (New York: Longmans, Green, 1902).
77. Mircea Eliade, *The Sacred and the Profane: The Nature of Religion* (New York: Harcourt Brace, 1957), p. 99. "By reactualizing sacred history, by imitating the divine behavior, man puts and keeps himself close to the gods—that is, in the real and significant" (p. 202). "Acting as a fully responsible human being, man imitates the paradigmatic actions of the gods, repeats their

actions, whether in the case of a simple physiological function such as eating or of a social, economic, cultural, military, or other activity" (p. 98).

78. F. E. Williams [cited in Lucien Lévy-Bruhl, *La Mythologie primitive* (Paris, 1935), pp. 162, 163–64], quoted in Eliade, p. 98. "He did not pray to the mythical hero for aid and favor; he identified himself with him. . . . This is as much to say that religious man wishes to be *other* than he is on the plane of his profane experience. Religious man is not *given*; he *makes* himself, by approaching the divine models" (Eliade, pp. 98–100).

79. Jewett, "Queen's Twin," p. 201.
80. Jewett, "Queen's Twin," p. 201.
81. Jewett, "Queen's Twin," p. 192.
82. Jewett, "Queen's Twin," p. 200.
83. Jewett, "Queen's Twin," p. 202.
84. Jewett, "Queen's Twin," p. 205.
85. Jewett, "Queen's Twin," p. 205.
86. Jewett, "Queen's Twin," p. 207.
87. Jewett, "Queen's Twin," p. 208.
88. Jewett, "Queen's Twin," p. 208.
89. Jewett, "Queen's Twin," p. 209. In a letter to Hamilton Wright Mabie (editor and author, among other things, of the essay "My Search for the Goddess" mentioned in Chapter 2), Jewett thanks him for his decision to reprint "The Queen's Twin," then goes on: "I have had a very pleasant letters [*sic*] from East and West since the Queen died, to ask for imaginary Mrs. Martin and how she bore her great loss—but Mrs. Martin only stood for her author's interest, or, as it appears afresh, the interest of a good many others.—It gave me great pleasure sometime [*sic*] to know that the Queen herself liked the story and said some delightful things about it—It was printed in the *Cornhill* at the same time that the *Atlantic* printed it here" (Jewett to Hamilton Wright Mabie, 20 February, n.y., South Berwick, Maine, Library of Congress, Manuscript Division, L.C. 0215–1007, pp. 216, 217).

Jewett's original interest in writing the story may have been prompted by a more personal source, the death of her sister Caroline in 1898. She wrote to Grace Norton: "It is impossible to get over the feeling that something of me died and not the living brightness and affectionateness of my sister" (Jewett to Grace Norton, Saturday morning, 1898, Houghton Library, Harvard University). Letters between the Jewett sisters now in the SPNEA Archives reveal that one of Sarah's family nicknames was "the Queen of Sheba."

CHAPTER 10

1. Jewett, *Firs*, p. 128.   2. Jewett, *Firs*, p. 130.
3. Jewett, *Firs*, pp. 130–31.   4. Jewett, *Firs*, p. 131.
5. Jewett, *Firs*, pp. 132–33.
6. Jewett, "William's Wedding," p. 213. *The Tory Lover* was published in 1901. In an unpublished letter Alice Brown, who once described Jewett as a symbolist in prose, first thanks her for a copy of *The Tory Lover*, then tactfully dismisses the novel by writing that she "grudges" any time Jewett takes away from the characters and style of *Pointed Firs*. Having done *that* so perfectly, Jewett has spoiled her readers for anything else [Alice Brown to Sarah Orne Jewett, 129 State Street, Montpelier, Vermont, n.d. ["1901?" marked on

manuscript, perhaps by Annie Fields], bMS. Am 1743 (28)], Houghton Library, Harvard University.

7. Jewett, "William's Wedding," p. 213.

8. Jewett, "William's Wedding," p. 214.

9. Jewett, "William's Wedding," p. 214.

10. Jewett, "William's Wedding," p. 215.

11. Jewett, "William's Wedding," p. 216.

12. Jewett, "William's Wedding," p. 216.

13. Jewett, "William's Wedding," p. 217.

14. Jewett, "William's Wedding," p. 219.

15. Jewett, "William's Wedding," p. 220.

16. Jewett, "William's Wedding," pp. 217–18.

17. Jewett, "William's Wedding," p. 221.

18. Jewett, "William's Wedding," p. 221.

19. Jewett, "William's Wedding," p. 223.

20. Jewett, "William's Wedding," p. 224.

21. Jewett, "William's Wedding," p. 224.

22. Jewett, "William's Wedding," p. 224.

23. Jewett, "William's Wedding," p. 226.

24. Jewett, "William's Wedding," p. 226.

25. Edward Garnett, "Books Too Little Known: Miss Sarah Orne Jewett's Tales," *Academy and Literature* 65 (11 July 1903): 23; reprinted in *Appreciation*, p. 23.

26. Garnett, p. 23.

27. Barton L. St. Armand, "Jewett and Marin: The Inner Vision," in *Appreciation*, pp. 302–33.

28. Ortner, pp. 14, 30. de Beauvoir, *passim*.

29. Jewett, *Firs*, p. 108.

30. Jewett wrote to Annie Fields that December: "I have just been reading Mr. Arnold's essay on George Sand, and finished it with tears in my eyes. How beautiful, and how full of inspiration it is! We cannot be grateful enough to either of them, and yet how little I really know her books! I am willing to study French very hard this winter in order to read her comfortably in the spring!" (Sarah Orne Jewett to Annie Fields, Sunday afternoon, December 1888, in Fields, *Letters*, p. 38. George Sand (Dudevant), *Little Fadette: A Domestic Story* (1849; rpt. London: The Scholar's Press, 1928), p. 3.

31. Sand, pp. 3–4.

32. Sand, p. 4.

33. Jewett, *Firs*, p. 4.

34. Jewett, *Firs*, p. 59.

35. Jewett, Manuscript diary 1871–79, MS. Am 1743.1 (341), Houghton Library, Harvard University, inside front cover; quoted in Josephine Donovan's fine assessment, "Sarah Orne Jewett's Critical Theory: Notes Toward a Feminine Literary Mode," in Nagel, p. 216. See also Richard Cary's affectionate essay, "The Literary Rubrics of Sarah Orne Jewett," in Nagel, pp. 198–211.

36. Donovan, "Jewett's Critical Theory," p. 217.

37. Sarah Orne Jewett to Annie Fields, Saturday night [1899 or 1900], Fields, *Letters*.

38. Renza, p. 175.

39. Jewett, *Firs*, p. 218.

40. Jewett, *Firs*, p. 218.

41. Ammons, "Going in Circles," p. 92.

42. Donovan, "Jewett's Critical Theory," p. 217. See also chap. 6, "Criticism and Influence," in Donovan's *Sarah Orne Jewett*.

43. Russ, "What Can a Heroine Do?" in *Images of Women in Fiction: Feminist Perspectives,* ed. Susan Koppelman Cornillon (Bowling Green, OH: Bowling Green University Popular Press, 1972), p. 13.

44. Russ, p. 13.

45. Jewett to Horace Scudder, South Berwick, 13 July 1873, in Matthiessen, *Sarah Orne Jewett,* pp. 45–46.

46. William Dean Howells, *A Chance Acquaintance,* quoted in Cary, "Introduction," *Deephaven.* Cary acknowledges that this passage was brought to his attention by Van Wyck Brooks.

47. Jewett, *Deephaven,* p. 66.

48. Jewett, in Fields, *Letters,* p. 81.

49. Renza, p. 167.

50. Kermode, p. 132; Jean-Paul Sartre, *Nausea,* trans. Lloyd Alexander (New York: New Directions, 1964). Elizabeth Ammons's "Going in Circles" uses Gilligan's work to illuminate the circular patterns in *Pointed Firs.* Perspectives on Jewett's modernism may also be found in Willa Cather's Preface to *The Best Stories of Sarah Orne Jewett* (1925) and Marjorie Pryse's "Introduction to the Norton Edition" (1981), as well as Sandra Zagarell's "Narrative of Community," Joseph Boone's *Tradition Counter Tradition,* and Josephine Donovan's "Sarah Orne Jewett's Critical Theory." Donovan addresses Jewett's "plotlessness" and "an escape from a masculine time of history into transcending feminine space" (p. 223). While Donovan and I both see rituals of return to the maternal center, I lay more stress on the importance of separation for the "daughter's" development. Jewett's art, like Persephone's torch, illuminates through the integration of love and consciousness. See also Sharon O'Brien, *Willa Cather: The Emerging Voice,* especially chaps. 15 and 16.

51. Kermode, pp. 136–37.

52. Sarah Orne Jewett, "Miss Tempy's Watchers," in *The Country of the Pointed Firs and Other Stories* (1888, rpt. New York: W. W. Norton, 1982), p. 251.

Works Cited

Abel, Elizabeth. "(E)Merging Identities: The Dynamics of Female Friendships in Contemporary Fiction by Women." *Signs* 6 (Spring 1981): 413–35.

Adams, Henry. *The Education of Henry Adams.* 1907. Reprint. Boston: Houghton Mifflin, 1961.

———. *Mont-Saint-Michel and Chartres.* 1904. Reprint. Garden City, NY: Doubleday-Anchor, 1959.

Alcott, Louisa May. *Little Women.* 1868. Reprint. New York: Modern Library, 1983.

Alden, H. M. "The Eleusinia." Part 1, *Atlantic Monthly* 4 (September 1859): 295–303; Part 2, *Atlantic Monthly* 6 (August 1860): 157–68.

Ammons, Elizabeth. "Going in Circles: The Female Geography of *The Country of the Pointed Firs.*" *Studies in the Literary Imagination* 16 (Autumn 1983): 83–92.

———. "Heroines in Uncle Tom's Cabin." *American Literature* 49 (May 1977): 116–79 (reprinted in *Critical Essays on Harriet Beecher Stowe,* edited by Elizabeth Ammons. Boston: G. K. Hall, 1980).

———. "Jewett's Witches." In *Critical Essays on Sarah Orne Jewett,* edited by Gwen Nagel. Boston: G. K. Hall, 1984.

———. "The Shape of Violence in Jewett's 'A White Heron.'" *Colby Library Quarterly* 22:1 (March 1986): 6–16.

———. "Stowe's Dream of the Mother-Savior: *Uncle Tom's Cabin* and American Women Writers before the 1920s." In *New Essays on Uncle Tom's Cabin,* edited by Eric J. Sundquist. Cambridge, London, and New York: Cambridge University Press, 1986.

Auerbach, Nina. *Communities of Women: An Idea in Fiction.* Cambridge, MA: Harvard University Press, 1978.

———. "Magi and Maidens: The Romance of the Victorian Freud." *Critical Inquiry* 8:2 (Winter 1981): 281–300.

Bachofen, Johann Jakob. *Das Mutterrecht* (1861). *Myth, Religion, and Mother Right.* Translated by Ralph Manheim. Princeton, NJ: Bollingen Foundation, Princeton University Press, 1967.

Bakan, David. *The Duality of Human Experience: Isolation and Communion in Western Man.* Boston: Beacon, 1966.

Balint, Alice. *The Early Years of Life: A Psycho-Analytic Study.* New York: Basic Books, 1954.

Balint, Alice, and Michael Balint. *Primary Love and Psycho-Analytic Technique.* Edited by Michael Balint. London: Tavistock; New York: Liveright, 1956.

Ball, B. W. "Woman's Rights in Ancient Athens." *Atlantic Monthly* 27 (March 1871): 273–86.

Bamberger, Joan. "The Myth of Matriarchy: Why Men Rule in Primitive Society." In *Woman, Culture, and Society,* edited by Michelle Z. Rosaldo and Louise Lamphere. Stanford, CA: Stanford University Press, 1974.

Barthes, Roland. *Writing Degree Zero.* New York: Hill and Wang, 1968.

Baym, Nina. "Melodramas of Beset Manhood: How Theories of American Fiction Exclude Women Authors." *American Quarterly* 33:2 (Summer 1981): 123–39.

———. *Women's Fiction: A Guide to Novels by and about Women in America, 1820–1870.* Ithaca, NY: Cornell University Press, 1978.

Berkson, Dorothy. "Millennial Politics and the Feminine Fiction of Harriet Beecher Stowe." In *New Essays on Uncle Tom's Cabin,* edited by Eric J. Sundquist. Cambridge, London, and New York: Cambridge University Press, 1986.

Berthoff, Warner. "The Art of Jewett's *Pointed Firs.*" *New England Quarterly* 32 (March 1959): 31–53.

Bettelheim, Bruno. *The Uses of Enchantment: The Meaning and Importance of Fairy Tales.* New York: Vintage, 1977.

Bishop, Fermin. "The Sense of the Past in Sarah Orne Jewett." *University of Wichita Bulletin,* University Studies No. 41 (February 1959): 3–10 (reprinted in Cary, *Appreciation*).

Blanc-Bentzon, Marie Thérèse. "Le Roman de la femme-medecin." *Revue des Deux Mondes* 67 (1 February 1885): 598–632 (translation reprinted in Cary, *Appreciation*).

Bloch, Ruth H. "American Feminine Ideals in Transition: The Rise of the Moral Mother, 1785–1815." *Feminist Studies* 4 (June 1978): 101–26.

Bloom, Harold. *The Anxiety of Influence.* New York: Oxford University Press, 1973.

Boas, George. Preface to *Myth, Religion, and Mother Right,* by Johann Jakob Bachofen. Translated by Ralph Manheim. Princeton, NJ: Princeton University Press, 1967.

Boone, Joseph Allen. *Tradition Counter Tradition: Love and the Form of Fiction.* Chicago: University of Chicago Press, 1987.

Bowditch, Mrs. Ernest. "The Jewett Library." *Colby Library Quarterly* 5 (December 1961): 357–65.

Bowlby, John. *Attachment and Loss.* Vol. 1, *Attachment.* London: Penguin, 1969.

Brown, Herbert Ross. *The Sentimental Novel in America, 1789–1860.* Durham, NC: Duke University Press, 1940.

Buhle, Mari Jo. *Women and American Socialism, 1870–1920.* Urbana, IL: University of Illinois Press, 1981.

Campbell, Joseph. *The Flight of the Wild Gander: Explorations in the Mythological Dimension.* New York: Viking, 1951.

———. *The Hero with a Thousand Faces.* Princeton, NJ: Princeton University Press, Bollingen, 1949.

———. Introduction to *Myth, Religion, and Mother Right,* by Johann Jakob Bachofen. Translated by Ralph Manheim. Princeton, NJ: Princeton University Press, 1967.

Cary, Richard. "The Literary Rubrics of Sarah Orne Jewett." In *Critical Essays on Sarah Orne Jewett,* edited by Gwen Nagel. Boston: G. K. Hall, 1984.

———. *Sarah Orne Jewett.* New York: Twayne, 1962.

————, ed. *Appreciation of Sarah Orne Jewett: Twenty-Nine Interpretive Essays*. Waterville, ME: Colby College Press, 1973.

————, ed. *Deephaven and Other Stories*. New Haven, CT: College and University Press, 1966.

————, ed. *Sarah Orne Jewett Letters*, rev. and enl. ed. Waterville, ME: Colby College Press, 1967.

Cather, Willa. "148 Charles Street." *Not Under Forty*. New York: Knopf, 1953.

————. "Miss Jewett." *Not Under Forty*. New York: Knopf, 1953.

————, ed. *The Best Short Stories of Sarah Orne Jewett*. 2 vols. Boston: Houghton Mifflin, 1925.

Child, Lydia Maria. "The Intermingling of Religions." *Atlantic Monthly* 28 (October 1871): 385–95.

Chodorow, Nancy. "Family Structure and Feminine Personality." In *Women, Culture and Society*, edited by Louise Lamphere and Michelle Z. Rosaldo. Stanford, CA: Stanford University Press, 1974.

————. *The Reproduction of Mothering: Psychoanalysis and the Sociology of Gender*. Berkeley, CA: University of California Press, 1978.

Chopin, Kate. *The Awakening*. 1899. Reprint. New York: W. W. Norton, 1976.

Cixous, Helene. "The Laugh of Medusa." *Signs* 1:4 (Summer 1976): 875–94.

Colette. *The Pure and the Impure*. New York: Farrar, Straus, and Giroux, 1966.

Collins, Margery, and Christine Pierce. "Holes and Slime: Sexism in Sartre's Psychoanalysis." In *Women and Philosophy*, edited by Carol C. Gould and Mary W. Wartofsky. New York: Capricorn Books, 1976.

Conway, Jill. "Stereotypes of Femininity in a Theory of Sexual Evolution." *Victorian Studies* 14 (September 1970): 47–62.

Cooke, Rose Terry. *"How Celia Changed Her Mind" and Selected Stories*. Edited by Elizabeth Ammons. New Brunswick, NJ: Rutgers University Press, 1986.

————. *Root-Bound, and Other Sketches*. Boston: Congregational Sunday School and Publishing Society, 1885.

Cott, Nancy F. *The Bonds of Womanhood: "Woman's Sphere" in New England, 1780–1835*. New Haven, CT: Yale University Press, 1977.

————. "Passionlessness: An Interpretation of Victorian Sexual Ideology, 1790–1850." In *A Heritage of Her Own*, edited by Nancy F. Cott and Elizabeth H. Pleck. New York: Simon and Schuster, 1979.

Coxe, Margaret. *The Young Lady's Companion: in a series of letters*. Columbus, Ohio: I. N. Whiting, 1839.

Crozier, Alice. *The Novels of Harriet Beecher Stowe*. New York: Oxford University Press, 1969.

Crumpacker, Laurie. "Harriet Beecher Stowe: A Study of Nineteenth-Century Androgyny." In *American Novelists Revisited: Essays in Feminist Criticism*, edited by Fritz Fleischman. Boston: G. K. Hall, 1982.

Dall, Caroline Healy. *Margaret and Her Friends, or Ten Conversations upon the Mythology of the Greeks and Its Expression in Art*. Boston: Roberts Brothers, 1895.

Daly, Mary. *Beyond God the Father: Toward a Philosophy of Women's Liberation*. Boston: Beacon, 1973.

———. *The Church and the Second Sex, with a New Feminist Post-Christian Introduction by the Author.* New York: Harper and Row–Colophon, 1975.

—*Gyn/Ecology: The Metaethics of Radical Feminism.* Boston: Beacon, 1978.

Davis, Elizabeth Gould. *The First Sex.* Baltimore: Penguin, 1971.

de Beauvoir, Simone. *The Second Sex.* Translated by H. M. Parshley. New York: Knopf, 1952.

Degler, Carl. *At Odds: Women and Family in America from the Revolution to Present.* New York: Oxford University Press, 1980.

Diner, Helen. *Mothers and Amazons.* New York: Julian, 1965.

Dinnerstein, Dorothy. *The Mermaid and the Minotaur: Sexual Arrangements and Human Malaise.* New York: Harper and Row, 1976.

Donahue, Marie. "Sarah Orne Jewett's 'Dear Old House and Home.'" *Downeast Magazine,* August 1977, 62–67.

Donovan, Josephine. "Nan Prince and the Golden Apples." *Colby Library Quarterly* 22:1 (March 1986): 17–27.

———. *New England Local Color Literature: A Women's Tradition.* New York: Ungar, 1983.

———. *Sarah Orne Jewett.* New York: Ungar, 1981.

———. "Sarah Orne Jewett's Critical Theory: Notes toward a Feminine Literary Mode." In *Critical Essays on Sarah Orne Jewett,* edited by Gwen Nagel. Boston: G. K. Hall, 1984.

———. "The Unpublished Love Poems of Sarah Orne Jewett." *Frontiers: A Journal of Women Studies* 4:3 (1979): 26–31.

———. "A Woman's Vision of Transcendence: A New Interpretation of the Works of Sarah Orne Jewett." *Massachusetts Review* 21:2 (Summer 1980): 365–80.

Douglas, Ann. *The Feminization of American Culture.* New York: Knopf, 1977.

Douglas [Wood], Ann. "The Literature of Impoverishment: The Women Local Colorists in America 1865–1914." *Women's Studies* 1 (1972): 3–45.

Douglas, Mary. *Purity and Danger: An Analysis of the Concepts of Pollution and Taboo.* Baltimore: Penguin, 1966.

Downey, Jean. "A Biographical and Critical Study of Rose Terry Cooke." Ph.D. diss., University of Ottawa, 1956.

Driver, Ann Barstow. "Review Essay: Religion." *Signs* 2:2 (Winter 1976): 434–42.

Duclaux [Agnes Mary Frances Robinson]. *The Life of Ernest Renan.* Boston: Houghton Mifflin, 1898.

Eakin, Paul. "Sarah Orne Jewett and the Meaning of Country Life." *American Literature* 38 (January 1967): 508–31 (reprinted in Cary, *Appreciation*).

Eliade, Mircea. *The Sacred and the Profane: The Nature of Religion.* New York: Harcourt Brace, 1957.

Ellmann, Mary. *Thinking about Women.* New York: Harcourt, Brace & World, 1968.

Emerson, Ralph Waldo. "The Poet" (1843). In *Selections from Ralph Waldo Emerson,* edited by Stephen E. Whicher. Boston: Houghton Mifflin, 1957.

English, Dierdre, and Barbara Ehrenreich. *Witches, Midwives, and Nurses: A History of Women Healers.* Old Westbury, NY: Feminist Press, 1972.

Etherington, Norman A. "Rider Haggard, Imperialism, and the Layered Personality." *Victorian Studies* 22 (Autumn 1978): 71–87.

Faderman, Lillian. "Female Same-Sex Relationships in Novels by Longfellow, Holmes, and James." *New England Quarterly* 51:3 (September 1978): 309–22.

———. *Surpassing the Love of Men: Romantic Friendship between Women from the Renaissance to the Present.* New York: William Morrow, 1981.

Fairbairn, W. E. D. *An Object-Relations Theory of the Personality.* New York: Basic Books, 1952.

Fee, Elizabeth. "Science and the Woman Problem: Historical Perspectives." In *Sex Differences,* edited by Michael Tietelbaum. New York: Doubleday-Anchor, 1976.

———. "The Sexual Politics of Victorian Anthropology." *Feminist Studies* 1 (1973): 23–29.

Fetterley, Judith. Introduction to "Miss Lucinda." In *Provisions: A Reader from 19th-Century American Women,* edited by Judith Fetterley. Bloomington, IN: Indiana University Press, 1985.

Fiedler, Leslie. *Love and Death in the American Novel.* New York: Stein and Day, 1966.

Fields, Annie Adams. "The Mysteries of Eleusis." *The Singing Shepherd.* Boston and New York: Houghton Mifflin, 1895.

———. *Orpheus: A Masque.* Boston: Houghton Mifflin, 1900.

———. *The Return of Persephone.* Boston: privately printed, 1877 (reprinted in Fields, *Under the Olive*).

———. *Under the Olive.* Boston: Houghton Mifflin, 1881.

———, ed. *The Letters of Sarah Orne Jewett.* Boston: Houghton Mifflin, 1911.

Fike, Francis. "An Interpretation of *Pointed Firs. New England Quarterly* 34 (December 1961): 478–91 (reprinted in Cary, *Appreciation*).

Fiske, John. "Athenian and American Life." *Atlantic Monthly* (November 1974): 556–60.

———. *Myths and Mythmakers.* 1872. Reprint. Boston: Houghton Mifflin, 1900.

———. "The Origins of Folk-Lore." *Atlantic Monthly* 27 (February 1871): 145–61.

Flagg, Wilson. "Simples and Simplers." *Atlantic Monthly* 29 (June 1872): 743–49.

Flax, Jane. "The Conflict Between Nurturance and Autonomy in Mother-Daughter Relationships within Feminism." *Feminist Studies* 4:2 (June 1978): 171–89.

Folsom, Marcia McClintock. "'Tact Is a Kind of Mind-Reading': Empathic Style in Sarah Orne Jewett's *The Country of the Pointed Firs.*" *Colby Library Quarterly* 18 (1982): 66–78 (reprinted in Nagel, *Critical Essays*).

Frazer, Sir James George. *The Golden Bough: A Study in Magic and Religion,* vol. 1, abridged. 1922. Reprint. New York: Macmillan, 1963.

Freibert, Lucy, and Barbara White, eds. *Hidden Hands: An Anthology of American Women Writers, 1790–1870.* New Brunswick, NJ: Rutgers University Press, 1985.

Freud, Sigmund. "Female Sexuality" (1929, 1931). *Complete Psychological Works of Sigmund Freud* (Standard Edition). Vol. 21 (1927–1931). Translated and edited by James Strachey. London: Hogarth Press, 1961.

Frost, John Eldridge. *Sarah Orne Jewett.* Kittery Point, ME: The Gundalow Club, 1960.

Frye, Northrop. *The Anatomy of Criticism: Four Essays*. Princeton, NJ: Princeton University Press, 1957.

Gage, Mathilda Joslyn. *Woman, Church, and the State*. 1900. Reprint. New York: Arno, 1972.

Gardiner, Judith Kegan. "The Heroine As Her Author's Daughter." In *Feminist Criticism: Essays on Theory, Poetry and Prose*, edited by Cheryl L. Brown and Karen Olson. Metuchen, NJ: Scarecrow, 1978.

———. "On Female Identity and Writing by Women." *Critical Inquiry* 8:2 (Winter 1982): 347–61.

Garnett, Edward. "Books Too Little Known: Miss Sarah Orne Jewett's Tales." *Academy and Literature* 65 (11 July 1903): 23 (reprinted in Cary, *Appreciation*).

Gaskell (Stevenson), Elizabeth Cleghorn. *Cranford*. New York: Harper, 1864.

Geertz, Clifford. "Thick Description: Toward an Interpretive Theory of Culture." *The Interpretation of Cultures*. New York: Basic Books, 1973.

Gilbert, Sandra, and Susan Gubar. *The Madwoman in the Attic: The Woman Writer and the Nineteenth Century Literary Imagination*. New Haven, CT: Yale University Press, 1979.

Gilligan, Carol. *In a Different Voice*. Cambridge, MA: Harvard University Press, 1982.

Gilman, Charlotte Perkins. *Herland*. 1915. Reprint. New York: Pantheon, 1979.

Goldenberg, Naomi. "A Feminist Critique of Jung." *Signs* 2:2 (1976): 444–49.

Gollin, Rita K. "Annie Adams Fields, 1834–1915." *Legacy: A Journal of Nineteenth-Century American Women Writers* 4:1 (Spring 1987): 27–33.

Gordon, Ann D., and Mari Jo Buhle. "Sex and Class in Colonial and Nineteenth-Century America." In *Liberating Women's History*, edited by Bernice A. Carroll. Urbana, IL: University of Illinois Press, 1976.

Green, David Bonnell. "Bibliographical Note." *The World of Dunnet Landing: A Sarah Orne Jewett Collection*. Lincoln, NE: University of Nebraska Press, 1962.

———. "The World of Dunnett Landing." *New England Quarterly* 34 (December 1961): 514–17.

Green, Martin. *The Great American Adventure*. Boston: Beacon, 1984.

Grimm, Jakob Ludwig Karl. *The Complete Grimms' Fairy Tales*. Translated by Margaret Hunt; revised, corrected and completed by James Stern. New York: Pantheon, 1972.

Guthrie, W. K. C. *The Greeks and Their Gods*. Reprint. Boston: Beacon Press, 1955.

Hall, Nor. *Mothers and Daughters: Reflections on the Archetypal Feminine*. Minneapolis, MN: Rusoff, 1976.

Hawthorne, Nathaniel. *The Marble Faun, or, The Romance of Monte Beni*. 1860. Reprint. New York: New American Library, 1960.

———. *Tanglewood Tales for Boys and Girls: Being a Second Wonder-Book*. Boston: Ticknor, Reed, and Fields, 1853.

———. *A Wonder-Book for Girls and Boys*. Boston: Ticknor, Reed, and Fields, 1852; London, 1851.

Higginson, Thomas Wentworth. "The Greek Goddesses." *Atlantic Monthly* 24 (July 1869): 97–108.

Hobbs, Glenda. "Pure and Passionate: Female Friendship in Sarah Orne Jewett's 'Martha's Lady.'" *Studies in Short Fiction* 17 (1980): 21–29.

Hohmann, Marti. "Sarah Orne Jewett to Lily Munger: Twenty-Three Letters." *Colby Library Quarterly* 22:1 (March 1986): 28–35.

Homerus. *The Homeric Hymns: A New Prose Translation and Essays, Literary and Mythological.* Edited and translated by Andrew Lang. New York: Longmans, Green; London: G. Allen, 1899.

Horn, Robert L. "The Power of Jewett's *Deephaven.*" *Colby Library Quarterly* 9 (December 1972): 617–31.

———. "Universality in the Fiction of Sarah Orne Jewett." Ph.D. diss., University of Wisconsin, 1968.

Hovet, Theodore. "'Once Upon a Time': Sarah Orne Jewett's 'A White Heron.'" *Studies in Short Fiction* 15:1 (Winter 1978): 63–68.

Howells, William Dean. *A Chance Acquaintance.* Boston and New York: Houghton Mifflin, 1915. Reprint. Bloomington, IN: Indiana University Press, 1971.

James, Henry. *The Bostonians: A Novel.* 1886. Reprint. New York: Crowell, 1974.

———. "Mr. and Mrs. James T. Fields." *Atlantic Monthly* 116 (July 1915): 21–31.

———. *The Wings of the Dove.* 1902. Reprint. New York: Modern Library, 1937.

James, William. *The Varieties of Religious Experience.* New York: Longmans, Green, 1902.

———. *"The Will to Believe" and Other Essays in Popular Philosophy.* New York: Longmans, Green, 1896.

Jewett, Sarah Orne. "An Autumn Holiday." *Country By-Ways.* Boston: Houghton Mifflin, 1881.

———. "The Best China Saucer." *Play-Days: A Book of Stories for Children.* Boston: Houghton, Osgood, 1878.

———. "A Bit of Shore Life." *Old Friends and New.* Boston: Houghton, Osgood, 1879.

———. "The Christmas Ghosts." drafts 1 and 2, MS. 1743.22 (15). Houghton Library, Harvard University.

———. "Confessions of a Housebreaker." *The Mate of the Daylight, and Friends Ashore.* Boston: Houghton Mifflin, 1884.

———. *A Country Doctor.* Boston and New York: Houghton Mifflin, 1884.

———. *The Country of the Pointed Firs* (1896). In *The Country of the Pointed Firs and Other Stories,* selected and introduced by Mary Ellen Chase, with an introduction by Marjorie Pryse. New York: W. W. Norton, 1982.

———. "The Decay of Churches." MS. 1743.22 (25). Houghton Library, Harvard University.

———. *Deephaven* (1877). In *Deephaven and Other Stories,* edited by Richard Cary. New Haven, CT: College and University Press, 1966.

———. "Dr. Theodore Herman Jewett." MS. Am 1743.22 (28). Houghton Library, Harvard University.

———. "For Country Girls." MS. Am 1743.22 (38). Houghton Library, Harvard University.

———. "The Foreigner" (1900). In *The Country of the Pointed Firs and Other*

Stories, selected and introduced by Mary Ellen Chase, with an introduction by Marjorie Pryse. New York: W. W. Norton, 1982.

———. "The Friendship of Women." MS. Am 1743.22 (41). Houghton Library, Harvard University.

———. "From a Mournful Villager." *Country By-Ways.* Boston: Houghton Mifflin, 1881.

———. "Good Luck: A Girl's Story." *Country By-Ways.* Boston: Houghton Mifflin, 1881.

———. *The Letters of Sarah Orne Jewett,* edited by Annie Fields. Boston: Houghton Mifflin, 1911.

———. "A Little Ancestress." MS 1743.25 (134). Houghton Library, Harvard University.

———. "Looking Back on Girlhood." In *The Uncollected Short Stories of Sarah Orne Jewett,* edited by Richard Cary. Waterville, ME: Colby College Press, 1971.

———. Manuscript Diary 1867. MS. Am 1743.26 (3). Houghton Library, Harvard University.

———. Manuscript Diary 1871–72. Houghton Library, Harvard University.

———. Manuscript Diary 1871–79. MS. Am 1743.1 (341). Houghton Library, Harvard University.

———. "Miss Sydney's Flowers." *Old Friends and New.* Boston: Houghton, Osgood, 1879.

———. "Miss Tempy's Watchers" (1888). In *The Country of the Pointed Firs and Other Stories,* selected and introduced by Mary Ellen Chase, with an introduction by Marjorie Pryse. New York: W. W. Norton, 1982.

———. "A Modern Idyll," MS. Am 1743.22 (70). Houghton Library, Harvard University.

———. "A Neighbor's Landmark." *The Life of Nancy.* Boston: Houghton Mifflin, 1894.

———. "The New Wife." MS. Am 1743.25 (83). Houghton Library, Harvard University.

———. "An October Ride." *Country By-Ways.* Boston: Houghton Mifflin, 1881.

———. "Outgrown Friends." MS. Am 1743.22 (87). Houghton Library, Harvard University.

———. "The Queen's Twin" (1899). In *The Country of the Pointed Firs and Other Stories,* selected and introduced by Mary Ellen Chase, with an introduction by Marjorie Pryse. New York: W. W. Norton, 1982.

———. "Recollections of Dr. William Perry of Exeter." MS. Am 1743.22 (102). Houghton Library, Harvard University.

———. "River Driftwood" (1881). In *Deephaven and Other Stories,* edited by Richard Cary. New Haven, CT: College and University Press, 1966.

———. "Thoughts about Housekeeping." MS. 1743.22 (115). Houghton Library, Harvard University.

———. "Tom's Husband." *The Mate of the Daylight, and Friends Ashore.* Boston: Houghton Mifflin, 1884.

———. *The Tory Lover.* Boston: Houghton Mifflin, 1901.

———. "The Town Poor" (1890). In *The Country of the Pointed Firs and Other Stories,* selected and arranged by Willa Cather. Garden City, NY: Doubleday-Anchor, 1956.

———. "A White Heron" (1886). In *The Country of the Pointed Firs and Other Stories,* selected and arranged by Willa Cather. Garden City, NY: Doubleday-Anchor, 1956.

———. "The White Rose Road." *Strangers and Wayfarers.* Boston and New York: Houghton Mifflin, 1890.

———. "William's Wedding" (1910). In *The Country of the Pointed Firs and Other Stories,* selected and introduced by Mary Ellen Chase, with an introduction by Marjorie Pryse. New York: W. W. Norton, 1982.

———. "A Winter Drive." *Country By-Ways.* Boston: Houghton Mifflin, 1881.

Jobes, Katherine T. "From Stowe's Eagle Island to Jewett's 'A White Heron.'" *Colby Library Quarterly* 10 (December 1974): 515–21.

Jung, Carl. "Psychological Aspects of the Kore." In *Essays on a Science of Mythology: The Myths of the Divine Child and the Divine Maiden,* rev. ed. Translated by R. F. C. Hull. New York: Harper and Row, 1963.

Kaplan, Justin. *Mr. Clemens and Mark Twain: A Biography.* New York: Simon and Schuster, 1966.

Kelley, Mary. *Private Woman, Public Stage: Literary Domesticity in Nineteenth-Century America.* New York and London: Oxford University Press, 1984.

Kerényi, Károly. *Eleusis: Archetypal Image of Mother and Daughter.* Translated by Ralph Manheim. New York: Bollingen Foundation, Pantheon, 1967.

Kermode, Frank. *The Sense of an Ending.* New York: Oxford University Press, 1966.

Kolodny, Annette. *The Lay of the Land: Metaphor As Experience and History in American Life and Letters.* Chapel Hill, NC: University of North Carolina Press, 1975.

Lamphere, Louise. "Beyond Dichotomies." Review of *Gender and Kinship: Essays Toward a Unified Analysis* (edited by Jane Fishburne Collier and Sylvia Junko Yanagisako). *Women's Review of Books* 5:5 (February 1988): 17–18.

———. "Strategies, Cooperation, and Conflict among Women in Domestic Groups." In *Women, Culture, and Society,* edited by Michelle Z. Rosaldo and Louise Lamphere. Stanford, CA: Stanford University Press, 1974.

Landy, Marcia. "The Silent Women: Toward a Feminist Critique." In *The Authority of Experience: Essays in Feminist Criticism,* edited by Arlyn Diamond and Lee R. Edwards. Amherst, MA: University of Massachusetts Press, 1977.

Leach, Edmund. "Genesis as Myth." In *Interpretations of Cultures: Myth and Cosmos,* edited by John Middleton. Garden City, NY: The Natural History Press, 1967.

Lerner, Gerda. "The Lady and the Mill Girl: Changes in the Status of Women in the Age of Jackson, 1790–1840." In *A Heritage of Her Own,* edited by Nancy F. Cott and Elizabeth H. Pleck. New York: Simon and Schuster, 1979.

Lévi-Strauss, Claude. *The Elementary Structures of Kinship.* Translated by J. H. Bell and J. R. von Sturmer. Boston: Beacon, 1969.

———. *From Honey to Ashes: Introduction to a Science of Mythology.* Vol. 2. New York: Harper and Row, 1966.

———. *The Raw and the Cooked: Introduction to a Science of Mythology.* Vol. 1. New York: Harper and Row, 1964, 1969.

Lévy-Bruhl, Lucien. *La Mythologie primitive*. Paris: F. Alcan, 1935.

Lovejoy, Arthur O., Gilbert Chinard, George Boas, and Ronald Crane. *A Documentary History of Primitivism and Related Ideas*. Baltimore: Johns Hopkins Press, 1935.

Mabie, Hamilton Wright. "My Search for the Goddess." In *Liber Scriptorum*, edited by Rossiter Johnson, John Denison Champlin, George Cary Eggleston. New York: Authors Club, 1893.

Magowan, Robin. "The Art of Pastoral Narrative: Sand, Fromentin, Jewett." Ph.D. diss., Yale University, 1964.

———. "Fromentin and Jewett: Pastoral Narrative in the Nineteenth Century." *Comparative Literature* 16 (Fall 1964): 331–37.

———. "The Outer Island Sequence in *Pointed Firs*." *Colby Library Quarterly* 6 (June 1964): 418–24.

———. "Pastoral and the Art of Landscape in *The Country of the Pointed Firs*." *New England Quarterly* 36 (June 1963): 229–40 (reprinted in Cary, *Appreciation*).

Marks, Elaine. "'Women with Women: Community among Women in Fiction." Paper presented to the Women and Literature Section, Midwest Modern Language Association Convention, Minneapolis, Fall 1978.

Marks, Elaine, and Isabelle de Courtivron, eds. *New French Feminisms*. Amherst, MA: University of Massachusetts Press, 1979.

Martin, Jay. *Harvests of Change: American Literature, 1865–1914*. Princeton, NJ: Princeton University Press, 1967.

Marx, Leo. *The Machine in the Garden: Technology and the Pastoral Ideal in America*. New York: Oxford University Press, 1964.

Masteller, Jean Carwile. "The Women Doctors of Howells, Phelps, and Jewett: The Conflict of Marriage and Career." In *Critical Essays on Sarah Orne Jewett*, edited by Gwen Nagel. Boston: G. K. Hall, 1984.

Matthiessen, F. O. *Sarah Orne Jewett*. Boston and New York: Houghton Mifflin, 1929.

Mieggi, Giovanni. *Virgin Mary*. Philadelphia: Westminster, 1955.

Mitchell, Juliet. *Psycho-Analysis and Feminism: Freud, Reich, Laing, and Women*. New York: Random House–Vintage, 1975.

Mobley, Marilyn. "Rituals of Flight and Return: The Ironic Journeys of Sarah Orne Jewett's Female Characters." *Colby Library Quarterly* 22:1 (March 1986): 36–42.

Moers, Ellen. *Literary Women: The Great Writers*. Garden City, NY: Doubleday-Anchor, 1977.

Morgan, Ellen. "The Atypical Woman: Nan Prince in the Literary Transition to Feminism." *The Kate Chopin Newsletter* 2 (Fall 1976): 33–37.

Mylonas, George E. *Eleusis and the Eleusinian Mysteries*. Princeton, NJ: Princeton University Press, 1969.

Nagel, Gwen. "'This Prim Corner of Land Where She Was Queen': Sarah Orne Jewett's New England Gardens." *Colby Library Quarterly* 22:1 (March 1986): 43–62.

———, ed. *Critical Essays on Sarah Orne Jewett*. Boston: G. K. Hall, 1984.

Nagel, Gwen L., and James Nagel, comps. *Sarah Orne Jewett: A Reference Guide*. Boston: G. K. Hall, 1978.

Neumann, Erich. *The Great Mother: An Analysis of the Archetype*. Translated by Ralph Manheim. Princeton, NJ: Bollingen Foundation, Princeton University Press, 1955.

Newton, Sir Charles Thomas. *A History of Discoveries at Halicarnassus, Cnidus, and Branchidae.* London: Day and Sons, 1862.

Ninck, Martin Hermann. *Wodan und germanischer Schicksalsglaube.* Jena: E. Diederichs, 1935.

Nodding, Nel. *Caring: A Feminine Approach to Ethics and Moral Education.* Berkeley, CA: University of California Press, 1984.

Noyes, Sylvia Gray. "Mrs. Almira Todd, Herbalist-Conjurer." *Colby Library Quarterly* 9 (December 1972): 643–49.

O'Brien, Sharon. *Willa Cather: The Emerging Voice.* New York: Oxford University Press, 1987.

Olsen, Tillie. *Silences.* New York: Delacorte, 1978.

O'Neill, William L. *Everyone Was Brave: The Rise and Fall of Feminism in America.* Chicago: Quadrangle, 1969.

Ortner, Sherry. "Is Female to Male As Nature Is to Culture?" *Feminist Studies* 1:2 (Fall 1972): 5–31 (reprinted in Lamphere and Rosaldo, *Women, Culture, and Society*).

Otto, Walter F. "The Meaning of the Eleusinian Mysteries." *The Mysteries, Papers from the Eranos Yearbooks.* Vol. 2. New York and London: Pantheon, 1955.

Papashvily, Helen. *All the Happy Endings: A Study of the Domestic Novel in America, the Women Who Wrote It, the Women Who Read It, in the Nineteenth Century.* New York: Harper and Brothers, 1956.

Parker, Gail. *The Oven Birds: American Women on Womanhood, 1820–1920.* Garden City, NY: Doubleday-Anchor, 1972.

Parsons, Theophilus. *The Finite and the Infinite.* Boston: Roberts, 1872.

Pater, Walter Horatio. "The Myth of Demeter and Persephone." *Greek Studies: A Series of Essays.* New York: Macmillan, 1894.

Pattee, Fred Lewis. *The Feminine Fifties.* New York: D. Appleton, 1940.

Perrault, Charles. *Popular Tales.* Oxford: Clarendon Press, 1878.

Phelps [Ward], Elizabeth Stuart. *The Gates Ajar.* Boston: Fields, Osgood, 1869.

Plaskow, Judith, and Joan Arnold Romero, eds. *Women and Religion*, rev. ed. Missoula, MT: Scholar's Press and the American Academy of Religion, 1974.

Pomeroy, Sarah B. "A Classical Scholar's Perspective on Matriarchy." In *Liberating Women's History: Theoretical and Critical Essays*, edited by Berenice A. Carroll. Urbana, IL: University of Illinois Press, 1976.

Pool, Eugene Hillhouse. "The Child in Sarah Orne Jewett." *Colby Library Quarterly* 7 (September 1967): 503–9 (reprinted in Cary, *Appreciation*).

Portales, Marco A. "History of a Text: Jewett's *The Country of the Pointed Firs.*" *New England Quarterly* 55:4 (December 1982): 586–92.

Pratt, Annis. *Archetypal Patterns in Women's Fiction.* Bloomington, IN: University of Indiana Press, 1981.

———. "Women and Nature in Modern Fiction." *Contemporary Literature* 13 (Autumn 1972): 476–90.

Pryse, Marjorie. "Introduction to the Norton Edition." *The Country of the Pointed Firs and Other Stories,* selected and introduced by Mary Ellen Chase, with an introduction by Marjorie Pryse. New York: W. W. Norton, 1982.

————. "Women 'at Sea': Feminist Realism in Sarah Orne Jewett's 'The Foreigner.'" *American Literary Realism* 15 (1982): 244–52 (reprinted in Nagel, *Critical Essays*).

Raymond, Janice. *A Passion for Friends: Towards a Philosophy of Female Affection.* Boston: Beacon, 1986.

Reed, Evelyn. *Woman's Evolution: From Matriarchal Clan to Matriarchal Society.* New York: Pathfinder, 1975.

Renza, Louis. *"A White Heron" and the Question of Minor Literature.* Madison, WI: University of Wisconsin Press, 1984.

Reuther, Rosemary Radford. *New Women/New Earth: Sexist Ideologies and Human Liberation.* New York: Seabury, 1975.

————. *Religion and Sexism: Images of Women in the Jewish and Christian Tradition.* New York: Simon and Schuster, 1974.

Rhode, Robert D. "Sarah Orne Jewett and 'The Palpable Present Intimate,'" *Colby Library Quarterly* 8 (September 1968): 146–55 (reprinted in Cary, *Appreciation*).

————. *Setting in the American Short Story of Local Color, 1885–1900.* The Hague: Mouton, 1975.

Rich, Adrienne. "Aunt Jennifer's Tigers." *The Fact of a Doorframe, Poems Selected and New, 1950–1984.* New York: W. W. Norton, 1984.

————. *Of Woman Born: Motherhood As Experience and Institution.* New York: W. W. Norton, 1976.

Robinson, Lillian S. "Dwelling in Decencies: Radical Criticism and the Feminist Perspective." *College English* 32 (May 1971): 879–89.

Roman, Judith. "A Closer Look at the Jewett–Fields Relationship." In *Critical Essays on Sarah Orne Jewett,* edited by Gwen Nagel. Boston: G. K. Hall, 1984.

Romines, Ann. "In *Deephaven*: Skirmishes Near the Swamp." In *Critical Essays on Sarah Orne Jewett,* edited by Gwen Nagel. Boston: G. K. Hall, 1984.

Rosaldo, Michelle Z. "Women, Culture and Society: A Theoretical Overview." In *Women, Culture, and Society,* edited by Louise Lamphere and Michelle Z. Rosaldo. Stanford, CA: Stanford University Press, 1974.

Russ, Joanna. "What Can a Heroine Do?" In *Images of Women in Fiction: Feminist Perspectives,* edited by Susan Koppelman Cornillon. Bowling Green, OH: Bowling Green University Popular Press, 1972.

St. Armand, Barton L. "Jewett and Marin: The Inner Vision." *Colby Library Quarterly* 9 (December 1972): 632–43 (reprinted in Cary, *Appreciation*).

————. "Paradise Deferred: The Image of Heaven in the Work of Emily Dickinson and Elizabeth Stuart Phelps." *American Quarterly* 29 (Spring 1977): 55–78.

Sand (Dudevant), George. *Little Fadette: A Domestic Story.* 1849. Reprint. London: The Scholar's Press, 1928.

Sartre, Jean-Paul. *Nausea.* Translated by Lloyd Alexander. New York: New Directions, 1964.

Schleiermacher, Friedrich. *The Christian Faith.* Vol. 1. 1821; rev. ed. 1830. Reprint. New York: Harper and Row, 1963.

————. *On Religion: Speeches to Its Cultured Despisers.* 1799. Reprint. New York: Harper and Row, 1958.

Short, Clarice. "Studies in Gentleness." *Western Humanities Review* 11 (Autumn 1957): 387–93 (reprinted in Cary, *Appreciation*).

Showalter, Elaine. "Feminist Criticism in the Wilderness." *Critical Inquiry* 8:2 (Winter 1981): 179–205.

———. *A Literature of Their Own: Women Novelists from Brontë to Lessing*. Princeton, NJ: Princeton University Press, 1977.

Sklar, Kathryn Kish. *Catherine Beecher: A Study in American Domesticity*. New Haven, CT: Yale University Press, 1973.

Smith, Daniel Scott. "Family Limitation, Sexual Control, and Domestic Feminism in Victorian America." *Feminist Studies* 1 (Winter-Spring 1973): 40–57.

Smith-Rosenberg, Carroll. "The Female World of Love and Ritual: Relations between Women in Nineteenth-Century America." *Signs* 1:1 (1975): 1–29.

Sougnac, Jean. *Sarah Orne Jewett*. Paris: Jouve et Cie., 1937.

Spofford, Harriet Prescott. *A Little Book of Friends*. Boston: Little, Brown, 1916.

Stanton, Elizabeth Cady. "The Matriarchate, or Mother-Age." In *Transactions of the National Council of Women of the United States*. Philadelphia, 1891 (reprinted in *Up from the Pedestal*, edited by Aileen S. Kraditor. Chicago: Quadrangle, 1968).

———. *The Woman's Bible*. 1895. Reprint. New York: Arno, 1972.

Stewart, Grace. *A New Mythos: The Novel of the Artist as Heroine, 1877–1977*. St. Albans, VT: Eden, 1979.

Stone, Merlin. *When God Was a Woman*. New York: Dial, 1976.

Stouck, David. "*The Country of the Pointed Firs*: A Pastoral of Innocence." *Colby Library Quarterly* 9 (December 1970): 213–20 (reprinted in Cary, *Appreciation*).

Stowe, Harriet Beecher. *The Pearl of Orr's Island*. 1862. Reprint. Hartford, CT: The Stowe-Day Foundation, 1979.

Sulloway, Frank J. *Freud: Biologist of the Mind*. New York: Basic, 1979.

Tanner, Nancy. "Matrifocality in Indonesia and Africa and among Black Americans." In *Women, Culture, and Society*, edited by Michelle Z. Rosaldo and Louise Lamphere. Stanford, CA: Stanford University Press, 1974.

Taylor, William R., and Christopher Lasch. "Two 'Kindred Spirits': Sorority and Family in New England, 1836–1846." *New England Quarterly* 36:1 (March 1963): 23–41.

Tennyson, Alfred (Lord). *Demeter and Other Poems*. New York and London: Macmillan, 1889.

Thaxter, Rosamond. *Sandpiper, The Life of Celia Thaxter*. Sanbornville, NH: Wake-Brook House, 1962.

Thompson, Charles Miner. "The Art of Miss Jewett." *Atlantic Monthly* 94 (October 1904): 485–97 (reprinted in Cary, *Appreciation*).

Thorp, Margaret F. *Sarah Orne Jewett*. University of Minnesota Pamphlets on American Writers, No. 61. Minneapolis, MN: University of Minnesota Press, 1966.

Toth, Susan Allen. "Character Studies in Rose Terry Cooke: New Faces for the Short Story." *Kate Chopin Newsletter* 2 (1976): 19–26.

———. "Sarah Orne Jewett and Friends: A Community of Interest." *Studies in Short Fiction* 9 (Summer 1972): 223–41.

———. "The Value of Age in the Fiction of Sarah Orne Jewett." *Studies in Short Fiction* 8 (Summer 1971): 433–41 (reprinted in Cary, *Appreciation*).

Trecker, Janice Law. "Sex, Science, and Education." *American Quarterly* 26 (October 1974): 352–66.

Tryon, W. S. "Annie Adams Fields." In *Notable American Women, 1607–1950: A Biographical Dictionary,* Vol. 1, edited by Edward T. James and Janet W. James. Cambridge, MA: Harvard University Press, 1971.

Ulanov, Ann B. *The Feminine in Jungian Psychology and Christian Theology.* Evanston, IL: Northwestern University Press, 1971.

Ullman, Stephen. "Semantic Universals." In *Universals of Language,* edited by Joseph H. Greenberg. Cambridge, MA: MIT Press, 1963.

Voelker, Paul. "*The Country of the Pointed Firs:* A Novel by Sarah Orne Jewett." *Colby Library Quarterly* 9:4 (December 1970): 201–13 (reprinted in Cary, *Appreciation*).

Waggoner, Hyatt. "The Unity of *The Country of the Pointed Firs.*" *Twentieth Century Literature* 5 (July 1959): 67–73 (reprinted in Cary, *Appreciation*).

Weber, Carl, ed. *Letters of Sarah Orne Jewett in the Colby College Library.* Waterville, ME: Colby College Library, 1947.

Weber, Clara Carter, and Carl J. Weber, comps. *A Bibliography of the Published Writings of Sarah Orne Jewett.* Waterville, ME: Colby College Press, 1949.

Webster, Paula. "Matriarchy: A Vision of Power." In *Toward an Anthropology of Women,* edited by Rayna R. Reiter. New York: Monthly Review Press, 1975.

Welter, Barbara. "The Cult of True Womanhood." *American Quarterly* 18 (Summer 1966): 151–74.

———. "The Feminization of American Religion: 1800–1860." In *Dimity Convictions: The American Woman in the Nineteenth Century.* Athens, OH: Ohio University Press, 1976.

Westbrook, Perry D. *Acres of Flint: Sarah Orne Jewett and Her Contemporaries.* Metuchen, NJ: Scarecrow Press, 1951; rev. ed., 1981.

Whitehead, Harriet. "Review: *Woman's Evolution: From Matriarchal Clan to Matriarchal Society* by Evelyn Reed." *Signs* 2:2 (1976): 746–48.

Whittier, John Greenleaf. "Godspeed." In *The Complete Poetical Works of John Greenleaf Whittier,* edited by Horace Scudder. Boston and New York: Houghton, Mifflin, 1894.

Williams, Sister Mary, C.S.J. "The Pastoral in New England Local Color: Celia Thaxter, Sarah Orne Jewett, and Alice Brown." Ph.D. diss., Stanford University, 1972.

Wilson, Forrest. *Crusader in Crinoline: The Life of Harriet Beecher Stowe.* Philadelphia: J. B. Lippincott, 1941.

Woodberry, G. E. "Review of *Demeter and Other Poems* by Alfred Lord Tennyson." *Atlantic Monthly* 65 (March 1890): 421.

Zagarell, Sandra A. "Narrative of Community: The Identification of a Genre." *Signs* 13:31 (Spring 1988): 498–527.

Index

3 5282 00370 2027